D1737701

HTML5 and CSS3: Building Responsive Websites

Design robust, powerful, and above all, modern websites across all manner of devices with ease using HTML5 and CSS3

A course in three modules

BIRMINGHAM - MUMBAI

HTML5 and CSS3: Building Responsive Websites

Published on: October 2016

Production reference: 1250117

Published by Packt Publishing Ltd.
Livery Place
35 Livery Street
Birmingham B3 2PB, UK.

ISBN 978-1-78712-481-3

www.packtpub.com

Credits

Authors

Thoriq Firdaus

Ben Frain

Benjamin LaGrone

Reviewers

Saumya Dwivedi

Gabriel Hilal

Joydip Kanjilal

Anirudh Prabhu

Taroon Tyagi

Esteban S. Abait

Christopher Scott Hernandez

Mauvis Ledford

Sophie Williams

Dale Cruse

Ed Henderson

Rokesh Jankie

Content Development Editor

Amedh Pohad

Graphics

Kirk D'Penha

Production Coordinator

Deepika Naik

Preface

Responsive web design is an explosive area of growth in modern web development due to the huge volume of different device sizes and resolutions that are now commercially available. The Internet is going mobile. Desktop-only websites just aren't good enough anymore. With mobile internet usage still rising, and tablets changing internet consumption habits, you need to know how to build websites that will just "work," regardless of the devices used to access them.

This Learning Path course explains all the key approaches necessary to create and maintain a modern responsive design using HTML5 and CSS3.

What this learning path covers

Module 1, Responsive Web Design Beginner's Guide, is a step-by-step beginner's guide, where you will learn to build engaging responsive websites. With coverage of Responsive Grid System, Bootstrap, and Foundation, you will discover three of the most robust frameworks in responsive web design. Next, you'll learn to create a cool blog page, a beautiful portfolio site, and a crisp professional business site and make them all totally responsive. You'll also find out which framework works best for your project specifications. The module teaches you how to build presentable, responsive websites through examples, tips, and best practices of code writing and project organization. Additionally, you will also learn how to use CSS preprocessors, LESS, and Sass, which allows you to compose leaner style rules.

Module 2, Responsive Web Design with HTML5 and CSS3, is packed with examples, and a thorough explanation of modern techniques and syntax, it provides a comprehensive resource for all things "responsive." You'll explore the most up-to-date techniques and tools needed to build great responsive designs, ensuring that your projects won't just be built "right" for today, but in the future too. The module covers every essential aspect of responsive web design. In addition, it extends the responsive design methodology by applying the latest and most useful techniques provided by HTML5 and CSS3, making designs leaner and more maintainable than ever before. It also explains common best practice methods of writing and delivering code, images, and files.

Module 3, HTML5 and CSS3 Responsive Web Design Cookbook, is your guide to obtaining full access to next generation devices and browser technology. Create responsive applications that make snappy connections for mobile browsers and give your website the latest design and development advantages to reach mobile devices. The topics in this module include responsive elements and media, responsive typography, responsive layouts, using media queries, utilizing modern responsive frameworks, developing mobile-first web applications, optimizing responsive content, and achieving unobtrusive interaction using JavaScript and jQuery. Each recipe features actual lines of code that you can apply.

At the end of this course you will learn to get and use all the tools you need to build and test your responsive web project performance and take your website to the next level.

What you need for this learning path

Module 1:

You need to have a basic understanding of HTML and CSS; at least, you should know what an HTML element is and how to style an HTML element with CSS in its fundamental form. Some degree of familiarity and experience with HTML5, CSS3, and command lines, though not essential, will be a great help to get the most out of this module. We will explain each step and all the techniques in full, along with some handy tips and references.

Furthermore, you will also need a computer running Windows, OS X, or Ubuntu; an Internet browser (preferably Google Chrome or Mozilla Firefox); and a code editor (in this module, we will use Sublime Text).

Module 2:

- A text editor
- An evergreen browser

Module 3:

You will need an IDE (Integrated Development Environment); NetBeans or Eclipse is recommended (there are instructions on how to get one inside), image editing software such as Photoshop or GIMP, a web host, and a local web server such as Apache or a local hosting application such as XAMPP or MAMPP.

Who this learning path is for

This course is for web developers who are familiar with HTML and CSS but want to understand the essentials of responsive web design. It is for those developers who are willing to seek innovative techniques that deliver fast, intuitive interfacing with the latest mobile Internet devices.

Reader feedback

Feedback from our readers is always welcome. Let us know what you think about this course—what you liked or disliked. Reader feedback is important for us as it helps us develop titles that you will really get the most out of.

To send us general feedback, simply e-mail feedback@packtpub.com, and mention the course's title in the subject of your message.

If there is a topic that you have expertise in and you are interested in either writing or contributing to a course, see our author guide at www.packtpub.com/authors.

Customer support

Now that you are the proud owner of a Packt course, we have a number of things to help you to get the most from your purchase.

Downloading the example code

You can download the example code files for this course from your account at
`http://www.packtpub.com`. If you purchased this course elsewhere, you can visit
`http://www.packtpub.com/support` and register to have the files e-mailed directly
to you.

You can download the code files by following these steps:

1. Log in or register to our website using your e-mail address and password.
2. Hover the mouse pointer on the **SUPPORT** tab at the top.
3. Click on **Code Downloads & Errata**.
4. Enter the name of the course in the **Search** box.
5. Select the course for which you're looking to download the code files.
6. Choose from the drop-down menu where you purchased this course from.
7. Click on **Code Download**.

You can also download the code files by clicking on the **Code Files** button on the
course's webpage at the Packt Publishing website. This page can be accessed by
entering the course's name in the **Search** box. Please note that you need to be logged
in to your Packt account.

Once the file is downloaded, please make sure that you unzip or extract the folder
using the latest version of:

- WinRAR / 7-Zip for Windows
- Zipeg / iZip / UnRarX for Mac
- 7-Zip / PeaZip for Linux

The code bundle for the course is also hosted on GitHub at `https://github.com/`
`PacktPublishing/HTML5-and-CSS3-Building-Responsive-Websites`. We also
have other code bundles from our rich catalog of books, courses and videos available
at `https://github.com/PacktPublishing/`. Check them out!

Errata

Although we have taken every care to ensure the accuracy of our content, mistakes do happen. If you find a mistake in one of our courses—maybe a mistake in the text or the code—we would be grateful if you could report this to us. By doing so, you can save other readers from frustration and help us improve subsequent versions of this course. If you find any errata, please report them by visiting http://www.packtpub.com/submit-errata, selecting your course, clicking on the **Errata Submission Form** link, and entering the details of your errata. Once your errata are verified, your submission will be accepted and the errata will be uploaded to our website or added to any list of existing errata under the Errata section of that title.

To view the previously submitted errata, go to https://www.packtpub.com/books/content/support and enter the name of the course in the search field. The required information will appear under the **Errata** section.

Piracy

Piracy of copyrighted material on the Internet is an ongoing problem across all media. At Packt, we take the protection of our copyright and licenses very seriously. If you come across any illegal copies of our works in any form on the Internet, please provide us with the location address or website name immediately so that we can pursue a remedy.

Please contact us at copyright@packtpub.com with a link to the suspected pirated material.

We appreciate your help in protecting our authors and our ability to bring you valuable content.

Questions

If you have a problem with any aspect of this course, you can contact us at questions@packtpub.com, and we will do our best to address the problem.

Module 3: HTML5 and CSS3 Responsive Web Design Cookbook

Module 1

Responsive Web Design Beginner's Guide

Build powerful and engaging responsive websites with ease

1
Responsive Web Design

I still remember, back when I was a kid, a mobile phone came with a mere tiny size monochromatic screen. All we could do at that time was make a phone call, text, and play a simple game. Today, mobile devices have drastically advanced in many ways.

New mobile devices are built with varying screen sizes; some even come with higher DPI or resolution. Most new mobile devices are now equipped with a touch-enabled screen, allowing us to interact with the device conveniently using a tap or a swipe of fingers. The screen orientation is switchable between portrait and landscape. The software is also more capable compared to older devices. The mobile browser, in particular, is now able to render and display web pages that are as good as a browser in a desktop computer.

In addition, the number of mobile users has exploded in the last couple of years. We can now see many people around spending countless hours facing their mobile devices, a phone, or a tablet, doing things such as running their businesses on the go or simple Internet browsing. The number of mobile users is likely to grow in the years to come and may even outnumber the total number of desktop users.

That is to say, mobiles have changed the Web and changed the way people use the Internet and enjoy websites. These advancements in mobile devices and the increasing mobile Internet usage prompts questions on a new paradigm to build websites that are accessible and function well in varying circumstances. This is where **Responsive Web Design** *comes in.*

In this chapter, we will cover the following topics:

- Glance at the basics of responsive web design, viewport meta tag, and CSS3 media queries
- Take a look at the responsive frameworks that we will use to build responsive websites in the following chapters

Responsive web design in a nutshell

Responsive web design is one of the most discussed topics in the web design and development community. So, I believe many of you have heard about it to a certain extent.

Ethan Marcotte was the one who coined the term "responsive web design". He suggests in his article *Responsive Web Design* (`http://alistapart.com/article/responsive-web-design/`), that the Web should seamlessly adjust and adapt to the environment where the users view the website rather than addressing it exclusively for a specific platform. In other words, the website should be responsive, it should be presentable on any screen size, regardless of the platform on which it is viewed.

Take the Time website (`http://time.com/`) as an example. The web page fits nicely on a desktop browser with a large screen size and also on a mobile browser with a limited viewable area. The layout shifts and adapts as the viewport size changes. As you can see in the following screenshot, on the mobile browser, the background color of the header is dark grey, the image is scaled down proportionally, and the Tap bar appears where Time hides the latest news, magazine, and videos sections:

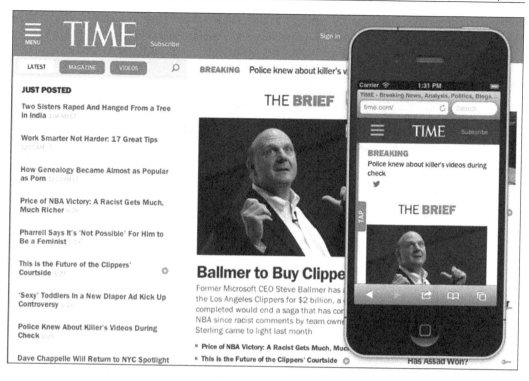

There are two components to build responsive websites, namely, **viewport meta tag** and **media queries**.

Viewport meta tag

Before smartphones, such as the iPhone, became mainstream, every website was built to be around 1000 px in width or 980 px wide and it was zoomed out to fit into the mobile phone screen, which eventually made the website unreadable. Hence, the <meta name="viewport"> was created.

In a nutshell, the viewport meta tag is used to define the web page scale and its visible area (viewport) in the browser. The following code is an example of a viewport meta tag in action:

```
<meta name="viewport" content="width=device-width, initial-scale=1">
```

The preceding viewport meta tag specification defines the web page viewport width to follow the device. It also defines the web page scale upon opening the web page for the first time at 1:1, in a way that the sizes and the dimensions of the web page content should be persistent; they should not be scaled up or scaled down.

In favor of comprehending how the viewport meta tag would affect a web page layout, I have created two web pages for comparison; one with the viewport meta tag added in and the other one without it. You can see the difference in the following screenshot:

The first website shown in the preceding image is issued with the viewport meta tag using the exact same specification as in our previous code example. As we have specified `width=device-width`, the browser acknowledges that the website viewport is at the same size as the device screen, so that it will not squish the web page to fit in the entire screen. The `initial-scale=1` will retain the title and the paragraph in their original size.

In the second website's example, as we did not add the viewport `meta` tag, the browser assumed that the web page should be displayed entirely. So, the browser forced the whole website down to fit within the whole screen area, making the title and the text totally unreadable.

A word on screen size and viewport

You may have found on many web design forums or blogs that viewport and screen size are mentioned interchangeably quite often. But, as a matter of fact, they are two different things.

Screen size refers to the device's actual screen size. A 13-inch laptop, for example, commonly has a screen size of 1280*800 pixels. The viewport, on the other hand, describes the viewable area in the browser where it displays websites. The following diagram illustrates this:

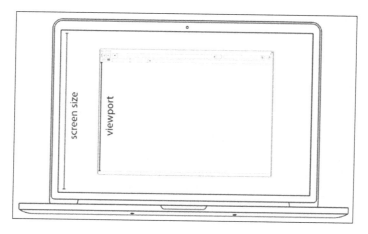

Media queries

The media types module in CSS enables us to target style rules to specific media. If you have created a print style sheet before, you certainly are familiar with the concept of media types. CSS3 introduced a new media type called media queries, which allow us to apply styles within the specified range of the viewport width, also known as breakpoints.

The following is one simple example; we decrease the p font size from 16px to 14px of the website when the website's viewport size is at 480px or lower.

```
p {
font-size: 16px;
}
@media screen and (max-width: 480px) {
p {
    font-size: 14px;
}
}
```

The following diagram illustrates the preceding code:

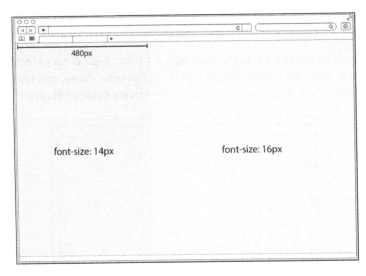

We can also combine multiple ranges of viewport widths by using the and operator. Following our preceding example, we can set the p font size to 14px when the viewport size is between 480px and 320px in the following manner:

```
@media screen and (min-width: 320px) and (max-width: 480px) {
p {
font-size: 11px;
   }
}
```

Viewport and media queries

We will be dealing with viewport meta tag and media queries while building responsive websites in *Module 2, Responsive Web Design with HTML5 and CSS3*, which covers these two in greater detail.

A look into responsive frameworks

Building a responsive website can be very tedious work. There are many measurements to be considered while building a responsive website, one of which would be creating the responsive grid.

The grid helps us build websites with proper alignment. If you have ever used 960. gs (http://960.gs/), which is one of the popular CSS frameworks, you would have experienced how easy it is to organize the web page layout by adding preset classes, such as grid_1 or push_1, in the elements.

However, the 960.gs grid is set in a fixed unit, namely, pixel (px), which is not applicable when it comes to building a responsive website. We need a framework with the grid set in percentage (%) unit to build responsive websites; we need a responsive framework.

A responsive framework provides the building blocks to build responsive websites. Generally, it includes the classes to assemble a responsive grid, the basic styles for typography and form inputs, and a few styles to address various browser quirks. Some frameworks even go further with a series of styles to create common design patterns and web user interfaces such as buttons, navigation bars, and image slider. These predefined styles allow us to develop responsive websites faster with less hassle. The following are a few other reasons why using a responsive framework is a favorable option to build responsive websites:

- **Browser compatibility**: Assuring the consistency of a web page on different browsers is really painful and more distressing than developing the website itself. However, with a framework, we can minimize the work to address browser compatibility issues. The framework developers have most likely tested the framework on various desktop browsers and mobile browsers with the most constrained environment prior to releasing it publicly.

- **Documentation**: A framework, in general, also comes with comprehensive documentation that records the bits and pieces on using the framework. The documentation will be very helpful for entry users to begin studying the framework. It is also a great advantage when we are working with a team. We can refer to the documentation to get everyone on the same page and follow the standard code of writing conventions.

- **Community and extensions**: Some popular frameworks such as Bootstrap and Foundation have an active community that helps address the bugs in the framework and extends the functionality. The jQuery UI Bootstrap (http://jquery-ui-bootstrap.github.io/jquery-ui-bootstrap/) is perhaps a good example in this case. The jQuery UI Bootstrap is a collection styles for jQuery UI widgets to match the feel and look of Bootstrap's original theme. It's now common to find free WordPress and Joomla themes that are based on these frameworks.

Through the course of this module, we will be building three responsive websites by using three different responsive frameworks, namely Responsive.gs, Bootstrap, and Foundation.

The Responsive.gs framework

Responsive.gs (`http://responsive.gs/`) is a lightweight, responsive framework, which is merely 1 KB in size when compressed. Responsive.gs is based on a width of 940 px, and made in three variants of grids, that is, 12, 16, and 24 columns. What's more, Responsive.gs is shipped with box-sizing polyfill, which enables CSS3 box-sizing in Internet Explorer 6, 7, and 8, and makes it decently presentable in those browsers.

> Polyfill is a piece of code that enables certain web features and capabilities that are not built in the browser natively. Usually, it addresses the older versions of Internet Explorer. For example, you can use HTML5Shiv (`https://github.com/aFarkas/html5shiv`) so that new HTML5 elements, such as `<header>`, `<footer>`, and `<nav>`, are recognized in Internet Explorer 6, 7, and 8.

A word on CSS box model

HTML elements, which are categorized as block-level elements, are essentially boxes drawn with the content width, height, margin, padding, and border through CSS. Prior to CSS3, we were facing constraints when specifying a box. For instance, when we specify a `<div>` tag with a width and height of `100px`, as follows:

```
div {
    width: 100px;
    height: 100px;
}
```

The browser will render `div` as a `100px` square box, as shown in the next diagram:

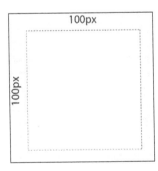

However, this will only be true if the padding and border have not been added in. As a box has four sides, a padding of 10px (`padding: 10px;`) will actually add 20px to the width and height—10px for each side, as shown in the following diagram:

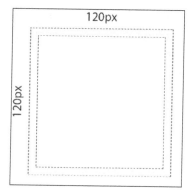

While it takes up space on the page, the element's margin space is reserved outside the element rather than as part of the element itself; thus, if we give an element a background color, the margin area will not take that color.

CSS3 box sizing

CSS3 introduced a new property called `box-sizing`, which lets us specify how the browser should calculate the CSS box model. There are a couple of values that we can apply within the `box-sizing` property.

Value	Description
`content-box`	This is the default value of the box model. This value specifies the padding and the border-box's thickness outside the specified width and height of the content, as we have demonstrated in the preceding section.
`border-box`	This value will do the opposite of what the content-box does; it includes the padding and the border box as the width and height of the box.
`padding-box`	At the time of writing this module, this value is experimental and has just been added recently. This value specifies the box dimensions.

In each of the projects in this module, we will be using the `border-box` value so that we can determine the box dimensions with ease for the websites. Let's take our preceding example to understand this, but this time we will set the `box-sizing` model to `border-box`. As mentioned in the preceding table, the `border-box` value will retain the box's width and the height as `100px`, regardless of the padding and border addition. The following illustration shows a comparison between the outputs of the two different values, `content-box` (the default value) and `border-box`:

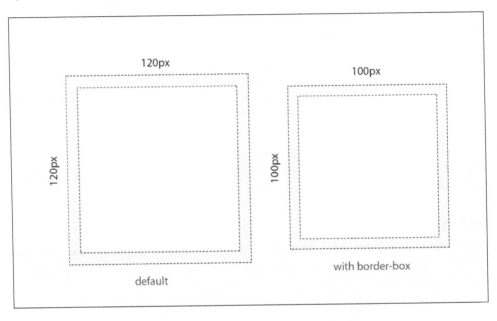

In this module, we will use Responsive.gs and explore more of it in the next two chapters to build a simple responsive blog.

The Bootstrap framework

Bootstrap (http://getbootstrap.com/) was originally built by Mark Otto (http://markdotto.com/) and initially intended only for internal use on Twitter. In short, Bootstrap was then launched for free for public consumption.

 Bootstrap has long been associated with Twitter, but since the author has departed from Twitter and Bootstrap itself has grown beyond his expectations, Bootstrap now stands on its own brand (http://blog.getbootstrap.com/2012/09/29/onward/).

If you refer to the initial development, the responsive feature was not yet added. It was then added in Version 2 due to the increasing demand for creating responsive websites.

Bootstrap also comes with many more added features as compared to Responsive.gs. It is packed with preset user interface styles, which comprise common user interfaces used on websites such as buttons, navigation bars, pagination, and forms, so you don't have to create them from scratch again when starting a new project. On top of that, Bootstrap is also powered with some custom jQuery plugins such as image slider, carousel, popover, and modal box.

You can use and customize Bootstrap in many ways. You can directly customize the Bootstrap theme and its components directly through the CSS style sheets, the Bootstrap customize and download page (http://getbootstrap.com/customize/), or the Bootstrap LESS variables and mixins, which are used to generate the style sheets.

In this module, we will go into Bootstrap in *Chapter 5*, *Developing a Portfolio Website with Bootstrap*, and *Chapter 6*, *Polishing the Responsive Portfolio Website with LESS*, to build a responsive portfolio website.

The Foundation framework

Foundation (http://foundation.zurb.com/) is a framework created by ZURB, a design agency based in California. Similar to Bootstrap, Foundation is not just a responsive CSS framework; it is shipped with a preset grid, components, and a number of jQuery plugins to present interactive features.

Some high-profile brands, such as McAfee (http://www.mcafee.com/common/privacy/english/slide.html), which is one of the most respectable brands for computer antivirus, have built their websites using Foundation.

The Foundation style sheet is powered by Sass, a Ruby-based CSS preprocessor. We will be discussing more about Sass, along with the Foundation features in the last two chapters of this module; therein, we will be developing a responsive website for a startup company.

There are many complaints that the code in responsive frameworks is excessive; as a framework such as Bootstrap is used widely, it has to cover every design scenario and thus, it comes with some extra styles that you might not need for your website. Fortunately, we can easily minimize this issue by using the right tools, such as CSS preprocessors, and following a proper workflow.

Frankly, there isn't a perfect solution; and using a framework certainly isn't for everyone. It all comes down to your needs, your website's needs, and in particular, your client's needs and budgets. In reality, you will have to weigh these factors to decide whether you will go with a responsive framework or not. Jem Kremer has an extensive discussion in this regard in her article *Responsive Design Frameworks: Just Because You Can, Should You?* (http://www. smashingmagazine.com/2014/02/19/responsive-design-frameworks-just-because-you-can-should-you/)

A brief introduction to CSS preprocessors

Both Bootstrap and Foundation use CSS preprocessors to generate their style sheets. Bootstrap uses LESS (http://lesscss.org/)—though the official support for Sass has just been released recently. Foundation, on the contrary, uses Sass as the only way to generate its style sheets (http://sass-lang.com/).

CSS preprocessor is not an entirely new language. If you have known CSS, you should be accustomed to the CSS preprocessor immediately. The CSS preprocessor simply extends CSS by allowing the use of programming features such as variables, functions, and operations.

The following is an example of how we write CSS with the LESS syntax:

```
@color: #f3f3f3;

body {
  background-color: @color;
}
p {
  color: darken(@color, 50%);
}
```

When the preceding code is compiled, it takes the `@color` variable that we have defined and places the value in the output, as follows:

```
body {
  background-color: #f3f3f3;
}
p {
  color: #737373;
}
```

The variable is reusable throughout the style sheet and this enables us to retain style consistency and make the style sheet more maintainable.

We are going to use and explore CSS preprocessors, LESS, and Sass further during the course of building responsive websites with Bootstrap (*Chapter 5, Developing a Portfolio Website with Bootstrap* and *Chapter 6, Polishing the Portfolio Website with LESS*) and Foundation (*Chapter 7, A Responsive Website for Business with Foundation*, and *Chapter 8, Extending Foundation*).

Have a Go Hero — delve into responsive web design

Our discussion on responsive web design here, though essential, is merely the tip of the iceberg. There is so much more about responsive web design than what we have recently covered in the preceding sections. I would suggest that you take your time to get yourself more insight and remove any apprehension on responsive web design, including the concept, the technicalities, and some constraints.

The following are some of the best recommendations for references:

◆ The *Responsive Web Design* article by Ethan Martcotte (`http://alistapart.com/article/responsive-web-design`), is where it all begins

◆ Also a good place to start is *Responsive Web Design* by Rachel Shillcock (`http://webdesign.tutsplus.com/articles/responsive-web-design--webdesign-15155`)

◆ *Don't Forget the Viewport Meta Tag* by Ian Yates (`http://webdesign.tutsplus.com/articles/quick-tip-dont-forget-the-viewport-meta-tag--webdesign-5972`)

◆ *How To Use CSS3 Media Queries To Create a Mobile Version of Your Website* by Rachel Andrew (`http://www.smashingmagazine.com/2010/07/19/how-to-use-css3-media-queries-to-create-a-mobile-version-of-your-website/`)

◆ Read about the future standards on responsive image using HTML5 Picture Element *Responsive Images Done Right: A Guide To <picture> And srcset* by Eric Portis (`http://www.smashingmagazine.com/2014/05/14/responsive-images-done-right-guide-picture-srcset/`)

◆ A roundup of methods to make data table responsive (`http://css-tricks.com/responsive-data-table-roundup/`)

Pop Quiz — responsive web design main components

Q1. In his article, which we have referred to about two times in this chapter, Ethan Marcotte mentioned the main technical ingredients that formulate a responsive website. What are those main components?

1. Viewport Meta Tag and CSS3 Media Queries.

2. Fluid grids, flexible images, and media queries.

3. Responsive images, breakpoints, and polyfills.

Q2. What is a viewport?

1. The screen size of the device.

2. The region where the web page is rendered.

3. The meta tag to set the web page's viewport size.

Q3. Which one of these is the correct way to declare CSS3 Media Queries?

1. `@media (max-width: 320px) { p{ font-size:11px; }}`

2. `@media screen and (max-device-ratio: 320px) { div{ color:white; }}`

3. `<link rel="stylesheet" media="(max-width: 320px)" href="core.css" />`

Responsive web design inspiration sources

Now, before we jump into the next chapters and start building responsive websites, it may be a good idea to spend some time looking for ideas and inspiration for responsive websites; to see how they are built and how the layout is organized on desktop browsers, as well as on mobile browsers.

It's a common thing for websites to be redesigned from time to time to stay fresh. So, instead of making a pile of website screenshots, which may no longer be relevant in the next several months because of the redesign, we're better going straight to the websites that curate websites, and the following are the places to go:

- MediaQueries (`http://mediaqueri.es/`)
- Awwwards (`http://www.awwwards.com/websites/responsive-design/`)
- CSS Awards (`http://www.cssawards.net/structure/responsive/`)
- WebDesignServed (`http://www.webdesignserved.com/`)
- Bootstrap Expo (`http://expo.getbootstrap.com/`)
- Zurb Responsive (`http://zurb.com/responsive`)

Summary

In this chapter, we glanced at the short story behind responsive web design, as well as the viewport meta tag and CSS3 media queries, which formulate responsive websites. This chapter also concluded that we are going to work on three projects by using the following frameworks: Responsive.gs, Bootstrap, and Foundation.

Using a framework is an easier and faster way to get responsive websites up and running, rather than building everything from scratch on our own. Alas, as mentioned, using a framework also has some negative aspects. If it is not done properly, the end result could all go wrong. The website could be stuffed and stuck with unnecessary styles and JavaScript, which at the end makes the website load slowly and hard to maintain.

We need to set up the right tools; not only will they facilitate the projects, but they will also help us in making the website more easy to maintain, and this is what we are going to do in the next chapter.

2
Web Development Tools

Every professional has a set of tools that facilitates their work and gets the job done. Likewise, we will also need our own tools to do our bit of building responsive websites. So, before we start working on the projects in this module, the following are the tools we have to prepare.

Tools that we will have to prepare include:

- A code editor for writing codes
- A compiler that will compile the CSS preprocessor syntax into plain CSS
- A local server to host the websites locally during the development stage
- A bower to manage the website libraries

Choosing a code editor

As soon as we start writing code for HTML, CSS, and JavaScript, we need a code editor. A code editor is an indispensible tool to develop websites. Technically, you will only need text editors such as TextEdit in OS X or Notepad in Windows to write and edit code. However, by using a code editor, your eyes will be less irritated.

Similar to Microsoft Word, which has been specially designed to make word and paragraph formatting more intuitive, a code editor is designed with a set of special features that improves code writing experiences such as syntax highlighting, auto-completion, code snippets, multiple line selection, and supporting a large number of languages. Syntax highlighting will display code in different colors, enhancing code readability and make it easy to find errors in the code.

My personal preference for a code editor, and the one that I will use in this module, is Sublime Text (`http://www.sublimetext.com/`). Sublime Text is a cross-platform code editor available for Windows, OS X, and Linux. It can be downloaded free for evaluation for an unlimited time.

 Keep in mind that while Sublime Text allows us to evaluate free of cost for an unlimited time, it may sometimes bug you to purchase the license. If you start feeling annoyed, please consider purchasing the license.

Sublime Text Package Control

One thing that I love most from Sublime Text is Package Control where we can search, install, list, and remove extensions from Sublime Text conveniently. However, Package Control does not come pre-installed with Sublime Text. So, assuming you have installed Sublime Text (which I think you should have), we will install Package Control in Sublime Text.

Time for action – installing Sublime Text Package Control

Perform the following steps to install Sublime Text Package Control; this will allow us to install Sublime Text extension easily:

1. The easiest way to install Package Control in Sublime Text is through the Sublime Text console. Open the console by navigating to the **View | Console** menu in Sublime Text. You should now see a new input field show up at the bottom, as shown in the following screenshot:

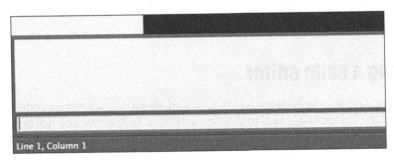

2. Due to the overhaul made in Sublime Text 3 that changed almost the entire API, the Package Control is now separated in two versions, one for Sublime Text 2 and the other one for Sublime Text 3. Each version requires a different piece of code to install Package Control. If you are using Sublime Text 2, copy the code from `https://sublime.wbond.net/installation#st2`. If you are using Sublime Text 3, copy the code from `https://sublime.wbond.net/installation#st3` instead.

3. Paste the code that you have copied from step 2 into the console input field, as shown in the following screenshot:

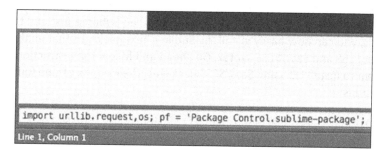

```
import urllib.request,os; pf = 'Package Control.sublime-package';
```
Line 1, Column 1

4. Press *Enter* to run the codes and eventually install Package Control. Keep in mind that the process may take a while depending on your Internet connection speed.

What just happened?

We just installed Package Control to search, install, list, and remove extensions in Sublime Text easily. You can access Package Control through **Command Palette...**, which can be accessed by navigating to the **Tools | Command Palette...** menu. Alternatively, you can press a key shortcut to access it faster. Windows and Linux users can press *Ctrl* + *Shift* + *P*, while OS X users can press *Command* + *Shift* + *P*. Then, search for **Command Palette...** to list all available commands for Package Control.

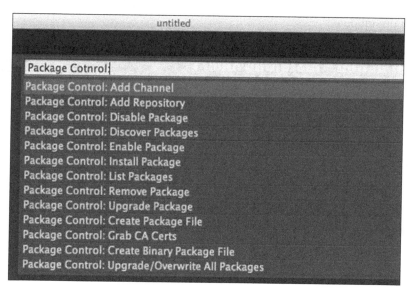

Have a go hero – install the LESS and Sass syntax-highlighting package

As mentioned in the first chapter, we are going to use these CSS preprocessors to compose styles in two of the projects in this module. Having installed Sublime Text and the Package Control already, you can now easily install the Sublime Text packages that enable color highlighting for LESS and Sass/SCSS syntax. Go ahead and follow the instructions that we have just shown to install LESS and Sass/SCSS packages, their syntax can be found at the following locations:

 ◆ LESS Syntax for Sublime Text (`https://github.com/danro/LESS-sublime`)
 ◆ Syntax Highlighting for Sass and SCSS (`https://github.com/P233/Syntax-highlighting-for-Sass`)

Setting up a local server

Having a local server set up and running on our computer is necessary while developing a website. When we use a local server to store our website, we will be able to access it through `http://localhost/` in the browsers, and we will also be able to access it on mobile phone browsers and tablets, which will not be possible when we run the website under `file:///  protocol`. Besides, some scripts may only be functioning under the HTTP protocol (`http://`).

There are many applications that make setting up a local server a breeze with only a few clicks, and XAMPP (`https://www.apachefriends.org/`) is the application that we will be using in this module.

Time for action – installing XAMPP

XAMPP is available for Windows, OS X, and Linux. Download the installer from `https://www.apachefriends.org/download.html`; pick the installer in accordance with the platform you are using right now. Each platform will have a different installer with different extensions; Windows users will get `.exe`, OSX users will get `.dmg`, while Linux users will get `.run`. Perform the following steps to install XAMPP in Windows:

1. Launch the XAMPP `.exe` installer.
2. If the Windows User Account Control prompts **Do you want to allow the following program to make changes to this computer?** click on **Yes**.

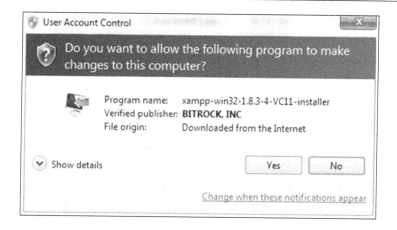

3. When the **XAMPP Setup Wizard** window appears, click on **Next** to start the setup.

4. XAMPP allows us to select which components to install. In this case, our web server requirement is the bare minimum. We will only need Apache to run the server, so we deselect the other options. (Note: the **PHP** option is grayed out; it cannot be unchecked):

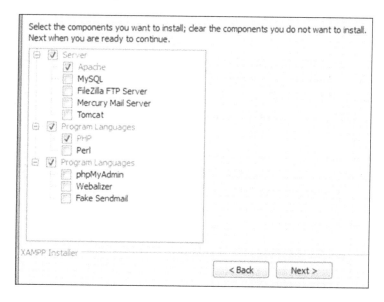

5. After confirming the components that will be installed, click on the **Next** button to proceed.

6. You will be prompted for the location to install XAMPP. Let's just leave it to the default location at `C:\xampp` and then click on **Next**.

7. Then, simply click on **Next** for the next two dialogs to start installing XAMPP. Wait until the process is complete.

8. When the process is complete, you should see the window stating **Setup has finished installing XAMPP**. Click on the **Finish** button to finalize the process and close the window.

Perform the following steps to install XAMPP in OS X:

1. For OS X users, open the XAMPP `.dmg` file. A new **Finder** window should appear, containing the actual installer file which is typically named `xampp-osx-*-installer` (the asterisk (*) represents the XAMPP version), as shown in the following screenshot:

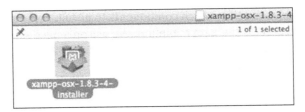

2. Double-click on the **installer** file to start the installation. XAMPP requires your computer credentials to run the installer. So, enter your computer name and password and click on **OK** to give it access.

3. The **XAMPP Setup Wizard** window appears afterwards; click on **Next** to start the setup.

4. Unlike Windows, which lists the components per item, the OS X version only shows two components, namely **XAMPP Core Files** and **XAMPP Developer Files**. Herein, we will only need the **XAMPP Core Files**, which comprises Apache, MySQL, and PHP that we need to run the server. So, deselect the **XAMPP Developer** option and then click on the **Next** button to proceed.

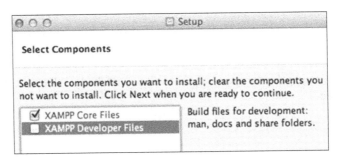

5. You will be prompted that XAMPP will be installed in the `Applications` folder. Unlike Windows, this directory can't be edited. So, click on **Next** to proceed.

6. Then, simply click on the **Next** button for the next two dialogs to start installing XAMPP. Wait until it is complete.

7. When the installation is complete, you will see **Setup has finished installing XAMPP** displayed in the window. Click on the **Finish** button to finalize the process and close the window.

Perform the following steps to install XAMPP in Ubuntu:

1. Download the XAMPP installer for Linux. The installer comes in the `.run` extension and is available for 32-bit and 64-bit systems.

2. Open the terminal and navigate to the folder where the installer is downloaded. Assuming it's in the `Downloads` folder, type:

```
cd ~/Downloads
```

3. Make the `.run` installer file executable with `chmod u+x`, followed by the `.run` installer filename:

```
chmod u+x xampp-linux-*-installer.run
```

4. Execute the file with the `sudo` command followed by the `.run` installer file location, as follows:

```
sudo ./xampp-linux-x64-1.8.3-4-installer.run
```

5. The command from Step 4 will bring up the **XAMPP Setup Wizard** window. Click on **Next** to proceed, as shown in the following screenshot:

6. The installer lets you select which components to install on the computer. Similar to the OS X version, there are two components shown in the option: **XAMPP Core Files** (containing Apache, MySQL, PHP, and a bunch of other things to run the server) and **XAMPP Developer Files**. As we do not need **XAMPP Developer Files**, we can deselect it and then click on the **Next** button.

7. The installer will show you that it will install XAMPP in /opt/lampp. The folder location can't be customized. Just click on the **Next** button to proceed.

8. Click on the **Next** button for the next two dialog screens to install XAMPP.

What just happened?

We have just set up a local server in our computer with MAMP. You can now access the local server with the http://localhost/ address through the browsers. For OS X users, however, the address is your computer username followed by .local. Say that your username is john the local server is accessible through john.local. The local server directory path is different for each platform:

◆ In Windows: C:\xampp\htdocs

◆ In OSX: /Applications/XAMPP/htdocs

♦ In Ubuntu: `/opt/lampp/htdocs`

 Ubuntu users may want to change the permissions and create a `symlink` folder on the desktop to reach the `htdocs` folder conveniently. To do so, you can run the `sudo chown username:groupname /opt/lampp/htdocs` command through the terminal from the desktop location. Replace `username` and `groupname` to match your own.

The `ln -s /opt/lamp/htdocs` folder is where we will have to put our project folders and files. From now on, we will refer to this folder simply as `htdocs`. XAMPP is also equipped with a graphical application where you can turn the server on and off, as shown in the following screenshot:

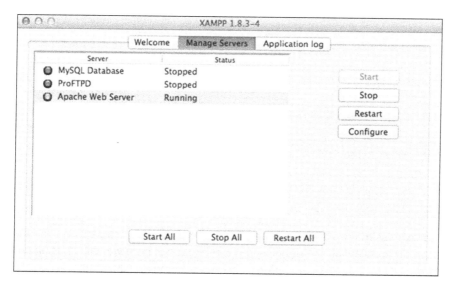

 Ubuntu users, you'll have to run `sudo /opt/lampp/manager-linux.run` or `manager-linux-x64.run`.

Choosing a CSS preprocessor compiler

As we will be using LESS and Sass to generate the style sheets of our responsive website, we will need a tool that will compile or change them into normal CSS format.

Back when CSS preprocessors were just gaining momentum, the only way to compile them was through command lines, which may have been the stumbling block for many people to even try CSS preprocessors at that time. Fortunately, we now have plenty of applications with a nice graphical interface to compile CSS preprocessors; the following is the list for your reference:

Tools	Language	Platform	Price
WinLESS (`http://winless.org/`)	LESS	Windows	Free
SimpLESS (`http://wearekiss.com/simpless`)	LESS	Windows, OSX	Free
ChrunchApp (`http://crunchapp.net`)	LESS	Windows, OSX	Free
CompassApp (`http://compass.handlino.com`)	Sass	Windows, OSX, Linux	$10
Prepros (`http://alphapixels.com/prepros/`)	LESS, Sass, and so on	Windows, OSX	Freemium ($24)
Codekit (`https://incident57.com/codekit/`)	LESS, Sass, and so on	OSX	$29
Koala (`http://koala-app.com/`)	LESS, Sass, and so on	Windows, OSX, Linux	Free

I will try to cover as many platforms as possible. Regardless of which platform you are using, you will be able to follow all the projects in this module. So, here we will be using Koala. It's free and available on three major platforms, namely, Windows, OSX, and Linux.

Installing Koala in each platform is pretty straightforward.

Browser for development

Ideally, we have to test our responsive websites in as many browsers as possible, including beta browsers such as Firefox Nightly (`http://nightly.mozilla.org/`) and Chrome Canary (`http://www.google.com/intl/en/chrome/browser/canary.html`). This is to ensure that our website is functioning well in different environments. However, during the development, we may pick one primary browser for development and as the point of reference of how the website should be put on display.

In this module, we will be using Chrome (`https://www.google.com/intl/en/chrome/browser/`). It is my humble opinion that Chrome, besides running fast, is also a very powerful web development tool. Chrome comes with a set of tools that are ahead of the other browsers. The following are two of my favorite tools in Chrome when it comes to developing responsive websites.

Source maps

One of the pitfalls of using CSS preprocessors is when debugging the style sheet. As the style sheet is generated and the browser refers to the CSS style sheet, we will find it hard to discover where exactly the code is declared within the CSS preprocessor's style sheet.

We may tell the compiler to generate comments containing the line numbers of where the code is actually written, but source maps solve this snag more elegantly. Rather than generating a bunch of comments that eventually pollute the style sheet, we can generate a `.map` file on compiling CSS preprocessors. Through this `.map` file, browsers such as Chrome, with source maps enabled, will be able to point directly to the source when we inspect an element, as shown in the following screenshot:

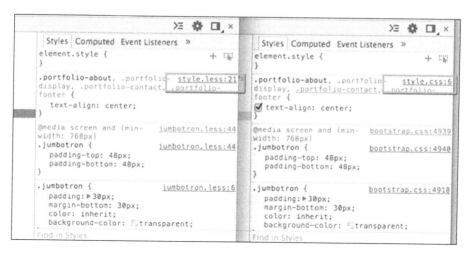

As you can see from the preceding screenshot, the Chrome DevTools shown on the left with source maps enabled refer directly to the `.less` files that allow us to debug the website with ease. Whereas, the source maps of the one shown on the right is disabled, so it refers to `.css`, and debugging the website would require a bit of struggle.

The source maps feature is, by default, enabled in the latest version of Chrome. So, make sure that your Chrome is up-to-date.

Mobile emulator

There isn't any substitution for testing a responsive website in a real device, a phone, or a tablet. Each device has its own merits; some factors, such as the screen dimension, the screen resolution, and the version of mobile browser, will affect your website displayed on the device. Yet, if that is not possible, we can use a mobile emulator as an alternative.

Chrome is also shipped with a mobile emulator that works out-of-the-box. This feature contains a number of presets for many mobile devices including iPhone, Nexus, and Blackberry. This feature not only emulates the device's user agent, it also turns on a number of device specifications, including the screen resolution, pixel ratio, viewport size, and touch screen. This feature can be extremely useful for debugging our responsive website early during development, without requiring an actual mobile device.

The mobile emulator is accessible through the **Emulation** tab of the Chrome DevTool **Console** drawer, as shown in the following screenshot:

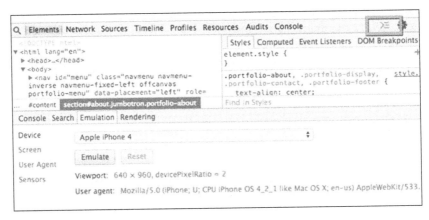

With the mobile emulator built into Chrome, we do not need to set up yet another emulator from a third-party application or Chrome extensions. Here, we will use it to test our responsive websites.

 Firefox has a similar feature to Chrome's mobile emulator, though it comparably only has very few features. You can enable this feature by navigating to the **Tools | Web Developer | Responsive Design View** menu.

Managing project dependency with Bower

We will need a number of libraries to manage a project dependency with Bower. In the web development context, we refer to a library as a collection of code, usually CSS and JavaScript, to add features on the website. Often, the website is dependent on a particular library for it to function its prime feature. As an example, if I built a website to convert currencies, the website will require Account.js (`http://josscrowcroft.github.io/accounting.js/`); it is a handy JavaScript library to convert regular numbers into currency format with the currency symbol.

It is common that we may add about five or more libraries on a single website, but maintaining all the libraries used in the website and making sure that they are all up-to-date could become cumbersome. This is where Bower is useful.

Bower (`http://bower.io/`) is a frontend package manager. It is a handy tool that streamlines the way we add, update, and remove libraries or dependencies (libraries that are required for the project) in our project. Bower is a Node.js module, so we first have to install Node.js (`http://nodejs.org/`) on our computer to be able to use Bower.

Time for action – installing Node.js

Perform the following steps to install Node.js in Windows, OS X, and Ubuntu (Linux). You may skip directly to the section of the platform you are using.

Perform the following steps to install Node.js in Windows:

1. Download the Node.js Windows installer from the Node.js download page (`http://nodejs.org/download/`). Choose your flavor for your Windows system, the 32-bit or 64-bit version, and the `.msi` or `.exe` installer.

    32-bit or 64-bit

    Follow this page to discover if your Windows computer is running on a 32-bit or a 64-bit system `http://windows.microsoft.com/en-us/windows/32-bit-and-64-bit-windows`.

2. Run the installer (`.exe` or `.msi` file).

3. Click on the **Next** button of the Node.js welcome message.

4. As usual, when you are installing a software or application, you will first be prompted by the application's license agreement. Once you have read the license, click on **I accept the terms in the License Agreement** and then click on the **Next** button to proceed.

5. Then, you will be prompted for the folder where Node.js should be installed. Leave it as the default folder, which is in `C:\Program Files\nodejs\`.

6. As you can see from the following screenshot, the installer then prompts to ask if you want to customize the item to be installed. Leave it as it is and click on the **Next** button to proceed, as shown in the following screenshot:

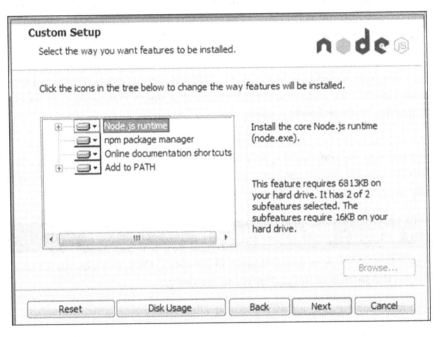

7. Afterwards, click on the **Install** button to start installing Node.js.

8. The installation process is quite fast; it takes only a few seconds. If you see the notification that says **Node.js has been successfully installed**, you may click on the **Finish** button to close the installation window.

Perform the following steps to install Node.js in OS X:

1. Download the Node.js installer for OS X, which comes in the `.pkg` extension.

2. The installer will show you a welcome message and show you the location where it will install Node.js (`/usr/local/bin`), as shown in the following screenshot:

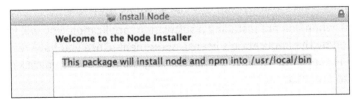

3. The installer then shows the user license agreement. If you read and agree to the license, click on the **Agree** button and then click on the **Next** button.

4. The Node.js installer for OS X allows you to select which Node.js feature to install prior to installing it into your computer. Here, we will install all the features; simply click on the **Install** button to start installing Node.js, as shown in the following screenshot:

 If you want to customize your Node.js install, click on the **Customize** button at the bottom left, as shown in the previous screenshot.

Perform the following steps to install Node.js in Ubuntu:

Installing Node.js in Ubuntu is quite straightforward. Node.js can be installed through Ubuntu's **Advanced Packaging Tool (APT)** or `apt-get`. If you are using Ubuntu version 13.10 or the latest version, you can launch the terminal and run the following two commands consecutively:

```
sudo apt-get install nodejs
sudo apt-get install npm
```

If you are using Ubuntu version 13.04 or earlier, run the following command instead:

```
sudo apt-get install -y python-software-properties python g++ make
sudo add-apt-repository ppa:chris-lea/node.js
sudo apt-get update
sudo apt-get install nodejs
```

What just happened?

We have just installed Node.js and `npm` command, which enable us to use Bower later on through the **Node.js Package Manager (NPM)**. The `npm` command line should now be accessible through the Windows command prompt or the OS X and Ubuntu terminals. Run the following command to test if the `npm` command works:

```
npm -v
```

This command returns the NPM version installed in the computer, as shown in the following screenshot:

Additionally, for Windows users, you may see a message at the top of the command prompt window saying **Your environment has been set up for using Node.js and npm**, as shown in the following screenshot:

This shows that you can perform the node and npm command within the command prompt. As we have set Node.js and npm is up and running, we are now going to install Bower.

Have a go hero – get yourself familiar with command lines

Throughout this module, we will be dealing with a number of command lines to install Bower, as well as Bower packages. Yet, if you are from a graphic design background like I was, where we mostly work on a graphical application, operating a command line for the first time could be really awkward and intimidating. Hence, I would suggest you take time and get yourself familiar with the basic command lines. The following are a few references worth checking out:

◆ *A Designer's Introduction to the Command Line* by Jonathan Cutrell (https://webdesign.tutsplus.com/articles/a-designers-introduction-to-the-command-line--webdesign-6358)

◆ *Navigating the Terminal: A Gentle Introduction* by Marius Masalar (https://computers.tutsplus.com/tutorials/navigating-the-terminal-a-gentle-introduction--mac-3855)

- *Introduction to the Windows Command Prompt* by Lawrence Abrams (`http://www.bleepingcomputer.com/tutorials/windows-command-prompt-introduction/`)

- *Introduction to Linux Command* by Paul Tero (`http://www.smashingmagazine.com/2012/01/23/introduction-to-linux-commands/`)

Time for action – installing Bower

Perform the following steps to install Bower:

1. If you are using Windows, open the command prompt. If you are using OS X or Ubuntu, open the terminal. For installing Bower, Git is required. Please ensure that Git is downloaded and installed (https://git-scm.com/downloads).

2. Run the following command:

   ```
   npm install -g bower
   ```

 If you are having trouble installing Bower in Ubuntu, run the command with `sudo`.

What just happened?

We have just installed Bower on the computer, which enables the `bower` command. The `-g` parameter that we included in the preceding command installs Bower globally, so that we are able to execute the `bower` command in any directory in the computer.

Bower commands

After installing Bower, we have access to a set of command lines to operate Bower functionalities. We will run these commands in the terminal, or in the command prompts if you are using Windows, just like we installed Bower with the `npm` command. All commands start with `bower` and are followed by the command keyword. The following is the list of commands that we may use frequently:

Command	Function
`bower install <library-name>`	Installs a library into the project. When we perform this function, Bower creates a new folder called `bower_components` to save all the library files.
`bower list`	Lists all installed package names in the project. This command also shows the new version if available.

Command	Function
`bower init`	Sets the project as the Bower project. This command also creates `bower.json`.
`bower uninstall <library-name>`	Removes the library name from the project.
`bower version <library-name>`	Retrieves the installed library version.

 You can run `bower --help` for the complete list of commands.

Pop quiz – web development tools and command lines

Q1. We have just installed Sublime Text along with Package Control. What is the Package Control used for?

1. To install and remove the Sublime Text package easily.

2. To install LESS and Sass/SCSS packages.

3. To manage packages in Sublime Text.

Q2. We have also installed XAMPP. Why did we need to install XAMPP?

1. To host the websites locally.

2. To develop websites locally.

3. To manage the project locally.

Summary

In this chapter, we have installed Sublime Text, XAMPP, Koala, and Bower. All these tools will facilitate us in building the websites. As we have got the tools prepared, we can now start working on the projects. So, let's move on to the next chapter and start the very first project.

3
Constructing a Simple Responsive Blog with Responsive.gs

In the previous chapter, we installed a number of software that will facilitate our projects. Here, we will start off our very first project. In this project, we are going to build a responsive blog.

Having a blog is essential for a company. Even several Fortune 500 companies such as FedEx (`http://outofoffice.van.fedex.com/`*), Microsoft (*`https://blogs.windows.com/`*) and General Motors (*`http://fastlane.gm.com/`*) have official corporate blogs. A blog is a great channel for the company to publish official news as well as to connect with their customers and the masses. Making the blog responsive is the way to go to make the blog more accessible to the readers who may access the site through a mobile device, such as a phone or tablet.*

As the blog that we are going to build in this first project will not be that complex, this chapter would be an ideal chapter for those who have just come across responsive web design.

So let's get started.

To sum up, in this chapter, we will cover the following topics:

- ◆ Dig into Responsive.gs components
- ◆ Examine the blog blueprint and design
- ◆ Organize the website files and folders
- ◆ Look into HTML5 elements for semantic markup
- ◆ Construct the blog markup

Responsive.gs components

As we mentioned in *Chapter 1*, *Responsive Web Design*, Responsive.gs is a lightweight CSS framework. It comes only with the bare minimum requirements for building responsive websites. In this section, we are going to see what is included in Responsive.gs.

The classes

Responsive.gs is shipped with a series of reusable classes to form the responsive grid that makes it easier and faster for web designers to build web page layout. These classes contain preset style rules that have been carefully calibrated and tested. So we can simply drop in these classes within the HTML element to construct the responsive grid. The following is a list of the classes in Responsive.gs:

Class name	Usage
container	We use this class to set the web page container and align it to the center of the browser window. This class, however, does not give the element width. Responsive.gs gives us the flexibility to set the width as per our requirement.
row, group	We use these two classes to wrap a group of columns. Both of these classes are set with so called self-clearing floats that fix some layout issues caused by the element with the CSS float property.
	Check the following references for further information about the CSS float property and the issue it may cause to a web page layout:
	◆ *The Mystery Of The CSS Float Property* by Louis Lazaris (http://www.smashingmagazine.com/2009/10/19/the-mystery-of-css-float-property/)
	◆ *All About Floats* by Chris Coyier (http://css-tricks.com/all-about-floats/)
col	We use this class to define the column of the web page. This class is set with the CSS float property. So any elements set with this class have to be contained within an element with the row or group class to avoid the issues caused by the CSS float property.
gutters	We use this class to add spaces between the columns set with the preceding col class.

Class name	Usage
span_{x}	This class defines the column width. So we use this class in tandem with the col class.
	Responsive.gs comes in three variants of grid, which gives us flexibility while organizing the web page layout. Responsive.gs is available in the 12-, 16-, and 24-columns format. These variants are set in three separate style sheets. If you download Responsive.gs package and then unpack it, you will find three style sheets named responsive.gs.12col.css, responsive.gs.16col.css, and responsive.gs.24col.css.
	The only difference between these style sheets is the number of span_ classes defined within it. It is apparent that the 24-column format style sheet has the most number of span_{x} classes; the class stretches from span_1 to span_24. If you need greater flexibility on dividing your page, then using the 24-column format of Responsive.gs is the way to go. Though each column may be too narrow.
clr	This class is provided to address the floating issue. We use this class in the occasion where using the row class would not be semantically appropriate.

Now, let's see how we apply them in an example to discover how they really work. Many times, you will see that a web page is divided into a multiple columns structure. Take that into account as our example here; we can do the following to construct a web page with two columns of content:

```
<div class="container">
<div class="row gutters">
  <div class="col span_6">
    <h3>Column 1</h3>
    <p>Lorem ipsum dolor sit amet, consectetur adipisicing
elit. Veniam, enim.</p>
  </div>
  <div class="col span_6">
    <h3>Column 2</h3>
    <p>Lorem ipsum dolor sit amet, consectetur adipisicing
elit. Reiciendis, optio.</p>
  </div>
</div>
</div>
```

As you can see from the preceding code snippet, we first added `container` that wraps all the contents. Then, it is followed by `div` with a `row` class to wrap the columns. At the same time, we also added the `gutters` class so that there will be blank space between the two columns. In this example, we used the 12-column format. Therefore, to split the page into two equal columns, we added the `span_6` class for each column. This is to say that the number of `span_{x}` classes should be equal to 12, 16, or 24 in accordance with the variant we are using in order for the columns to cover the entire container. So, if we used the 16-columns format, for example, we may add `span_8` instead.

In the browser, we will see the following output:

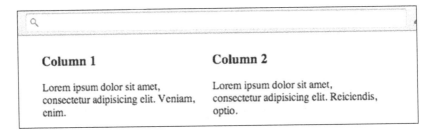

Using HTML5 elements for semantic markups

Paul Boag, in his article *Semantic code: What? Why? How?* (`http://boagworld.com/dev/semantic-code-what-why-how/`) wrote:

> *HTML was originally intended as a means of describing the content of a document, not as a means to make it appear visually pleasing.*

Unlike traditional content outlets such as newspapers or magazines, which are apparently intended for humans, the Web is read both by humans and machines such as search engines and screen readers that help visually impaired people navigate websites. So making our website structure semantic is really encouraged. Semantic markup allows these machines to understand the content better and also makes the content more accessible in different formats.

On that account, HTML5 introduces a bunch of new elements in its mission to make the web more semantic. The following is a list of elements that we are going to use for the blog:

Element	Description
`<header>`	The `<header>` element is used to specify the head of a section. While this element may be used commonly to specify the website header, it is also appropriate to use this element to specify, for example, the article header where we place the title and other supporting pieces of the article. We can use `<header>` multiple times in a single page where it is fitting.
`<nav>`	The `<nav>` element is used to represent a group of links that is intended as the primary navigation of the website or a section of a page.
`<article>`	The `<article>` element is quite self-explanatory. This element specifies the article of a website, such as the blog entry or the main page content.
`<main>`	The `<main>` element defines the main portion of a section. This element can be used to do things such as wrapping the article content.
`<figure>`	The `<figure>` element is used to specify document figures such as diagrams, illustrations, and images. The `<figure>` element can be used along with `<figcaption>` to add the figure's caption, if needed.
`<figcaption>`	As mentioned, `<figcaption>` represents the caption of the document's figure. Thus, it must be used in tandem with the `<figure>` element.
`<footer>`	Similar to the `<header>` element, the `<footer>` element is commonly used to specify the website footer. But it can also be used to represent the end or the lowest part of a section.

 Refer to the cheat sheet http://websitesetup.org/html5-cheat-sheet/, to find more new HTML elements in HTML5.

HTML5 search input types

Besides the new elements, we will also add one particular new type of input on the blog, search. As the name implies, the search input type is used to specify a search input. In the desktop browsers, you may not see a significant difference. You may also not immediately see how the search input type give advantages to the website and the users.

The search input type will boost the experience of mobile users. Mobile platforms such as iOS, Android, and the Windows Phone have been equipped with contextual screen keyboards. The keyboard will change according to the input type. You can see in the following screenshot that the keyboard displays the **Search** button, which allows users to perform a search more conveniently:

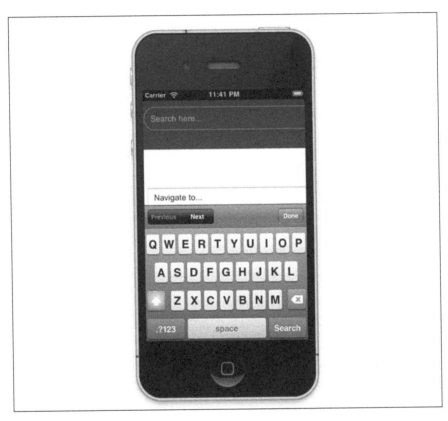

HTML5 placeholder attribute

HTML5 introduced a new attribute named `placeholder`. The specs described this attribute as a short hint (a word or short phrase) intended to aid the user with data entry when the control has no value, as shown in the following example:

```
<input type="search" name="search_form " placeholder="Search here…">
```

You will see that **Search here...** in the `placeholder` attribute is shown in the input field, as shown in the following screenshot:

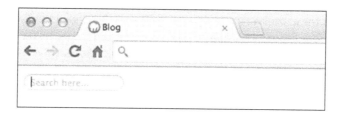

In the past, we relied on JavaScript to achieve a similar effect. Today, with the `placeholder` attribute, the application gets much simpler.

HTML5 in Internet Explorer

These new HTML elements make our document markup more descriptive and meaningful. Unfortunately, Internet Explorer 6, 7, and 8 will not recognize them. Thus, the selectors and style rules that address these elements are inapplicable; it is as if these new elements are not included in the Internet Explorer dictionary.

This is where a polyfill named HTML5Shiv comes into play. We will include HTML5Shiv (`https://github.com/aFarkas/html5shiv`) to make Internet Explorer 8 and its lower versions acknowledge these new elements. Read the following post (`http://paulirish.com/2011/the-history-of-the-html5-shiv/`) by Paul Irish for the history behind HTML5Shiv; how it was invented and developed.

Furthermore, older Internet Explorer versions won't be able to render the content in the HTML5 `placeholder` attribute. Fortunately, we can patch mimic the `placeholder` attribute functionality in the old Internet Explorer with a polyfill (`https://github.com/UmbraEngineering/Placeholder`). We will use it later on the blog as well.

A look into polyfills in the Responsive.gs package

Responsive.gs is also shipped with two polyfills to enable certain features that are not supported in Internet Explorer 6, 7, and 8. From now on, let's refer to these browser versions as "old Internet Explorer", shall we?

Box sizing polyfills

The first polyfill is available through an **HTML Component (HTC)** file named `boxsizing.htc`.

An HTC file is much the same as JavaScript and is commonly used in tandem with the Internet Explorer proprietary CSS property `behavior` to add a specific functionality to Internet Explorer. The `boxsizing.htc` file that comes with Responsive.gs will apply a similar functionality as in the CSS3 `box-sizing` property.

Responsive.gs includes the `boxsizing.htc` file within the style sheets as follows:

```
* {
  -webkit-box-sizing: border-box;
  -moz-box-sizing: border-box;
  box-sizing: border-box;
  *behavior: url(/scripts/boxsizing.htc);
}
```

As shown in the preceding code snippet, Responsive.gs applies the `box-sizing` property and includes the `boxsizing.htc` file with the asterisk selector. This asterisk selector is also known as wildcard selector; it selects all the elements within the document, and that being said, `box-sizing`, in this case, will affect all elements within the document.

> The `boxsizing.htc` file path must be an absolute path or relative to the HTML document in order for polyfill to work. This is a hack. It is something we forcibly use to make old Internet Explorer behave like a modern browser. Using an HTC file such as the preceding one is not considered valid as per the W3C standards.
>
> Please refer to this page by Microsoft regarding HTC files (`http://msdn.microsoft.com/en-us/library/ms531018(v=vs.85).aspx`).

CSS3 media queries polyfill

The second polyfill script that comes along with Responsive.gs is `respond.js` (`https://github.com/scottjehl/Respond`), which will "magically enable" CSS3 `respond.js` to work out of the box. There is no need for configuration; we can simply link the script within the `head` tag as follows:

```
<!--[if lt IE 9]>
<script src="respond.js"></script>
<![endif]-->
```

In the preceding code, we encapsulated the script inside `<!--[if lt IE 9]>` to make the script load only within the old Internet Explorer.

Examining the blog's wireframe

Building a website is much the same as building a house; we need to examine the specification of every corner before we stack up all the bricks. So, before we jump in to building the blog, we will examine the blog's wireframe to see how the blog is laid out and also see the things that will be displayed on the blog.

Let's take a look at the following wireframe. This wireframe shows the blog layout when it is viewed on the desktop screen:

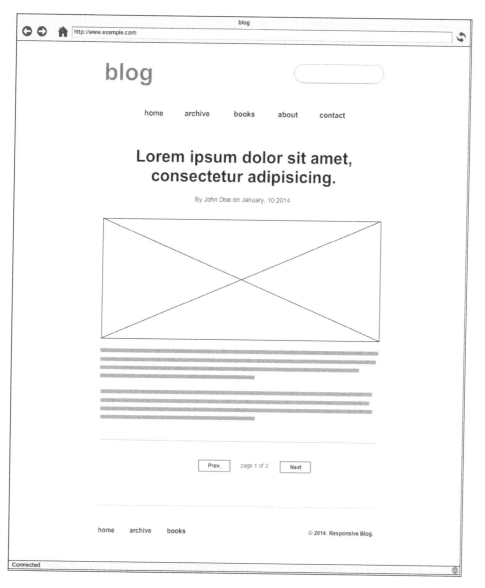

As you can see in the preceding screenshot, the blog will be plain and simple. In the header, the blog will have a logo and a search form. Down below the header, consecutively, we will place the menu navigation, the blog post, the pagination for navigating to the next or previous list of posts, and the footer.

The blog post, as in general, will comprise the title, the publishing date, the post's featured image, and the post excerpt. This wireframe is an abstraction of the blog's layout. We use it as our visual reference of how the blog layout will be arranged. So, in spite of the fact that we have shown only one post within the preceding wireframe, we will actually add a few more post items on the actual blog later on.

The following is the blog layout when the viewport width is squeezed:

When the viewport width gets narrow, the blog layout adapts. It is worth noticing that when we shift the layout, we should not alter the content flow as well as the UI hierarchy. Assuring the layout consistency between the desktop and the mobile version will help the users get familiar with a website quickly, regardless of where they are viewing the website. As shown in the preceding wireframe, we still have the UI set in the same order, albeit, they are now stacked vertically in order to fit in the limited area.

One thing that is worth mentioning from this wireframe is that the navigation turns into an HTML dropdown selection. We will discuss how to do so during the course of building the blog.

Now, as we have prepared the tools and checked out the blog layout, we are ready to start off the project. We will start off by creating and organizing the project directories and assets.

Organizing project directories and files

Often, we will have to link to certain files, such as style sheets and images. Unfortunately, websites are not a clever thing; they cannot find these files on their own. So, we must set the filepath correctly to avoid broken link errors.

This is why having organized directories and files is essential when it comes to building websites. It will be exceptionally important when we are working on a very large project with a team of people and with dozens to hundreds of files to handle. Poorly managed directories could drive anyone in the team insane.

Having well-organized directories will help us minimize potential errors of broken links. It will also make the project more maintainable and easily scalable in the future.

Time for action – creating and organizing project directories and assets

Perform the following steps to set up the project's working directory:

1. Go to the `htdocs` folder. As a reminder, this folder is the folder in the local server located at:

   - `C:\xampp\htdocs` in Windows
   - `/Applications/XAMPP/htdocs` in OSX
   - `/opt/lampp/htdocs` in Ubuntu

2. Create a new folder named `blog`. From now on, we will refer to this folder as the project directory.

3. Create a new folder named `css` to store style sheets.

4. Create a new folder named `image` to store images.

5. Create a new folder named `scripts` to store JavaScript files.

6. Create a new file named `index.html`; this HTML file will be the main page of the blog. Download the Responsive.gs package from `http://responsive.gs/`. The package comes in the `.zip` format. Extract the package to unleash the files within the package. There, you will find a number of files, including style sheets and JavaScript files, as you can see from the following screenshot:

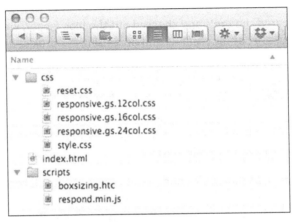

The files that ship in Responsive.gs

7. Move `responsive.gs.12col.css` to the `css` folder of the project directory; it is the only style sheet of Responsive.gs that we need.

8. Move `boxsizing.htc` to the `scripts` folder of the project directory.

9. The `respond.js` file that ships in the Responsive.gs package is out-of-date. Let's download the latest version of Respond.js from the GitHub repository (`https://github.com/scottjehl/Respond/blob/master/src/respond.js`) instead, and put it in the `scripts` folder of the project directory.

10. Download HTML5Shiv from `https://github.com/aFarkas/html5shiv`. Put the JavaScript file `html5shiv.js` within the `scripts` folder.

11. We will also use the placeholder polyfill that is developed by James Brumond (`https://github.com/UmbraEngineering/Placeholder`). James Brumond developed four different JavaScript files for cater to different scenarios.

12. The script that we are going to use here is `ie-behavior.js`, because this script specifically addresses Internet Explorer. Download the script (`https://raw.githubusercontent.com/UmbraEngineering/Placeholder/master/src/ie-behavior.js`) and rename it as `placeholder.js` to make it more apparent that this script is a placeholder polyfill. Put it in the `scripts` folder of the project directory.

13. The blog will need a few images to use as the post's featured image. In this module, we will use the images shown in the following screenshot, consecutively taken by Levecque Charles (`https://twitter.com/Charleslevecque`) and Jennifer Langley (`https://jennifer-langley.squarespace.com/photography/`):

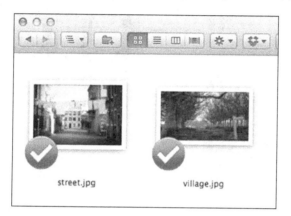

 Find more free high-definition images at Unsplash (`http://unsplash.com/`).

14. We will add a favicon to the blog. A favicon is a tiny icon that appears on the browser tab beside the title, which will be helpful for readers to quickly identify the blog. The following is a screenshot that shows a number of pinned tabs in Chrome. I bet that you are still able to recognize the websites within these tabs just by seeing the favicon:

Google Chrome pinned tabs

15. Further, we will also add the iOS icon. In Apple devices such as iPhone and iPad, we can pin websites on the home screen to make it quick to access the website. This is where the Apple icon turns out to be useful. iOS (the iPhone/iPad operating system) will show the icon we provide, as shown in the following screenshot, as if it was a native application:

Website added to the iOS home screen

16. These icons are provided in the source files that come along with this module. Copy these icons and paste them in the image folder that we have just created in step 5, as shown in the following screenshot:

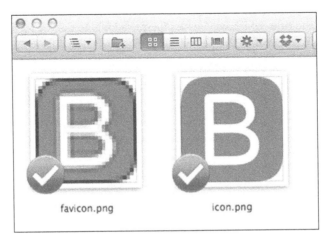

Create favicons and iOS icons quickly and easily with AppIconTemplate. AppIconTemplate (`http://appicontemplate.com/`) is a Photoshop template that makes it easy for us to design the icon. The template is also shipped with Photoshop Actions to generate the icons with a few clicks.

What just happened?

We have just created a directory for this project and put a couple of files in the directory. These files include the Responsive.gs style sheets and JavaScript files, images and icons, and a number of polyfills. We have also created an `index.html` file that will be the home page for the blog. At this point, the project directory should contain files as shown in the following screenshot:

The current files and folders in the working directory

Have a go hero – making the directory structure more organized

Many people have their own preferences for how to organize their project's directory structure. The one shown in the previous section was just an example, of how I personally manage the directory for this project.

Try going further to make the directory more organized and meet your own preference for organization. A few common ideas are as follows:

- Make the folder name shorter, that is, `js` and `img`, instead of JavaScript and Image
- Group the folders `js`, `img`, and `css` all together in a new folder named `assets`

Pop quiz – using polyfill

Earlier in this module, we discussed polyfill and also mentioned a few polyfill scripts that we are going to implement in the blog.

Q1. When do you think would be an appropriate time to use the polyfill?

1. When the blog is viewed in Internet Explorer 6.
2. When the feature is not supported in the browser.
3. When we need to add new feature on the website.
4. We can use it at anytime.

The blog HTML structures

We have laid the structure of the project directories and files in the previous section. Let's now start constructing the blog markup. As we mentioned, we will use a number of HTML5 elements to form a more meaningful HTML structure.

Time for action – constructing the blog

Perform the following steps to build the blog:

1. Open the index.html file that we have created in step 6 of the previous section *Time for action – creating and organizing project directories and assets*. Let's start by adding the most basic HTML5 structure as follows:

```
<!DOCTYPE html>
<html lang="en">
<head>
  <meta charset="UTF-8">
  <title>Blog</title>
</head>
<body>

</body>
</html>
```

Here, set DOCTYPE, which has been brought to the bare minimum form. The DOCTYPE format in HTML5 is now shorter and cleaner than the DOCTYPE format of its HTML4 counterpart. Then, we set the language of our page, which in this case is set to en (English). You may change it to your local language; find the code for your local language at http://en.wikipedia.org/wiki/List_of_ISO_639-1_codes.

We have also set the character encoding to `UTF-8` to enable the browser to render the Unicode characters, such as `U+20AC`, to the readable format €.

2. Below the `charset` meta tag in the `head` tag, add the following meta:

```
<meta http-equiv="X-UA-Compatible" content="IE=edge">
```

Internet Explorer can sometimes behave oddly, where it suddenly switches to compatibility mode and renders the page as viewed in Internet Explorer 8 and 7. This meta tag addition will prevent that from happening. It will force Internet Explorer to render the page with the highest support of the latest standards available in Internet Explorer.

3. Below the `http-equiv` meta tag, add the following meta viewport tag:

```
<meta name="viewport" content="width=device-width, initial-scale=1">
```

As we mentioned in *Chapter 1*, *Responsive Web Design*, the preceding viewport meta tag specification defines the web page viewport width to follow the device viewport size. It also defines the web page scale at 1:1 upon opening the web page the first time.

4. Link the Apple icon with the `link` tag, as follows:

```
<link rel="apple-touch-icon" href="image/icon.png">
```

As per Apple's official instructions, you would normally need to include multiple sources of icons to cater to iPhone, iPad, and the devices with a Retina screen. That isn't actually necessary for our blog. The trick is that we deliver the largest size required, which is 512 px square, through a single source, as shown in the previous screenshot.

Head over to the Apple documentation, specifying a web page icon for Web Clip (`https://developer.apple.com/library/ios/documentation/AppleApplications/Reference/SafariWebContent/ConfiguringWebApplications/ConfiguringWebApplications.html`), for further reference.

5. Add a description meta tag below the title, as follows:

```
<meta name="description" content="A simple blog built using Responsive.gs">
```

6. This description of the blog will show up in **Search Engine Result Page (SERP)**. In this step, we will construct the blog header. First, let's add the HTML5 `<header>` element along with the classes for styling, to wrap the header content. Add the following within the `body` tag:

```
<header class="blog-header row">

</header>
```

7. Within the `<header>` element that we added in step 9, add a new `<div>` element with the `container` and `gutters` class, as follows:

```
<header class="blog-header row">
<div class="container gutters">

</div>
</header>
```

Referring to the table shown earlier in the chapter, the `container` class will align the blog header content to the center of the browser window, while the `gutters` class will add spaces between the columns, which we will add in the next steps.

8. Create a new column to contain the blog logo/name with a `<div>` element along with the Responsive.gs `col` and `span_9` class to set the `<div>` element as column and specify the width. Don't forget to add the class to add custom styles:

```
<header class="blog-header row">
<div class="container gutters">
        <div class="blog-name col span_9">
<a href="/">Blog</a>
</div>
</div>
</header>
```

9. Referring to the blog wireframe, we will have a search form next to the blog logo/name. On that account, create another new column with a `<div>` element together with the `col` and `span_3` class of Responsive.gs, and the input search type. Add the `<div>` element below the logo markup as follows:

```
<header class="blog-header row">
<div class="container gutters">
        <div class="blog-name col span_9">
    <a href="/">Blog</a>
</div>
<div class="blog-search col span_3">
            <div class="search-form">
                <form action="">
  <input class="input_full" type="search"        placeholder="Search
  here...">
```

```
    </form>
                </div>
        </div>
    </div>
    </header>
```

As we mentioned earlier in this chapter, we used an input search type to serve a better user experience. This input will show the mobile screen keyboard with a special key that allows users to hit the **Search** button and immediately run the search. We also added placeholder text with the HTML5 `placeholder` attribute to show the users that they can perform a search in the blog through the input field.

10. After constructing the header blog, we will construct the blog navigation. Here we will use the HTML5 `nav` element to define a new section as navigation. Create a `nav` element along with the supporting classes to style. Add the `nav` element below the header construction as follows:

```
. . .
    </div>
    </header>
<nav class="blog-menu row">

</nav>
```

11. Inside the `nav` element, create a `div` element with the `container` class to align the navigation content to the center of the browser window:

```
<nav class="blog-menu">
<div class="container">
</div>
</nav>
```

12. In accordance to the wireframe, the blog will have five items on the link menu. We will lay out this link with the `ul` element. Add the links within the container, as shown in the following code snippet:

```
<nav class="blog-menu row">
  <div class="container">
      <ul class="link-menu">
        <li><a href="/">Home</a></li>
        <li><a href="#">Archive</a></li>
        <li><a href="#">Books</a></li>
        <li><a href="#">About</a></li>
        <li><a href="#">Contact</a></li>
    </ul>
</div>
</nav>
```

13. Having done with constructing the navigation, we will construct the content section of the blog. Following the wireframe, the content will consist a list of posts. First, let's add the HTML5 <main> element to wrap the content below the navigation as follows:

```
. . .
</ul>
</nav>
<main class="blog-content row">

</main>
```

We use the <main> element as we consider the posts as the prime section of our blog.

14. Similar to the other blog sections—the header and the navigation—we add a container <div> to align the blog posts to the center. Add this <div> element within the <main> element:

```
<main class="blog-content row">
    <div class="container">

</div>
</main>
```

15. We will now create the blog post markup. Think of the blog post as an article. Thus, here we will use the <article> element. Add the <article> element within the container <div> that we will add in step 17 as follows:

```
<main class="blog-content row">
<div class="container">
    <article class="post row">

    </article>
</div>
</main>
```

16. As mentioned, the <header> element is not limited to define a header. The blog can be used to define the head of a section. In this case, apart from the blog header, we will use the <header> element to define the articles head section that contains the article title and publishing date.

17. Add the <header> element within the article element:

```
<article class="post row">
<header class="post-header">
<h1 class="post-title">
<a href="#">Useful Talks &amp; Videos for Mastering CSS</a>
    </h1>
        <div class="post-meta">
```

```
    <ul>
       <li class="post-author">By John Doe</li>
       <li class="post-date">on January, 10 2014</li>
    </ul>
    </div>
  </header>
  </article>
```

18. A picture is worth a thousand words. So, it's the norm to use an image to support the post. Here, we will display the image below the post header. We will group the featured image together with the post excerpt as the post summary, as shown in the following code:

```
...
  </header>
  <div class="post-summary">
  <figure class="post-thumbnail">
  <img src="image/village.jpg" height="1508" width="2800" alt="">
  </figure>
  <p class="post-excerpt">Lorem ipsum dolor sit amet,   consectetur
  adipisicing elit. Aspernatur, sequi, voluptatibus, consequuntur
  vero iste autem aliquid qui et rerum vel ducimus ex enim
  quas!...<a href="#">Read More...</a></p>
    </div>
  </article>
```

Add a few more posts subsequently. Optionally, you may exclude the post featured image in the other posts.

19. After adding a pile of posts, we will now add the post pagination. The pagination is a form of common page navigation that allows us to jump to the next or previous list of posts. Normally, the pagination is located at the bottom of the page after the last post item.

The pagination of a blog consists of two links to navigate to the next and previous page, and a small section to place the page numbers to show what page the user is currently in.

20. So, add the following code after the last post:

```
...
</article>
<div class="blog-pagination">
<ul>
  <li class="prev"><a href="#">Prev. Posts</a></li>
  <li class="pageof">Page 2 of 5</li>
  <li class="next"><a href="#">Next Posts</a></li>
</ul>
</div>
```

21. Finally, we will construct the blog footer. We can define the blog footer using the HTML5 `<footer>` element. The footer structure is identical to the one for the header. The footer will have two columns; each respectively contains the blog footer links (or, as we call it, secondary navigation) and copyright statement. These columns are wrapped with a `<div>` container. Add the following footer in the main section, as follows:

```
    ...
</main>
<footer class="blog-footer row">
   <div class="container gutters">
      <div class="col span_6">
<nav id="secondary-navigation"  class="social-   media">
          <ul>
             <li class="facebook">
<a href="#">Facebook</a>
  </li>
             <li class="twitter">
<a href="#">Twitter</a></li>
             <li class="google">
<a href="#">Google+</a>
    </li>
          </ul>
        </nav>
      </div>
      <div class="col span_6">
<p class="copyright">&copy; 2014. Responsive  Blog.</p>
      </div>
      </div>
</footer>
```

What just happened?

We have just finished constructing the blog's HTML structure—the header, the navigation, the content, and the footer. Assuming that you have been following our instructions closely, you can access the blog at `http://localhost/blog/` or `http://{coputer-username}.local/blog/` in OS X.

However, as we haven't applied any styles, you will find that the blog is looking plain and the layout is yet to be organized:

The blog appearance at the current stage

We will style the blog in the next chapter.

Have a go hero – creating more blog pages

In this module, we only build the blog's home page. However, you are free to extend the blog by creating more pages, such as adding an about page, a single post content page, and a page with a contact form. You may reuse the HTML structure that we have built in this chapter. Remove anything within the `<main>` element and replace it with content as per your requirement.

Pop quiz – HTML5 elements

Let's end this chapter with simple questions regarding HTML5:

Q1. What is the `<header>` element used for?

1. It is used to represent the website header.

2. It is used to represent a group of introductory and navigational aids.

Q2. What is the `<footer>` element used for?

    1.   It is used to represent the website footer.

    2.   It is used to represent the end or the lowest part of a section.

Q3. Is it allowed to use the `<header>` and `<footer>` elements multiple times within a single page?

    1.   Yes, as long as it's semantically logical.

    2.   No, it's considered redundant.

Summary

In this chapter, we started our first project. Earlier in the chapter, we explored the Responsive. gs components, looked into how Responsive.gs constructs a responsive grid, and what classes are used to shape the grid.

We also discussed HTML5, including the new elements, namely, the polyfills to mimic HTML5 features in the browsers that do not support particular features natively. Then, we used HTML5 to construct the blog markup.

In the next chapter, we will be focusing more on marking the blog up using CSS3 and adding some JavaScript. We will also be debugging the blog for errors that turn up in old Internet Explorer.

4
Enhancing the Blog Appearance

In the previous chapter, we constructed the blog markup from the header section to the footer section using HTML5 elements. The blog, however, is currently faceless. If you opened the blog in a browser, you will just see it bare; we have not yet written the styles that add up to its appearance.

Throughout the course of this chapter, we will focus on decorating the blog with CSS and JavaScript. We will be using CSS3 to add the blog styles. CSS3 brings a number of new CSS properties, such as `border-radius`, `box-shadow`, *and* `box-sizing`, *that allow us to decorate websites without the need to add images and extra markup.*

However, the CSS properties, as mentioned previously, are applicable only within the latest browser versions. Internet Explorer 6 to 8 are not able to recognize those CSS properties, and won't be able to output the result in the browsers. So, as an addition, we will also utilize a number of polyfills to make our blog presentable in the old Internet Explorer.

It's going to be an adventurous chapter. Let's go.

In this chapter, we shall cover the following topics:

- ◆ Looking into CSS3 properties and CSS libraries, which we are going to use in the blog
- ◆ Compile and minify style sheets and JavaScripts with Koala
- ◆ Compose the blog style rules with the mobile-first approach
- ◆ Optimize the blog for desktop
- ◆ Patch the blog in Internet Explorer with polyfills

Using CSS3

CSS3 ships with long-awaited properties, `border-radius` and `box-shadow`, that simplify old and tedious methods that were used to present rounded corner and drop shadow in HTML. On top of that, it also brings a new type of pseudo-element that enables us to style the placeholder text shown in input fields through the HTML5 `placeholder` attribute.

Let's take a look at how they work.

Creating rounded corners with CSS3

Back in the 90s, creating a rounded corner was complicated. Adding a pile of HTML markup, slicing out images, and formulating multiple line style of rules is inevitable, as presented in the post by Ben Ogle at `http://benogle.com/2009/04/29/css-round-corners.html`.

CSS3 makes it much simpler to create rounded corners with the `border-radius` property, and the following is an example:

```
div {
  width: 100px; height: 100px;
  border-radius: 30px;
}
```

The preceding style rule will round the box corner (read the *A word on CSS Box Model* section in *Chapter 1, Responsive Web Design*) each for `30px`, as shown in the following figure:

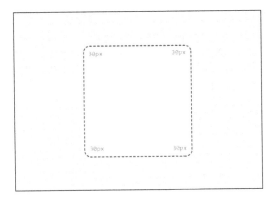

Furthermore, we can also round only to specific corners. The following code snippet, for example, will round only the top-right corner:

```
div {
  width: 100px; height: 100px;
  border-top-right-radius: 30px;
}
```

Creating drop shadow

Much the same as creating rounded corners, using images was unavoidable to create shadow effects in the website in the past. Now, adding a drop shadow has been made easy with the introduction of the box-shadow property. The box-shadow property consists of five parameters (or values):

The first parameter specifies where the shadow takes place. This parameter is optional. Set the value to inset to let the shadow appear inside the box or leave it empty to display the shadow outside.

The second parameter specifies the **shadow vertical** and **horizontal distance** from the box.

The third parameter specifies the **shadow blur** that fades the shadow; a bigger number will produce a bigger but faded shadow.

The fourth parameter specifies the **shadow expansion**; this value is slightly contradicted to the shadow blur value. This value will enlarge yet also intensify the shadow depth.

The last parameter specifies the color. The color can be in any web-compatible color format, including Hex, RGB, RGBA, and HSL.

Carrying on the preceding example, we can add up box-shadow, as follows:

```
div {
  width: 100px;
  height: 100px;
  border-radius: 30px;
  box-shadow: 5px 5px 10px 0 rgba(0,0,0,0.5);
}
```

The preceding code will output the shadow, as shown in the following figure:

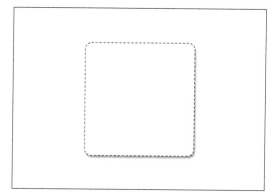

Add `inset` at the beginning if you want to show the shadow inside the box, as follows:

```
div {
    width: 100px;
    height: 100px;
    border-radius: 30px;
    box-shadow: inset 5px 5px 10px 0 rgba(0,0,0,0.5);
}
```

 The CSS3 `box-shadow` property can be applied in many creative ways, and the following is an example by Paul Underwood, for your inspiration: `http://www.paulund.co.uk/creating-different-css3-box-shadows-effects`

CSS3 browser supports and the use of vendor prefix

Both the `border-radius` and `box-shadow` properties have been well-implemented in many browsers. Technically, if we would cater only to the latest browser versions, we do not need to include the so-called vendor prefix.

Yet, if we intend to enable these two properties, `border-radius` and `box-shadow`, back in the earliest browser versions, where they were still marked as experimental by the browser vendors such as Safari 3, Chrome 4, and Firefox 3, adding the vendor prefix is required. Each browser has its prefix as follows:

- `-webkit-`: This is the Webkit-based browsers prefix, which currently includes Safari, Chrome, and Opera.
- `-moz-`: This is the Mozilla Firefox prefix.
- `-ms-`: This is the Internet Explorer prefix. But Internet Explorer has been supporting `border-radius` and `box-shadow` since Internet Explorer 9 without the need to add this prefix.

Let's carry on our previous examples (again). With the addition of the vendor prefix to cater to the earliest versions of Chrome, Safari, and Firefox, the code would be as follows:

```
div {
    width: 100px;
    height: 100px;
    -webkit-border-radius: 30px;
    -moz-border-radius: 30px;
    border-radius: 30px;
    -webkit-box-shadow: 5px 5px 10px 0 rgba(0,0,0,0.5);
    -moz-box-shadow: 5px 5px 10px 0 rgba(0,0,0,0.5);
    box-shadow: 5px 5px 10px 0 rgba(0,0,0,0.5);
}
```

The code may turn out to be a bit longer; still it is preferable over having to cope with complicated markups and multiple style rules.

Chrome and its new browser engine, Blink

Chrome decided to fork Webkit and built its own browser engine on top of it, named Blink (`http://www.chromium.org/blink`). Opera, which previously discarded its initial engine (Presto) for Webkit, follows along the Chrome movement. Blink eliminates the use of the vendor prefix, so we would not find `-blink-` prefix or such like. In Chrome's latest versions, instead of using the vendor prefix, Chrome disables experimental features by default. Yet, we can enable it through the options in the `chrome://flags` page.

Customizing to placeholder text styles

With the addition of HTML5, the placeholder attribute brings the question of how to customize the placeholder text. By default, browsers display the placeholder text with a light gray color. How do we change, for example, the color or the font size?

At the time of writing this, each browser has its own way in this regard. WebKit-based browsers, such as Safari, Chrome, and Opera, use `::-webkit-input-placeholder`. Internet Explorer 10 uses `:-ms-input-placeholder`. Firefox 4 to 18, on the other hand, use `pseudo-class`, `:-moz-placeholder`, but it has then been replaced with the pseudo-element `::-moz-placeholder` (notice the double colons) since Firefox 19 to keep up with the standard.

These selectors cannot be used in tandem within a single style rule. So, the following code snippet will not work:

```
input::-webkit-input-placeholder,
input:-moz-placeholder,
input::-moz-placeholder,
input:-ms-input-placeholder {
  color: #fbb034;
}
```

They have to be declared in a single style rule declaration, as follows:

```
input::-webkit-input-placeholder {
  color: #fbb034;
}
input:-moz-placeholder {
  color: #fbb034;
}
input::-moz-placeholder {
  color: #fbb034;
```

```
}
input:-ms-input-placeholder {
  color: #fbb034;
}
```

This is definitely inefficient; we added extra lines only to achieve the same output. There isn't another viable option at the moment. The standard for styling the placeholder is still in discussion (see the CSSWG discussion at `http://wiki.csswg.org/ideas/placeholder-styling` and `http://wiki.csswg.org/spec/css4-ui#more-selectors` for more details).

Using CSS libraries

The underlying thing that distinguishes between a CSS library and a CSS framework is the problem it addresses. For example, a CSS framework, such as Blueprint (`http://www.blueprintcss.org/`), is designed as a foundation or starting point of a new website. It generally ships with various pieces of libraries to encompass many circumstances. A CSS library, on the other hand, addresses a very specific thing. Generally, a CSS library is also not tied down to a particular framework. `Animate.css` (`http://daneden.github.io/animate.css/`) and `Hover.css` (`http://ianlunn.github.io/Hover/`) are two perfect examples in this regard. Both of them are CSS libraries. They can be used along with any framework.

Herein, we will integrate two CSS libraries into the blog, namely `Normalize` (`http://necolas.github.io/normalize.css/`) and `Formalize` (`http://formalize.me/`). These CSS libraries will standardize basic element styles across different browsers and minimize styling errors that may unexpectedly occur.

Working with Koala

Once we have explored all the things that we are going to include in this project, let's set up the tool to put them together. In *Chapter 1, Responsive Web Design*, we have installed Koala. Koala is a free and open source development tool that ships with many features. In this first project, we will use Koala to compile style sheets and JavaScripts into a single file, as well as minify the codes to result in a smaller file size.

There will be about five style sheets that we are going to include in the blog. If we load all these style sheets separately, the browsers will have to pull off five HTTP requests, as shown in the following screenshot:

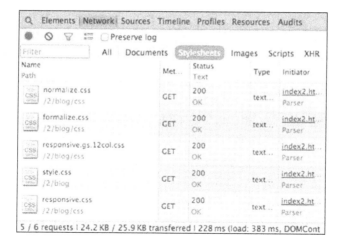

As shown in the preceding screenshot, the browser performs five HTTP requests to load all the style sheets, which have a size of 24.4 KB in total and require around 228 ms in total to load.

Combining these style sheets into a single file and squishing the codes therein will speed up the page-load performance. The style sheet can also become significantly smaller, which eventually will also save bandwidth consumption.

As shown in the following screenshot, the browser only performs one HTTP request; the style sheet size is reduced to 13.5KB, and takes only 111 ms to load. The page loads about 50 percent faster in comparison with the preceding example:

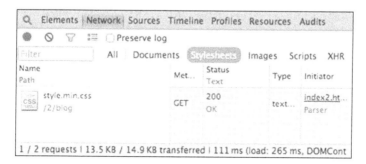

Best practices to speed up website performance:

Head over to YSlow! performance rules (`https://developer.yahoo.com/performance/rules.html`) or Google PageSpeed Insight rules (`https://developers.google.com/speed/docs/insights/rules`) for further steps to make a website load faster, aside from combining style sheets and JavaScripts.

Time for action – integrating project directory into Koala and combining the style sheets

In this section, we will integrate the configured Koala to compile and output the style sheets, by performing the following steps:

1. Create a new style sheet in the `css` folder named `main.css`. This is the prime style sheet, where we will compose our own style rules for the blog.

2. Create a new style sheet named `style.css`.

3. Download `normalize.css` (`http://necolas.github.io/normalize.css/`), and put it in the `css` folder of the project directory.

4. Download `formalize.css` (`http://formalize.me/`), and also put it in the `css` folder of the project directory.

5. Open `style.css` in Sublime Text.

6. Import the supporting style sheets using the `@import` rule in the following order, as follows:

   ```
   @import url("css/normalize.css");
   @import url("css/formalize.css");
   @import url("css/responsive.gs.12col.css");
   @import url("css/main.css");
   @import url("css/responsive.css");
   ```

7. Launch Koala. Then, drag-and-drop the project directory into the Koala sidebar. Koala will show and list recognizable files, as shown in the following screenshot:

8. Select `style.css` and tick **Auto Compile** to compile `style.css` automatically whenever Koala detects a change in it. Have a look at the following screenshot:

9. Select the **Combine Import** option to let Koala combine the content within the style sheets (the content that was included in `style.css`) with the `@import` rule. Take a look at the following screenshot:

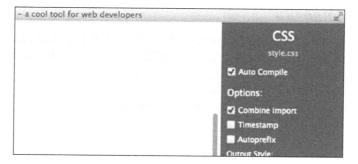

10. Set **Output Style:** to **compress**. Take a look at the following screenshot:

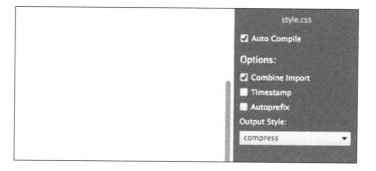

This will compress the style rules into a single line, which eventually will make the `style.css` file size smaller.

11. Click on the **Compile** button. Take a look at the following screenshot:

This will compile `style.css` and generate a new file named `style.min.css` as the output.

12. Open `index.html` and link `style.min.css`. using the following code:

```
<link href="style.min.css" rel="stylesheet">
```

What just happened?

We have just integrated the project directory within Koala. We have also created two new style sheets, namely, `main.css` and `style.css`. We have also put together five style sheets, including `main.css`, in the `style.css` file using the `@import` rule. We combined these files and generated a new style sheet named `style.min.css`, which can be found inline with `style.css`, as shown in the following screenshot:

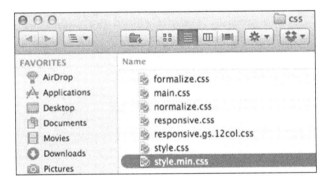

Finally, we link the minified style sheet, `style.min.css`, in `index.html`.

Have a go hero – renaming the output

The `style.min.css` name is the default name set by Koala; it inserts the suffix, `min`, to every minified output. Though it is the most popular naming convention for minified web source files, style sheets, and JavaScript, Koala allows you to rename the output to match your personal liking. To do so, click on the edit icon that is highlighted with a circle in the following screenshot:

The following are a few alternative naming ideas you can try:

◆ `style-min.css` (with dash)

◆ `styles.min.css` (with the `s`)

◆ `blog.css` (refers to the website name)

However, don't forget to change the name specified in the `<link>` element that refers to the style sheet as well if you decided to rename the output other than `style.min.css` as we managed in the preceding steps.

Pop quiz – website performance rules

Q1. Which of the following rules is not the one to improve website performance?

1. Minifying resources such as CSS and JavaScript.

2. Compressing image files.

3. Leveraging browser cache.

4. Using CSS shorthand properties.

5. Using CDN to deliver web resources.

Thinking mobile first

Before we get our hands on the code, let's talk about the mobile-first approach that will drive our decision on writing part of the blog style rules.

Mobile-first is one of the buzzwords in the web design community. Mobile-first is a new way of thinking on building websites of today, which also guides the pattern to build websites that are optimized for mobile use. As mentioned in *Chapter 1, Responsive Web Design*, mobile users are growing and desktop is no longer the main platform where users can access the web.

The mobile-first concept drives us to think and prioritize mobile use on building the website blocks, including how we compose style rules and media queries. In addition, adopting mobile-first thinking, as Brad Frost demonstrated in his blog post (`http://bradfrostweb.com/blog/post/7-habits-of-highly-effective-media-queries/`), allows producing leaner codes than the other way around (desktop to mobile). Herein, we will first optimize and address the blog for mobile and then enhance to the desktop version afterwards.

Mobile-first is beyond the capacity of this module, we'll make Mobile-first web applications later in *Module 3, HTML5 and CSS3 Responsive Web Design Cookbook*. The following are some of my recommendation sources to dig into this topic further:

- Mobile First by Luke Wroblewski (`http://www.abookapart.com/products/mobile-first`)
- Mobile First Responsive Web Design by Brad Frost (`http://bradfrostweb.com/blog/web/mobile-first-responsive-web-design/`)
- Building a Better Responsive Website by Jeremy Girard (`http://www.smashingmagazine.com/2013/03/05/building-a-better-responsive-website/`)

Composing the blog styles

In the preceding sections, we added third-party styles that lay down the blog appearance fundamentals. Starting in this section, we are going to compose our own style rules for the blog. We will begin from the header then go down to the footer.

Time for action – composing the base style rules

In this section, we are going to write blog base styles. These style rules encompass the content font family, the font size, and a number of elements therein in general.

First of all, it is my personal opinion that using the default system font such as Arial and Times is so boring.

Due to the browser support and font license restriction, we were only able to use fonts that were installed in the user's operating system. Consequently, for more than a decade, we're stuck to a very limited choice of fonts we can use on the Web, and many websites use the same set of fonts, such as Arial, Times, and even Comic Sans. So, yes, these are boring fonts.

Today, with the advancement in `@font-face` specification, as well as the license of font usage on the Web, we are now able to use fonts on the website outside the font selection of the user's computer. There are also now larger collections of fonts that we can embed on the Web for free, such as the ones that we can find in Google Font (`http://www.google.com/fonts`), Open Font Library (`http://openfontlibrary.org/`), Font Squirrel (`http://www.fontsquirrel.com`), Fonts for Web (`http://fontsforweb.com/`), and Adobe Edge Web Font (`https://edgewebfonts.adobe.com/`).

I really encourage web designers to explore more the possibility of, and build, a more enriched website using the custom fonts on their websites.

Perform the following steps to compose the base style rules:

1. To make our blog look more refreshing, we will use a couple of custom fonts from the Google Font library. Google Font has made it easy for us to use fonts on the Web. Google has taken care of the hassle of writing the syntax, as well as ensuring that the font formats are compatible in all major browsers.

Speaking of which, refer to the Paul Irish post, *Bulletproof @ font-face syntax* (`http://www.paulirish.com/2009/bulletproof-font-face-implementation-syntax/`), for further help on composing CSS3 `@font-face` syntax that works across all browsers.

2. In addition, we won't be befuddled with the font license, as Google Font is completely free. All we have to do is add a special style sheet as explained in this page `https://developers.google.com/fonts/docs/getting_started#Quick_Start`. In our case, add the following link before the prime style sheet link:

```
<link href='http://fonts.googleapis.com/css?family=Droid+Serif:400
,700,400italic,700italic|Varela+Round' rel='stylesheet'>
```

Upon doing so, we will be able to use the Droid Serif font family, along with Varela Round; see these font specimens and characters in the following web pages:

- **Droid Serif** (`http://www.google.com/fonts/specimen/Droid+Serif`)
- **Varela Round** (`http://www.google.com/fonts/specimen/Varela+Round`)

3. Set the entire element box sizing to `border-box`. Add the following line (as well as the other lines in the next steps) in `main.css`:

```
* {
    -webkit-box-sizing: border-box;
    -moz-box-sizing: border-box;
    box-sizing: border-box;
    *behavior: url(/scripts/boxsizing.htc);
}
```

4. We are going to set the blog main font, that is, the font that applies to the entire content of the blog. Herein, we will use Droid Serif of Google Font. Add the following style rules after the list of `@import` style sheet:

```
body {
    font-family: "Droid Serif", Georgia, serif;
    font-size: 16px;
}
```

5. We are going to apply a different font family for the headings (h1, h2, h3, h4, h5, and h6) in order to set it apart from the body content. Herein, we will apply the second custom font family that we brought from the Google Font collection, Varela Round.

6. Add the following line to apply Varela Round to the headings:

```
h1, h2, h3, h4, h5, h6 {
    font-family: "Varela Round", Arial, sans-serif;
    font-weight: 400;
}
```

The browsers, by default, set the headings' weight to `bold` or `600`. However, Varela Round only ships with normal font weight, which equates to `400`. So, as shown in the preceding code snippet, we have also set the `font-weight` to `400` to prevent the so-called *faux-bold*.

Refer to the A List Apart article, *Say No to Faux Bold* (`http://alistapart.com/article/say-no-to-faux-bold`) for further information about faux-bold.

7. In this step, we will also customize the default anchor tag or link styles. It's my personal preference to remove the underline of the default link style.

 Even Google removes the underline of its search result (`http://www.theverge.com/2014/3/13/5503894/google-removes-underlined-links-site-redesign`).

Furthermore, we also change the link color to `#3498db`. It's blue, but subtler than the blue color applied as the default link style, as shown in the following screenshot:

8. Add the following lines to change the default link color:

```
a {
    color: #3498db;
    text-decoration: none;
}
```

9. We will set the color of the link to hover state, as well. This color appears when the mouse cursor is over the link. Herein, we set the link hover color to `#2a84bf`, the darker version of the color we set in step 4. Have a look at the following screenshot:

10. Add the following line to set the color of the link when it is in hover state, as follows:

```
a:hover {
    color: #2a84bf;
}
```

11. Make the image fluid with the following style rules, as follows:

```
img {
  max-width: 100%;
  height: auto;
}
```

In addition, these style rules will prevent the image from exceeding its container when the actual image width is larger than the container.

 Refer to A List Apart article *Fluid Images* (`http://alistapart.com/article/fluid-images`) for further detail on fluid images.

What just happened?

We have just added style rules that address some elements in the blog, namely, the headings, the link, and the image. At this stage, there isn't a significant difference yet that appears in the blog, except the font family change in the content and the headings, as well as the link color. Have a look at the following screenshot:

Have a go hero – customizing the link color

Please note that the link color, `#2a84bf`, is my personal selection. There are a number of considerations when choosing a color, such as the brand, the audience, and the content. The link doesn't have to be `#2a84bf`. The link color in the Starbucks website (`http://www.starbucks.co.id/about-us/pressroom`), for example, is green, which refers to its brand identity.

So, don't be afraid to explore and try new colors. The following are a few color ideas:

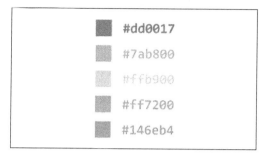

Next, we will compose the blog header and navigation style rules. The style rules will mostly be applied through the element's classes. So, before proceeding, please refer to *Chapter 2, Web Development Tools*, to see the class names and ID that we added in the elements.

Time for action – enhancing the header and the navigation appearance with CSS

The steps are as follows:

1. Open `main.css`.

2. Add some whitespace surrounding the header with `padding`, and also set the header color to `#333`, as follows:

```
.blog-header {
padding: 30px 15px;
background-color: #333;
}
```

3. To make the logo look prominent, we will set it with Varela Round font, which is the same font family we used for the headings. We also make it bigger and transform the letters all to uppercase, as follows:

```
.blog-name {
font-family: "Varela Round", Arial, sans-serif;
font-weight: 400;
font-size: 42px;
text-align: center;
text-transform: uppercase;
}
```

4. The logo link color currently is `#2a84bf`, which is the common color we set for links `<a>`. This color does not suit well with the background color. Let's change the color to white instead, as follows:

```
.blog-name a {
    color: #fff;
}
```

5. Set the search input styles, as follows:

```
.search-form input {
  height: 36px;
  background-color: #ccc;
  color: #555;
  border: 0;
  padding: 0 10px;
  border-radius: 30px;
}
```

These style rules set the input color, border color, and the background colors. It turns the input into something as shown in the following screenshot:

6. As you can see in the preceding screenshot, the placeholder text is barely readable as the color blends with the input background color. So, let's make the text color a bit darker, as follows:

```
.search-form input::-webkit-input-placeholder {
  color: #555;
}
.search-form input:-moz-placeholder {
  color: #555;
}
.search-form input::-moz-placeholder {
  color: #555;
}
.search-form input:-ms-input-placeholder {
  color: #555;
}
```

If you use OS X or Ubuntu, you will see the glowing color that highlights the input when it is currently targeted, as shown in the following screenshot:

In OS X, the glowing color is blue. In Ubuntu, it will be orange.

7. I would like to remove this glowing effect. The glowing effect is technically shown through `box-shadow`. So, to remove this effect, we simply set the input `box-shadow` to `none`, as follows:

```
.search-form input:focus {
  -webkit-box-shadow: none;
  -moz-box-shadow: none;
  box-shadow: none;
}
```

It's worth noting that the glowing effect is part of the **User Experience** (**UX**) design, telling the users that they are currently within the input field. This UX design is particularly helpful if the users were only able to navigate the website with a keyboard.

8. So, we will have to create an effect that brings a similar UX as a replacement. Herein, we will replace the glowing effect that we removed by lightening the input background color. The following is the complete code of this step:

```
.search-form input:focus {
  -webkit-box-shadow: none;
  -moz-box-shadow: none;
  box-shadow: none;
  background-color: #bbb;
}
```

The input background color becomes lighter when it is in focus, as shown in the following screenshot:

9. We will write the style for the navigation. First, align the menu to the center, and add some whitespace at the top and the bottom of the navigation with the margin. Have a look at the following code:

```
.blog-menu {
  margin: 30px 0;
  text-align: center;
}
```

10. Remove the left-hand side padding of `<ul>`, as follows:

```
.blog-menu ul {
  padding-left: 0;
}
```

11. Add some whitespace between the menus with a margin, and remove the list bullet, as follows:

```
.blog-menu li {
  margin: 15px;
  list-style-type: none;
}
```

12. Customize the menu color and font, as follows:

```
.blog-menu a {
  color: #7f8c8d;
  font-size: 18px;
   text-transform: uppercase;
   font-family: "Varela Round", Arial, sans-serif;
}
.blog-menu a:hover {
   color: #3498db;
}
```

What just happened?

We have just decorated the header and the navigation. Corresponding to the mobile-first way of thinking, which we discussed earlier in this section, we first aim the styles to optimize the blog presentation in mobile.

Activate the Chrome mobile emulator, and you will see that the blog is optimized for a smaller screen size already; the logo and the menu, as shown in the following screenshot, are aligned to the center rather than aligned to the left:

Have a go hero – customizing the header

The blog header is given a dark color, #333. I truly understand that this color may look boring to some of you. Hence, freely customize the color as well as the style of the logo and the search input field. Some ideas are as follows:

- Use CSS3 gradients or image for the header background
- Replace the logo with an image through the CSS image replacement method
- Reduce the search input border radius, change the background color, and adjust the placeholder text color

Having managed the blog header as well as the navigation, we proceed to the blog content section. The content section includes the blog post items, and the blog pagination.

Time for action – enhancing the content section appearance with CSS

Perform the following steps to style the blog content:

1. Add whitespace on all sides of the content section with `padding` and `margin`, as follows

```
.blog-content {
  padding: 15px;
  margin-bottom: 30px;
}
```

2. Separate each blog post with some whitespace and borderline, as follows:

```
.post {
  margin-bottom: 60px;
  padding-bottom: 60px;
  border-bottom: 1px solid #ddd;
}
```

3. Align the title to the center, adjust the title font size a little, and change the color with the following style rules:

```
.post-title {
  font-size: 36px;
  text-align: center;
  margin-top: 0;
}
.post-title a {
  color: #333;
}
.post-title a:hover {
  color: #3498db;
}
```

4. Below the title, we have `post-meta`, which consists of the post author name and the post publishing date. Similar to the title, we also adjust the font size and the whitespace, and change the font color, as follows:

```
.post-meta {
  font-size: 18px;
  margin: 20px 0 0;
  text-align: center;
  color: #999;
}
.post-meta ul {
  list-style-type: none;
  padding-left: 0;
}
.post-meta li {
  margin-bottom: 10px;
}
```

5. The post thumbnail, as you can see in the following screenshot, looks small and squished due to the margin on all its sides:

6. Let's remove these margins, as follows:

```
.post-thumbnail {
  margin: 0;
}
```

Some of the images, as shown in the following screenshot, have a caption:

7. Let's style it to make it look distinctive from the rest of the content and also show that it is an image caption. Add the following lines of code to style the caption:

```
.post-thumbnail figcaption {
  color: #bdc3c7;
  margin-top: 15px;
  font-size: 16px;
  font-style: italic;
}
```

8. Adjust the post excerpt font size, color, and line height, as follows:

```
.post-excerpt {
  color: #555;
  font-size: 18px;
  line-height: 30px;
}
```

9. Starting in this step, we will write the style of the blog pagination. First, let's make some adjustments to the font size, the font family, the whitespace, the position, and the alignment, as shown in the following code:

```
.blog-pagination {
  text-align: center;
  font-size: 16px;
  position: relative;
  margin: 60px 0;
}
.blog-pagination ul {
  padding-left: 0;
}
.blog-pagination li,
.blog-pagination a {
  display: block;
  width: 100%;
}
.blog-pagination li {
  font-family: "Varela Round", Arial, sans-serif;
  color: #bdc3c7;
  text-transform: uppercase;
  margin-bottom: 10px;
}
```

10. Decorate the pagination link with rounded corner borders, as follows:

```
.blog-pagination a {
  -webkit-border-radius: 30px;
  -moz-border-radius: 30px;
  border-radius: 30px;
  color: #7f8c8d;
  padding: 15px 30px;
  border: 1px solid #bdc3c7;
}
```

11. Specify the link decoration when the mouse cursor hovers over the links, as follows:

```
.blog-pagination a:hover {
  color: #fff;
  background-color: #7f8c8d;
  border: 1px solid #7f8c8d;
}
```

12. Finally, place the page number indicator at the top of the pagination links with the following style rules:

```
.blog-pagination .pageof {
  position: absolute;
  top: -30px;
}
```

What just happened?

We just styled the blog content section—including the page navigation (pagination), and the following screenshot shows how the content section looks:

Have a go hero – improving the content section

Most of the style rules we applied in the content section are decorative. It's something that you don't have to follow forcefully. Feel free to improve the styles to follow your personal taste.

You can perform the following modifications:

◆ Customize the post title font family and the colors

◆ Apply border colors or rounded corners for the post image

◆ Change the pagination border colors, or make the background more colorful

Next, we will style the footer, the last section of the blog.

Time for action – enhancing the footer section appearance with CSS

Perform the following steps to enhance the footer style:

1. Adjust the footer font, color, and the margin, as follows:

```
.blog-footer {
  background-color: #ecf0f1;
  padding: 60px 0;
  font-family: "Varela Round", Arial, sans-serif;
  margin-top: 60px;
}
.blog-footer,
.blog-footer a {
  color: #7f8c8d;
}
```

2. The footer contains social media links. Let's adjust the styles that encompass the margin, padding, alignment, colors, and whitespace, as follows:

```
.social-media {
  margin: 0 0 30px;
}
.social-media ul {
  margin: 0;
  padding-left: 0;
}
.social-media li {
  margin: 0 8px 10px;
  list-style: none;
}
.social-media li,
```

```
.social-media a {
  font-size: 18px;
}
.social-media a:hover {
  color: #333;
}
```

3. Set the margin-top out of the copyright container.

```
.copyright {
  margin-top: 0;
}
```

4. Align the footer content to the center, as follows:

```
.social-media,
.copyright {
  text-align: center;
}
```

What just happened?

We have just styled the footer section, and the following screenshot shows how the blog footer will look:

Optimize the blog for desktop

The blog is currently optimized for mobile, or narrow viewport size. If you view it in a larger viewport size, you will find that some elements are misplaced or are not properly aligned. The blog logo and the navigation, for example, are currently aligned to the center, as you can see in the following screenshot:

As per our blueprint that we have shown you in *Chapter 3, Constructing a Simple Responsive Blog with Responsive.gs*, the logo should align to the left-hand side and each menu link should be displayed inline. In the upcoming steps, we will fix these through Media Queries; we will optimize the blog for desktop view.

Time for action – composing style rules for desktop

Perform the following steps to compose style rules for desktop:

1. Open `responsive.css` in Sublime Text.

2. Add the following media query:

```
@media screen and (min-width: 640px) {
  // add style rules here
}
```

We will add all the style rules in the following steps within this media query. This media query specification will apply the style rules within the viewport width starting from 640 px and up.

1. Align the blog logo to the left-hand side, as follows:

```
.blog-name {
  text-align: left;
  margin-bottom: 0;
}
```

2. Display the list item of the navigation menu, post meta, and social media inline, as follows:

```
.blog-menu li,
.post-meta li,
.social-media li {
      display: inline;
}
```

3. Increase the post title size, as follows:

```
.post-title {
  font-size: 48px;
}
```

4. Also, display the blog pagination links inline, as follows:

```
.blog-pagination li,
.blog-pagination a {
  display: inline;
}
```

5. Put the pagination page indicator in its initial position—inline with the blog pagination link, as follows:

```
.blog-pagination .pageof {
  position: relative;
  top: 0;
  padding: 0 20px;
}
```

6. Align the social media links in the footer to the left and the copyright notice to the right, as follows:

```
.social-media {
  text-align: left;
}
.copyright {
  text-align: right;
}
```

What just happened?

We have just added style rules that address the blog for the desktop view. If you are now viewing the blog in the viewport width that is larger than 640 px, you should find that the elements in the blog such as the logo and the navigation menu are in their common position, as shown in the following screenshot:

Making Internet Explorer more capable with polyfills

With the use of glorious CSS3 and HTML5 features, comes a consequence: the layout failed and is broken in the old Internet Explorer, as you can see in the following screenshot:

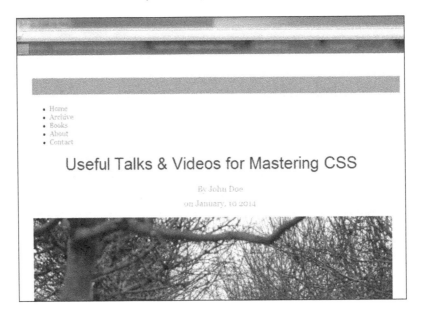

If you are okay with it, you can skip this section and head over to the next project immediately. However, if you feel adventurous, let's proceed to this section and fix those bugs.

Time for action – patch Internet Explorer with polyfills

Perform the steps to patch Internet Explorer with polyfills:

1. We have a number of polyfills in the scripts folder namely `html5shiv.js`, `respond.js`, and `placeholder.js`. Let's combine these scripts into a single file.

2. First, create a new JavaScript file named `polyfills.js` that will hold the content of those polyfill scripts.

3. Open `polyfills.js` in Sublime Text.

4. Add the following lines to import the polyfill scripts:

    ```
    // @koala-prepend "html5shiv.js"
    // @koala-prepend "respond.js"
    // @koala-prepend "placeholder.js"
    ```

    > The `@koala-prepend` directive is the Koala proprietary directive to import JavaScript files. Read more about it in the Koala documentation page at `https://github.com/oklai/koala/wiki/JS-CSS-minify-and-combine`.

5. In Koala, select `polyfills.js`, and click on the **Compile** button, as shown in the following screenshot:

By this step, Koala will have generated the minified file named `polyfills.min.js`.

6. Open `index.html`, and link `polyfills.js` before `</head>`, as follows:

```
<!--[if lt IE 9]>
<script type="text/javascript" src="scripts/polyfills.min.js"></
script>
<![endif]-->
```

> Since this script is only needed in Internet Explorer 8 and below, we encapsulate them with the Internet Explorer Conditional Comment, `<!--[if lt IE 9]>`, as you can see in the preceding code snippet.
>
> Refer to the QuirksMode article for further information about Internet Explorer Conditional Comments at `http://www.quirksmode.org/css/condcom.html`.

What just happened?

We just applied polyfills in the blog to patch Internet Explorer rendering issues with HTML5 and Media Queries. These polyfills work out-of-the-box. Refresh Internet Explorer, and voila! Have a look at the following screenshot:

The style rules are applied, the layout is in position, and the placeholder text is there.

Have a go hero – polish the blog for Internet Explorer

We will end this project. But, as you can see from the preceding screenshot, there are still many things to address to make the blog appearance in the old Internet Explorer as good as in the latest browsers. For example:

- Referring to the preceding screenshot, the placeholder text is currently aligned to the top. You can fix it and make it align vertically to the center.

- You can also apply a polyfill named CSS3Pie (`http://css3pie.com/`) that brings the CSS3 border radius in Internet Explorer to make the search input field rounded as it is in the latest browser versions.

Summary

We completed the first project; we have built a simple, responsive blog using Responsive. gs. The end result of the blog may not be that enticing for you. It is also far from polished, particularly in the old Internet Explorer; as mentioned, there are still many things to address in that regard. Still, I hope you can take something useful from the process, the techniques, and the codes therein.

To summarize, here is what we have done in this chapter, enhanced and polished the blog with CSS3, used Koala to combine and minimize style sheets and JavaScript files, and applied polyfills to patch Internet Explorer issues with HTML5 and CSS3.

In the next chapter, we will start the second project. We are going to explore another framework to build a more extensive and responsive website.

5
Developing a Portfolio Website with Bootstrap

Bootstrap (`http://getbootstrap.com/`) is one of the sturdiest frontend development frameworks. It ships with amazing features, such as a responsive grid, user interface components, and JavaScript libraries that let us build responsive websites up and running quickly.

Bootstrap is so popular that the web development community positively supports it by developing extensions in a variety of forms to add extra features. In case the standard features that come with Bootstrap are not sufficient, there can be an extension to cover your particular requirements.

In this chapter, we will start our second project. We will employ Bootstrap to build a responsive portfolio website. So, this chapter apparently would be useful for those who work in creative fields such as photography, graphic design, and illustrating.

Herein, we will also employ a Bootstrap extension to empower the portfolio website with off-canvas navigation. Following Bootstrap, we will turn to LESS as the foundation of the website style sheets.

Let's move on.

The discussion that we are going to cover in this chapter will include the following topics:

◆ Explore Bootstrap components
◆ Look into the Bootstrap extension to bring off-canvas navigation

- Examine the portfolio website blueprint and design
- Set up and organize the project directories and assets with Bower and Koala
- Construct the portfolio website HTML structure

The Bootstrap components

Unlike the Responsive.gs framework that we used in the first project, Bootstrap is shipped with extra components, which are commonly used in the Web. Hence, before we step further into developing the portfolio website, first let's explore these components, mainly those of which we will employ within the website, such as the responsive grid, the buttons, and the form elements.

 Frankly, the official Bootstrap website (http://getbootstrap.com/) is always the best source to be up-to-date with anything related to Bootstrap. So, herein, I would like to point out the key things that are straightforward.

The Bootstrap responsive grid

Bootstrap comes with a Responsive Grid System, along with the supporting classes that form the columns and the rows. In Bootstrap, we build the column using these prefix classes: col-xs-, col-sm-, col-md-, and col-lg-. This is then followed by the column number, ranging from 1 to 12, to define the column size as well as to aim the column for a specific viewport size. See the following table for more detail on the prefixes:

Prefix	Description
col-xs-	This specifies the column for the Bootstrap-defined smallest (extra small) viewport size, which is equal to or less than 768 px
col-sm-	This specifies the column for the Bootstrap-defined small viewport size, which is equal to or greater than 768 px.
col-md-	This specifies the column for the Bootstrap-defined medium viewport size, which is equal to or greater than 992 px
col-lg-	This specifies the column for the Bootstrap-defined large viewport size, which is equal to or greater than 1,200 px

In the following example, we set out three columns in a row, with each column assigned a col-sm-4 class:

```
<div class="row">
  <div class="col-sm-4"></div>
  <div class="col-sm-4"></div>
  <div class="col-sm-4"></div>
</div>
```

So, each column will have the same size, and they will scale down up to the Bootstrap-defined small viewport size (≥ 768px). The following screenshot shows how the preceding markup turns out in the browser (by adding a few styles):

View the example in the viewport size, which is smaller than 768 px, and all these columns will start to stack up—the first column at the top and the third column at the very bottom, as shown in the following screenshot:

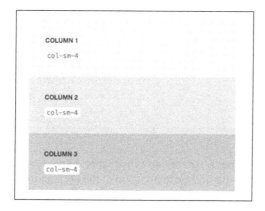

Furthermore, we can add multiple classes to specify the column proportion within multiple viewport sizes, as follows:

```
<div class="row">
  <div class="col-sm-6 col-md-2 col-lg-4"></div>
  <div class="col-sm-3 col-md-4 col-lg-4"></div>
  <div class="col-sm-3 col-md-6 col-lg-4"></div>
</div>
```

Given the preceding example, the columns will have the same size within the Bootstrap-defined large viewport size (≥ 1,200 px), as shown in the following screenshot:

The column proportion then starts to shift when we view it in the medium viewport size following the assigned classes on each column. The first column width will become smaller, the second column will retain the same proportion, while the third column will be larger, as shown in the following screenshot:

The column proportion will start to shift again when the website is at the threshold of the Bootstrap-defined medium- and small-viewport size, which is approximately at 991px, as shown in the following screenshot:

 For further assistance on constructing a Bootstrap grid, head over to the Grid System section of the Bootstrap official website (`http://getbootstrap.com/css/#grid`).

Bootstrap buttons and forms

Other components that we will incorporate into the website are buttons and forms. We will create an online contact through which users will be able get in touch. In Bootstrap, the button is formed with the `btn` class followed by `btn-default` to apply Bootstrap default styles, as shown in the following code:

```
<button type="button" class="btn btn-default">Submit</button>
<a class="btn btn-default">Send</a>
```

Replace the `btn-default` class with `btn-primary`, `btn-success`, or `btn-info` to give the buttons the colors specified, as shown in the following code:

```
<button type="button" class="btn btn-info">Submit</button>
<a class="btn btn-success">Send</a>
```

The code snippet defines the button size with these classes: `btn-lg` to make the button large, `btn-sm` to make it small, and `btn-xs` to make the button even smaller, as shown in the following code:

```
<button type="button" class="btn btn-info btn-lg">Submit</button>
<a class="btn btn-success btn-sm">Send</a>
```

The following screenshot shows how the button-size changes with the look, when the preceding classes are added:

Bootstrap allows us to display buttons in a number of ways, such as displaying a series of buttons inline together or adding a dropdown toggle in a button. For further assistance and details on constructing these types of buttons, head over to the button groups (`http://getbootstrap.com/components/#btn-groups`) and the button dropdown (`http://getbootstrap.com/components/#btn-dropdowns`) sections of Bootstrap's official website.

The Bootstrap buttons groups and buttons with a dropdown toggle

Bootstrap also provided a handful of reusable classes to style the form elements, such as `<input>` and `<textarea>`. To style the form elements, Bootstrap uses the `form-control` class. The style is light and decent, as shown in the following screenshot:

For more information regarding styling and arranging the form element in Bootstrap, refer to the form section of the Bootstrap official page (`http://getbootstrap.com/css/#forms`).

Bootstrap Jumbotron

Bootstrap describes Jumbotron as follows:

> *"A lightweight, flexible component that can optionally extend the entire viewport to showcase key content on your site" (http://getbootstrap.com/ components/#jumbotron)*

Jumbotron is a special section to display the website's first-line message, such as the marketing copy, catchphrases, or special offers, and additionally a button. Jumbotron is typically placed above the fold and below the navigation bar. To construct a Jumbotron section in Bootstrap, apply the `jumbotron` class, as follows:

```
<div class="jumbotron">
  <h1>Hi, This is Jumbotron</h1>
<p>Place the marketing copy, catchphrases, or special offerings.</p>
  <p><a class="btn btn-primary btn-lg" role="button">Got it!</a></p>
</div>
```

With the Bootstrap default styles, the following is how the Jumbotron looks:

This is the Jumbotron appearance with the default style

 Further details about Bootstrap Jumbotron can be found in the Bootstrap components page at `http://getbootstrap.com/ components/#jumbotron`.

Bootstrap third-party extensions

It's impossible to cater to everyone's needs, and the same thing applies to Bootstrap as well. A number of extensions are created in many forms—from CSS, JavaScript, icons, starter templates, and themes—to extend Bootstrap. Find the full list on this page (`http:// bootsnipp.com/resources`).

In this project, we will include an extension named Jasny Bootstrap (`http://jasny.github.io/bootstrap/`), developed by Arnold Daniels. We will use it primarily to incorporate off-canvas navigation. The off-canvas navigation is a popular pattern in responsive design; the menu navigation will first set off the visible area of the website and will only slide-in typically by clicking or tapping, as illustrated in the following screenshot:

The off-canvas section slide-in when users click on the three-stripe icon

Jasny Bootstrap off-canvas

Jasny Bootstrap is an extension that adds extra building blocks to the original Bootstrap. Jasny Bootstrap is designed with Bootstrap in mind; it follows Bootstrap conventions in almost every aspect of it, including the HTML markups, the class naming, and the JavaScript functions as well as the APIs.

As mentioned, we will use this extension to include off-canvas navigation in the portfolio website. The following is an example code snippet to construct off-canvas navigation with Jasny Bootstrap:

```
<nav id="offcanvas-nav" class="navmenu navmenu-default navmenu-fixed-
left offcanvas" role="navigation">
  <ul class="nav navmenu-nav">
    <li class="active"><a href="#">Home</a></li>
    <li><a href="#">Link</a></li>
    <li><a href="#">Link</a></li>
  </ul>
</nav>
```

```
<div class="navbar navbar-default navbar-fixed-top">
<button type="button" class="navbar-toggle" data-toggle="offcanvas"
data-target="#offcanvas-nav" data-target="body">
    <span class="icon-bar"></span>
    <span class="icon-bar"></span>
    <span class="icon-bar"></span>
  </button>
</div>
```

As you can see from the preceding code snippet, constructing off-canvas navigation requires a bunch of HTML elements, classes, and attributes in the mix. To begin with, we need two elements, <nav> and <div>, to contain respectively the menu and the button to toggle the navigation menu on and off. The <nav> element is given an ID as a unique reference of which menu to target via the data-target attribute in <button>.

A handful of classes and attributes are added within these elements to specify the colors, backgrounds, position, and functions:

- ◆ navmenu: Jasny Bootstrap has a new type of navigation, called navmenu. The navmenu class will display the navigation vertically, and placed on the side—right-hand or left-hand—of the website content, instead of at the top.

- ◆ navmenu-default: The class that will set the navmenu class with the default styles, which is dominated by light gray. Use the navmenu-inverse class instead if you prefer a dark color. Have a look at the following screenshot:

Two default colors of off-canvas navigation

- The `navmenu-fixed-left` class positions the navmenu on the left-hand side. Use the `navmenu-fixed-right` class to set it on the right-hand side instead.

- The `offcanvas` class is the prime class to set the navigation menu off the canvas.

- The `data-target="#offcanvas-nav"` code in `<button>` acts as a selector that refers to a specific navigation menu with the given ID.

- The `data-toggle="offcanvas"` code tells the button to toggle the off-canvas navigation. In addition, the original Bootstrap ships with several types of `data-toggle` to hook up different widgets, such as the modal (`data-toggle="modal"`), dropdown (`data-toggle="dropdown"`), and tab (`data-toggle="tab"`).

- The data-target="body" lets the website body slide along with the off-canvas navigation at the same time when being toggled on and off. Jasny Bootstrap calls it as push menu; follow this page (`http://jasny.github.io/bootstrap/examples/navmenu-push/`) to see it in action.

 In addition, Jasny Bootstrap provides two extra types of off-canvas navigation, named slide-in menu (`http://jasny.github.io/bootstrap/examples/navmenu/`) and reveal menu (`http://jasny.github.io/bootstrap/examples/navmenu-reveal/`)—follow the inclusive URL to see them in action.

Digging into Bootstrap

Exploring every inch of Bootstrap component is beyond the capacity of this module. Hence, we only discussed a couple of things from Bootstrap that will be essential to the project. Aside from the Bootstrap official website (`http://getbootstrap.com/`), the following are a couple of dedicated references that dig deep into Bootstrap that you can look into:

- Bootstrap tutorials for beginners by Coder's Guide (`http://www.youtube.com/watch?v=YXVoqJEwqoQ`), a series of video tutorials that help beginners to get up and running with Bootstrap

- *Twitter Bootstrap Web Development How-To, David Cochran, Packt Publishing* (`http://www.packtpub.com/web-development/twitter-bootstrap-web-development-how-instant`)

- *Mobile First Bootstrap, Alexandre Magno, Packt Publishing* (`http://www.packtpub.com/web-development/mobile-first-bootstrap`)

- *Learning Bootstrap, Packt Publishing* (`https://www.packtpub.com/web-development/learning-bootstrap`)

Using font icons

Retina or **high-definition** (**HD**) display makes everything on the screen look sharper and more vibrant. But, the problem lies with the legacy images or web icons brought before the advent of HD display. These images typically are served as a bitmap or a raster image, and they turn blurry on this screen, as shown in the following screenshot:

A series of icons that blur on the edges, as displayed in retina display

We do not want that to happen in our website, so we will have to use a font icon that is more scalable and stays sharp in a high-definition screen.

To tell the truth, Bootstrap ships with a font icon set called Glyphicon. Sadly, it does not come with the social media icons that we need. After going through a number of font-icon sets, I finally opted for Ionicons (`http://ionicons.com/`). Herein, we will use the alternative version that comes with LESS, which is official repository (`https://github.com/driftyco/ionicons`), so we will be able to integrate with Bootstrap seamlessly, which also happens to use LESS.

Examining the portfolio website layout

Before we start building the blocks and edges of the website, let's take a look the website wireframe. This wireframe will be the reference and give us the picture of how the website layout will be organized both in the mobile and desktop view.

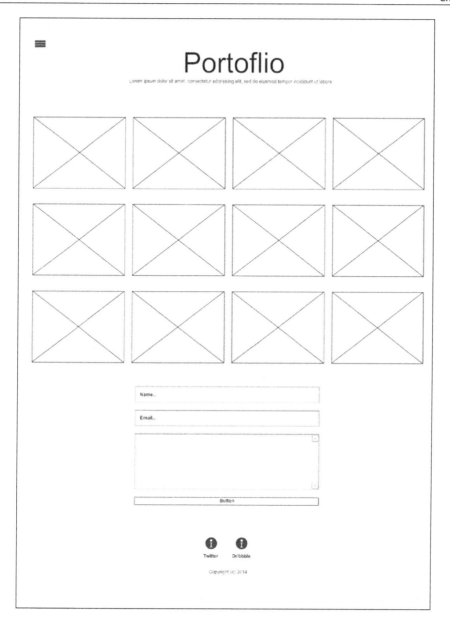

The preceding screenshot shows the website layout for the desktop or—technically—the wide viewport size.

The website will have a button positioned at the top-left of the website with a so-called **hamburger** icon to slide in the off-canvas menu. Then comes the website's first line, which says the website name and a line of catchphrase. The subsequent section will contain the portfolio images, while the last section will contain an online form and social media icons.

The mobile view looks more simplified, yet maintaining the same logical structure as in the desktop view layout, as shown in the following screenshot:

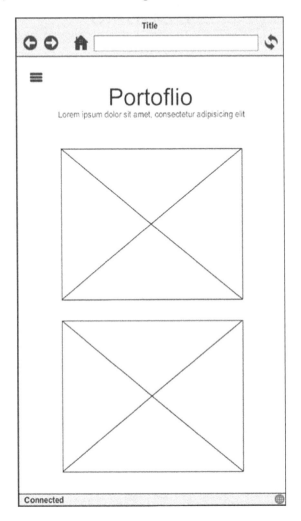

Project directories, assets, and dependencies

Let's start off the project by organizing the project directories and assets that include the dependencies, images, and font icon.

 What is dependency? Dependency herein is a file or a package of files, such as CSS and JavaScript library, that is needed to run the project and build the website.

In this project, we will put Bower (`http://bower.io/`) into practice to organize the project dependencies. Bower, as we briefly mentioned in *Chapter 1*, *Responsive Web Design*, is a frontend package manager that streamlines the way to install, remove, and update frontend development libraries, such as jQuery, Normalize, and HTML5Shiv.

Time for action – organizing project directories, assets, and installing project dependencies with Bower

In this section, we are going to add the project dependencies that include the Bootstrap, Jasny Bootstrap, Ionicons, and HTML5Shiv. We will install them using Bower so that we are able to maintain them—remove and update them—more seamlessly in the future.

In addition, since this might be the first time for many of you using Bower, I will walk you through the process at a slow pace, bit by bit. Please perform the following steps thoroughly:

1. In the `htdocs` folder, create a new folder, and name it `portfolio`. This is the project directory, where we will add all project files and folders to.

2. In the `portfolio` folder, create a new folder named `assets`. We will put the project assets, such as image, JavaScript, and style sheet in this folder.

3. In the assets folder, create these following folders:

   - `img` to contain the website images and image-based icons
   - `js` to contain the JavaScript files
   - `fonts` to contain the font icon set
   - `less` to contain the LESS style sheets
   - `css` as the output folder of LESS

4. Create `index.html` as the website's main page.

5. Add the images for the website in the `img` folder; this includes the portfolio images and the icons for a mobile device, as shown in the following screenshot:

▼ 📁 img	May
6layers.jpg	May
apple-icon.png	May
blur.jpg	May
brain.jpg	May
color.jpg	May
compass.jpg	May
contour.jpg	May
favicon.png	May
flame.jpg	May
hotcold.jpg	May
infinity.jpg	May
lifeguard.jpg	May
meteor.jpg	May
thewave.jpg	May

This website has around 14 images including the icons for mobile devices. I would like to thank my friend Yoga Perdana (`https://dribbble.com/yoga`) for allowing me to use his wonderful work in this module. You can find these images bundled along with this module. But, certainly, you can replace them with your very own images.

6. We will install the dependencies—packages, libraries, JavaScript, or CSS that are required to run the project, as well as to build the website—through Bower. But, before running any Bower command to install the dependencies, we would like to set the project as a Bower project using the `bower init` command to define the project specification in `bower.json`, such as the project name, the version, and the author.

7. To begin with, open a terminal or command prompt if you are using Windows. Then, navigate to the project directory using the `cd` command, as follows:

   ❑ In Windows: `cd \xampp\htdocs\portfolio`

   ❑ In OS X: `cd /Applications/XAMPP/htdocs/portfolio`

   ❑ In Ubuntu: `cd /opt/lampp/htdocs/portfolio`

8. Type `bower init`, as shown in the following screenshot:

 This command, `bower init`, initiates our project as a Bower project. This command also leads to a number of prompts to fill to describe the project such as the project name, the project version, the author, and so on.

9. First, we specify the project name. In this case, I would like to name the project `responsive-portfolio`. Type the name as follows, and press *Enter* to proceed. Have a look at the following screenshot:

10. Specify the project version. Since the project is new, let's simply set it to `1.0.0`, as shown in the following screenshot:

```
● ○ ○                    bower init — bower — node — 80×24
+  portfolio  bower init
? name: responsive-portfolio
? version: (0.0.0) 1.0.0
```

11. Press *Enter* to proceed.

12. Specify the project description. This prompt is entirely optional. You may leave it empty if you think it's not required for your project. In this case, I will describe the project as `a responsive portfolio website built with Bootstrap`, as shown in the following screenshot:

```
● ○ ○                    bower init — bower — node — 80×24
+  portfolio  bower init
? name: responsive-portfolio
? version: 1.0.0
? description: a responsive portfolio website buildt with Bootstrap
```

13. Specify the main file of the project. This certainly will vary depending on the project. Herein, let's set the main file to `index.html`, the website's home page, as shown in the following screenshot:

```
● ○ ○                    bower init — bower — node — 80×24
→  portfolio  bower init
? name: responsive-portfolio
? version: 1.0.0
? description: a responsive portfolio website buildt with Bootstrap
? main file: index.html
```

14. This prompts the question, "what types of modules does this package expose?" It specifies what the package is used for. In this case, simply select the global option, as shown in the following screenshot:

```
● ○ ○                    bower init — bower — node — 80×24
→  portfolio  bower init
? name: responsive-portfolio
? version: 1.0.0
? description: a responsive portfolio website buildt with Bootstrap
? main file: index.html
? what types of modules does this package expose?:
  ○ amd
  ○ es6
 >⬡ globals
  ○ node
  ○ yui
```

15. Press the Space Bar key to select it, and press *Enter* to continue.

 This prompt describes what the module technology in the project (our project) is meant for. Our project is not attached to a particular technology or module; it's just a plain static website with HTML, CSS, and a few lines of JavaScript. We are not building Node, YUI, or AMD modules. Thus, it is best to select the `globals` option.

16. The **keywords** prompt tells the project relation. In this case, I would like to fill it as `portfolio`, `responsive`, `bootstrap`, as shown in the following screenshot. Press *Enter* to continue:

```
● ○ ○                bower init — bower — node — 80×24
→  portfolio  bower init
?  name: responsive-portfolio
?  version: 1.0.0
?  description: a responsive portfolio website buildt with Bootstrap
?  main file: index.html
?  what types of modules does this package expose?: globals
?  keywords: portfolio, responsive, bootstrap
```

The **keywords** prompt is optional. You can leave it empty if you want by pressing the *Enter* key with the value left empty.

17. The **authors** prompt specifies the author of the project. This prompt is prepopulated with your computer user name and e-mail that you have registered in the system. Yet, you can overwrite it by specifying a new name and pressing *Enter* to continue, as shown in the following screenshot:

```
● ○ ○                bower init — bower — node — 80×24
→  portfolio  bower init
?  name: responsive-portfolio
?  version: 1.0.0
?  description: a responsive portfolio website buildt with Bootstrap
?  main file: index.html
?  what types of modules does this package expose?: globals
?  keywords: portfolio, responsive, bootstrap
?  authors: (Thoriq Firdaus <tfirdaus@creatiface.com>)
```

 If the project has multiple authors, you can specify each author with a comma separator, as follows:

authors: `John Doe, Jane Doe`.

18. Specify the project license. Herein, we will simply set it to the `MIT` license. The `MIT` license grants anyone to do whatever he or she wants with the code in the project, including modification, sublicensing, and commercial use. Have a look at the following screenshot:

```
⊙ ○ ○              bower init — bower — node — 80×24
→  portfolio  bower init
?  name: responsive-portfolio
?  version: 1.0.0
?  description: a responsive portfolio website buildt with Bootstrap
?  main file: index.html
?  what types of modules does this package expose?: globals
?  keywords: portfolio, responsive, bootstrap
?  authors: Thoriq Firdaus <tfirdaus@creatiface.com>
?  license: (MIT) MIT█
```

 Refer to Choose A License (`http://choosealicense.com/`) to find other types of licenses.

19. Specify the home page of the project. This could be your own website repository. In this case, I would like to set it with my personal domain, `creatiface.com`, as shown in the following screenshot:

```
⊙ ○ ○              bower init — bower — node — 80×24
→  portfolio  bower init
?  name: responsive-portfolio
?  version: 1.0.0
?  description: a responsive portfolio website buildt with Bootstrap
?  main file: index.html
?  what types of modules does this package expose?: globals
?  keywords: portfolio, responsive, bootstrap
?  authors: Thoriq Firdaus <tfirdaus@creatiface.com>
?  license: MIT
?  homepage: creatiface.com█
```

20. In the **set currently installed components as dependencies?:** command, type n
(no), as we haven't installed any dependencies or packages yet, as shown in the
following screenshot:

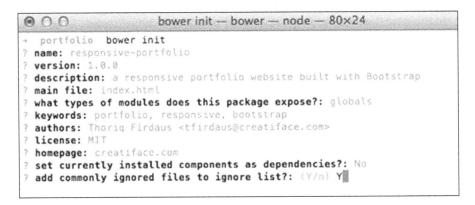

```
● ○ ○                bower init — bower — node — 80×24
→  portfolio  bower init
?  name: responsive-portfolio
?  version: 1.0.0
?  description: a responsive portfolio website buildt with Bootstrap
?  main file: index.html
?  what types of modules does this package expose? globals
?  keywords: portfolio, responsive, bootstrap
?  authors: Thoriq Firdaus <tfirdaus@creatiface.com>
?  license: MIT
?  homepage: creatiface.com
?  set currently installed components as dependencies?: (Y/n) n
```

21. The **Add commonly ignored files to ignore list?** command will create the
.gitignore file containing a list of common files to exclude from the Git
repository. Type Y for yes. Have a look at the following screenshot:

```
● ○ ○                bower init — bower — node — 80×24
→  portfolio  bower init
?  name: responsive-portfolio
?  version: 1.0.0
?  description: a responsive portfolio website built with Bootstrap
?  main file: index.html
?  what types of modules does this package expose? globals
?  keywords: portfolio, responsive, bootstrap
?  authors: Thoriq Firdaus <tfirdaus@creatiface.com>
?  license: MIT
?  homepage: creatiface.com
?  set currently installed components as dependencies?: No
?  add commonly ignored files to ignore list?: (Y/n) Y
```

I will use Git to manage the code revision and will upload it to a Git
repository, such as Github or Bitbucket, hence I selected Y (yes). If,
however, you are not familiar with Git yet, and do not plan to host
the project in a Git repository, you may ignore this prompt and type
n. Git is beyond the scope of this module's discussion. To learn more
about Git, the following is the best reference I recommend:

Learn Git for beginners by GitTower (http://www.git-tower.
com/learn/).

22. For the **would you like to mark this package as private which prevents it from being accidentally published to the registry?** command type Y as we won't register our project to the Bower registry. Have a look at the following screenshot:

```
● ○ ○                    bower init — bower — node — 80×24
*   portfolio   bower init
?   name: responsive-portfolio
?   version: 1.0.0
?   description: a responsive portfolio website built with Bootstrap
?   main file: index.html
?   what types of modules does this package expose?: globals
?   keywords: portfolio, responsive, bootstrap
?   authors: Thoriq Firdaus <tfirdaus@creatiface.com>
?   license: MIT
?   homepage: creatiface.com
?   set currently installed components as dependencies?: No
?   add commonly ignored files to ignore list?: Yes
?   would you like to mark this package as private which prevents it from
cidentally published to the registry?: (y/N) Y
```

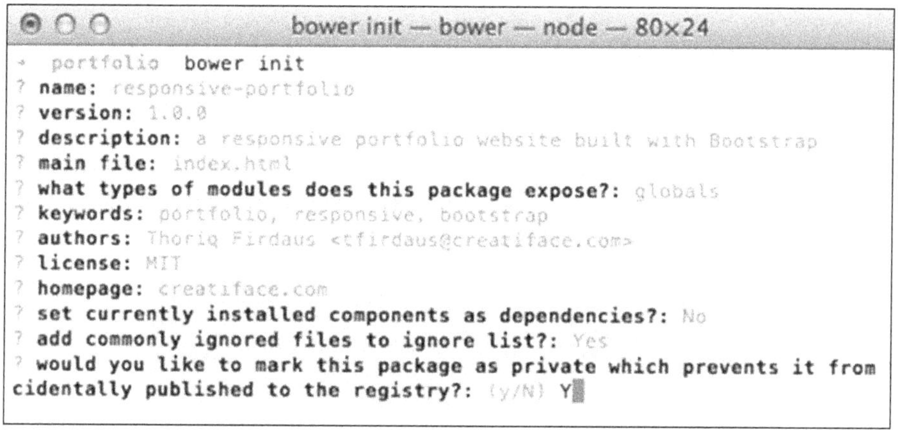

23. Examine the output. If it looks good, type Y to generate the output within the bower.json file, as shown in the following screenshot:

```
● ○ ○                    bower init — bower — node — 80×24
    ],
    description: 'a responsive portfolio website built with Bootstrap',
    main: 'index.html',
    moduleType: [
      'globals'
    ],
    keywords: [
      'portfolio',
      'responsive',
      'bootstrap'
    ],
    license: 'MIT',
    homepage: 'creatiface.com',
    private: true,
    ignore: [
      '**/.*',
      'node_modules',
      'bower_components',
      'test',
      'tests'
    ]
}
?   Looks good?: (Y/n)
```

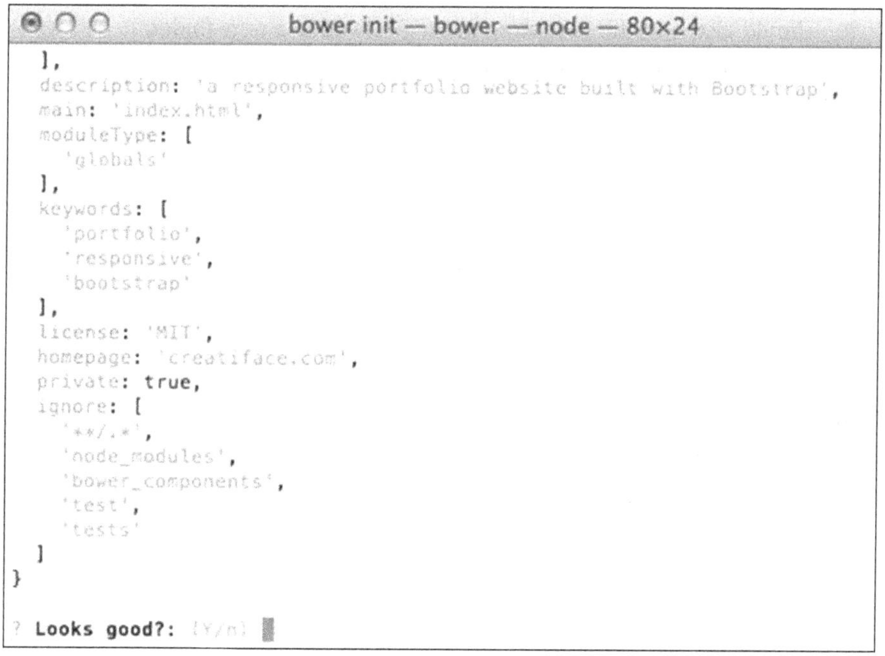

24. There are a number of libraries we want to install. To begin with, let's install Bootstrap with the `bower install bootstrap --save` command, as shown in the following screenshot:

```
● ○ ○
→  portfolio  bower install bootstrap --save
```

The `--save` parameter following the command will register Bootstrap as the project dependency in `bower.json`. If you open it, you should find it recorded under the dependencies, as shown in the following screenshot:

```
21        "**/.*",
22        "node_modules",
23        "bower_components",
24        "test",
25        "tests"
26     ],
27     "dependencies": {
28        "bootstrap": "3.1.1"
29     }
30  }
31
```

You should also find the Bootstrap package saved in a new folder, `bower_components`, along with jQuery, which is a Bootstrap dependency, as shown in the following screenshot:

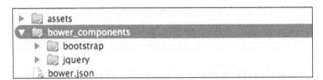

```
▶ 📁 assets
▼ 📁 bower_components
   ▶ 📁 bootstrap
   ▶ 📁 jquery
     📄 bower.json
```

25. Install the Bootstrap extension, Jasny Bootstrap, with the `bower install jasny-bootstrap -save` command.

26. Install Ionicons with the LESS style sheet, with the `bower install ionicons` command.

27. The Ionicons package ships with the font files. Move them to the `fonts` folder of the project directory, as shown in the following screenshot:

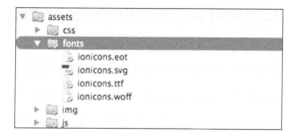

28. Finally, install HTML5Shiv to enable the new elements of HTML5 in Internet Explorer 8 and below, with the `bower install html5shiv --save` command.

What just happened?

We just created folders and the website home page document, `index.html`. Images and icons that are going to be displayed on the website are also prepared. We also recorded the project specification in `bower.json`. Through this file, we can tell that the project is named `responsive-portfolio`, currently at version 1.0.0, and has a couple of dependencies, as follows:

- Bootstrap (`https://github.com/twbs/bootstrap`)

- Jasny Bootstrap (`http://jasny.github.io/bootstrap/`)

- Ionicons with LESS (`https://github.com/lancehudson/ionicons-less`)

- HTML5Shiv (`https://github.com/aFarkas/html5shiv`)

We have downloaded these libraries via the `bower install` command, which is leaner than having to download and extract the `.zip` package. All the libraries should have been added within a folder named `bower_components`, as shown in the following screenshot:

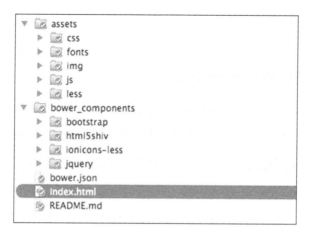

Have a go hero – specifying Bower custom directory

Bower, by default, creates a new folder named `bower_components`. Bower allows us to configure the folder name through the Bower configuration file, `.bowerrc`. Change the folder name as per your preference by creating `.bowerrc`. Follow this reference (`http://bower.io/docs/config/`) to configure bower.

Pop quiz – test your understanding on Bower commands

Q1. We have shown you how to install and update libraries with Bower. The question now is: how to remove the library that has been installed?

1. Run the `bower remove` command.

2. Run the `bower uninstall` command.

3. Run the `bower delete` command.

Q2. Besides installing and removing the library, we can also search the availability of the library in the Bower registry. How to search a library through the Bower registry?

1. Run `bower search` followed by a keyword.

2. Run `bower search` followed by the library name.

3. Run `bower browse` followed by a keyword.

Q3. Bower also allows us to look into the detail of the package properties, such as the package version, dependencies, author, etc. What command do we perform to look into these details?

1. `bower info`.

2. `bower detail`.

3. `bower property`.

Updating Bower components

As the dependencies are installed with Bower, maintaining the project will be more streamlined. These libraries can be updated to the newer version at a later time. With the use of Bower commands, updating the libraries that we have just installed is practically leaner than downloading the `.zip` package and manually moving the files into the project directory.

Run the `bower list` command to see all installed Bower packages, and check whether a new version of the packages is available, as shown in the following screenshot:

```
→  portfolio  bower list
bower check-new      Checking for new versions of the project dependencie
responsive-portfolio#1.0.0
├─┬ bootstrap#3.1.1 (latest is 3.2.0)
│ └── jquery#2.1.1
├── html5shiv#3.7.2
├── ionicons-less#1.4.1
├─┬ jasny-bootstrap#3.1.3
│ ├── bootstrap#3.1.1 (3.2.0 available)
│ └── jquery#2.1.1
→  portfolio ▊
```

Then, install the new version using the `bower install` command and followed by the Bower package name along with the version number. To install Bootstrap version 3.2.0, for example, run the `bower install bootstrap#3.2.0 --save` command.

 We actually should be able to update packages with the `bower update` command. Yet, it seems this command does not work as expected in accordance with a number of reports in the following Bower Issue thread (`https://github.com/bower/bower/issues/1054`). So, using the `bower install` command, as shown previously, is the way to go at the moment.

The portfolio website HTML structure

Now that we have put together the essential stuff to build the website. Let's start building the website's HTML structure. As in the last project, herein, we will be using a couple of new HTML5 elements to build the semantic structure.

Time for action – building the website HTML structure

In this section, we are going to build the website's HTML structure. You will find that a few of the elements that we are going to add herein will be similar to the ones we added in the first website, responsive blog. Hence, the following steps will be straightforward. If you have followed the first through to the end, these steps should also be easy to follow. Let's carry on.

1. Open `index.html`. Then, add the basic HTML structure, as follows:

```html
<!DOCTYPE html>
<html lang="en">
<head>
  <meta charset="UTF-8">
```

```
    <title>Portfolio</title>
</head>
<body>

</body>
</html>
```

2. Below `<meta charset="UTF-8">`, add a meta tag to address the Internet Explorer rendering compatibility:

```
<meta http-equiv="X-UA-Compatible" content="IE=edge">
```

The preceding meta tag specification will force Internet Explorer to use the latest engine's version therein to render the page.

> For more in regard to `X-UA-Compatible`, refer to the Modern.IE article, *How to Use X-UA-Compatible* (`https://www.modern.ie/en-us/performance/how-to-use-x-ua-compatible`).

3. Below the `http-equiv` meta tag, add the meta viewport tag:

```
<meta name="viewport" content="width=device-width, initial-scale=1">
```

The preceding viewport meta tag specification defines the web page viewport width to follow the device viewport size, as well as scale the page at a ratio of 1:1 upon opening the web page the first time.

4. Below the viewport meta tag, add the link to the favicon and apple-touch-icon, which will display the website's icon in Apple devices, such as iPhone, iPad, and iPod:

```
<link rel="apple-touch-icon" href="assets/img/apple-icon.png">
<link rel="shortcut icon" href="assets/img/favicon.png" type="image/png">
```

5. Add the website's meta description below `<title>`:

```
<meta name="description" content="A simple portoflio website built using Bootstrap">
```

The description specified within this meta tag will be displayed in the **Search Engine Result Page (SERP)**.

6. You may also specify the author of the page with a meta tag below the meta description tag, as follows.

```
<meta name="author" content="Thoriq Firdaus">
```

7. Inside `<body>`, add the website off-canvas navigation HTML, as follows:

```
<nav id="menu" class="navmenu navmenu-inverse navmenu-fixed-left
offcanvas portfolio-menu" role="navigation">
        <ul class="nav navmenu-nav">
            <li class="active"><a href="#">Home</a></li>
            <li><a href="#">Blog</a></li>
            <li><a href="#">Shop</a></li>
            <li><a href="#">Speaking</a></li>
            <li><a href="#">Writing</a></li>
            <li><a href="#">About</a></li>
        </ul>
    </nav>
```

Aside from the essential classes that we have mentioned in the Jasny Bootstrap off-canvas section in this chapter, we have also added a new class named `portfolio-menu` in the `<nav>` element to apply our very own styles to the off-canvas navigation.

8. Add the Bootstrap `navbar` structure, along with `<button>` to slide the off-canvas in and out:

```
<div class="navbar navbar-default navbar-portfolio portfolio-
topbar">
<button type="button" class="navbar-toggle" data-
toggle="offcanvas" data-target="#menu" data-canvas="body">
        <span class="icon-bar"></span>
<span class="icon-bar"></span>
<span class="icon-bar"></span>
</button>
</div>
```

9. Below `navbar`, add the `<main>` element, as follows:

```
<main class="portfolio-main" id="content" role="main">
</main>
```

As described in W3C (`http://www.w3.org/TR/html-main-element/`), the `<main>` element defines the main content of the website. So, this is where we will put the website content including the portfolio images.

10. Add Bootstrap Jumbotron, containing the portfolio website name and a line of catchphrase. Since I will display the work of a friend of mine, Yoga Perdana, I wish to show off his name, along with his catchphrase that is displayed in his Dribbble page profile (`https://dribbble.com/yoga`), as follows:

```
<main class="portfolio-main" id="content" role="main">
<section class="jumbotron portfolio-about" id="about">
<h1 class="portfolio-name">Yoga Perdana</h1>
```

```
<p class="lead">Illustrator &amp; Logo designer. I work using
digital tools, specially vector.</p>
</section>
</main>
```

You may freely add your name or company name in this matter.

11. Below the Bootstrap Jumbotron section, add a new section with the HTML5 `<section>` element, along with a heading that defines this section, as follows:

```
...
<section class="jumbotron portfolio-about" id="about">
<h1 class="portfolio-name">Yoga Perdana</h1>
<p class="lead">Illustrator &amp; Logo designer. I work using
digital tools, specially vector.</p>
</section>
<section class="portfolio-display" id="portfolio">
  <h2>Portfolio</h2>
</section>
```

12. Add a Bootstrap container (`http://getbootstrap.com/css/#overview-container`) below the heading that will contain the portfolio images using the following code:

```
<section class="portfolio-display" id="portfolio">
<h2>Portfolio</h2>
    <div class="container">
</div>
</section>
```

13. Arrange the portfolio images into columns and rows. We have 12 portfolio images, which means we may have four images/columns in a row. The following is the first row:

```
...
<div class="container">
<div class="row">
<div class="col-md-3 col-sm-6 portfolio-item">
    <figure class="portfolio-image">
<img class="img-responsive" src="assets/img/6layers.jpg"
height="300" width="400" alt="">
<figcaption class="portfolio-caption">6 Layers</figcaption>
            </figure>
   </div>
<div class="col-md-3 col-sm-6 portfolio-item">
    <figure class="portfolio-image">
<img class="img-responsive" src="assets/img/blur.jpg" height="300"
width="400" alt="">
```

```
<figcaption class="portfolio-caption">Blur</figcaption>
</figure>
  </div>
<div class="col-md-3 col-sm-6 portfolio-item">
        <figure class="portfolio-image">
<img class="img-responsive" src="assets/img/brain.jpg"
height="300" width="400" alt="">
<figcaption class="portfolio-caption">Brain</figcaption>
</figure>
  </div>
  <div class="col-md-3 col-sm-6 portfolio-item">
      <figure class="portfolio-image">
<img class="img-responsive" src="assets/img/color.jpg"
height="300" width="400" alt="">
<figcaption class="portfolio-caption">Color</figcaption>
</figure>
  </div>
</div>
</div>
```

Each column is assigned with a special class to allow us to apply customized styles. We also added a class in `<figure>` that wraps the image, as well as the `<figcaption>` element that wraps the image caption for the same purpose.

14. Add the remaining images into columns and rows. Since, in this case, we have 12 images, there should be three rows displayed in the website. Each row contains four images, including one row that we've added in step 13.

15. Below the portfolio section, add the website message form containing three form fields and a button, as shown in the following code:

```
...
</section>
<div class="portfolio-contact" id="contact">
      <div class="container">
        <h2>Get in Touch</h2>
<form id="contact" method="post" class="form" role="form">
            <div class="form-group">
<input type="text" class="form-control input-lg" id="input-name"
placeholder="Name">
</div>
                <div class="form-group">
<input type="email" class="form-control input-lg" id="input-email"
placeholder="Email">
                </div>
                <div class="form-group">
```

```
<textarea class="form-control" rows="10"></textarea>
            </div>
 <button type="submit" class="btn btn-lg btn-primary">Submit</
button>
            </form>
</div>
</div>
```

Herein, we made the website form simple with only three form fields. But, you may add extra form fields, as per your own requirement.

16. Finally, we will add the website footer with the HTML5 `<footer>` element. The footer, as we have seen from the website wireframe, contains the social media icons and the website copyright statement.

17. Add the following HTML markup below the website's main content:

```
...
</main>
<footer class="portfolio-footer" id="footer">
        <div class="container">
          <div class="social" id="social">
            <ul>
<li class="twitter"><a class="icon ion-social-twitter"
href="#">Twitter</a></li>
<li class="dribbble"><a class="icon ion-social-dribbble-outline"
href="#">Dribbble</a></li>
                </ul>
            </div>
<div class="copyright">Yoga Perdana &copy; 2014</div>
        </div>
    </footer>
```

What just happened?

We just constructed the portfolio website HTML structure with a couple of HTML5 elements and Bootstrap reusable classes. You should be able to see the website through the following address `http://localhost/portfolio/` or `http://{computer-username}/portfolio/` if you are using OS X. No styles have yet been applied to the website at this stage; we haven't linked any style sheet in the page. So, the screenshot following the upcoming tip is how the website looks currently.

The full code shown in the preceding steps can also be obtained from the following Gist `http://git.io/oIh31w`.

- Home
- Blog
- Shop
- Speaking
- Writing
- About

Yoga Perdana

Illustrator & Logo designer. I work using digital tools, specially vector.

Portfolio

6 Layers

Blur

Have a go hero – extending the portfolio website

Bootstrap ships a variety of components. Yet, we use only a couple, including the grids, Jumbotron, buttons, and forms. Extend the website by adding extra Bootstrap components, as follows:

- Pagination (http://getbootstrap.com/components/#pagination)
- Breadcrumbs (http://getbootstrap.com/components/#breadcrumbs)
- Responsive embed (http://getbootstrap.com/components/#responsive-embed)
- Panels (http://getbootstrap.com/components/#panels)
- Wells (http://getbootstrap.com/components/#wells)

In addition, try creating more web pages and link them through the off-canvas navigation menus.

Pop quiz – Bootstrap button classes

Bootstrap specified a number of reusable classes to quickly shape and form elements with the preset styles.

Q1. Which of the following classes is not used in Bootstrap grid?

1. `col-sm-pull-8`
2. `col-md-push-3`
3. `col-xs-offset-5`
4. `col-lg-6`
5. `col-xl-7`

Q2. Which of the following classes does Bootstrap use to style a button?

1. `btn-link`
2. `btn-submit`
3. `btn-send`
4. `btn-cancel`
5. `btn-enter`

Summary

This chapter starts the second project of this module. We are building a portfolio website using one of the most popular frontend development frameworks, Bootstrap. We also explored a new enticing tool in web development named Bower, which streamlines the website dependencies management.

They both are a great combination of tools. Bootstrap lets us build responsive websites quickly with the modular components and reusable classes, while Bower makes the project more maintainable—easily.

In the next chapter, we will deal more with LESS and JavaScript to decorate the website.

6
Polishing the Responsive Portfolio Website with LESS

In the preceding chapter, we constructed the portfolio website structure with HTML5 and a couple of Bootstrap drop-in classes. The website as you might have seen isn't yet decorated. We haven't yet composed our very own styles or linked the style sheet to the page. So, this chapter's focus will be on website decoration.

Bootstrap primarily uses LESS to generate the styles of its components. Following suit, we will also use LESS to style the portfolio website. LESS brings a number of features, such as variables and mixins, that would allow us to write leaner and more efficient style rules. At the end of the day, you will also find customizing and maintaining website styles with LESS is easier than with plain CSS.

Furthermore, we've also used a Bootstrap extension called Jasny Bootstrap to include off-canvas navigation into the portfolio website. At this stage, nothing will happen to the off-canvas navigation; we only set out the HTML structure. So, in this chapter, apart from compiling the website styles, we will also compile the JavaScript library of both Bootstrap and Jasny Bootstrap to make the off-canvas navigation function.

In this chapter, we will discuss many things, including the following topics:

- Learn the basic LESS syntax, such as variables and mixins
- Organize the style sheet references with LESS `@import` directive
- Configure Koala to compile LESS into regular CSS

- Look into the source map to debug LESS
- Compose the website custom styles with LESS
- Compile JavaScript to activate off-canvas navigation

Basic LESS syntax

LESS (`http://lesscss.org/`) is a JavaScript-based CSS preprocessor developed by Alexis Sellier (`http://cloudhead.io/`), also known as CloudHead. As mentioned, Bootstrap uses LESS to compose its component styles—though it only recently released the Sass version officially. As mentioned, we will follow Bootstrap to use LESS to compose our own style rules and manage style sheets.

In a nutshell, LESS extends CSS by bringing some programming features, such as variable, function, and operation. CSS is a straightforward language and fundamentally very easy to learn. However, maintaining static CSS is practically exhaustive, particularly when we have to deal with a thousand lines of style rules and multiple style sheets. The capabilities that LESS offers, such as variable, mixins, function, and operation (which we are going to take a look at shortly) will allow us to develop style rules that will be easier to maintain and organize.

Variables

A variable is the most fundamental feature in LESS. A variable in LESS, as in other programming languages, is used to store a constant or a value that can be reused later limitlessly within the entire style sheet. In LESS, a variable is declared with an @ sign and is followed by the variable name. The variable name can be a combination of numbers and letters. In the following example, we will create a couple of LESS variables to store some colors in the HEX format and assign them in the succeeding style rules to pass the colors, as shown in the following code:

```
@primaryColor: #234fb4;
@secondaryColor: #ffb400;
a {
  color: @primaryColor;
}
button {
  background-color: @secondaryColor;
}
```

Using a LESS compiler, such as Koala, the preceding codes will be compiled into static CSS, as follows:

```
a {
  color: #234fb4;
}
button {
  background-color: #ffb400;
}
```

Using variables is not only limited to storing colors as we just demonstrated. We can use variables for any type of values, for example:

```
@smallRadius: 3px;
```

One of the advantages of using a variable is that, if we have to make a change, we will only need to change the value within the variable. The change we make will take place in every occurrence of that variable in the style sheet. This is certainly a time saver. Scanning through the style sheet and making the change singly or perhaps with the **search** and **replace** feature of the code editor might cause unintended changes if not done carefully.

> You will find the term *compile* and *compiler* often. The word compile herein means that we convert the LESS into standard CSS format that can be rendered in the browser. Compiler is the tool used to do so. In this case, the tool we are using is Koala.

Nesting style rules

LESS lets us nest style rules into one another. Traditionally with plain CSS, when we want to apply style rules to elements, say, under a `<nav>` element, we can compose the style rules in the following way:

```
nav {
  background-color: #000;
  width: 100%;
}
nav ul {
  padding: 0;
  margin: 0;
}
nav li {
  display: inline;
}
```

As we can see from the preceding example, we repeat the `nav` selector each time we apply styles to a particular element nested under the `<nav>` element. By using LESS, we are able to eliminate this repetition and simplify it by nesting the style rules, as follows:

```
nav {
  background-color: #000;
  width: 100%;
  ul {
    padding: 0;
    margin: 0;
  }
  li {
    display: inline;
  }
}
```

Eventually, the preceding style rules will return the same result—only we write the style rules more efficiently this time.

Mixins

Mixins are one of the most powerful features in LESS. Mixins simplify style rules declaration by allowing us to create a group of CSS properties that can be included in other style rules in the style sheets. Let's take a look at the following code snippet:

```
.links {
  -webkit-border-radius: 3px;
  -mox-border-radius: 3px;
  border-radius: 3px;
  text-decoration: none;
  font-weight: bold;
}
.box {
-webkit-border-radius: 3px;
  -moz-border-radius: 3px;
  border-radius: 3px;
  position: absolute;
  top: 0;
  left: 0;
}
.button {
  -webkit-border-radius: 3px;
  -mox-border-radius: 3px;
  border-radius: 3px;
}
```

In the preceding example, we declared `border-radius` in three different style rules along with the vendor prefix to cover earlier versions of Firefox- and Webkit-based browsers. In LESS, we are able to simplify `border-radius` declaration by creating a mixin. A mixin in LESS is simply specified with a class selector. Given the preceding example, let's create a mixin named `.border-radius` to contain the `border-radius` properties, as follows:

```
.border-radius {
  -webkit-border-radius: 3px;
  -moz-border-radius: 3px;
  border-radius: 3px;
}
```

Afterwards, we include `.border-radius` into the succeeding style rules to pass the containing properties into them, as follows:

```
.links {
  .border-radius;
  text-decoration: none;
  font-weight: bold;
}
.box {
  .border-radius;
  position: absolute;
  top: 0;
  left: 0;
}
.button {
  .border-radius;
}
```

This code will produce exactly the same output as in the first code snippet of this section when compiled into static CSS.

Parametric mixins

Furthermore, we can also extend the mixins into so-called **parametric mixins**. This feature allows us to add arguments or variables and turn the mixins to be configurable. Let's take the same example as in the preceding section. But, this time, we will not assign a fixed value; instead, we replace it with a variable, as follows:

```
.border-radius(@radius) {
  -webkit-border-radius: @radius;
  -moz-border-radius: @radius;
  border-radius: @radius;
}
```

Now, we can insert this mixin into other style rules and assign a different value to each:

```
a {
  .border-radius(3px);
  text-decoration: none;
  font-weight: bold;
}
div {
  .border-radius(10px);
  position: absolute;
  top: 0;
  left: 0;
}
button {
  .border-radius(12px);
}
```

When we compile it into regular CSS, each style rule is applied with a different border-radius value, as follows:

```
a {
  -webkit-border-radius: 3px;
  -moz-border-radius: 3px;
  border-radius: 3px;
  text-decoration: none;
  font-weight: bold;
}
div {
  -webkit-border-radius: 10px;
  -moz-border-radius: 10px;
  border-radius: 10px;
  position: absolute;
  top: 0;
  left: 0;
}
button {
  -webkit-border-radius: 12px;
  -moz-border-radius: 12px;
  border-radius: 12px;
}
```

Specify a default value in a parametric mixin

Furthermore, we can specify a default value in a parametric mixin, which will be useful in case a parameter is not passed. When we set a parameter in a mixin, as we did in the preceding example, LESS will take the parameter as a requirement. If we do not pass a parameter in it, LESS will return an error. So, let's take the preceding example and extend it with a default value, say, 5px, as follows:

```
.border-radius(@radius: 5px) {
  -webkit-border-radius: @radius;
  -moz-border-radius: @radius;
  border-radius: @radius;
}
```

The preceding parametric mixin will return the border radius of 5px by default. The default value will be overwritten if we pass a custom value within brackets.

Merging mixins with extend syntax

Extend syntax is the long-awaited feature to come into LESS. One main issue with LESS mixins is that it simply copies the containing CSS properties of a mixin, thus producing duplicate code. Again, if we are dealing with a large-scale website with a thousand lines of codes, the amount of duplicated code would make the style sheet size unnecessarily large.

In Version 1.4, LESS introduced extend syntax. The extend syntax comes in a form that is similar to a CSS pseudo-class, :extend. The extend syntax will group CSS selectors that inherit the properties set containing the mixin. Compare the following two examples.

To begin with, we include a mixin without the :extend syntax:

```
.border-radius {
  -webkit-border-radius: 3px;
  -moz-border-radius: 3px;
  border-radius: 3px;
}
.box {
  .border-radius;
  position: absolute;
  top: 0;
  left: 0;
}
.button {
  .border-radius;
}
```

The preceding LESS code is short, but when it is compiled into CSS, the code extends to around 17 lines, as the `border-radius` properties are repeated or simply copied in every style rule, as follows:

```
.border-radius {
  -webkit-border-radius: 3px;
  -moz-border-radius: 3px;
  border-radius: 3px;
}
.box {
  -webkit-border-radius: 3px;
  -moz-border-radius: 3px;
  border-radius: 3px;
  position: absolute;
  top: 0;
  left: 0;
}
.button {
  -webkit-border-radius: 3px;
  -moz-border-radius: 3px;
  border-radius: 3px;
}
```

In this second example, we will put the :extend syntax into practice into the same mixin:

```
.border-radius {
  -webkit-border-radius: 3px;
  -moz-border-radius: 3px;
  border-radius: 3px;
}
.box {
  &:extend(.border-radius);
  position: absolute;
  top: 0;
  left: 0;
}
.button {
  &:extend(.border-radius);
}
```

The following is how the code turns into plain CSS; it becomes even shorter than the initial uncompiled LESS codes.

```
.border-radius,
.box
```

```
.button {
  -webkit-border-radius: 3px;
  -moz-border-radius: 3px;
  border-radius: 3px;
}
.box {
  position: absolute;
  top: 0;
  left: 0;
}
```

Generating value with mathematical operations

We can also perform math operations with LESS-like addition, subtraction, division, and multiplication. Operations could be pretty useful to determine a length, such as the element's width and height. In the following example, we will calculate the proper box width by subtracting it with the padding so that it can be fit into the parent container.

First, we will define the variable for the padding with the `@padding` variable:

```
@padding: 10px;
```

Then, we specify the box width and subtract it with the `@padding` variable:

```
.box {
  padding: @padding;
  width: 500px - (@padding * 2);
}
```

Remember that the padding takes two sides of the box, whether it is right and left or top and bottom, so that is why we multiply `@padding` in the width property by two. Finally when we compile this LESS operation into the regular CSS, this code will look as follows:

```
.box {
  padding: 10px;
  width: 480px;
}
```

In other cases, we can do the same to the height property, as follows:

```
.box {
  padding: @padding;
  width: 500px - (@padding * 2);
  height: 500px - (@padding * 2);
}
```

Generating color with mathematical operations and LESS functions

Believe it or not, in LESS, we can alter colors with math operations. It's like mixing paint colors, except we do it by addition, subtraction, division, and multiplication. For instance:

```
.selector {
  color: #aaa + 2;
}
```

When compiled, the color turns into the following:

```
.selector {
  color: #acacac;
}
```

Furthermore, LESS also provides a handful of functions that allow us to turn colors darker or lighter to a certain extent. The following example will lighten the color in the @color variable by 50%.

```
@color: #FF0000;
.selector {
  color: lighten(@color, 50%);
}
```

Alternatively, to darken the color, use the darken() function, as follows:

```
@color: #FF0000;
.selector {
  color: darken(@color, 50%);
}
```

 A complete list of the LESS color function can be found in the following page of LESS's official website (http://lesscss.org/functions/#color-operations).

Referential import

This is one of my favorite features in LESS. The referential import, as the name implies, allows us to import an external style sheet merely as reference. Prior to the emerging of this feature, all style rules in the style sheet imported with the `@import` directive will be appended, which is more often than not unnecessary.

Since Version 1.5, LESS introduced the `(reference)` option that marks `@import` as reference, thus preventing the external style rules from being appended. Add the `(reference)` mark after `@import`, as follows:

```
@import (reference) 'partial.less';
```

Using a variable in an import statement

One of the constraints that LESS used to encounter was when using a variable within the `@import` directive (`https://github.com/less/less.js/issues/410`). It is one of the most requested features to present in LESS and finally has been resolved since LESS 1.4. We are now able to declare a variable in an `@import` statement by naming the variable within curly braces, for example, `@{variable-name}`.

The use of a variable along with `@import` will allow us to define the style sheet path once, through a variable. Then, call the path using the variable, as follows:

```
@path: 'path/folder/less/';
@import '@{path}mixins.less';
@import '@{path}normalize.less';
@import '@{path}print.less';
```

This approach is visibly neater and more efficient than having to add the full path every time we import a new style sheet, as follows:

```
@import 'path/folder/less/mixins.less';
@import 'path/folder/less/normalize.less';
@import 'path/folder/less/print.less';
```

 Refer to the **Import Directive** section of the LESS official website (`http://lesscss.org/features/#import-directives-feature`) for further assistance on importing an external style sheet with LESS.

Using source map for easier style debugging

While CSS preprocessors like LESS allows us to write style rules more efficiently, the browsers are still only able to read plain CSS, which will cause a new problem particularly when debugging issues in the style sheet.

Since the browser is referring to the generated CSS instead of the source file (LESS), we will likely be clueless of the exact lines where the style rules are actually declared in a source file. A source map addresses this issue by mapping the generated CSS back to the source files. In a browser that supports source map, you will find the browser refers directly to the source file. In the case of LESS, the browser will refer to the `.less` style sheet as shown in the following screenshot:

```
Styles   Computed   Event Listeners   DOM Breakpoints   Properties                          +
element.style {
}
textarea.form-control {                                                        forms.less:150
    height: ▶ auto;
}
.form-control {
☑ display: block;
☑ width: ▶ 100%;                                                               forms.less:115
☑ height: ▶ 34px;
☑ padding: ▶ 6px 12px;
☑ font-size: 14px;
☑ line-height: 1.42857143;
☑ color: ■#555;
☑ background-color: ☐#fff;
☑ background-image: none;
☑ border: ▶ 1px solid ▦#ccc;
☑ border-radius: ▶ 4px;
```

In this project, we will generate a source map of the generated CSS. So, if we encounter bugs, it is a lot easier to address it. We can immediately figure out exactly where the style rules reside.

Head over to the following references for further information about the source map:

- Working with CSS preprocessors by Google (`https://developer.chrome.com/devtools/docs/css-preprocessors`)

- An Introduction to Source Map (`http://blog.teamtreehouse.com/introduction-source-maps`)

- Using LESS Source Maps (`http://roots.io/using-less-source-maps/`)

More on LESS

LESS has plenty of features and will only grow with more additions in the years to come. It's impractical to include and discuss them all at once in this module. So, the following are a few references to dig in deeper:

- LESS's official website (`http://lesscss.org/`); the best source to be up-to-date with LESS

- *LESS Web Development Essentials, Bass Jobsen, Packt Publishing* (`https://www.packtpub.com/web-development/less-web-development-essentials`)

- Instant LESS CSS preprocessor (`https://www.packtpub.com/web-development/instant-less-css-preprocessor-how-instant`)

External style sheet references

We walked through a big amount of basic syntax in LESS in the preceding section. Now, we will start to actually work with LESS, speaking of which, before we are able to write our own style rules as well as reuse variables, mixins, and functions that are shipped in Bootstrap and the Jasny Bootstrap package, we will have to import them into our own style sheet with the LESS `@import` directive.

Time for action – creating style sheets and organizing external style sheet references

Perform the following steps to manage the style sheet references:

1. Go to the project directory and create a new style sheet named `var-bootstrap.less` in `assets/less` directory. This style sheet contains the copy of Bootstrap's predefined variables. This copy will allow us to customize the variables without affecting the initial specifications.

2. Hence, copy the Bootstrap variables in the `variables.less` style sheet of the `/bootstrap/less` directory. Paste the complete variables into `var-bootstrap.less` that we only created in step 1.

 For your convenience, you may also copy Bootstrap variables directly from the Github repository (`http://git.io/7LmzGA`).

3. Create a new style sheet named `var-jasny.less`. Similar to `var-bootstrap.less`, this style sheet will contain the copy of the Jasny Bootstrap variables.

4. Obtain the Jasny Bootstrap variables in `variables.less` of the `jasny-bootstrap/less` directory. Paste all the variables in the `var-jasny.less` style sheet we just created in step 3.

 Alternatively, copy the variables directly from the Jasny Bootstrap repository (`http://git.io/SK1ccg`).

5. Create a new style sheet named `frameworks.less`.

6. We are going to use this style sheet to import the Bootstrap and Jasny Bootstrap style sheets residing in the `bower_component` folder.

7. In `frameworks.less`, create a variable named `@path-bootstrap` to define the path, pointing to the folder named `less`, where all the LESS style sheets of Bootstrap reside:

```
@path-bootstrap: '../../bower_components/bootstrap/less/';
```

8. Similarly, create a variable that defines the path, pointing to the Jasny Bootstrap `less` folder, as follows:

```
@path-jasny: '../../bower_components/jasny-bootstrap/less/';
```

9. Also create one to define the Ionicons path:

```
@path-ionicons: '../../bower_components/ionicons-less/less/';
```

10. Import the style sheets that contain variables using the following code:

```
@import 'var-bootstrap.less';
@import 'var-jasny.less';
```

11. Import the Bootstrap and Jasny Bootstrap style sheets, which are only required to build the portfolio website. Specify the paths using the variables we created in steps 6 to 8, as follows:

```
// Mixins
@import '@{path-bootstrap}mixins.less';

// Reset
@import '@{path-bootstrap}normalize.less';
@import '@{path-bootstrap}print.less';

// Core CSS
@import '@{path-bootstrap}scaffolding.less';
@import '@{path-bootstrap}type.less';
@import '@{path-bootstrap}grid.less';
@import '@{path-bootstrap}forms.less';
@import '@{path-bootstrap}buttons.less';

// Icons
```

```less
@import '@{path-ionicons}ionicons.less';

// Components
@import '@{path-bootstrap}navs.less';
@import '@{path-bootstrap}navbar.less';
@import '@{path-bootstrap}jumbotron.less';

// Offcanvas
@import "@{path-jasny}navmenu.less";
@import "@{path-jasny}offcanvas.less";

// Utility classes
@import '@{path-bootstrap}utilities.less';
@import '@{path-bootstrap}responsive-utilities.less';
```

 You can also copy the preceding code from Gist (`http://git.io/WpBVAA`).

 To minimize extraneous style rules, which really are not needed for the website, we excluded a number of Bootstrap and Jasny Bootstrap style sheets from `frameworks.less` as you can see previously.

12. Create a new style sheet named `style.less`. This is the style sheet where we are going to compose our very own style rules.

13. Import the Bootstrap variables and the mixins within `style.less`:

```less
@path-bootstrap: '../../bower_components/bootstrap/less/';
@import 'var-bootstrap.less';
@import 'var-jasny.less';
@import (reference) '@{path-bootstrap}mixins.less';
```

What just happened?

To sum up, we just created style sheets and put them in order. At first, we created two style sheets named `var-bootstrap.less` and `var-jasny.less` to store the Bootstrap and Jasny Bootstrap variables. As mentioned, we made these copies to avoid directly altering the originals. We have also created a style sheet named `frameworks.less`, containing references to the Bootstrap and Jasny Bootstrap style sheets.

Finally, we created the website primary style sheet named `style.less` and imported the variables and mixins so that they are reusable inside the `style.less`.

Have a go hero – name and organize the style sheets

In the preceding steps, we organized and named the folders as well as the files to my personal preferences. Even so, you don't have to follow the naming conventions absolutely. Do organize and name them in your own way.

 The most important thing to note is that the @import statement refers to the correct file name.

The following are a few ideas:

- Rename `var-bootstrap.less` to simply `vars.less`.
- Alternatively, create a new folder name `vars` or `configs` to put the `var-bootstrap.less` and `var-jasny.less` style sheet in it.
- Did you know that you can also import the LESS style sheet without declaring the `.less` extension. For the sake of simplicity, you can omit the extensions, for example:

```
@import (reference) '@{path-bootstrap}mixins.less';
```

Pop quiz – which of the following option is not LESS Import option?

Q1. In one of the section of this chapter, we discussed `(reference)`, which imports yet treats external LESS style sheets only as a reference. In addition to `(reference)`, LESS also provides more options to import a style sheet. So, which of the following is not the LESS import option?

1. `(less)`
2. `(css)`
3. `(multiple)`
4. `(once)`
5. `(default)`

Q2. How do you use variable within an `@import` statement?

1. `@import '@{variable}style.less';`
2. `@import '@[variable]style.less';`
3. `@import '@(variable)style.less';`

Working with Koala

The HTML and the style sheets have been prepared. It's now time to put them together to shape a solid portfolio website. We will compose the website styles using LESS syntax. Herein, we will also use Koala as in the first project. This time, we will compile LESS into plain CSS.

Time for action – compiling LESS into CSS using Koala

Perform the following steps to compile LESS into CSS using Koala:

1. Add the project directory in the Koala sidebar, as follows:

2. Select all the style sheets except `frameworks.less` and `style.less`. Right-click and select **Toggle Auto Compile**. Have a look at the following screenshot:

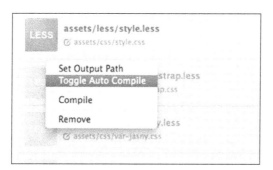

This will turn off the **Auto Compile** option on the selected style sheets and prevent Koala from compiling these style sheet unintentionally.

3. On the other hand, ensure that **Auto Compile** is checked for the two remaining style sheets, `frameworks.less` and `style.less`:

4. Make sure that the `frameworks.less` and `style.less` output is set to `/assets/css` directory, as shown in the following screenshot:

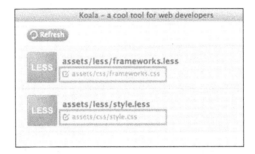

5. Check the **Source Map** option for both style sheets to generate the source map files, which will help us when debugging:

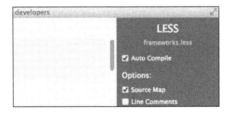

6. Select the output styles for the two style sheets, `frameworks.less` and `style.less`, to **compress**:

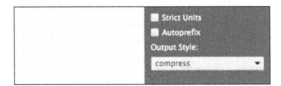

This option will generate a small-sized CSS style sheet, as the codes within the style sheet will be compressed into a single line. Hence, the style sheet will load faster in the browser and also save bandwidth consumption on the user's side.

7. Select `frameworks.less` and click on the **Compile** button to compile it into CSS:

8. Do the same for `style.less`. Select it and click on the **Compile** button to compile it into CSS. Open `index.html` in the code editor, and link both of the style sheets inside `<head>`, as follows:

```
<link href="assets/css/frameworks.css" rel="stylesheet">
<link href="assets/css/style.css" rel="stylesheet">
```

What just happened?

In the preceding steps, we compiled the website primary style sheets, `frameworks.less` and `style.less`, from LESS to CSS. You should now have them along with the source maps in the `assets/css/` directory. The code is compressed, thus resulting in a relatively small file size, as shown in the following screenshot:

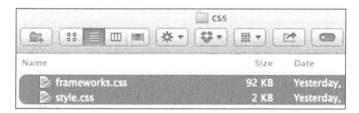

The style sheets are relatively small in size. As shown, frameworks.css is 92 kb, while style.css is only 2 kb

Additionally, we also linked these CSS style sheets in `index.html`. However, since we have not yet written our own styles, the websites are decorated with the default Bootstrap styles, as shown in the following screenshot:

Polishing the portfolio website with LESS

This is the section you might be waiting for, to style the portfolio website. It is apparently a pleasing experience to see the website start to have shapes, colors, and look. In this section, we will customize the default styles and compose our style rules using the LESS syntax that we have covered earlier in this chapter.

Time for action – composing the website styles with LESS syntax

Perform the following steps to style the website:

1. Add a new font family from Google Font. Herein, I opted for Varela Round (`http://www.google.com/fonts/specimen/Varela+Round`). Place the following Google Font link before any other style sheets:

   ```
   <link href='http://fonts.googleapis.com/css?family=Varela+Round'
   rel='stylesheet' type='text/css'>
   ```

2. We will customize the default styles by changing some variables. Open `var-bootstrap.less` in Sublime Text. First, we change the `@brand-primary` variable that defines the Bootstrap primary color; change it from `#428bca` to `#46acb8`:

3. Also, change the color in the `@brand-success` variable from `#5cb85c` to `#7ba47c`:

4. Change the `@headings-font-family` variable, which defines the font family used in the headings, from `inherit` to `"Varela Round"`, as follows:

   ```
   @headings-font-family: "Varela Round", @font-family-sans-serif;
   ```

5. The Bootstrap default style shows a glowing effect when the user focusses on a form field. The color of this effect is specified in `@input-border-focus`. Change the color from `#66afe9` to `#89c6cb`:

6. In the top section of the website, you can see that the navbar still has the Bootstrap default style with the gray background and border color, as shown in the following screenshot:

7. These two colors are specified in `@navbar-default-bg` and `@navbar-default-border`, respectively. Change both of these variable values to transparent, as follows:

```
@navbar-default-bg: transparent;
@navbar-default-border: transparent;
```

8. Similarly, the default style of the Jumbotron section is set with a gray background color. To remove this color, set the `@jumbotron-bg` variable to `transparent`, as follows:

```
@jumbotron-bg: transparent;
```

9. We will be back editing a few more Bootstrap variables later on. For the meantime, let's write our own style rules. To begin with, we will show the navbar toggle button, which is hidden by the Bootstrap default styles. In our case, this button will be used to slide the off-canvas navigation on and off. Let's force this button to be visible with the following style rules:

```
.portfolio-topbar {
  .navbar-toggle {
```

```
   display: block;
 }
}
```

10. As you can see from the following screenshot, the toggle button with the so-called hamburger icon (http://gizmodo.com/who-designed-the-iconic-hamburger-icon-1555438787) is now visible:

11. Currently, this button is positioned on the right-hand side. Referring to the website blueprint, it should be on the left. Add float:left to put it on the left-hand side and margin-left:15px to add a little whitespace to the button's left, as follows:

```
.portfolio-topbar {
  .navbar-toggle {
    display: block;
    float: left;
    margin-left: 15px;
  }
}
```

12. Herein, I want to customize the toggle button's default styles, which are also specified through a couple of variables in var-bootstrap.less. Hence, open var-bootstrap.less in Sublime Text.

13. First of all, we will remove the button borders by changing the value of the @navbar-default-toggle-border-color variable from #ddd to transparent, as follows:

```
@navbar-default-toggle-border-color: transparent;
```

14. We will also remove the gray background color that appears when we hover over the button. Remove the gray background color out of it by changing the @navbar-default-toggle-hover-bg variable from #ddd to transparent, as follows:

```
@navbar-default-toggle-hover-bg: transparent;
```

15. I want the hamburger icon to look bolder and strong. So, herein, we want to change the colors to black. Change the value of `@navbar-default-toggle-icon-bar-bg` from `#888` to `#000`:

```
@navbar-default-toggle-icon-bar-bg: #000;
```

16. At this stage, the website content is aligned to the left-hand side, which is the default browser alignment for any content. Following the website blueprint, the website content should be centered. Use `text-align: center`, as follows, to align the content to the center:

```
.portfolio-about,
.portfolio-display,
.portfolio-contact,
.portfolio-footer {
    text-align: center;
}
```

17. Add the following to turn the website name to all-caps (all capital letters), making it bigger and bolder:

```
.portfolio-about {
  .portfolio-name {
    text-transform: uppercase;
  }
}
```

18. On the other hand, make the catchphrase line subtler by specifying the text color to gray light. Herein, we can simply use Bootstrap's predefined variable named `@gray-light` to apply the gray color, as follows:

```
.portfolio-about {
  .portfolio-name {
    text-transform: uppercase;
  }
  .lead {
    color: @gray-light;
  }
}
```

19. In the portfolio section, specify the background color with gray light, which is lighter than the color in `@gray-lighter` variable. The addition of the background color aims to lay a bit of emphasis on the portfolio section.

20. In this project, we opt to use the LESS `darken()` function to slightly darken the white color, as follows:

```
.portfolio-display {
  background-color: darken(#fff, 1%);
}
```

> The background color may alternatively be achieved by lightening the black color by 99 percent using the LESS `lighten()` function as `background-color: lighten(#000, 99%);`.

21. At this stage, if we take a look at the portfolio section, it seems there are merely little spaces at the top and the bottom, as pointed out in the following screenshot:

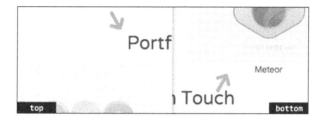

22. Give the portfolio section more space to breathe at the top and bottom by adding `padding-top` and `padding-bottom`, as follows:

```
.portfolio-display {
  background-color: darken(#fff, 1%);
  padding-top: 60px;
  padding-bottom: 60px;
}
```

23. To sum up, we added two headings in the website, including one in the portfolio section, to explicitly display the section name. These headings will share the same style rules. So, in that case, we better create a mixin that specifically defines the heading styles.

24. Define the mixin as well as the CSS properties to apply the heading styles, as follows:

```
.heading {
  color: lighten(#000, 70%);
  text-transform: uppercase;
  font-size: 21px;
  margin-bottom: 60px;
}
```

25. Add the following style rules for the section heading, which will make it look subtler and in tune with the background color of the portfolio section:

```
.portfolio-display {
...
  h2 {
    &:extend(.heading);
  }
}
```

26. As shown in the following screenshot, there is only very little space in between each row; the rows are too close to each other, as follows:

So, put more space by specifying `margin-bottom` for each portfolio item, as follows:

```
.portfolio-item {
  margin-bottom: 30px;
}
```

27. Add styles for the portfolio image, as follows:

```
.portfolio-image {
  padding: 15px;
  background-color: #fff;
margin-right: auto;
margin-left: auto;
}
```

28. Also, add the styles for the caption, as follows:

```
.portfolio-caption {
  font-weight: 500;
  margin-top: 15px;
  color: @gray;
}
```

29. What do you think about showing a transition effect when we hover over the portfolio image? That will look nice, won't it? In this case, I would like to show a shadow surrounding the portfolio image upon hover.

30. Add the effect using Bootstrap's predefined mixins, `.transition()` and `.box-shadow()`, as follows:

```
.portfolio-image {
  padding: 15px;
  background-color: #fff;
margin-right: auto;
margin-left: auto;
  .transition(box-shadow 1s);
  &:hover {
    .box-shadow(0 0 8px fade(#000, 10%));
  }
}
```

31. Below the portfolio section, we have the website contact form, which has already been applied with the Bootstrap default styling. So, let's customize it with our own style rules.

32. First, we will add more spaces at the top and the bottom of the contact form section with `padding`.

33. Add the styles for the heading with the `.heading` mixin we created in step 18:

```
.portfolio-contact {
...
  h2 {
    &:extend(.heading);
  }
}
```

34. The form currently spans the container fully. So, add the following style rules to set the maximum width, yet still display the form in the middle of the container, as follows:

```
.portfolio-contact {
...
  .form {
    width: 100%;
    max-width: 600px;
    margin-right: auto;
    margin-left: auto;
  }
}
```

35. Add the following style rules to make the form elements—`<input>`, `<textarea>`, `<button>`—look flatter. These style rules remove the shadow and lower the border radius. Have a look at the following code:

```
.portfolio-contact {
...
  .form {
    width: 100%;
    max-width: 600px;
    margin-right: auto;
    margin-left: auto;
    input, textarea, button {
      box-shadow: none;
      border-radius: @border-radius-small;
    }
  }
}
```

36. Add the following lines to style the button and make it live with a transition effect, as follows:

```less
.portfolio-contact {
...
  .form {
    width: 100%;
    max-width: 600px;
    margin-right: auto;
    margin-left: auto;
    input, textarea, button {
      box-shadow: none;
      border-radius: @border-radius-small;
    }
    .btn {
      display: block;
      width: 100%;
      .transition(background-color 500ms);
    }
  }
}
```

37. Starting this step, we will add style rules for the footer, the last section of the website. The footer contains the social media links, Dribbble and Twitter, and a copyright statement at the very bottom.

38. First, as in the preceding sections, we put more whitespace at the top and bottom of the section with padding:

```less
.portfolio-footer {
  padding-top: 60px;
  padding-bottom: 60px;
}
```

39. Then, we put more spaces between the social media links and the copyright statement with margin-bottom:

```less
.portfolio-footer {
  padding-top: 60px;
  padding-bottom: 60px;
.social {
    margin-bottom: 30px;
}
}
```

40. Add the following lines to remove the `<ul>` element `padding` derived from default browser styles:

```
.portfolio-footer {
...
  .social {
    margin-bottom: 30px;
    ul {
      padding-left: 0;
    }
  }
}
```

41. Add the highlighted lines in the following code to display the social media links beside each other:

```
.portfolio-footer {
...
  .social {
    margin-bottom: 30px;
    ul {
      padding-left: 0;
    }
    li {
      list-style: none;
      display: inline-block;
      margin: 0 15px;
    }
  }
}
```

42. Give the social media links the color of their respective social media brands, as follows:

```
.portfolio-footer {
...
  .social {
    ...
    a {
      font-weight: 600;
      color: @gray;
      text-decoration: none;
      .transition(color 500ms);
      &:before {
        display: block;
        font-size: 32px;
        margin-bottom: 5px;
      }
    }
```

```
      .twitter a:hover {
        color: #55acee;
      }
      .dribbble a:hover {
        color: #ea4c89;
      }
    }
  }
```

> Get more colors of popular websites in BrandColors (`http://brandcolors.net/`).

43. Finally, make the copyright statement color subtler with the gray color:

```
.portfolio-footer {
  ...
    .copyright {
      color: @gray-light;
    }
}
```

What just happened?

In the preceding steps, we just styled the website by customizing a number of Bootstrap variables as well as composing our own style rules. Compile `style.less` to generate the CSS. Additionally, you can obtain all the style rules we applied from this Gist (`http://git.io/-FWuiQ`).

The website should now be presentable. The following screenshot shows how the website looks in the desktop view:

The website is also responsive; the layout will adapt to the viewport width size, as shown in the following screenshot:

Have a go hero – being more creative

Many of the style rules that we have just applied in the preceding section are merely decorative. Feel free to add more creativity and customization, as follows:

- Explore the website's new color schemes. Use handy tools, such as Kuler, (`https://kuler.adobe.com/`) to generate color scheme
- Apply different font families
- Present more awesome transition effects with CSS3

Pop quiz — using LESS function and extend syntax

Q1. How do you make a color lighter with LESS?

1. `lighter(#000, 30%);`

2. `lighten(#000, 30%);`

3. `lightening(#000, 30%);`

Q2. How do you make a color transparent?

1. `fadeout(#000, 10%);`

2. `transparentize(#000, 10%);`

3. `fade-out(#000, 10%);`

Q3. Which one of the following is an incorrect way to extend a mixin in LESS?

1. `.class:extend(.another-class);`

2. `.class::extend(.another-class);`

3.
```
.class {
:extend(.another-class);
}
```

Improve and make the website functioning with JavaScript

The off-canvas navigation has not yet been activated. If you click on the toggle button, the off-canvas navigation will not slide in. Furthermore, if you view the portfolio website in Internet Explorer 8, you will find that a number of style rules are not applied. This is because Internet Explorer 8 does not recognize the HTML5 elements that are used in the website. To sort these issues out, we will have to make use of some JavaScript libraries..

Time for action – compiling JavaScript with Koala

1. Create a new JavaScript file named `html5shiv.js` in `assets/js` directory.

2. Import `html5shiv.js` from the HTML5Shiv package we downloaded through Bower into this file:

   ```
   // @koala-prepend "../../bower_components/html5shiv/dist/
   html5shiv.js"
   ```

3. Create a new JavaScript file named `bootstrap.js`.

4. In `bootstrap.js`, import the JavaScript libraries that are required to turn the off-canvas navigation functionality on, as follows:

```
// @koala-prepend "../../bower_components/jquery/dist/jquery.js"
// @koala-prepend "../../bower_components/bootstrap/js/transition.js"
// @koala-prepend "../../bower_components/jasny-bootstrap/js/offcanvas.js"
```

5. Open Koala and ensure that the **Auto Compile** option for `html5shiv.js` and `bootstrap.js` is checked, as shown in the following screenshot:

6. Also, make sure that the output path of these two JavaScript files is set to the `/assets/js` directory, as shown in the following screenshot:

7. Compile both these JavaScript files by clicking on the **Compile** button in Koala, as follows:

Once these JavaScript files are compiled, you should find the minified version of these files, `html5shiv.min.js` and `bootstrap.min.js`, as shown in the following screenshot:

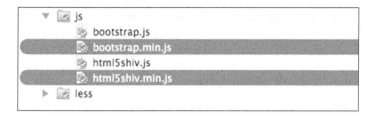

8. Open `index.html` in Sublime Text, and link `html5shiv.js` within the `<head>` section using the Internet Explorer conditional comment tag, as follows:

    ```
    <!--[if lt IE 9]>
    <script type="text/javascript" src="assets/js/html5shiv.min.js"></script>
    <![endif]-->
    ```

9. Link `bootstrap.min.js` at the bottom of `index.html`, as follows:

    ```
    <script type="text/javascript" src="assets/js/bootstrap.min.js"></script>
    ```

What just happened?

We just compiled jQuery and Bootstrap JavaScript libraries to enable the off-canvas functionality. We also enabled HTML5 elements in Internet Explorer 8 using HTML5Shiv. By now, the website is fully functional.

> You can view the website through this Github page (`http://tfirdaus.github.io/rwd-portfolio/`).

You should be able to slide in and out the off-canvas navigation, and the styles should now be visible in Internet Explorer 8. Take a look at the following screenshot:

The off-canvas navigation menu is slid in.

Summary

We just accomplished the second project of this module. In this project, we built a portfolio website using Bootstrap. Bootstrap makes it easy and quick to build a responsive website along with the website components using the drop-in classes provided.

At the top of that, we also used a Bootstrap extension called Jasny Bootstrap to include off-canvas navigation, which is one of the missing popular responsive design patterns in the original Bootstrap. When it comes styling the website, we used LESS, a CSS preprocessor that allows us to write the style rules more efficiently.

To sum up, we did many things in this project to get the website up and running. I hope you've learned many things along the way.

In the next chapter, we will start off the third project of this module using the Foundation framework. Stay tuned!

7
A Responsive Website for Business with Foundation

In this era, where many people are connected to the Internet, having a website becomes an essential for a company of any size—a small company or a Fortune 500 company with multibillion businesses. Therefore, in this third project of this module, we are going to build a responsive website for business.

To build the website, we will adopt a new framework called Foundation. Foundation is built by ZURB, a web-development agency based in California. It's a meticulously crafted framework with a stack of interactive widgets. On the technical side, Foundation styles are built on top of Sass and SCSS. Hence, we will also walk through the subject during the course of working on the project.

To work towards this project, first let's assume that you have a business idea. It might be a bit exaggerated, but it's a brilliant idea that could potentially turn into a multibillion-dollar business and change the world. You have an awesome product baked, and now it's time to build the website. You are very excited and cannot wait to rock the world.

So, without further ado, let's get the project started.

This chapter will primarily revolve around Foundation, and the topics that we are going to cover herein include:

- Examining the website design and layout in wireframe
- Looking into Foundation features, components, and add-ons
- Managing the project directories and assets
- Obtaining the Foundation package through Bower
- Constructing the website HTML structure

Examining the website layout

First and foremost, unlike the previous two projects we did, we are going to examine the website layout in wireframe before going any further in the chapter. After examining it, we will discover the Foundation components that are required for the website, along with the components and assets that may not be available in the Foundation package. The following is the website layout in the normal desktop screen size:

Logo		features	pricing	blog	login	sign up

Lorem ipsum dolor sit.

Lorem ipsum dolor sit amet, consectetur adipisicing elit,
sed do eiusmod tempor incididunt ut labore et dolore
magna aliqua.

Button

Lorem ipsum dolor sit amet,
consectetur adipisicing elit, sed do
eiusmod tempor incididunt ut labore
et dolore magna aliqua.

Lorem ipsum dolor sit amet,
consectetur adipisicing elit, sed do
eiusmod tempor incididunt ut labore
et dolore magna aliqua.

Lorem ipsum dolor sit amet,
consectetur adipisicing elit, sed do
eiusmod tempor incididunt ut labore
et dolore magna aliqua.

Lorem ipsum dolor sit amet,
consectetur adipisicing elit, sed do
eiusmod tempor incididunt ut labore
et dolore magna aliqua.

Lorem ipsum dolor sit amet, consectetur adipisicing elit, sed do
eiusmod tempor incididunt ut labore et dolore magna aliqua.

Basic	Team	Enterprise
$10/month	$50/month	$300/month
• 1Gb Storage • 1 User • 24/7 Support	• 50 Gb Storage • Up to 10 Users • 24/7 Support	• Unlimited Storage • Unlimited Users • 25/7 Priority Support
Sign Up	Sign Up	Sign Up

about	contact	help	careers	terms	privacy

Facebook   Twitter

The preceding wireframe shows that the website will have five sections. The first section, plainly, is the header. The header section will contain the website logo, menu navigation, a few lines of catchphrases, and a button—many call it a call-to-action button.

 The following are a couple of references in regard to guidelines, best practices, and examples of call-to-action buttons. These are old posts, yet the underlying guidelines, tips, and principles are timeless; it's still valid and relevant to date.

- Call to Action Buttons: Examples and Best Practices (`http://www.smashingmagazine.com/2009/10/13/call-to-action-buttons-examples-and-best-practices/`).
- "Call To Action" Buttons: Guidelines, Best Practices And Examples (`http://www.hongkiat.com/blog/call-to-action-buttons-guidelines-best-practices-and-examples/`).
- How To Design Call to Action Buttons That Convert (`http://unbounce.com/conversion-rate-optimization/design-call-to-action-buttons/`).

Normally, people need to get as much information as they can about the advantages and disadvantages before deciding to buy. So, under the header, we will display the list of items of the product or the key features offered.

In addition to the features list, we will also display customer testimonials within a slider. According to `www.entrepreneur.com` (`http://www.entrepreneur.com/article/83752`), displaying customer testimonials is one of the effective ways to drive more customers or sales, which is eventually good for business.

Below the testimonial section, the website will display the plan and price tables. And the last section will be the footer, containing secondary website navigation and links to Facebook and Twitter.

Let's now see how the website's layout will be in a smaller viewport size, which is as follows:

Much like the websites we built in the previous projects, all the content will be stacked. The catchphrases and the call-to-action button are aligned to the center. The menu in the navigation is now depicted as the hamburger icon. Next, we will see what Foundation has to offer in its package to build the website.

A look into Foundation

Foundation (`http://foundation.zurb.com/`) is one of the most popular frontend development frameworks. It is used by a number of notable companies, such as Pixar, Washington Post, Warby Parker (`https://www.warbyparker.com/`), and so on. As mentioned, Foundation ships with common web components and interactive widgets. Herein, we will look into the components, as well as the widgets we are going to employ for the website.

The grid system

The grid system is an integral part of a framework. It is one thing that makes managing web layout feel like a breeze. Foundation's grid system comprises twelve columns that can adapt to narrow viewport size through the drop-in classes provided. Similar to both the frameworks we explored in the previous chapters, the grid consists of rows and columns. Every column has to be wrapped within a row for the layout to span properly.

In Foundation, apply the `row` class to define an element as a row, and apply the element with the `columns` or `column` class to define it as a column. For example:

```
<div class="row">
<div class="columns">
</div>
<div class="columns">
</div>
</div>
```

You may also omit the *s* from `columns`, as follows:

```
<div class="row">
<div class="column">
</div>
<div class="column">
</div>
</div>
```

The column size is defined through the following series of classes:

- `small-{n}`: This specifies the grid column width in the small viewport size scope (approximately 0 px – 640 px).
- `medium-{n}`: This specifies the grid column width in the medium viewport size scope (approximately 641 px – 1,024 px).

◆ `large-{n}`: This specifies the grid column width in the large viewport size scope (approximately 1,025 px – 1,440 px).

 The `{n}` variable we gave in the preceding class names represents a number that spans from 1 to 12. The sum of the column number within a row should be no more than 12.

These classes can be applied in conjunction within a single element. For example:

```
<div class="row">
<div class="small-6 medium-4 columns"></div>
<div class="small-6 medium-8 columns"></div>
</div>
```

The preceding example gives the following result in the browser:

Resize the viewport size such that it is small enough and that the columns' width shifts following the assigned classes. In this case, each column has an equal width since both of them are assigned with the `small-6` class:

 Generally, you may resize the viewport size by dragging the browser window. If you are using Chrome, you can activate the device mode and mobile emulator (`https://developer.chrome.com/devtools/docs/device-mode`). Or, if you use Firefox, you can enable the responsive design view (`https://developer.mozilla.org/en-US/docs/Tools/Responsive_Design_View`), which will allow you to resize the viewport size without having to drag the Firefox window.

The buttons

The button is essential for any kind of website, and we will certainly add a button in some places in the website. Foundation uses the `button` class to define an element as a button. You can assign the class to the elements, such as `<a>` and `<button>`. This class applies the default button styles, as shown in the following screenshot:

Furthermore, you can include additional classes to define the button color or context. Use one of the classes—`secondary`, `success`, `alert`—to set the button color:

You can also specify the button size using one of the following classes: `tiny`, `small`, or `large`:

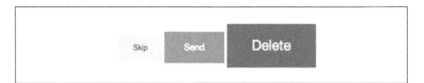

Make the button fancier with rounded corners using one of the classes, `radius` and `round`:

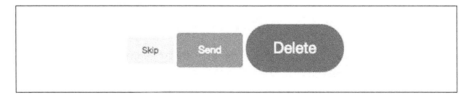

There are a few more classes to form a button. Additionally, Foundation also provides multiple types of buttons, such as button groups, split buttons, and dropdown buttons. Hence, you may go to the **Buttons** section of the Foundation documents to find more about them.

The navigation and top bar

One of the important sections on a website is the navigation. The navigation helps users to browse the website from one page to another. Foundation, in this case, provides a couple of navigation types, and among them, one is called the top bar. Foundation's top bar will reside at the very top of the website before any content or section. The following is how the top bar will appear with the Foundation default style:

The top bar is responsive. Try resizing the browser's viewport size such that it is small enough, and you will find that the navigation is concealed within the menu, which requires us to click on **MENU** to reveal the full list of the menu items:

The Foundation top bar is primarily formed with the `top-bar` class to apply the styles, the `data-topbar` attribute to run the JavaScript function related to the top bar, and finally `role="navigation"` for better accessibility.

So, the following code is how we start to build the top bar in Foundation:

```
<nav class="top-bar" data-topbar role="navigation">
  ...
</nav>
```

Foundation splits the top bar content into two sections. The left-hand side area is called the title area, consisting of the website name or logo. Foundation constructs this section with the list element, as follows:

```
<ul class="title-area">
<li class="name">
    <h1><a href="#">Hello</a></h1>
  </li>
  <li class="toggle-topbar menu-icon">
<a href="#"><span>Menu</span></a>
</li>
</ul>
```

The second section is simply called the top bar section. Typically, this section contains the menu, buttons, and search form. Foundation sets this section using the `top-bar-section` class, along with the `left` and `right` class to specify the alignment. So, to put it all together, the following is the complete code to build a basic Foundation top bar, as you see in the preceding screenshots:

```
<nav class="top-bar" data-topbar role="navigation">
  <ul class="title-area">
    <li class="name">
      <h1><a href="#">Hello</a></h1>
    </li>
    <li class="toggle-topbar menu-icon">
<a href="#"><span>Menu</span></a>
</li>
  </ul>
<section class="top-bar-section">
    <ul class="right">
      <li class="active"><a href="#">Home</a></li>
      <li><a href="#">Blog</a></li>
      <li><a href="#">About</a></li>
      <li><a href="#">Contact</a></li>
    </ul>
  </section>
</nav>
```

Certainly, you will have to link the Foundation CSS style sheet beforehand in the document to see the top bar look.

The pricing tables

Whether you are selling products or services, you should name your price.

As we will build a website for business, we will need to display pricing tables. Fortunately, Foundation has included this component at its core, hence we won't need a third-party extension. For flexibility, Foundation structures a pricing table with the list element, as follows:

```
<ul class="pricing-table pricing-basic">
   <li class="title">Basic</li>
   <li class="price">$10<small>/month</small></li>
   <li class="description">Perfect for personal use.</li>
   <li class="bullet-item">1GB Storage</li>
   <li class="bullet-item">1 User</li>
   <li class="bullet-item">24/7 Support</li>
<li class="cta-button">
<a class="button success round" href="#">Sign Up</a>
</li>
</ul>
```

Each item in the list is set with a class, which I'm sure has explained itself through the name. Given the preceding HTML structure and the default style given through the Foundation CSS, the output turns out quite nicely, as shown in the following screenshot:

Moving around Orbit

The carousel or slider is one of the most popular design patterns on the web. Despite the debate with respect to its accessibility, many people still love to have it on their website— and so do we. Herein, we want to employ Orbit (http://foundation.zurb.com/docs/components/orbit.html), the Foundation jQuery plugin to display a content slider.

Orbit is customizable in that we can fully control the output, as well as the behavior of the slide through classes, attributes, or JavaScript initiation. We can also add almost anything within the Orbit slides, including textual content, images, links, and the mix. And needless to say, we can style most of its parts.

How is Orbit constructed?

Foundation uses the list element to construct the slide container, as well as the slides, and initiates the functionality using the HTML5 data- attribute named data-orbit. The following is a basic example of the Orbit slider structure, containing two slides of images:

```
<ul class="example-orbit" data-orbit>
<li><img src="image.jpg" alt="" /></li>
<li class="active"><img src="image2.jpg" alt="" /></li>
</ul>
```

Deploying Orbit is downright easy, and technically, it can contain almost any type of content within the slide and not only images. We will look more in that regard later as we build the website.

 For the time being, feel free to explore the Orbit slider section (`http://foundation.zurb.com/docs/components/orbit.html`) in Foundation's official website, which, to my account is the best place to get into the Orbit slider.

Adding add-ons, the font Icons

Foundation also provides a handful of add-ons, one of which is Webicons (`http://zurb.com/playground/social-webicons`). Needless to say, we will need social icons, and since these icons are basically vectors, they are infinitely scalable and thus will remain crisp and sharp in any screen resolution——normal or high definition. Have a look at the following icon set:

A few of the glyphs in the icon set

Aside from this icon set, you can also find the following:

◆ A collection of starter templates (`http://foundation.zurb.com/templates.html`) that will be useful to kick-off a new website and webpage

◆ Responsive tables (`http://foundation.zurb.com/responsive-tables.html`)

◆ Stencils (`http://foundation.zurb.com/stencils.html`), which you will find useful for sketching and prototyping new websites

Further on Foundation

Detailing every corner and aspect of Foundation is beyond the scope of this module. These are, by far, the most essential components of the framework that we are going to employ in the project and the website.

Fortunately, Packt Publishing has published a couple of titles that exclusively cover Foundation. I suggest you have a look at one of the following books if you are keen on further exploring the framework:

- *Learning Zurb Foundation, Kevin Horek, Packt Publishing* (`https://www.packtpub.com/web-development/learning-zurb-foundation`)
- *ZURB Foundation Blueprints, James Michael Stone, Packt Publishing* (`https://www.packtpub.com/web-development/zurb-foundation-blueprints`)

Additional required assets

There are several files that we will need in addition to Foundation's own components. These files encompass the image cover for the website header, the icons that will represent the feature in the website feature list section, the favicon image as well as the Apple icons, the avatar image to display in the testimonial section, and finally (which is also important) the website logo.

In terms of the header image, we will use the following image photographed by Alejandro Escamilla, which shows a man working with his Macbook Air; the screen seems off though (`http://unsplash.com/post/51493972685/download-by-alejandro-escamilla`):

The icons to display alongside the feature list items are designed by Nick Frost from Ballicons (`http://ballicons.net/`). Among the icons in the collection that we will include in the website are the following:

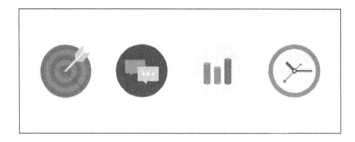

The following are the favicon and the Apple icon, which are generated using a Photoshop action called AppIconTemplate (`http://appicontemplate.com/`):

Favicon and the Apple icon

We will use the mystery man of WordPress as the default avatar. This avatar image will be displayed above the testimonial lines, as shown in the following wireframe:

The mystery man

The logo of this website is made with SVG for the sake of clarity and scalability. The logo is shown in the following screenshot:

You can get all these assets from the source files that come along with this module. Otherwise, grab them from the URL that we showed in the preceding paragraphs.

The project directories, assets, and dependencies

Once we assess the website layout, the framework features, and all the assets required, we will start working on the project. Herein, we will start getting the project directories and the assets organized. Also, we will grab and record all the project dependencies through Bower, the second project with Bootstrap. So, it's time for action.

Time for action – organizing the project directories, assets, and dependencies

1. In the `htdocs` folder, create a new folder, and name it `startup`. This is the folder in which the website will live.

2. Within the `startup` folder, create a folder named `assets` to contain all the assets like the style sheets, JavaScripts, images, and others.

3. Inside the `assets` folder create folders to group these assets:
    - `css` for the style sheets.
    - `js` to contain the JavaScripts.
    - `scss` to contain SCSS style sheet (more about SCSS in the next chapter).
    - `img` to contain the images.
    - `fonts` to contain the font icons.

4. Add the images, including the website logo, header image, icons, and the avatar image, as shown in the following screenshot:

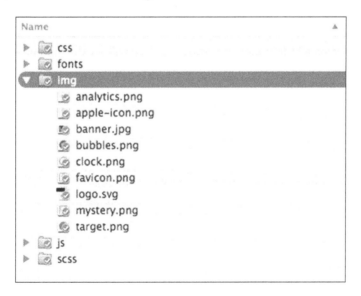

5. Now, we will download the project dependencies, which will include the Foundation framework, the icons, jQuery, and a couple of other libraries. Hence, let's open a terminal or command prompt if you are using Windows. Then, navigate to the project directory with the `cd` command:

   ❑ In Windows: `cd \xampp\htdocs\startup`

   ❑ In OSX: `cd /Applications/XAMPP/htdocs/startup`

   ❑ In Ubuntu: `cd /opt/lampp/htdocs/startup`

6. As we did in the second project, type the command, fill out the prompts to set the project specification, including the project name and the project version, as shown in the following screenshot:

```
→ startup git:(terminal)   bower init
[?] name: startup
[?] version: 1.0.0
[?] description: An example of corporate website built
[?] main file: index.html
[?] what types of modules does this package expose? global
[?] keywords: startup, responsive, foundation
[?] authors: Thoriq Firdaus <tfirdaus@creatiface.com>
[?] license: MIT
[?] homepage: https://github.com/tfirdaus/rwd-startup
[?] set currently installed components as dependencies?
[?] add commonly ignored files to ignore list? Yes
[?] would you like to mark this package as private which
```

When all the prompts are filled and completed, Bower will generate a new file named `bower.json` to put all the information in.

7. Before we install the project dependencies, we will set the dependencies folder destination. To do so, create a dot file named `.bowerrc`. Save the file with the following lines in it:

```
{
    "directory": "components"
}
```

This line will tell Bower to name the folder components instead of `bower_components`. And once the configuration is set, we are ready to install the libraries, starting with installing the Foundation package.

8. To install the Foundation package through Bower, type `bower install foundation --save`. Make sure that the `--save` parameter is included to record Foundation within the `bower.json file`.

> Apart from the Foundation primary package (files like the style sheet and JavaScript), this command will also grab libraries that are associated with Foundation, namely:
>
> Fastclick (`https://github.com/ftlabs/fastclick`)
>
> jQuery (`http://jquery.com/`)
>
> jQuery Cookie (`https://github.com/carhartl/jquery-cookie`)
>
> jQuery Placeholder (`https://github.com/mathiasbynens/jquery-placeholder`)
>
> Modernizr (`http://modernizr.com/`)

9. The Foundation font icon is set in a separate repository. To install it, type the `bower install foundation-icons --save` command.

10. The Foundation icon package comes with the style sheet that specifies and presents the icon through HTML classes and also the icon files. Herein, we need to make a copy of the font from the package folder into our own `fonts` folder. Have a look at the following screenshot:

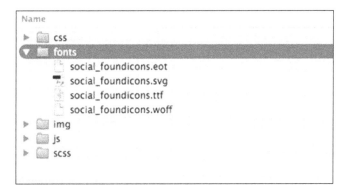

What just happened?

We just created the project directory, as well as folders to organize the project assets. In addition, we also installed the libraries that are required to build the website through Bower, which include the Foundation framework.

Having added in the images and the libraries, we will build the website's home page markup in the next section. So, without further ado, let's move on, and it's time for action again.

Time for action – building the website's HTML structure

1. Create a new HTML file named `index.html`. Then, open it in Sublime Text, our code editor of choice in this module.

2. Let's add the basic HTML5 structure as follows:

```
<!DOCTYPE html>
<html lang="en">
<head>
  <meta charset="UTF-8">
  <title>Startup</title>
</head>
<body>

</body>
</html>
```

3. Add the meta `X-UA-Compatible` variable with the content value `IE=edge` to allow Internet Explorer to use its latest cutting-edge rendering version:

```
<meta http-equiv="X-UA-Compatible" content="IE=edge">
```

4. Not to forget the meta `viewport` tag required to make the website responsive; add it in `<head>` as follows:

```
<meta name="viewport" content="width=device-width, initial-scale=1">
```

5. Add the favicon, as well as the Apple icon, below the meta viewport tag, as follows:

```
<link rel="apple-touch-icon" href="assets/img/apple-icon.png">
<link rel="shortcut icon" href="assets/img/favicon.png"
type="image/png">
```

6. Add the meta description for the search engine result purposes:

```
<meta name="description" content="A startup company website built
using Foundation">
```

7. The HTML markup for the content will follow the Foundation guidelines, as we have discussed in the early sections of this module. In addition, we may add extra classes in the elements to customize the styles. Let's start off by adding the website `<header>`, for which, add the following lines within `<body>`:

```
<header class="startup-header">
...
</header>
```

8. Next, add the website navigation bar within the header, as follows:

```
<header class="startup-header">
<div class="contain-to-grid startup-top-bar">
<nav class="top-bar" data-topbar>
     <ul class="title-area">
          <li class="name startup-name">
               <h1><a href="#">Startup</a></h1>
          </li>
<li class="toggle-topbar menu-icon">
               <a href="#"><span>Menu</span></a>
</li>
</ul>
          <section class="top-bar-section">
            <ul class="right">
                 <li><a href="#">Features</a></li>
<li><a href="#">Pricing</a></li>
<li><a href="#">Blog</a></li>
<li class="has-form log-in"><a href="" class="button secondary
round">Log In</a></li>
<li class="has-form sign-up"><a href="#" class="button round">Sign
Up</a></li>
               </ul>
</section>
</nav>
</div>
</header>
```

9. Below the navigation bar HTML markup, we add the catchphrase and call-to-action button, as follows:

```
<header class="startup-header">
  ...
<div class="panel startup-hero">
     <div class="row">
<h2 class="hero-title">Stay Cool and be Awesome</h2>
<p class="hero-lead">The most awesome web application in the
galaxy.</p>
</div>
     <div class="row">
<a href="#" class="button success round">Signup</a>
     </div>
</div>
</header>
```

10. Next, we will add the website's body content that will contain the product feature list section, the testimonial section, and the plan table price. First, add a `<div>` that will wrap the body content sections below the header, as follows:

```
<div class="startup-body">
  ...
</div>
```

11. Within `<div>`, we add the HTML markup for the feature list section, as follows:

```
<div class="startup-body">
<div class="startup-features">
<div class="row">
    <div class="medium-6 columns">
        <div class="row">
            <div class="small-3 medium-4 columns">
            <figure>
<img src="assets/img/analytics.png" height="128" width="128"
alt="">
            </figure>
</div>
        <div class="small-9 medium-8 columns">
          <h4>Easy</h4>
<p>This web application is super easy to use. No complicated
setup. It just works out of the box.</p>
 </div>
        </div>
        </div>
        <div class="medium-6 columns">
          <div class="row">
<div class="small-3 medium-4 columns">
                <figure>
                <img src="assets/img/clock.png" height="128"
width="128" alt="">
                </figure>
            </div>
            <div class="small-9 medium-8 columns">
              <h4>Fast</h4>
                <p>This web application runs in a
blink of eye. There is no other application that is on par with
our application in term of speed.</p>
                </div>
            </div>
          </div>
        </div>
        <div class="row">
          <div class="medium-6 columns">
            <div class="row">
<div class="small-3 medium-4 columns">
                <figure>
```

```
<img src="assets/img/target.png" height="128" width="128" alt="">
</figure>
                        </div>
<div class="small-9 medium-8 columns">
    <h4>Secure</h4>
<p>Your data is encyrpted with the latest Kryptonian technology.
It will never be shared to anyone. Rest assured, your data is
totally safe.</p>
                        </div>
                    </div>
                </div>
                <div class="medium-6 columns">
                    <div class="row">
                        <div class="small-3 medium-4 columns">
                            <figure>
                                <img src="assets/img/bubbles.png"
height="128" width="128" alt="">
                            </figure>
                        </div>
                        <div class="small-9 medium-8 columns">
                            <h4>Awesome</h4>
                            <p>It's simply the most awesome web
application and make you the coolest person in the galaxy. Enough
said.</p>
                        </div>
                    </div>
                </div>
            </div>
        </div>
</div>
</div>
```

The column division for this section refers to the layout shown in the website wireframe. So, as you can see from the preceding code that we just added, each feature list item is assigned with `medium-6` columns, hence the column width of each item will be equal.

12. Below the feature list section, we add the testimonial section's HTML markup, as follows:

```
<div class="startup-body">
...
<div class="startup-testimonial">
            <div class="row">
                <ul class="testimonial-list" data-orbit>
                    <li data-orbit-slide="testimonial-1">
                        <div>
                            <blockquote>Lorem ipsum dolor sit
amet, consectetur adipisicing elit. Dolor numquam quaerat
doloremque in quis dolore enim modi cumque eligendi eius.</
blockquote>
```

```
                              <figure>
                                  <img class="avatar" src="assets/
img/mystery.png" height="128" width="128" alt="">
                                  <figcaption>John Doe</figcaption>
                              </figure>
                          </div>
                      </li>
                      <li data-orbit-slide="testimonial-2">
                          <div>
                              <blockquote>Lorem ipsum dolor sit
amet, consectetur adipisicing elit.</blockquote>
                              <figure>
                                  <img class="avatar" src="assets/
img/mystery.png" height="128" width="128" alt="">
                                  <figcaption>Jane Doe</figcaption>
                              </figure>
                          </div>
                      </li>
                  </ul>
              </div>
          </div>
</div>
```

13. Referring to the layout in the wireframe, we should add the plan price table below the testimonial section, as follows:

```
<div class="startup-body">
<!-- ... feature list section … -->
<!-- ... testimonial section … -->
<div class="startup-pricing">
          <div class="row">
              <div class="medium-4 columns">
                  <ul class="pricing-table pricing-basic">
                      <li class="title">Basic</li>
                      <li class="price">$10<small>/month</
small></li>
                      <li class="description">Perfect for
personal use.</li>
                      <li class="bullet-item">1GB Storage</li>
                      <li class="bullet-item">1 User</li>
                      <li class="bullet-item">24/7 Support</li>
                      <li class="cta-button"><a class="button
success round" href="#">Sign Up</a></li>
                  </ul>
              </div>
              <div class="medium-4 columns">
                  <ul class="pricing-table pricing-team">
                      <li class="title">Team</li>
                      <li class="price">$50<small>/month</
small></li>
```

```
                                <li class="description">For a small
team.</li>
                                <li class="bullet-item">50GB Storage</li>
                                <li class="bullet-item">Up to 10 Users</
li>
                                <li class="bullet-item">24/7 Support</li>
                                <li class="cta-button"><a class="button
success round" href="#">Sign Up</a></li>
                        </ul>
                    </div>
                    <div class="medium-4 columns">
                        <ul class="pricing-table pricing-enterprise">
                            <li class="title">Enterprise</li>
                            <li class="price">$300<small>/month</
small></li>
                            <li class="description">For large
corporation</li>
                            <li class="bullet-item">Unlimited
Storage</li>
                            <li class="bullet-item">Unlimited Users</
li>
                            <li class="bullet-item">24/7 Priority
Support</li>
                            <li class="cta-button"><a class="button
success round" href="#">Sign Up</a></li>
                        </ul>
                    </div>
                </div>
            </div>
</div>
```

14. Finally, we add the website footer below the body content, as follows:

```
</div> <!—the body content end -->
<footer class="startup-footer">
        <div class="row footer-nav">
            <ul class="secondary-nav">
                <li><a href="#">About</a></li>
                <li><a href="#">Contact</a></li>
                <li><a href="#">Help</a></li>
                <li><a href="#">Careers</a></li>
                <li><a href="#">Terms</a></li>
                <li><a href="#">Privacy</a></li>
            </ul>
            <ul class="social-nav">
                <li><a class="foundicon-facebook"
href="#">Facebook</a></li>
                <li><a class="foundicon-twitter"
href="#">Twitter</a></li>
            </ul>
```

```
        </div>
        <div class="row footer-copyright">
            <p>Copyright 2014 Super Awesome App. All rights
reserved.</p>
        </div>
    </footer>
</body>
```

What just happened?

We just built the HTML markup for the website content and sections by following the Foundation guidelines. We also added extra classes along the way to customize the Foundation default styles later on.

Since building the HTML markup, we haven't added any of the styles; the website, at this point, looks white and plain, as shown in the following screenshot:

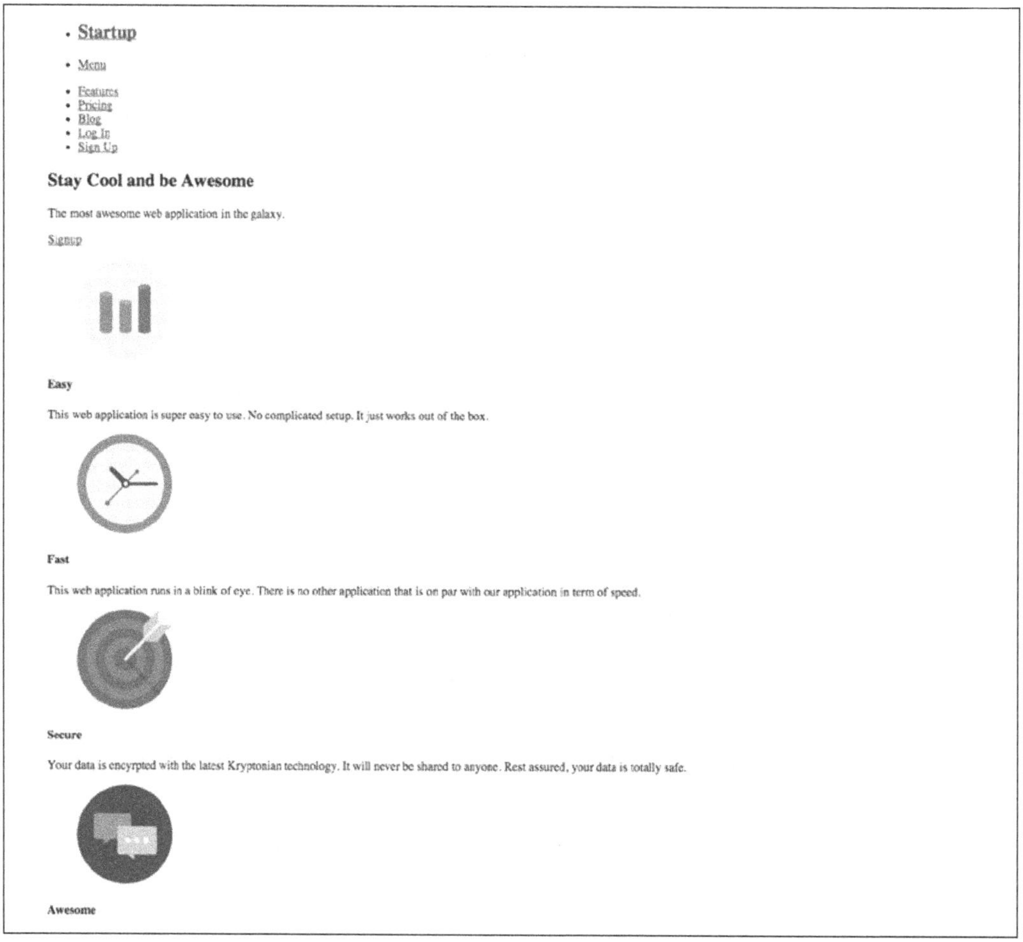

The full code of the HTML that we have just added can also be found at `http://git.io/qvdupQ`.

Summary

This chapter effectively started off our third project. In this project, we use Foundation to build a website for a start-up company. We walked through the Foundation features and adopted some of them into the website. We only added the website's HTML structure in this chapter though. The website, at this point, still looks plain and white. We have to compose the styles to define what the website looks and feels like, which is exactly what we will do in the next chapter.

We will compose the website styles using Sass, the CSS preprocessor that also defined the Foundation basic styles. Hence, at the beginning of the next chapter, first, we will learn to use Sass variable, mixins, functions, and other Sass features before we write the website styles.

It looks like there is still a lot of work left to do in order to accomplish this project. So, without further ado, let's move on to the next chapter.

8
Extending Foundation

*After constructing the website page markup in the previous chapter, we now start giving the website a look, feel, and colors. This time we will use **Sassy CSS** (**SCSS**), which also happens to be the underlying syntax of the Foundation default styles.*

SCSS is a syntax variation of a CSS preprocessor named Sass. The Sass original syntax uses indentation formatting that makes the codes look neat. SCSS, on the other hand, uses curly braces and semicolons just like regular CSS. The similarity helps everyone to quickly grasp the syntax, in particular those who are new to Sass.

Since we are going to employ SCSS, we will start off this chapter by walking you through a couple of Sass features and its utilities. You will learn to define variables and functions, perform operations, and comply with other directives, which allows us to compose the website style rules more efficiently.

This might sound challenging. And if you like a challenge, we can just get started right away.

This chapter will revolve around the following topics:

◆ Exploring Sass features and learning the syntax

◆ Looking into Bourbon, a Sass mixins library

◆ Organizing the style sheet structure and using the Import directive to include partial style sheets

◆ Setting up Koala to compile SCSS into CSS

- Customizing Foundation's default styles through variables
- Composing the website custom styles
- Optimizing the website layout for various viewport sizes
- Turning the website live by compiling the JavaScripts

Syntactically Awesome Style Sheets

Sass (http://sass-lang.com/) is a CSS preprocessor created by Hampton Catlin, Natalie Weizenbaum, and Chris Eppstein, which is the same team that also created Haml (http://haml.info/). Foundation, as mentioned at the beginning of this chapter, uses Sass to generate its CSS, and so will we. So, before we get our hands dirty, first we will delve into several Sass features, such as nesting, variables, mixins, functions, and others, that will allow us to write style rules more efficiently.

Nesting rules

Sass allows us to nest style rules into one another. This feature eventually allows us to write style rules that resemble the HTML structure of the web page. That way, the style rules can be more concise and more easy to scan through. Say, we added the header markup of our website, as follows:

```
<header>
  <h1><a href="#">Website</a></h1>
</header>
```

With Sass, we can construct the style rules, as follows:

```
header {
  background: #000;
  h1 {
    margin: 0;
    a {
      color: #fff;
    }
  }
}
```

It's worth noticing that even though Sass allows you to nest style rules, you should not abuse this facility. So, don't do something like the following code:

```
body {
  nav {
    ul {
      li {
        a {
          &:before {

          }
        }
      }
    }
  }
}
```

Consider it before nesting style rules. The main objective of this feature is to make the style rules look simpler, more concise, easier to scan through, and not to make it unnecessarily look more complex.

Storing a value with a variable

A variable is one useful piece in programming language that allows us to define a value once within a specified name. Each language has a slightly different way to declare a variable. For example, JavaScript uses the keyword `var`, LESS uses `@`, and Sass in this case uses the `$` sign.

One of the perfectly-suited implementations of a variable is to define the website colors, for example:

```
$primary: #000;
$secondary: #bdc3c7;
$tertiary: #2ecc71;
$quaternary: #2980b9;
$quinary: #e67e22;
```

So, instead of declaring the color value every time we need it, we can simply declare the representative variables. In the following example, we declare `$primary` as the body text color and `$secondary` as the background color:

```
body {
  background-color: $secondary;
  color: $primary;
}
```

When compiled to regular CSS, these variables are replaced with the defined value, as follows:

```
body {
  background-color: #bdc3c7;
  color: #000;
}
```

Using a variable with a proper name (of course), you will find it easier to write the variable rather than remembering the Hex or the RGB number; well, it is practically easier to write `$primary` than `#bdc3c7`, isn't it?

The Sass variable isn't exclusively aimed to define colors. We can also use a variable to define a string or plain text, as follows:

```
$var: "Hello World";
$body-font-family: "Helvetica Neue";
```

We can use a variable to store a number or a length:

```
$number: 9;
$global-radius: 3px;
```

We can use a variable to inherit the value of another variable:

```
$var: $anotherVar;
$header-font-family: $body-font-family;
```

We can use a variable to define the output of a function:

```
$h1-font-size: rem-calc(44);
```

Foundation centralized the declaration of its primary variables within a file named `_settings.scss`. We will look more into this matter later when we compose the website style rules.

Variable interpolation

There are certain circumstances when a variable is not applicable, such as when it is inserted within a string (plain text), as follows:

```
$var: "Hello";
$newVar: "$var World";
div {
  content: $newVar;
}
```

When compiled, the `$var` declaration within `$newVar` won't be replaced with the value of `"Hello"`. This is because Sass interprets `$var` as a string or plain text. Thus, the output of the following example will simply be:

```
div {
  content: "$var World";
}
```

Another example where a variable won't work is when a declaration is begun with an `@` rule or a directive, as follows:

```
$screen-size: (max-width: 600px);
@media $screen-size {
  div {
    display: none;
  }
}
```

This example simply returns an error to the Sass compiler because `@media` is supposed to be followed by either the `print` or `screen` keyword.

There are a few cases where we have to use interpolation to declare a variable. Variable interpolation happens to other programming languages, such as PHP, Ruby, and Swift. But I'm not going into the details of the technicalities of its workings, as I don't exactly know either. Simply put, interpolation allows us to embed a variable in a situation where it does not allow the variable to work—especially where it is a string that is actually expected.

Each programming language has its notation to enable interpolation. In this case, Sass uses `#{}`. Given one of the previous examples, we can write the variable as follows:

```
$var: "Hello";
$newVar: "#{$var} World";
div {
  content: $newVar;
}
```

And the result will be as follows:

```
div {
  content: "Hello World";
}
```

 Follow Hugo Giraudel posts (`https://webdesign.tutsplus.com/tutorials/all-you-ever-need-to-know-about-sass-interpolation--cms-21375`) for further assistance about variable interpolation in Sass.

Reusable code block with mixins

Now, we are going to look into Sass mixins. If you followed and accomplished the second project, you should know about LESS mixins. Mixins, both in Sass and LESS, have similar purposes; they allow developers to reuse code blocks and style rules within the entire style sheet and thus comply with the DRY principle (http://programmer.97things. oreilly.com/wiki/index.php/Don't_Repeat_Yourself). However, it is slightly different in terms of how we declare and reuse the mixins. This is how we declare a mixin in LESS:

```
.buttons {
  color: @link-color;
  font-weight: normal;
  border-radius: 0;
}
```

In Sass, we use the @mixins directive to create a mixin, for example:

```
$linkColor: $tertiary;
@mixin buttons {
  color: $linkColor;
  font-weight: normal;
  border-radius: 0;
}
```

Sass uses the @include directive to reuse the preceding code block within style rules. Given the preceding example, we can write:

```
.button {
    @include buttons;
}
```

The following is the output when the preceding example is compiled to CSS:

```
.button {
  color: #2ecc71;
  font-weight: normal;
  border-radius: 0;
}
```

That is a basic example of the application of Sass mixins.

A brief on the Sass mixin library

Some CSS3 syntaxes are so complex that writing them can be really tedious work. And this is where mixins can be particularly useful. Fortunately, with Sass being so popular and supported by so many generous developers, we don't have to port all CSS3 syntax into Sass mixins on our own. Instead, we can simply employ Sass's mixin library that makes our work as a web developer more enjoyable.

The Sass library comes with a collection of useful mixins and functions (we will talk about functions shortly) that we can use right away out-of-the-box. There are dozens of popular libraries available, and one that we are going to use herein is called Bourbon (`http://bourbon.io/`).

Bourbon compiles a number of mixins in a library that simplifies the way we declare CSS3 syntax, including syntax that is still marked as experimental, such as `image-rendering`, `filter`, and the CSS3 `calc` function. Now, which do you think is easier and faster to write when it comes to specifying the Hi-DPI Media Query?

 Hi-DPI Media Query is used to measure the device pixel density, for which we can use it to deliver higher-resolution graphics on web pages, specifically on devices with hi-definition screens. The following are some references for further information on the subject:

- High DPI Images for Variable Pixel Densities by Boris Smus (`http://www.html5rocks.com/en/mobile/high-dpi/`).
- Towards A Retina Web by Reda Lemeden (`http://www.smashingmagazine.com/2012/08/20/towards-retina-web/`).

Is the following standard syntax?

```
@media only screen and (-webkit-min-device-pixel-ratio: 2),
only screen and (min--moz-device-pixel-ratio: 2),
only screen and (-o-min-device-pixel-ratio: 2 / 1),
only screen and (min-resolution: 192dpi),
only screen and (min-resolution: 2dppx) {
  width: 500px;
}
```

Or, will it be the following one with the Bourbon mixin?:

```
@include hidpi(2) {
  width: 500px;
}
```

Without spending years researching, we can commonly agree that using the mixin should be a lot easier to write, as well as easier to remember.

 As mentioned, in addition to CSS3 mixins, Bourbon also ships with a couple of Sass functions, such as Triangle, which allows us to create CSS-based triangles. However, I'm not going to mention all the bits that are there in the Bourbon library. Since the library collection will most likely be updated or revised along with the introduction of new CSS specifications, it is better to refer to the list on the official documentation page (http://bourbon.io/docs/).

Creating and using a Sass function

A function is one piece of a feature that makes creating style rules more dynamic. A function in Sass is declared using the @function directive, which is then followed by the function name, a parameter with preferably its default value. In its simplest form, a Sass function may look as follows:

```
@function color($parameter: green) {

}
```

This function, however, won't output anything yet. To generate a result of this function, we need to add a @return value. Given the preceding example, we want to output the default value parameter, which says "hello". To do so, we write the @return value, which is then followed by $parameter, as follows:

```
@function color($parameter: green) {
  @return $parameter;
}
```

Use this function within a selector, as follows:

```
@function name($parameter: green) {
  @return $parameter;
}
.selector {
  color: name();
}
```

Compile it, and you get the following output:

```
.selector {
  color: green;
}
```

Customize the output by specifying a new value out of the default one, as follows:

```
.selector {
  color: name(yellow);
}
```

We will get a new output, as shown in the following code:

```
.selector {
  color: yellow;
}
```

This example merely shows the basic functionality of a function. There are a lot more examples on how we can utilize it in real cases to build reusable code series. So, I recommend you head over to the following references for further advanced discussion and find more examples.

Using pure Sass functions to make reusable logic more useful (`http://thesassway.com/advanced/pure-sass-functions`).

A couple of Sass functions (`http://hugogiraudel.com/2013/08/12/sass-functions/`).

Manipulating color with Sass functions

One thing that I love about using CSS preprocessors such as Sass, is how easy it is to determine and alter colors. Sass, in this case, provides a bunch of built-in functions to manipulate colors seamlessly. The following is a list of a few Sass color functions for your reference, which may be useful to manipulate colors in the website later on:

Functions	Description	Example

`lighten($color, $amount)`	Turns a color lighter by the specified amount.	`$black: #000000`
		
		`lighten($black, 10%);`
		
		In this example, we lighten `$black` by 10 percent. The output is #1a1a1a.

`darken($color, $amount)`	Turns a color darker than the specified amount.	`$white: #ffffff;`
		
		`darken($white, 10%)`
		
		In this example, we darken `$white` by 10 percent. The output will be #e6e6e6.

Functions	Description	Example

`fade-out($color, $amount)`	Turns the color to be more transparent than the specified amount.	`$black: #000000;`
		
		`fade-out($black, .5);`
		
		In this example, we change the `$black` color to be compiled into RGB format and set the transparency to 50 percent. The output is `rgba(0, 0, 0, 0.5)`.

 Please follow the Sass official documentation (`http://sass-lang.com/documentation/Sass/Script/Functions.html`) to find out the full list of the color functions available.

Useful Foundation's own function

The Foundation framework comes with an array of its own functions. Foundation uses these functions to build its own default styles, and we can also use them to build our own. One such useful function therein is `rem-calc()`, which allows us to calculate the `rem` unit with less hassle.

Em and Rem

The `rem` unit is a relative value that inherited concepts similar to em. Here is what Ian Yates expounded about the origin of em in his post (`https://webdesign.tutsplus.com/articles/taking-the-erm-out-of-ems--webdesign-12321`):

> *"Ems get their name from printing. Precisely when the term was first used is unclear, but as the uppercase M (pronounced emm) most closely represents the square printing block on which printing letters were placed, it came to lend its name to the measurement. Whatever the point size of the font in question, the block of the uppercase M would define the Em."*

But the problem with the em unit, as Jonathan Snook described in his post (`http://snook.ca/archives/html_and_css/font-size-with-rem`), is its compounding nature. Since the size is relative to its closest parent, in my experience the size output can be unpredictably frustrating at best; the size will be varying depending on where it is specified. Examine the following example:

```
body {
    font-size:16px;
}
div {
```

```
      font-size: 1.2em; /* 19px */
   }
ul {
      font-size: 1em; /* 19px */
   }
ul li {
      font-size: 1.2em; /* 23px */
   }
```

This is where the `rem` unit comes in. The `rem` unit measures the calculation directly against the font size of `<html>`, the root element of an HTML document—thus, it is also dubbed as root em. Regardless of where the unit is specified, the result will be precise, consistent, and more importantly, easy to figure out (it's like the `px` unit, but it's relative).

The `rem-calc` function accepts both integer and length. Hence, the following code examples work:

```
div {
   font-size: rem-calc(12);
}
span {
   font-size: rem-calc(10px);
}
p {
   font-size: rem-calc(11em);
}
```

In this case, they will turn out to be as follows:

```
div {
   font-size: 0.75rem;
}
span {
   font-size: 0.625rem;
}
p {
   font-size: 0.6875rem;
}
```

Have a go hero – diving into Sass

There is a lot more about Sass than we are able to cover in this module, such as placeholder, conditional statement, and operators, just to name a few. Thankfully, there are enough good references and books that have covered Sass, as well as its supporting utilities in greater depth, into which you can dig into on your own. The following are some of my best recommendations:

- *Sass and Compass for Designers, Ben Frain, Packt Publishing* (https://www.packtpub.com/web-development/sass-and-compass-designers)
- *Sass for Web Designers, Dan Cederholm, A Book Apart* (http://www.abookapart.com/products/sass-for-web-designers)
- The Sass Way—tutorials and tips on using Sass (http://thesassway.com/)
- A dedicated category on web design tutorials and for covering anything related to Sass (https://webdesign.tutsplus.com/categories/sass)

Before we resume the work, let's end this section with a couple of quizzes, shall we?

Pop quiz – multiple parameters in Sass function

In the preceding section, we discussed about Sass function, as well as showed you the simplest example out of it. In the example, we created a function with only one parameter. The fact is that we can add multiple parameters within a single Sass function.

Q1. So, which among the following examples is the correct way to create a function with multiple parameters?

1. Each parameter is separated with a semicolon.

   ```
   @function name($a:1px; $b:2px){
   @return $a + $b
   }
   ```

2. Each parameter is separated with an addition operator.

   ```
   @function name($a:2px + $b:2px){
   @return $a + $b
   }
   ```

3. Each parameter is separated with a comma.

   ```
   @function name($a:1px, $b:2px){
   @return $a + $b
   }
   ```

Pop quiz – Sass color manipulation

Q1. There are lots of Sass functions built-in. In this section, we named three, `lighten()`, `darken()`, and `fade-out()`, which I think are sufficient to help us to decorate the website of this project. The `fade-out()` function has an alias that also gives us the same result. So, which of the following is the name alias for the fade-out() function?

1. `transparentize($color, $amount)`

2. `transparency($color, $amount)`

3. `transparent($color, $amount)`

Project recap

In *Chapter 7, A Responsive Website for Business with Foundation*, we installed Foundation and Foundation Icons, along with their dependencies (jQuery, Fastclick, Modernizr, and so on) through Bower (`http://bower.io/`). We also prepared the website assets, namely, the images, image icons, and the website logo. In the last section of the chapter, we created `index.html` for the website home page, and we also constructed the markup using a couple of new HTML5 tags. So, the files and folders that are currently in the working directory are shown in the following screenshot:

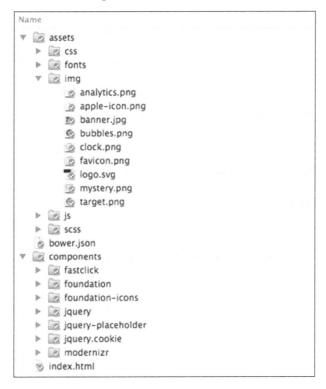

Style sheet organizations

Files that are still missing from our working directories are the style sheets to compose our customized styles for the website, and the Bourbon library that we briefly mentioned in the preceding section to provide us with some ready-to-use mixins and functions. This is what we are going to do in this section. We are going to create style sheets and organize them in a way to make them easily maintainable in the future.

Well, let's resume the work.

Time for action – organizing and compiling style sheets

Perform the following steps right to the end to properly organize the style sheets and compile them into CSS.

1. We need to install Bourbon. Launch a terminal or the command prompt, and type the following command:

    ```
    bower install bourbon --save
    ```

    This command installs the Bourbon package through the Bower registry and registers it within the bower.json file of the project.

     I've discussed the bower.json file exclusively in this post (https://webdesign.tutsplus.com/tutorials/ quick-tip-what-to-do-when-you-encounter-a- bower-file--cms-21162), check it out!

2. Create new style sheets named main.scss, responsive.scss, and styles. scss in the scss folder.

3. The _main.scss style sheet is the one where we will put all our own style rules. We will use the _responsive.scss file to exclusively put in the media queries of the website. And the styles.scss file is where we will compile those style sheets together.

     The underscore _ that began the file name is a special notation that tells the Sass compiler not to directly compile the file.

4. Still within the `scss` folder, create two more style sheets. This time, name them `_config.scss` and `foundation.scss`.

5. The `_config.scss` will contain a copy of all the variables used in Foundation, while `foundation.scss` will contain imported partials of Foundation style sheets. These copies will prevent us from directly modifying the original files, which will eventually be overridden when we update to the newest version.

6. Next, copy the whole content of the Foundation `_settings.scss` file to the `_config.scss` file that we recently created. In our case, the `_settings.scss` file is located in the `/components/foundation/scss/foundation/` directory.

7. Also, copy the whole content of Foundation's own `foundation.scss` and paste it to our own `foundation.scss` that we also recently created.

8. Then, we need to correct the path of the imported partials in our `foundation.scss` file. At this stage, all paths are pointing to the `foundation` folder, as follows:

```
@import "foundation/components/grid";
@import "foundation/components/accordion";
@import "foundation/components/alert-boxes";
... /* other imports */
```

This certainly is incorrect because we don't have a folder named `foundation` in the `scss` folder. Herein, we need to direct the path to the `components` folder instead, where the partials actually reside. So, change the path to be as follows:

```
@import "../../components/foundation/scss/foundation/components/
grid";
@import "../../components/foundation/scss/foundation/components/
accordion";
@import "../../components/foundation/scss/foundation/components/
alert-boxes";
... /* other imports */
```

 A comprehensive snippet of Foundation partial references can be found in the Gist (`http://git.io/1dITag`).

 In Sass, we don't have to specify the `.scss` or `.sass` extension when it comes to importing external files. The Sass compiler is clever enough to determine the extension on its own. And this is also because a plain CSS is also a valid Sass.

9. Another path that we have to correct is the path referring to the Foundation, `_functions.scss`, which contains the `rem-calc()` function. Open the `_config.scss` file, and change the line `@import "foundation/functions";` to `@import "../../components/foundation/scss/foundation/functions";`.

10. We are going to compile these style sheets into CSS using Koala. Launch Koala and add the working directory:

11. Within the style list in Koala, you won't find the SCSS style sheets with the underscore prefix. Koala, by default, ignores this file since it eventually won't be compiled into CSS.

12. However, you should find the two primary style sheets of the project listed therein, namely, `styles.scss` and `foundation.scss`. Be sure that this output is set to the `css` folder, as shown in the following screenshot:

13. Then, make sure that the option of `Auto Compile` is checked so that they will be automatically compiled into CSS, as we've made changes. Also, check the `Source Map` option to make debugging the style sheet easier. Have a look at the following screenshot:

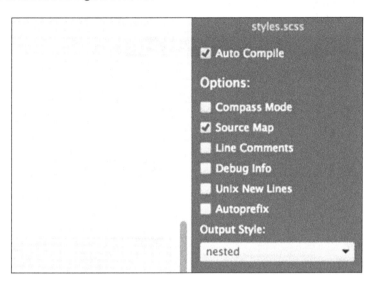

14. Click the **Compile** button of `styles.scss` and `foundation.scss` to compile them into CSS.

15. Open `index.html` and link both the compiled CSSs within the `<head>` tag, as follows:

```
<link rel="stylesheet" href="assets/css/foundation.css">
<link rel="stylesheet" href="assets/css/styles.css">
```

What just happened?

We just installed Bourbon and put together several new style sheets to style the website. Then, we compiled them into CSS, and then linked them to `index.html`. Hence, as you can see in the following screenshot, the website is now starting to take place—with the Foundation default styles:

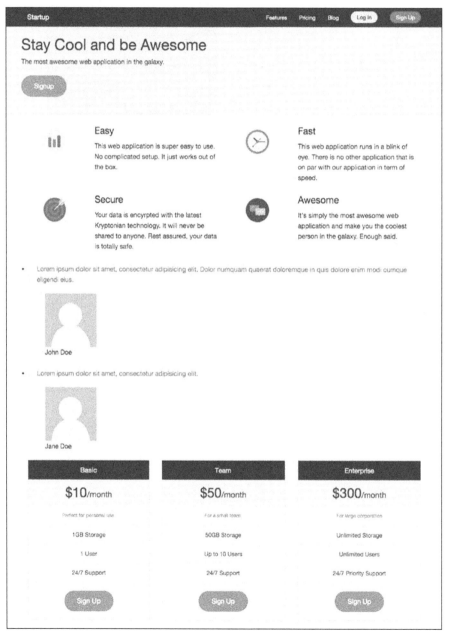

The website's look and feel

With the style sheets organized and compiled, now comes the time to customize the website's styles. As it happens, we don't have to write every bit of the style rules on our own. In this case, since we are using a framework (Foundation), sometimes customizing the website styles can be as easy as changing the default value in a variable.

Without further ado, let's move on.

Time for action – build on the website

Styling the website will involve multiple style sheets. Hence, follow the following steps carefully:

1. Import the following style sheets in `foundation.scss`:

   ```
   @import "config";
   @import "../../components/foundation/scss/normalize";
   @import "../../components/foundation-icons/foundation_icons_
   social/sass/social_foundicons.scss";
   ... /* other partials */
   ```

   That way, the variables, as well as the changes within `_config.scss`, will affect other component style sheets through Foundation. The `normalize` variable will standardize basic element styles, `social_foundicons.scss`; as you can guess, this allows us to apply Foundation's social icons.

2. Open `styles.scss` and import Bourbon, `_config.scss`, `main.scss`, and `responsive.scss`, as follows:

   ```
   @import "../../components/bourbon/dist/bourbon";
   @import "config";
   @import "main";
   @import "responsive";
   ```

3. Then, I want to apply a custom font from Google Font simply because the custom fonts look better than the average font system, such as Arial or Times. Herein, I picked a font named Varela Round (`https://www.google.com/fonts/specimen/Varela+Round`).

4. Open `index.html`, and add the font style sheet within the `<head>` tag, as follows:

   ```
   <link rel='stylesheet' href='http://fonts.googleapis.com/
   css?family=Varela+Round' type='text/css'>
   ```

5. Now, we will change the `font-family` stack, which is currently specified as the Foundation default font, to use Varela Round.

6. To do so, open `_config.scss`, uncomment the variable named `$body-font-family`, and insert `"Varela Round"`, as follows:

```
$body-font-family: "Varela Round", "Helvetica Neue", "Helvetica",
Helvetica, Arial, sans-serif;
```

Sass commenting

Typically, commenting will cause the code compiler or the engine to ignore the code—like a browser. However, it is also often used as an inline document, explaining what the code does.

Every programming language has its own way to comment on code. In CSS, it will be this way:

```
/* .property { content: ""' }*/
```

In Sass, we can either use the CSS way, as shown previously, or add `//`, as follows:

```
// .property { content: ""' }
```

When `//` is added at the beginning of the line, the compiler will completely ignore the line, and thus won't compile it.

7. We will style each of the website sections. To begin with, we will focus on the website header, and then, subsequently down to the footer. Let's start off by adding an image background. Open `_main.scss` and then add the following lines:

```
.startup-header {
  background: url('../img/banner.jpg') no-repeat center center
  fixed;
  background-size: cover;
}
```

CSS3 Background Size

Background size is a special CSS3 property that controls the background stretch. The value of the cover that we used in the preceding snippets will proportionally stretch the background image to entirely cover the container. Head to the following references for further assistance on the CSS3 Background Size:

- ◆ CSS Backgrounds and Borders Module Level 3 (http://www.w3.org/TR/css3-background/#the-background-size)

- ◆ *Perfect Full Page Background Image* by Chris Coyier (http://css-tricks.com/perfect-full-page-background-image/)

- ◆ Can I Use CSS3 Background Size? (http://caniuse.com/#feat=background-img-opts)

The image, however, is currently hidden at the back of the background color that applies to the top bar and a section in which Foundation named it Panel (`http://foundation.zurb.com/docs/components/panels.html`), as shown in the following screenshot:

8. Remove these background colors so that we can see through the background image. To do so, open the `_config.scss` file and uncomment the following lines:

```
$topbar-bg-color: #333;
$topbar-bg: $topbar-bg-color;
```

Change the value of the `$topbar-bg-color` variable from `#333` to `transparent`

```
$topbar-bg: transparent;
```

9. Uncomment this following line, which specifies the panel's background color:

```
$panel-bg: scale-color($white, $lightness: -5%);
```

Then, change the value to `transparent` as well:

```
$panel-bg: transparent;
```

Now, we can see the background image, which is shown in the following screenshot:

10. From the preceding screenshot, it is evident that the top bar and the panel background color have been removed, but some of the menu items still have it.

11. Let's remove these background colors. In `_config.scss`, uncomment the following line:

```
$topbar-dropdown-bg: #333;
```

And change the value to use the value of the `$topbar-bg` variable, as follows:

```
$topbar-dropdown-bg: $topbar-bg;
```

12. Save it and let a few seconds pass for the files to be compiled, and you should see now that the background color of those menu items are removed, as shown in the following screenshot:

13. Add `padding-top` to give more distance between the top bar and the upper boundary of the browser viewport:

```
.startup-header {
...
  .startup-top-bar {
    padding-top: rem-calc(30);
  }
}
```

And now, as you can see, there is more breadth therein:

The left-half of the image is before we add the padding-top,
and the right-half definitely is after we add the padding-top.

14. Give more padding at the top and bottom of the panel section; hence, we can view more of the background image. Nest the style rules under the `.startup-header`, as follows:

```
.startup-header {
  ...
  .startup-hero {
    padding-top: rem-calc(150px);
    padding-bottom: rem-calc(150px);
  }
}
```

15. Add the logo image, as follows:

```
.startup-name {
  max-width: 60px;
  a {
    text-indent: 100%;
    white-space: nowrap;
    overflow: hidden;
    background: url('../img/logo.svg') no-repeat center left;
    background-size: auto 90%;
    opacity: 0.9;
  }
}
```

Now we have the logo added, as follows:

16. Hover over the menu links in the top bar, and you will find it with a dark background color, as follows:

This background color is not quite right when it comes to the website's aesthetic as a whole, so let's remove that. In `_config.scss`, uncomment the following lines:

```
$topbar-link-bg-hover: #272727;
```

Then, change the value to transparent by inheriting the value of the `$topbar-bg` variable, as follows:

```
$topbar-link-bg-hover: $topbar-bg;
```

17. Turn the menu links to uppercase so that it looks slightly bigger. Set the variable named `$topbar-link-text-transform` in `_config.scss` from none to uppercase:

```
$topbar-link-text-transform: uppercase;
```

18. The next thing we will do is change the styles of the two buttons: `Login` and `Sign Up`. We will make it just a little bit more fashionable, and the following are all the new styles for these buttons; nest these lines under the `.startup-header`:

```
.startup-header {
...
.startup-top-bar {
  padding-top: rem-calc(30);
    ul {
$color: fade-out(#fff, 0.8);
$color-hover: fade-out(#fff, 0.5);
    background-color: transparent;
    .button {
@include transition (border 300ms ease-out, background-color 300ms
ease-out);
    }
    .log-in {
  padding-right: 0;
      > .button {
      background-color: transparent;
      border: 2px solid $color;
      color: #fff;
      &:hover {
      background-color: transparent;
      border: 2px solid $color-hover;
      color: #fff;
      }
    }
  }
    .sign-up {
    > .button {
    background-color: $color;
```

```
      border: 2px solid transparent;
      color: #fff;
      &:hover {
        background-color: $color-hover;
        border: 2px solid transparent;
      }
    }
  }
    }
    }
   }
}
```

Now, the buttons should look as shown in the following screenshot. Hover over the button, and you will see nice little transition effects that we added through the `transition()` mixin of Bourbon:

However, it's worth noticing that I consider this merely as decoration. It's up to you to customize the button styles.

19. With buttons on a transparent background, let's make three menu link items on the left-hand side, namely, **PRICES**, **PRICING**, and **BLOG**, slightly transparent as well. To do so, uncomment and change the variable named `$topbar-link-color` in `_config.scss` to `fade-out(#fff, 0.3)`, as follows:

```
$topbar-link-color: fade-out(#fff, 0.3);
```

20. Then, let's give the links a transition effect. Add the following lines in `_main.scss`:

```
.startup-header {
...
  .startup-top-bar {
    ...
    a {
      @include transition(color 300ms ease-out);
    }
  }
}
```

21. Next, we will add a dark transparent layer on the header. By adding this dark layer, the text in the header can be more distinct over the background image.

Add the following lines in `_main.scss`:

```scss
.startup-header {
...
  .startup-top-bar,
  .startup-hero {
    background-color: fade-out(#000, 0.5);
  }
}
```

22. Add the following lines as our last touch for the header section:

```scss
.startup-header {
...
  .startup-hero {
    padding-top: rem-calc(150px);
    padding-bottom: rem-calc(150px);
    .hero-lead {
      color: darken(#fff, 30%);
    }
  }
...
}
```

Now, we have a nice header for the website, as you can see in the following screenshot:

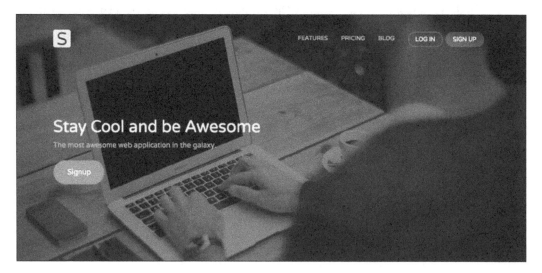

23. With the website styled, we will move to the next section. Below the header, we have the feature section that contains a number of key features of our products and services. And these are all the styles for the feature section:

```
...
.startup-features {
  padding: rem-calc(90 0);
  figure {
    margin: 0;
  }
  .columns {
    margin-bottom: rem-calc(15);
  }
}
```

In the preceding snippet, we remove the margin from the figure element that wraps the image icon. This will give the image icons figure more room to span, as you can see in the following screenshot:

Easy

This web application is super easy to use. No complicated setup. It just works out of the box.

Easy

This web application is super easy to use. No complicated setup. It just works out of the box.

Secure

Your data is encyrpted with the latest Kryptonian technology. It will never be shared to anyone. Rest assured, your data is totally safe.

Secure

Your data is encyrpted with the latest Kryptonian technology. It will never be shared to anyone. Rest assured, your data is totally safe.

Other than that, `margin-bottom`, as well as the padding we added in conjunction with it , simply gives this section more whitespace.

24. Below the feature section, we have the section that shows happy customers speaking. We call it the testimonial section. Add the following style rules to build on it:

```
.startup-testimonial {
  padding: rem-calc(90 0);
  text-align: center;
  background-color: darken(#fff, 2%);
  blockquote {
    font-size: rem-calc(24);
  }
```

```
figure {
  margin-top: 0;
  margin-bottom: 0;
  .avatar {
    border-radius: 50%;
    display: inline-block;
    width: 64px;
  }
}
figcaption {
  margin-top: rem-calc(20);
  color: darken(#fff, 30%);;
}
}
```

25. Also, remove the `blockquote` element's left-hand side border by changing the value of `$blockquote-border` in `_config.scss`, as follows:

```
$blockquote-border: 0 solid #ddd;
```

Note that the preceding styles are merely decoration. At this stage, this is how the testimonial section looks:

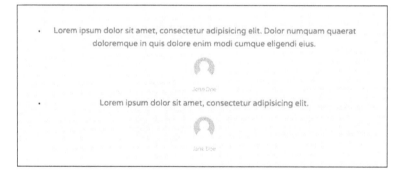

Don't freak out, it's not broken. The remaining styles will be added through the Orbit Slider plugin once it is enabled. We will take a look at the steps for this shortly.

26. Next, we will style the price and plan tables. These are all the styles for the table price, and their main purpose is to give each table a distinct color.

```
.startup-pricing {
  $basic-bg      : #85c1d0;
  $team-bg       : #9489a3;
```

```
    $enterprise-bg : #d04040;

    padding-top: rem-calc(120);
    padding-bottom: rem-calc(120);
    .pricing-table {
      background-color: darken(#fff, 2%);
    }
    .pricing-basic {
      .title {
        background-color: $basic-bg;
      }
      .price {
        background-color: lighten($basic-bg, 25%);
      }
    }
    .pricing-team {
      .title {
        background-color: $team-bg;
      }
      .price {
        background-color: lighten($team-bg, 25%);
      }
    }
    .pricing-enterprise {
    .title {
        background-color: $enterprise-bg;
      }
      .price {
        background-color: lighten($enterprise-bg, 25%);
      }
    }
  }
```

27. The footer section is bare and straightforward. There's nothing prominent. There is just a bunch of style rules to make the footer look nicer, as follows:

```
.startup-footer {
  $footer-bg: darken(#fff, 5%);
  text-align: center;
  padding: rem-calc(60 0 30);
  background-color: $footer-bg;
  border-top: 1px solid darken($footer-bg, 15%);
  .footer-nav {
    ul {
      margin-left: 0;
```

```
    }
    li {
      display: inline-block;
      margin: rem-calc(0 10);
    }
    a {
      color: darken($footer-bg, 30%);
      @include transition (color 300ms ease-out);
      &:hover {
        color: darken($footer-bg, 70%);
      }
    }
  }
  .social-nav {
    li a:before {
      margin-right: rem-calc(5);
      position: relative;
      top: 2px;
    }
    .foundicon-facebook:hover {
      color: #3b5998;
    }
    .foundicon-twitter:hover {
      color: #55acee;
    }
  }
  .footer-copyright {
    margin-top: rem-calc(30);
    color: darken($footer-bg, 15%);
  }
}
```

What just happened?

In this section, we focused on the website's appearance. We just added styles that eventually make the website look a lot nicer from the header and down to the footer. However, a few things are not workable at this stage, such as Orbit, and we have yet to test how the website looks in the smaller viewport size. So, that is exactly what we are going to address in the next section. This is how the website should now look at this stage:

Have a go hero – colors and creativities

I realize that good, bad, nice, and not nice are highly subjective. It all depends on individual preference and their degree of taste. So, if the website decoration, such as colors, fonts, and sizes, that we specified in the preceding steps are not up your alley, you can freely change them and add your own creativity.

Pop quiz – importing an external Sass style sheet

Q1. Hopefully, you followed the preceding steps fully through and paid attention to some of the minute details. We have imported a number of style sheets to compile them into a single style sheet. How do we make the Sass compiler ignore these imported style sheets so that the compiler won't compile them into a CSS file on its own?

1. Remove the extension file's extension in the import declaration.

2. Add an underscore as a prefix in the import declaration.

3. Add an underscore as a prefix in the file name.

Fine-tuning the website

As mentioned, there are a couple of things we need to do before we call the website done. First, we are going to enable Orbit and the toggle function of the top bar, and optimize the website styles, such as the positioning and the sizing, for smaller viewport size. It's time for action again.

Time for action – compiling JavaScript and styling the website with media queries

Perform the following steps to compile the JavaScript files and optimize the website for a small viewport size:

1. Create a new JavaScript file in the `assets/js` directory named `foundation.js`.

2. In `foundation.js`, import the following JavaScript files:

```
// @koala-prepend "../../components/foundation/js/vendor/jquery.js"
// @koala-prepend "../../components/foundation/js/foundation/
foundation.js"
// @koala-prepend "../../components/foundation/js/foundation/
foundation.topbar.js"
// @koala-prepend "../../components/foundation/js/foundation/
foundation.orbit.js"
```

3. Via Koala, compile `foundation.js`.

4. Then, open `index.html` and add the following lines right before `</body>` to enable the Orbit Slider functionalities:

```
<script src="assets/js/foundation.min.js"></script>
<script>
$(document).foundation({
    orbit: {
      timer_speed: 3000,
      pause_on_hover: true,
      resume_on_mouseout: true,
      slide_number: false
    }
  });
</script>
```

5. Now, we will refine the website layout for smaller viewport viewing with media queries. To do so, we need to uncomment the variables that define the media query ranges used in Foundation, so that we can use them in our style sheets as well:

```
$small-range: (0em, 40em);
$medium-range: (40.063em, 64em);
$large-range: (64.063em, 90em);
$xlarge-range: (90.063em, 120em);
$xxlarge-range: (120.063em, 99999999em);

$screen: "only screen";

$landscape: "#{$screen} and (orientation: landscape)";
$portrait: "#{$screen} and (orientation: portrait)";

$small-up: $screen;
$small-only: "#{$screen} and (max-width: #{upper-bound($small-range)})";

$medium-up: "#{$screen} and (min-width:#{lower-bound($medium-range)})";
$medium-only: "#{$screen} and (min-width:#{lower-bound($medium-range)}) and (max-width:#{upper-bound($medium-range)})";

$large-up: "#{$screen} and (min-width:#{lower-bound($large-range)})";
```

```
$large-only: "#{$screen} and (min-width:#{lower-bound($large-
range)}) and (max-width:#{upper-bound($large-range)})";

$xlarge-up: "#{$screen} and (min-width:#{lower-bound($xlarge-
range)})";
$xlarge-only: "#{$screen} and (min-width:#{lower-bound($xlarge-
range)}) and (max-width:#{upper-bound($xlarge-range)})";

$xxlarge-up: "#{$screen} and (min-width:#{lower-bound($xxlarge-
range)})";
$xxlarge-only: "#{$screen} and (min-width:#{lower-bound($xxlarge-
range)}) and (max-width:#{upper-bound($xxlarge-range)})";
```

 We can utilize these variables within our own style sheets, as follows:

```
@media #{$small-up} {
}
```

6. Now, we will define a couple of style rules through these media queries to adjust the website's styles, particularly the sizing, positioning, and whitespace.

7. And these are all the style rules to add in `_responsive.scss`.

```
@media #{$small-up} {
  .startup-name a {
    position: relative;
    left: rem-calc(15);
  }
}
@media #{$small-only} {
  .startup-header {
    .startup-name a {
      background-size: auto 80%;
    }
    .startup-top-bar {
      padding-top: rem-calc(15);
      .top-bar-section {
        text-align: center;
      }
```

```scss
      .sign-up {
        padding-top: 0;
      }
    }
    .startup-hero {
      text-align: center;
    }
  }
  .startup-footer {
    .secondary-nav {
      li, a {
        display: block;
      }
      a {
        padding: rem-calc(10);
      }
    }
  }
}
@media #{$medium-up} {
  .startup-top-bar {
    .log-in {
      padding-right: 3px;
    }
    .sign-up {
      padding-left: 3px;
    }
  }
}
@media #{$large-only} {
    .startup-name a {
    position: relative;
    left: rem-calc(0);
  }
}
```

What just happened?

We just compiled the JavaScript to enable the Orbit Slider and the toggle function of the top bar. And we also refined the website layout for a smaller viewport size. And the following screenshot shows how the website looks in a small viewport:

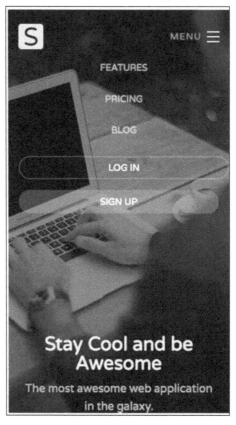

It is nice, isn't it?

Have a go hero – remove unnecessary Foundation components

We include all the Foundation components, even ones we are not using in the website. Hence, it is better to remove all the styles which do not give an advantage to the website. Open `_foundation.scss`, and comment the `@import` components that we do not need (at least at this moment) and recompile the style sheets.

Summary

We just finished working on the third project by building a responsive website for a new start-up company with Foundation. There are a lot of things we learned along the way to the end of this project, particularly about Sass. Sass is a powerful CSS preprocessor that allows us to compose styles in a more efficient and flexible form. We have learned to use variables, interpolation, mixins, and a couple of other Sass features.

Honestly speaking, the websites, including ones that we built in the previous chapters, are easy to build. Our work herein mostly involves making up the website appearance, such as the coloring and the sizing. Everything that matters most to make the website responsive, such as the Grid for example, has been covered by the frameworks we are using (Foundation, Bootstrap, and Responsive.gs).

To conclude, we hope the projects that we present in this module are a great start for you to build responsive websites on your own.

Module 2

Responsive Web Design with HTML5 and CSS3

Learn the HTML5 and CSS3 you need to help you design responsive and future-proof websites that meet the demands of modern web users

The Essentials of Responsive
Web Design

Only a few years ago, websites could be built at a fixed width, with the expectation that all end users would get a fairly consistent experience. This fixed width (typically 960px wide or thereabouts) wasn't too wide for laptop screens, and users with large resolution monitors merely had an abundance of margin either side.

But in 2007, Apple's iPhone ushered in the first truly usable phone browsing experience, and the way people access and interact with the Web changed forever.

In *Responsive Web Design with HTML5 and CSS3 - First Edition, Packt Publishing*, it was noted that:

> *"in the 12 months from July 2010 to July 2011, global mobile browser use had risen from 2.86 to 7.02 percent."*

In mid-2015, the same statistics system (`gs.statcounter.com`) reported that this figure had risen to 33.47%. By way of comparison, North America's mobile figure is at 25.86%.

By any metric, mobile device usage is rising ever upwards, while at the other end of the scale, 27 and 30 inch displays are now also commonplace. There is now a greater difference between the smallest and the largest screens browsing the Web than ever before.

Thankfully, there is a solution to this ever-expanding browser and device landscape. A responsive web design, built with HTML5 and CSS3, allows a website to 'just work' across multiple devices and screens. It enables the layout and capabilities of a website to respond to their environment (screen size, input type, device/browser capabilities).

Furthermore, a responsive web design, built with HTML5 and CSS3, can be implemented without the need for server based/back-end solutions.

Beginning our quest

Whether you're new to responsive web design, HTML5, or CSS3, or already well versed, I'm hoping this first chapter will serve one of two purposes.

If you're already using HTML5 and CSS3 in your responsive web designs, this first chapter should serve as a quick and basic refresher. Alternatively, if you're a newcomer, think of it as a 'boot camp' of sorts, covering the essentials so we're all on the same page.

By the end of this first chapter, we will have covered everything you need to author a fully responsive web page.

You might be wondering why the other nine chapters are here. By the end of this chapter, that should be apparent too.

Here's what we will cover in this first chapter:

- Defining responsive web design
- How to set browser support levels
- A brief discussion on tooling and text editors
- Our first responsive example: a simple HTML5 page
- The importance of the viewport meta tag
- How to make images scale to their container
- Writing CSS3 media queries to create design breakpoints
- The shortfalls in our basic example
- Why our journey has only just begun

Defining responsive web design

Responsive web design is the presentation of web content in the most relevant format for the viewport and device accessing it.

In its infancy, it was typical for a responsive design to be built starting with the 'desktop', fixed-width design. Content was then reflowed, or removed so that the design worked on smaller screens. However, processes evolved and it became apparent that everything from design, to content and development, worked much better when working in the opposite direction; starting with smaller screens and working up.

Before we get into this, there are a couple of subjects I'd like to address before we continue; browser support and text editors/tooling.

Setting browser support levels

The popularity and ubiquity of responsive web design makes it an easier sell to clients and stakeholders than ever before. Most people have some idea what responsive web design is about. The notion of a single codebase that will just work across all devices is a compelling offering.

One question that almost always comes up when starting a responsive design project is that of browser support. With so many browser and device variants, it's not always pragmatic to support every single browser permutation fully. Perhaps time is a limiting factor, perhaps money. Perhaps both.

Typically, the older the browser, the greater the work and code required to gain feature or aesthetic parity with modern browsers. Therefore, it may make more sense to have a leaner, and therefore faster, codebase by tiering the experience and only providing enhanced visuals and capabilities for more capable browsers.

In the previous edition of this module, *Responsive Web Design with HTML5 and CSS3 - First Edition, Packt Publishing*, some time was spent covering how to cater for very old desktop-only browsers. In this edition, we will not.

As I write this in mid-2015, Internet Explorer 6, 7, and 8 are all but gone. Even IE 9 only has a 2.45% worldwide share of the browser market (IE 10 is only 1.94% while IE 11 is rising nicely at 11.68%). If you have no alternative but to develop for Internet Explorer 8 and below, you have my sympathies and I'm afraid I must be upfront and advise you that there won't be a terrific amount you can use in this module.

For everyone else, you owe it to your client/paymaster to explain why developing for ailing browsers might be a mistake and investing development time and resource primarily for modern browsers and platforms makes good fiscal sense in every respect.

Ultimately however, the only statistics that really matter are yours. In all but extreme cases, the sites we build should at least be functional in every common browser. Beyond basic functionality, for any web project it makes sense to decide, in advance, what platforms you want to fully enhance the experience for, and which you are happy to concede visual/functional anomalies to.

You'll also find that practically, starting with the simplest 'base level' experience and enhancing (an approach known as **progressive enhancement**) is easier than coming at the problem from the opposite direction—building the ultimate experience first then attempting to provide fall backs for less capable platforms (an approach known as **graceful degradation**).

To exemplify why knowing this in advance matters, consider that if you were unlucky enough to have 25% of your website visitors using Internet Explorer 9 (for example), you'd need to consider what features that browser supports and tailor your solution accordingly. The same caution would be required if large amounts of your users are visiting with older mobile phone platforms such as Android 2. What you can consider a 'base' experience will vary depending upon the project.

If suitable data isn't available, I apply a simple and crude piece of logic to determine whether I should spend time developing a particular platform/browser version: if the cost of developing and supporting browser X is more than the revenue/benefit created by the users on browser X; don't develop specific solutions for browser X.

It's rarely a question of whether you could 'fix' an older platform/version. It's a question of whether you should.

When considering which platforms and browser versions support which features, if you aren't already, become familiar the `http://caniuse.com` website. It provides a simple interface for establishing what browser support there is for the features we will be looking at throughout.

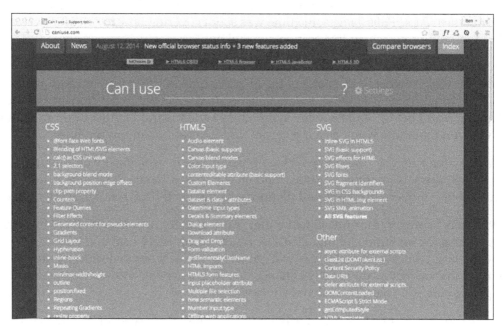

A brief note on tooling and text editors

It makes no difference what text editor or IDE system you use to build your responsive web designs. If the simplest of text editors allows you to write your HTML, CSS, and JavaScript efficiently, that's absolutely fine. Similarly there are no requisite pieces of tooling that are essential to get a responsive web design out of the door. All you actually need is something that enables you to write HTML, CSS, and JavaScript. Whether your preference is Sublime Text, Vim, Coda, Visual Studio, or Notepad - it matters little. Just use what works best for you.

However, be aware that there are more tools available now (often free) to negate many of the manual and time-intensive tasks of building web sites than ever before. For example, CSS processors (Sass, LESS, Stylus, PostCSS) can help with code organization, variables, color manipulations, and arithmetic. Tools like PostCSS can also automate horrible and thankless jobs like CSS vendor prefixing. Furthermore, 'Linting' and validation tools can check your HTML, JavaScript, and CSS code against standards as you work, eliminating many time wasting typos or syntax errors.

New tools come out constantly and they are continually improving. Therefore, whilst some relevant and beneficial tools will be mentioned by name as we go, be aware that something better may be just around the corner. Hence we won't be relying on anything other than standards based HTML and CSS in our examples. You should however, use whatever tools you can to produce your front-end code as quickly and reliably as possible.

Our first responsive example

In the first paragraph I promised that by the end of this chapter you would know all you needed to build a fully responsive web page. So far I've just been talking around the issue at hand. It's time to walk the walk.

Code samples

You can download all the code samples of this module by visiting `rwd.education/download.zip` or via GitHub at `https://github.com/benfrain/rwd`. It's worth knowing that where individual examples are built up throughout a chapter, only the final version of the example is provided in the code download. For example, if you download the code samples for *Chapter 2, Media Queries – Supporting Differing Viewports*, the examples will be in the state they are at by the end of *Chapter 2, Media Queries – Supporting Differing Viewports*. No intermediate states are provided other than in the text.

ur basic HTML file

We will start with a simple HTML5 structure. Don't worry at this point what each of the lines do (especially the content of the <head>, we will cover that in detail in *Chapter 4, HTML5 for Responsive Web Designs*).

For now, simply concentrate on the elements inside the <body> tag. I'm pretty sure nothing there will look too unusual; a few div's, a graphic for a logo, an image (a tasty looking scone), a paragraph or two of text and a list of items.

Here's an abridged version of the code. For brevity I have removed the paragraphs of text in the code below as we only need to concern ourselves with the structure. However, you should know that it's a recipe and description of how to make scones; quintessentially British cakes.

If you want to see the full HTML file, you can download it from the rwd.education website.

```
<!doctype html>
<html class="no-js" lang="en">
    <head>
        <meta charset="utf-8">
        <title>Our first responsive web page with HTML5 and CSS3</title>
        <meta name="description" content="A basic responsive web page - an example from Chapter 1">
        <link rel="stylesheet" href="css/styles.css">
    </head>
    <body>
        <div class="Header">
            <a href="/" class="LogoWrapper"><img src="img/SOC-Logo.png" alt="Scone O'Clock logo" /></a>
            <p class="Strap">Scones: the most resplendent of snacks</p>
        </div>
        <div class="IntroWrapper">
            <p class="IntroText">Occasionally maligned and misunderstood; the scone is a quintessentially British classic.</p>
            <div class="MoneyShot">
                <img class="MoneyShotImg" src="img/scones.jpg" alt="Incredible scones" />
                <p class="ImageCaption">Incredible scones, picture from Wikipedia</p>
            </div>
        </div>
        <p>Recipe and serving suggestions follow.</p>
        <div class="Ingredients">
```

```
            <h3 class="SubHeader">Ingredients</h3>
            <ul>

            </ul>
        </div>
        <div class="HowToMake">
            <h3 class="SubHeader">Method</h3>
            <ol class="MethodWrapper">

            </ol>
        </div>
    </body>
</html>
```

By default, web pages are flexible. If you were to open the example page, even as it is at this point (with no media queries present), and resize the browser window you'll see the text reflows as needed.

What about on different devices? With no CSS whatsoever, this is how that renders on an iPhone:

As you can see, it's rendering like a 'normal' web page would on an iPhone. The reason for that is that iOS renders web pages at 980px wide by default and shrinks them down into the viewport.

The viewable area of a browser is known technically as the **viewport**. The viewport is seldom equivalent to the screen size of a device, especially in instances where a user can resize a browser window.

Therefore, from now on, we will generally use this more accurate term when we are referring to the available space for our web page.

We can fix that prior problem easily by adding this snippet in the `<head>`:

```
<meta name="viewport" content="width=device-width">
```

This viewport `meta` tag is a non-standard (but de facto standard) way of telling the browser how to render the page. In this case, our viewport `meta` tag is effectively saying "make the content render at the width of the device". In fact, it's probably easier to just show you the effect this line has on applicable devices:

Great! The text is now rendering and flowing at a more 'native' size. Let's move on.

We will cover the `meta` tag and its various settings and permutations (and the standards based version of the same functionality) in *Chapter 2, Media Queries – Supporting Differing Viewports*.

Taming images

They say a picture is worth a thousand words. All this writing about scones in our sample page and there's no image of the beauties. I'm going to add in an image of a scone near the top of the page; a sort of 'hero' image to entice users to read the page.

Oh! That nice big image (2000px wide) is forcing our page to render more than a little wonky. We need to fix that. We could add a fixed width to the image via CSS but the problem there is that we want the image to scale to different screen sizes.

For example, our example iPhone is 320px wide so we could set a width of 320px to that image but then what happens if a user rotates the screen? The 320px wide viewport is now 480px wide. Thankfully it's pretty easy to achieve fluid images that will scale to the available width of their container with a single line of CSS.

I'm going to create the `css/styles.css` CSS file now that's linked in the head of the HTML page.

Here is the first thing I'm adding. Ordinarily I'd be setting a few other defaults, and we'll discuss those defaults in later chapters, but for our purposes I'm happy to open with just this:

```
img {
    max-width: 100%;
}
```

Now when the page is refreshed we see something more akin to what we might expect.

All this `max-width` based rule does is stipulate that all images should be a maximum of 100% of their width (in that they should expand to 100% of their size and no more). Where a containing element (such as the `body` or a `div` it sits within) is less than the intrinsic width of the image, it will simply scale up to the maximum available space.

Why not simply width: 100%?

To make images fluid you could also use the more widely used width property. For example, `width: 100%` but this has a different effect. When a property of `width` is used then the image will be displayed at that width, regardless of its own inherent size. The result in our example would be the logo (also an image) stretching to fill 100% of its container. With a container far wider than the image (as is the case with our logo) this leads a massively oversized image.

Excellent. Everything is now laid out as expected. No matter the viewport size, nothing is overflowing the page horizontally.

However, if we look at the page in larger viewports, the basic styles start to get both literally and figuratively stretched. Take a look at the example page at a size around 1400px:

Oh dear! In fact, even around 600px wide it's starting to suffer. Around this point it would be handy if we could rearrange a few things. Maybe resize the image and position it off to one side. Perhaps alter some font sizes and background colors of elements.

Thankfully, we can achieve all this functionality quite easily by employing CSS media queries to bend things to our will.

Enter media queries

As we have established, somewhere beyond the 600px wide point, our current layout starts to look stretched. Let's use CSS3 media queries to adjust the layout depending upon the screen width. Media queries allow us to apply certain CSS rules based upon a number of conditions (screen width and height for example).

Don't set breakpoints to popular device widths

'Breakpoint' is the term used to define the point in which a responsive design should change significantly.

When people first started making use of media queries it was common to see breakpoints in designs built specifically around the popular devices of the day. At the time it was typically iPhone (320px x 480px) and iPad (768px x 1024px) that defined these 'breakpoints'.

That practice was a bad choice then, and it would be an even worse one now. The problem is that by doing that we are catering a design to a specific screen size. We want a responsive design—something that is agnostic of the screen size viewing it; not something that only looks at its best at specific sizes.

Therefore, let the content and the design itself determine where a breakpoint is relevant. Maybe your initial layout starts to look wrong at 500px wide and greater, perhaps 800px. Your own project design should determine when a breakpoint is needed.

We will cover the entire gamut of CSS media queries in *Chapter 2, Media Queries – Supporting Differing Viewports*, inventively titled **Media Queries**.

However, for the purpose of whipping our basic example into shape, we will concentrate on just one type of media query; a minimum width media query. CSS rules within this type of media query only get applied if the viewport is a minimum defined width. The exact minimum width can be specified using a raft of different length units including percent, em, rem, and px. In CSS, a minimum width media query is written like this:

```
@media screen and (min-width: 50em) {
    /* styles */
}
```

The `@media` directive tells the browser we are starting a media query, the `screen` part (declaring 'screen' is technically not needed in this situation but we will deal with that in detail in the next chapter) tells the browser these rules should be applied to all screen types and the `and (min-width: 50em)` tells the browser that the rules should be limited to all viewports above 50em of size.

I believe it was Bryan Rieger (`http://www.slideshare.net/bryanrieger/rethinking-the-mobile-web-by-yiibu`) who first wrote that:

> *"The absence of support for media queries is in fact the first media query."*

What he meant by that is that the first rules we write, outside of a media query should be our 'base' rules which we then enhance for more capable devices.

For now, simply be aware that this approach re-enforces our smallest screen first mentality and allows us to progressively layer on detail as and when the design necessitates it.

Amending the example for a larger screen

We've already established that our design is starting to suffer at around 600px/37.5rem width.

Therefore, let's mix things up a little by way of a simple example of how we can lay things out differently at different viewport sizes.

Almost all browsers have a default text size of 16px so you can easily convert widths to rems by dividing the px value by 16. We will discuss why you might want to do this in *Chapter 2, Media Queries – Supporting Differing Viewports*.

First off, we will stop that main 'hero' image getting too big and keep it over on the right. Then the intro text can sit to the left.

We will then have the main portion of text, the 'method' that describes how to make the scones, on the left below with a small boxed out section detailing the ingredients over on the right.

All these changes can be achieved relatively simply by encapsulating these specific styles within a media query. Here's what things look like with the relevant styles added:

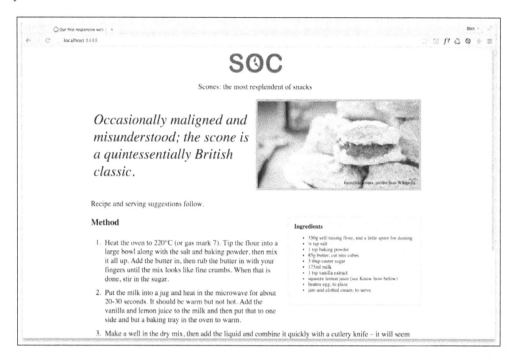

It still looks essentially the same as it did before on smaller screens but adjusts to the new layout as soon as the viewport is 50rem or wider.

Here are the layout styles that were added:

```
@media screen and (min-width: 50rem) {
    .IntroWrapper {
        display: table;
        table-layout: fixed;
        width: 100%;
    }

    .MoneyShot,
    .IntroText {
        display: table-cell;
        width: 50%;
        vertical-align: middle;
        text-align: center;
    }
}
```

```
.IntroText {
    padding: .5rem;
    font-size: 2.5rem;
    text-align: left;
}

.Ingredients {
    font-size: .9rem;
    float: right;
    padding: 1rem;
    margin: 0 0 .5rem 1rem;
    border-radius: 3px;
    background-color: #ffffdf;
    border: 2px solid #e8cfa9;
}

.Ingredients h3 {
    margin: 0;
}
}
```

That wasn't too bad was it? With only minimal code we have built a page that responds to the viewport size and offers a preferable layout as needed. By adding just a few more styles things look even easier on the eye. With those in place, our basic responsive page now looks like this on an iPhone:

And like this above 50rem width:

SOC

Scones: the most resplendent of snacks

Occasionally maligned and misunderstood; the scone is a quintessentially British classic.

Recipe and serving suggestions follow.

Method

1. Heat the oven to 220°C (or gas mark 7). Tip the flour into a large bowl along with the salt and baking powder, then mix it all up. Add the butter in, then rub the butter in with your fingers until the mix looks like fine crumbs. When that is done, stir in the sugar.

2. Put the milk into a jug and heat in the microwave for about 20-30 seconds. It should be warm but not hot. Add the vanilla and lemon juice to the milk and then put that to one side and but a baking tray in the oven to warm.

Ingredients

- 350g self-raising flour, and a little spare for dusting
- ¼ tsp salt
- 1 tsp baking powder
- 85g butter, cut into cubes
- 3 tbsp caster sugar
- 175ml milk
- 1 tsp vanilla extract
- squeeze lemon juice (see Know-how below)
- beaten egg, to glaze
- jam and clotted cream, to serve

These further visual embellishments don't add to the understanding of what's happening responsively, hence I have omitted them here but if you'd like to view the relevant code, download the chapter code at http://rwd.education or https://github.com/benfrain/rwd.

This has been a very basic example but it has encapsulated the essential methodology of building out a responsive web design.

To reiterate the essential things we have covered; start with 'base' styles, styles that can work on any device. Then layer enhancements on progressively as the viewport size and/or capabilities increase.

You can find the full specifications for CSS Media Queries (Level 3) here: http://www.w3.org/TR/css3-mediaqueries/

There is also a working draft for CSS Media Queries (Level 4) here: http://dev.w3.org/csswg/mediaqueries-4/

The shortcomings of our example

In this chapter we've covered all the essential component parts of a basic responsive HTML5 and CSS3 powered web page.

But you and I both know that this basic responsive example is rarely the limit of what we're tasked with building. Nor should it reflect the limit of what we are capable of building.

What about if we want our page to respond to different light conditions? What about changing the size of links when people use different pointing devices (a finger rather than a mouse for example)? What about being able to animate and move visual elements simply, using nothing but CSS?

Then there's the markup. How do go about marking up pages with more semantic elements; article, section, menu, and the like, or make forms with built in validation (no JavaScript needed)? And what if we want to change the visual order of elements at different viewports?

Let's not forget images. We have fluid images in this example but if people visit this page on a mobile phone, they will need to download a large graphic (2000px wide no less) that will only be shown on their phone at a fraction of that size. That will make the page considerably slower to load than needed. Surely there's a better way?

And what about logos and icons? We've used a PNG in this example, but we could easily use **scalable vector graphics** (**SVGs**) to enjoy graphics with resolution independence. That way they will look pin-sharp, regardless of the resolution of the viewing screen.

Hopefully you have time to stick around, as these are the very questions we will answer in the coming chapters.

Summary

Well done, you now know and understand the essential elements needed to create a fully responsive web page. However, as we have just discovered, there are plenty of places where things could be improved.

But that's fine. We don't just want the ability to make competent responsive web designs, we want to be able to create 'best of breed' experiences. So let's press on.

First up, we will wrap our heads around all that Level 3 and Level 4 CSS Media Queries have to offer. We have already seen how a web page can respond to viewport width but there's so much more we can do right now — and a lot more fun stuff coming to your browser soon. Let's go and take a look.

2
Media Queries – Supporting Differing Viewports

In the previous chapter, we had a brief look at the essential components for a responsive web page: a fluid layout, fluid images, and media queries.

This chapter will look in detail at media queries, hopefully providing all that's needed to fully understand their capability, syntax, and future development.

In this chapter, we shall:

- Learn why media queries are needed for a responsive web design
- Understand the media query syntax
- Learn how to use media queries in `link` tags, with CSS `@import` statements and within CSS files themselves
- Understand what device features we can test for
- Use media queries to facilitate visual changes dependent upon available screen space
- Consider whether media queries should be grouped together or written as and where needed
- Understand the `meta` viewport tag, to allow media queries to work as intended on iOS and Android devices
- Consider the capabilities being proposed for future media queries specifications

The CSS3 specification is made up of a number of modules. Media Queries (Level 3) are just one of these modules. Media queries allow us to target specific CSS styles depending upon the capabilities of a device. For example, with just a few lines of CSS we can change the way content is displayed, dependent upon things such as viewport width, screen aspect ratio, orientation (landscape or portrait), and so on.

Media queries are widely implemented. Pretty much everything other than ancient versions of Internet Explorer (8 and below) support them. In short, there's absolutely no good reason not to be using them!

Specifications at the W3C go through a ratification process. If you have a spare day, knock yourself out with the official explanation of the process at `http://www.w3.org/2005/10/Process-20051014/tr`. The simpler version is that specifications go from **Working Draft (WD)**, to **Candidate Recommendation (CR)**, to **Proposed Recommendation (PR)** before finally arriving, many years later, at W3C Recommendation (REC). Modules at a greater maturity level than others are generally safer to use. For example, CSS Transforms Module Level 3 (`http://www.w3.org/TR/css3-3d-transforms/`) has been at WD status since March 2009 and browser support for it is far poorer than CR modules such as media queries.

Why media queries are needed for a responsive web design

CSS3 media queries enable us to target particular CSS styles to particular device capabilities or situations. If you head over to the W3C specification of the CSS3 media query module (`http://www.w3.org/TR/css3-mediaqueries/`), you'll see that this is their official introduction to what media queries are all about:

> *"A media query consists of a media type and zero or more expressions that check for the conditions of particular media features. Among the media features that can be used in media queries are 'width', 'height', and 'color'. By using media queries, presentations can be tailored to a specific range of output devices without changing the content itself."*

Without media queries we would be unable to substantially alter the visuals of a website using CSS alone. They facilitate us writing defensive CSS rules that pre-empt such eventualities as portrait screen orientation, small or large viewport dimensions, and more.

Whilst a fluid layout can carry a design a substantial distance, given the gamut of screen sizes we hope to cover, there are times when we need to revise the layout more fully. Media queries make this possible. Think of them as basic conditional logic for CSS.

Basic conditional logic in CSS

True programming languages all have some facility in which one of two or more possible situations are catered for. This usually takes the form of conditional logic, typified by an `if/else` statement.

If programming vernacular makes your eyes itch, fear not; it's a very simple concept. You probably dictate conditional logic every time you ask a friend to order for you when visiting a cafe, "If they've got triple chocolate muffins I'll have one of those, if not, I'll have a slice of carrot cake". It's a simple conditional statement with two possible (and equally fine, in this case) results.

At the time of writing, CSS does not facilitate true conditional logic or programmatic features. Loops, functions, iteration, and complex math are still firmly in the domain of CSS processors (did I mention a fine book on the subject of the Sass pre-processor, called *Sass and Compass for Designers*?). However, media queries are one mechanism in CSS that allows us to author basic conditional logic. By using a media query the styles within are scoped depending upon whether certain conditions are met.

Programming features on their way

The popularity of CSS pre-processors has made the people working on CSS specifications take note. Right now there is a WD specification for CSS variables: `http://www.w3.org/TR/css-variables/`

However, browser support is currently limited to Firefox so it's really not something to consider using in the wild at present.

Media query syntax

So what does a CSS media query look like and more importantly, how does it work?

Enter the following code at the bottom of any CSS file and preview the related web page. Alternatively, you can open `example_02-01`:

```
body {
  background-color: grey;
}
```

```
@media screen and (min-width: 320px) {
  body {
    background-color: green;
  }
}
@media screen and (min-width: 550px) {
  body {
    background-color: yellow;
  }
}
@media screen and (min-width: 768px) {
  body {
    background-color: orange;
  }
}
@media screen and (min-width: 960px) {
  body {
    background-color: red;
  }
}
```

Now, preview the file in a browser and resize the window. The background color of the page will vary depending upon the current viewport size. We'll cover how the syntax works in more detail shortly. First, it's important to know how and where you can use media queries.

Media queries in link tags

Those that have been working with CSS since version 2 will know it's possible to specify the type of device (for example, `screen` or `print`) applicable to a style sheet with the media attribute of the `<link>` tag. Consider this example (which you'd place in the `<head>` tags of your markup):

```
<link rel="style sheet" type="text/css" media="screen" href="screen-styles.css">
```

Media queries add the ability to target styles based upon the capability or features of a device, rather than merely the type of device. Think of it as a question to the browser. If the browser's answer is "true", the enclosed styles are applied. If the answer is "false", they are not. Rather than just asking the browser "Are you a screen?" – as much as we could effectively ask with just CSS2 – media queries ask a little more. Instead, a media query might ask, "Are you a screen and are you in portrait orientation?" Let's look at that as an example:

```
<link rel="stylesheet" media="screen and (orientation: portrait)" href="portrait-screen.css" />
```

First, the media query expression asks the type (are you a screen?), and then the feature (is your screen in portrait orientation?). The `portrait-screen.css` style sheet will be applied for any screen device with a portrait screen orientation and ignored for any others. It's possible to reverse the logic of any media query expression by adding not to the beginning of the media query. For example, the following code would negate the result in our prior example, applying the file for anything that wasn't a screen with a portrait orientation:

```
<link rel="stylesheet" media="not screen and (orientation: portrait)"
href="portrait-screen.css" />
```

Combining media queries

It's also possible to string multiple expressions together. For example, let's extend one of our prior examples and also limit the file to devices that have a viewport greater than 800 pixels.

```
<link rel="stylesheet" media="screen and (orientation: portrait) and
(min-width: 800px)" href="800wide-portrait-screen.css" />
```

Further still, we could have a list of media queries. If any of the listed queries are true, the file will be applied. If none are true, it won't. Here is an example:

```
<link rel="stylesheet" media="screen and (orientation: portrait) and
(min-width: 800px), projection" href="800wide-portrait-screen.css" />
```

There are two points to note here. Firstly, a comma separates each media query. Secondly, you'll notice that after projection, there is no trailing and/or feature/value combination in parentheses. That's because in the absence of these values, the media query is applied to all media types. In our example, the styles will apply to all projectors.

You should be aware that you can use any CSS length unit to specify media queries with. **Pixels** (**px**) are the most commonly used but **ems** (**em**) and **rems** (**rem**) are equally appropriate. For some further info on the merits of each, I wrote a little more on the subject here: `http://benfrain.com/just-use-pixels`

Therefore, if you want a break point at 800px (but specified in em units) simply divide the number of pixels by 16. For example, 800px could also be specified as 50em (800 / 16 = 50).

Media queries with @import

We can also use the `@import` feature of CSS to conditionally load style sheets into our existing style sheet. For example, the following code would import the style sheet called `phone.css`, providing the device was screen based and had a maximum viewport of 360 pixels:

```
@import url("phone.css") screen and (max-width:360px);
```

Remember that using the `@import` feature of CSS, adds to HTTP requests (which impacts load speed) so use this method sparingly.

Media queries in CSS

So far, we have included them as links to CSS files that we would place within the `<head></head>` section of our HTML and as `@import` statements. However, it's more likely we will want to use media queries within CSS style sheets themselves. For example, if we add the following code into a style sheet, it will make all `h1` elements green, providing the device has a screen width of 400 pixels or less:

```
@media screen and (max-device-width: 400px) {
  h1 { color: green }
}
```

First we specify we want a media query with the `@media` at-rule, then we specify the type we want to match. In the preceding example, we want to apply the rules enclosed only to screens (and not, for example, `print`). Then, inside parenthesis we enter the specifics of the query. Then like any CSS rule, we open the braces and write the required styles.

At this point it's probably prudent of me to point out that in most situations, you don't actually need to specify `screen`. Here's the key point in the specification:

> *"A shorthand syntax is offered for media queries that apply to all media types; the keyword 'all' can be left out (along with the trailing 'and'). I.e. if the media type is not explicitly given it is 'all'."*

Therefore, unless you want to target styles to particular media types, just leave the `screen and` part out. That's the way we will be writing media queries in the example files from this point on.

What can media queries test for?

When building responsive designs, the media queries that get used most, usually relate to a device's viewport width (`width`). In my own experience, I have found little need (with the occasional exception of resolution and viewport height) to employ the other capabilities. However, just in case the need arises, here is a list of all capabilities that Media Queries Level 3 can test for. Hopefully some will pique your interest:

- `width`: The viewport width.
- `height`: The viewport height.
- `device-width`: The rendering surface's width (for our purposes, this is typically the screen width of a device).
- `device-height`: The rendering surface's height (for our purposes, this is typically the screen height of a device).
- `orientation`: This capability checks whether a device is portrait or landscape in orientation.
- `aspect-ratio`: The ratio of width to height based upon the viewport width and height. A 16:9 widescreen display can be written as `aspect-ratio: 16/9`.
- `device-aspect-ratio`: This capability is similar to `aspect-ratio` but is based upon the width and height of the device rendering surface, rather than viewport.
- `color`: The number of bits per color component. For example, `min-color: 16` will check that the device has 16-bit color.
- `color-index`: The number of entries in the color lookup table of the device. Values must be numbers and cannot be negative.
- `monochrome`: This capability tests how many bits per pixel are in a monochrome frame buffer. The value would be a number (integer), for example, `monochrome: 2`, and cannot be negative.
- `resolution`: This capability can be used to test screen or print resolution; for example, `min-resolution: 300dpi`. It can also accept measurements in dots per centimeter; for example, `min-resolution: 118dpcm`.
- `scan`: This can be either progressive or interlace features largely particular to TVs. For example, a 720p HD TV (the p part of 720p indicates "progressive") could be targeted with `scan: progressive` while a 1080i HD TV (the i part of 1080i indicates "interlaced") could be targeted with `scan: interlace`.
- `grid`: This capability indicates whether or not the device is grid or bitmap based.

All the preceding features, with the exception of scan and grid, can be prefixed with min or max to create ranges. For example, consider the following code snippet:

```
@import url("tiny.css") screen and (min-width:200px) and (max-width:360px);
```

Here, a minimum (min) and maximum (max) have been applied to width to set a range. The tiny.css file will only be imported for screen devices with a minimum viewport width of 200 pixels and a maximum viewport width of 360 pixels.

Features deprecated in CSS Media Queries Level 4

It's worth being aware that the draft specification for Media Queries Level 4 deprecates the use of a few features (http://dev.w3.org/csswg/mediaqueries-4/#mf-deprecated); most notably device-height, device-width, and device-aspect-ratio. Support for those queries will remain in browsers but it's recommended you refrain from writing any new style sheets that use them.

Using media queries to alter a design

By their very nature, styles further down a **cascading style sheet** (CSS file to you and me) override equivalent styles higher up (unless styles higher up are more specific). We can therefore set base styles at the beginning of a style sheet, applicable to all versions of our design (or at least providing our 'base' experience), and then override relevant sections with media queries further on in the document. For example, we might choose to set navigation links as text alone in limited viewports (or perhaps just smaller text) and then overwrite those styles with a media query to give us both text and icons at larger viewports where more space is available.

Let's have a look at how this might look in practice (example_02-02). First the markup:

```
<a href="#" class="CardLink CardLink_Hearts">Hearts</a>
<a href="#" class="CardLink CardLink_Clubs">Clubs</a>
<a href="#" class="CardLink CardLink_Spades">Spades</a>
<a href="#" class="CardLink CardLink_Diamonds">Diamonds</a>
```

Now the CSS:

```
.CardLink {
    display: block;
    color: #666;
    text-shadow: 0 2px 0 #efefef;
    text-decoration: none;
    height: 2.75rem;
    line-height: 2.75rem;
```

```
        border-bottom: 1px solid #bbb;
        position: relative;
    }

    @media (min-width: 300px) {
        .CardLink {
            padding-left: 1.8rem;
            font-size: 1.6rem;
        }
    }

    .CardLink:before {
        display: none;
        position: absolute;
        top: 50%;
        transform: translateY(-50%);
        left: 0;
    }

    .CardLink_Hearts:before {
        content: "♥";
    }

    .CardLink_Clubs:before {
        content: "♣";
    }

    .CardLink_Spades:before {
        content: "♠";
    }

    .CardLink_Diamonds:before {
        content: "♦";
    }

    @media (min-width: 300px) {
        .CardLink:before {
            display: block;
        }
    }
```

Here's a screen grab of the links in a small viewport:

And here's a grab of them at a larger viewport:

Any CSS can be wrapped in a media query

It's important to remember that anything you would normally write in CSS can also be enclosed inside a media query. As such, it's possible to entirely change the layout and look of a site in different situations (usually for differing viewport sizes) with media queries.

Media queries for HiDPI devices

Another common use case for media queries is to change styles when the site is viewed on a high-resolution device. Consider this:

```
@media (min-resolution: 2dppx) {
  /* styles */
}
```

Here our media query is specifying that we only want the enclosed styles to apply where the screen resolution is 2 dots per pixel unit (2dppx). This would apply to devices like the iPhone 4 (Apple's HiDPI devices are given the 'Retina' moniker) and a whole raft of Android devices. You could change that media query to apply to a wider range of devices by reducing the dppx value.

For the broadest possible support, when writing min-resolution media queries, ensure you have a prefixing tool running to provide relevant vendor prefixes. Don't worry if the term vendor prefixes doesn't make much sense right now as we deal with the subject in more detail in the next chapter.

Considerations for organizing and authoring media queries

We will take a brief tangent at this point to consider some of the different approaches that authors can take when writing and organizing their media queries. Each approach offers some benefits and some tradeoffs so it's worth at least knowing about these factors, even if you decide they are largely irrelevant for your needs.

Linking to different CSS files with media queries

From a browser perspective, CSS is considered to be a 'render blocking' asset. The browser needs to fetch and parse a linked CSS file before rendering of the page can complete.

However, modern browsers are smart enough to discern which style sheets (linked with media queries in the head) need to be analyzed immediately and which can be deferred until after the initial page rendering.

For these browsers, CSS files linked to with non-applicable media queries (for example if the screen is too small for the media query to apply) can be 'deferred' until after the initial page load, providing some performance advantage.

There's more on this topic over on Google's developer pages: `https://developers.google.com/web/fundamentals/performance/critical-rendering-path/render-blocking-css`

However, I would like to draw your attention to this part in particular:

> *"...note that "render blocking" only refers to whether the browser will have to hold the initial rendering of the page on that resource. In either case, the CSS asset is still downloaded by the browser, albeit with a lower priority for non-blocking resources."*

To reiterate, all the linked files will still be downloaded, the browser just won't hold up rendering of the page if they don't immediately apply.

Therefore, a modern browser loading a responsive web page (take a look at example_02-03) with four different style sheets linked with different media queries (to apply different styles for different viewport ranges) will download all four CSS files but probably only parse the applicable one initially before rendering the page.

The practicalities of separating media queries

Although we have just learned that the process of splitting media queries potentially offers some benefit, there is not always a large tangible advantage (apart from personal preference and/or compartmentalization of code) in separating different media query styles into separate files.

After all, using separate files increases the number of HTTP requests needed to render a page, which in turn can make the pages slower in certain other situations. Nothing is ever easy on the Web! It's therefore really a question of evaluating the entire performance of your site and testing each scenario on different devices.

My default stance on this is that, unless the project has considerable time available for performance optimizations, this is one of the last places I would look to make performance gains. Only once I am certain that:

- All images are compressed
- All scripts are concatenated and minified
- All assets are being served gzipped
- All static content is being cached via CDNs
- All surplus CSS rules have been removed

Perhaps then I would start looking to split up media queries into separate files for performance gains.

 gzip is a compression and decompression file format. Any good server should allow gzip for files such as CSS and this greatly decreases the size of the file as it travels from server to device (at which point it is decompressed to its native format). You can find a good summary of gzip on Wikipedia: http://en.wikipedia.org/wiki/Gzip

Nesting media queries 'inline'

In all but extreme circumstances, I recommend adding media queries within an existing style sheet alongside the 'normal' rules.

If you are happy to do the same, it leads to one further consideration: should media queries be declared underneath the associated selector? Or split off into a separate block of code at the end for all identical media queries? I'm glad you asked.

Combine media queries or write them where it suits?

I'm a fan of writing media queries underneath the original 'normal' definition. For example, let's say I want to change the width of a couple of elements, at different places in the style sheet, depending upon the viewport width I would do this:

```css
.thing {
    width: 50%;
}

@media screen and (min-width: 30rem) {
    .thing {
        width: 75%;
    }
}

/* A few more styles would go between them */

.thing2 {
    width: 65%;
}

@media screen and (min-width: 30rem) {
    .thing2 {
        width: 75%;
    }
}
```

This seems like lunacy at first. We have two media queries that both relate to when the screen has a minimum width of 30rem. Surely repeating the same `@media` declaration is overly verbose and wasteful? Shouldn't I be advocating grouping all the identical media queries into a single block like this:

```css
.thing {
    width: 50%;
}

.thing2 {
    width: 65%;
}
```

```
    }

@media screen and (min-width: 30rem) {
    .thing {
        width: 75%;
    }
    .thing2 {
        width: 75%;
    }
}
```

That is certainly one way to do it. However, from a maintenance point of view I find this more difficult. There is no 'right' way to do this but my preference is to define a rule for an individual selector once and have any variations of that rule (such as changes within media queries) defined immediately after. That way I don't have to search for separate blocks of code to find the declaration that is relevant to a particular selector.

> With CSS pre and post processors, this can be even more convenient as the media query 'variant' of a rule can be nested directly within the rule set. There's a whole section on that in one of my books *Sass and Compass for Designers*.

It would seem fair to argue against the former technique on the grounds of verbosity. Surely file size alone should be enough reason not to write media queries in this manner? After all, no one wants a big bloated CSS file to serve their users. However, the simple fact is that gzip compression (which should be compressing all the possible assets on your server) reduces the difference to a completely inconsequential amount. I've done various tests on this in the past so if it's something you would like to read more about, head over to: `http://benfrain.com/inline-or-combined-media-queries-in-sass-fight/`. The bottom line is, I don't believe you should concern yourself with file size if you would rather write media queries directly after the standard styles.

> If you want to author your media queries directly after the original rule but have all identical media queries definitions merged into one, there are a number of build tools (at the time of writing, Grunt and Gulp both have relevant plugins) that facilitate this.

The viewport meta tag

To get the most out of media queries, you will want smaller screen devices to display web pages at their native size (and not render them in a 980px window that you then have to zoom in and out of).

When Apple released the iPhone in 2007, they introduced a proprietary `meta` tag called the viewport `meta` tag which Android and a growing number of other platforms now also support. The purpose of the viewport `meta` tag is to provide a way for web pages to communicate to mobile browsers how they would like the web browser to render the page.

For the foreseeable future, any web page you want to be responsive, and render well across small screen devices, will need to make use of this `meta` tag.

> **Testing responsive designs on emulators and simulators**
>
> Although there is no substitute for testing your development work on real devices, there are emulators for Android and a simulator for iOS.
>
> For the pedantic, a simulator merely simulates the relevant device whereas an emulator actually attempts to interpret the original device code.
>
> The Android emulator for Windows, Linux, and Mac is available for free by downloading and installing the Android **Software Development Kit (SDK)** at `http://developer.android.com/sdk/`.
>
> The iOS simulator is only available to Mac OS X users and comes as part of the Xcode package (free from the Mac App Store).
>
> Browsers themselves are also including ever improving tools for emulating mobile devices in their development tools. Both Firefox and Chrome currently have specific settings to emulate different mobile devices/viewports.

The viewport `<meta>` tag is added within the `<head>` tags of the HTML. It can be set to a specific width (which we could specify in pixels, for example) or as a scale, for example `2.0` (twice the actual size). Here's an example of the viewport `meta` tag set to show the browser at twice (200 percent) the actual size:

```
<meta name="viewport" content="initial-scale=2.0,width=device-width"
/>
```

Let's break down the preceding `<meta>` tag so we can understand what's going on. The `name="viewport"` attribute is obvious enough. The `content="initial-scale=2.0` section is then saying, "scale the content to twice the size" (where 0.5 would be half the size, 3.0 would be three times the size, and so on) while the `width=device-width` part tells the browser that the width of the page should be equal to device-width.

The `<meta>` tag can also be used to control the amount a user can zoom in and out of the page. This example allows users to go as large as three times the device width and as small as half the device width:

```
<meta name="viewport" content="width=device-width, maximum-scale=3,
minimum-scale=0.5" />
```

You could also disable users from zooming at all, although as zooming is an important accessibility tool, it's rare that it would be appropriate in practice:

```
<meta name="viewport" content="initial-scale=1.0, user-scalable=no" />
```

The `user-scalable=no` being the relevant part.

Right, we'll change the scale to `1.0`, which means that the mobile browser will render the page at 100 percent of its viewport. Setting it to the device's width means that our page should render at 100 percent of the width of all supported mobile browsers. For the majority of cases, this `<meta>` tag would be appropriate:

```
<meta name="viewport" content="width=device-width,initial-scale=1.0"
/>
```

> Noticing that the viewport `meta` element is seeing increasing use, the W3C is making attempts to bring the same capability into CSS. Head over to `http://dev.w3.org/csswg/css-device-adapt/` and read all about the new `@viewport` declaration. The idea is that rather than writing a `<meta>` tag in the `<head>` section of your markup, you could write `@viewport { width: 320px; }` in the CSS instead. This would set the browser width to 320 pixels. However, browser support is scant, although to cover all bases and be as future proof as possible you could use a combination of `meta` tag and the `@viewport` declaration.

At this point, you should have a solid grasp of media queries and how they work. However, before we move on to a different topic entirely, I think it's nice to consider what may be possible in the near future with the next version of media queries. Let's take a sneak peak!

Media Queries Level 4

At the time of writing, while CSS Media Queries Level 4 enjoy a draft specification (`http://dev.w3.org/csswg/mediaqueries-4/`), the features in the draft don't enjoy many browser implementations. This means that while we will take a brief look at the highlights of this specification, it's highly volatile. Ensure you check browser support and double-check for syntax changes before using any of these features.

For now, while there are other features in the level 4 specification, we will concern ourselves only with scripting, pointer and hover, and luminosity.

Scripting media feature

It's a common practice to set a class on the HTML tag to indicate that no JavaScript is present by default and then replace that class with a different class when JavaScript runs. This provides a simple ability to fork code (including CSS) based upon that new HTML class. Specifically, using this practice you can then write rules specific to users that have JavaScript enabled.

That's potentially confusing so let's consider some example code. By default, this would be the tag as authored in the HTML:

```
<html class="no-js">
```

When JavaScript was run on the page, one of its first tasks would be to replace that no-js class:

```
<html class="js">
```

Once this is done, we can then write specific CSS rules that will only apply when JavaScript is present. For example, `.js .header { display: block; }`.

However, the scripting media feature of CSS Media Queries Level 4 aims to provide a more standardized manner to do this directly in the CSS:

```
@media (scripting: none) {
    /* styles for when JavaScript not working */
}
```

And when JavaScript is present:

```
@media (scripting: enabled) {
    /* styles for when JavaScript is working */
}
```

Finally, it also aims to provide the ability to ascertain when JavaScript is present but only initially. One example given in the W3C specification is that of a printed page that could be laid out initially but does not have JavaScript available after that. In such an eventuality, you should be able to do this:

```
@media (scripting: initial-only) {
    /* styles for when JavaScript works initially */
}
```

The current Editor's draft of this feature can be read here: http://dev.w3.org/csswg/mediaqueries-4/#mf-scripting

Interaction media features

Here is the W3C introduction to the pointer media feature:

> *"The pointer media feature is used to query about the presence and accuracy of a pointing device such as a mouse. If a device has multiple input mechanisms, the pointer media feature must reflect the characteristics of the "primary" input mechanism, as determined by the user agent."*

There are three possible states for the pointer features: none, coarse, and fine.

A coarse pointer device would be a finger on a touch screen device. However, it could equally be a cursor from a games console that doesn't have the fine grained control of something like a mouse.

```
@media (pointer: coarse) {
    /* styles for when coarse pointer is present */
}
```

A fine pointer device would be a mouse but could also be a stylus pen or any future fine grained pointer mechanism.

```
@media (pointer: fine) {
    /* styles for when fine pointer is present */
}
```

As far as I'm concerned, the sooner browsers implement these pointer features, the better. At present it's notoriously difficult to know whether or not a user has mouse, touch input, or both. And which one they are using at any one time.

The safest bet is always to assume users are using touch-based input and size user interface elements accordingly. That way, even if they are using a mouse they will have no difficulty using the interface with ease. If however you assume mouse input, and can't reliably detect touch to amend the interface, it might make for a difficult experience.

For a great overview of the challenges of developing for both touch and pointer, I recommend this set of slides called *Getting touchy* from Patrick H. Lauke: `https://patrickhlauke.github.io/getting-touchy-presentation/`

Read the Editor's draft of this feature here: `http://dev.w3.org/csswg/mediaqueries-4/#mf-interaction`

The hover media feature

As you might imagine, the hover media feature tests the users' ability to hover over elements on the screen. If the user has multiple inputs at their disposal (touch and mouse for example), characteristics of the primary input are used. Here are the possible values and example code:

For users that have no ability to hover, we can target styles for them with a value of `none`.

```
@media (hover: none) {
    /* styles for when the user cannot hover */
}
```

For users that can hover but have to perform a significant action to initiate it, `on-demand` can be used.

```
@media (hover: on-demand) {
    /* styles for when the user can hover but doing so requires
    significant effort */
}
```

For users that can hover, `hover` alone can be used.

```
@media (hover) {
    /* styles for when the user can hover */
}
```

Be aware that there are also `any-pointer` or `any-hover` media features. They are like the preceding hover and pointer but test the capabilities of any of the possible input devices.

Environment media features

Wouldn't it be nice if we had the ability to alter our designs based upon environmental features such as ambient light level? That way if a user was in a darker room, we could dim the lightness of the colors used. Or conversely, increase contrast in brighter sunlight. The environment media features aim to solve these very problems. Consider these examples:

```
@media (light-level: normal) {
    /* styles for standard light conditions */
}
@media (light-level: dim) {
    /* styles for dim light conditions */
}
@media (light-level: washed) {
    /* styles for bright light conditions */
}
```

Remember there are few implementations of these Level 4 Media Queries in the wild. It's also probable that the specifications will change before we can safely use them. It is however useful to have some feel for what new capabilities are on the way for us in the next few years.

Read the Editor's draft of this feature here: `http://dev.w3.org/csswg/mediaqueries-4/#mf-environment`

Summary

In this chapter, we've learned what CSS3 media queries are, how to include them in our CSS files, and how they can help our quest to create a responsive web design. We've also learned how to use the `meta` tag to make modern mobile browsers render pages as we'd like.

However, we've also learned that media queries alone can only provide an adaptable web design, one that snaps from one layout to another. Not a truly responsive one that smoothly transitions from one layout to another. To achieve our ultimate goal we will also need to utilize fluid layouts. They will allow our designs to flex between the break points that the media queries handle. Creating fluid layouts to smooth the transition between our media query break points is what we'll be covering in the next chapter.

3
Fluid Layouts and Responsive Images

Eons ago, in the mists of time (well the late 1990s), websites were typically built with their widths defined as percentages. These percentage-based widths fluidly adjusted to the screen viewing them and became known as fluid layouts.

In the years shortly after, in the mid to late 2000s, there was an intervening fixation on fixed width designs (I blame those pesky print designers and their obsession with pixel perfect precision). Nowadays, as we build responsive web designs we need to look back to fluid layouts and remember all the benefits they offer.

In *Chapter 2, Media Queries – Supporting Differing Viewports*, we ultimately conceded that while media queries allowed our design to adapt to changing viewport sizes, by snapping from one set of styles to another, we needed some ability to flex our design between the 'break points' that media queries provided. By coding a 'fluid' layout, we can facilitate this need perfectly; it will effortlessly stretch to fill the gaps between our media query break points.

In 2015, we have better means to build responsive web sites than ever. There is a new CSS layout module called **Flexible Box** (or **Flexbox** as it is more commonly known) that now has enough browser support to make it viable for everyday use.

It can do more than merely provide a fluid layout mechanism. Want to be able to easily center content, change the source order of markup, and generally create amazing layouts with relevant ease? Flexbox is the layout mechanism for you. The majority of this chapter deals with Flexbox, covering all the incredible capabilities it has to offer.

There is another key area to responsive web design we can address better now than ever before and that's responsive images. There are now specified methods and syntax for sending devices the most relevant version of an image for their viewport. We will spend the last section of this chapter understanding how responsive images work and how we can make them work for us.

In this chapter we will cover:

- How to convert fixed pixel sizes to proportional sizes
- Consider existing CSS layout mechanisms and their shortfalls
- Understand the Flexible Box Layout Module and the benefits it offers
- Learn the correct syntax for resolution switching and art direction with responsive images

Converting a fixed pixel design to a fluid proportional layout

Graphic composites made in a program like Photoshop, Illustrator, Fireworks (RIP), or Sketch all have fixed pixel dimensions. At some point, the designs need to be converted to proportional dimensions by a developer when recreating the design as a fluid layout in a browser.

There is a beautifully simple formula for making this conversion that the father of responsive web design, Ethan Marcotte, set down in his 2009 article, *Fluid Grids* (`http://alistapart.com/article/FLUIDGRIDS`):

target / context = result

If anything resembling math makes you quiver, think of it this way: divide the units of the thing you want, by the thing it lives in. Let's put that into practice as understanding it will enable you to convert any fixed dimension layouts into responsive/fluid equivalents.

Consider a very basic page layout intended for desktop. In an ideal world we would always be moving to a desktop layout from a smaller screen layout, but for the sake of illustrating the proportions we will look at the two situations back to front.

Here's an image of the layout:

The layout is 960px wide. Both header and footer are the full width of layout. The left hand side area is 200px wide, the right hand area is 100px wide. Even with my mathematically challenged brain I can tell you the middle section will be 660px wide. We need to convert the middle and side sections to proportional dimensions.

First up, the left hand side. It's 200 units wide (target). Divide that size by 960 units (the context) and we have a result: .208333333. Now, whenever we get our result with that formula we need to shift the decimal point two to the right. That would give us 20.8333333%. That's 200px described as a percentage of 960px.

OK, what about the middle section? 660 (target) divided by 960 (context) gives us .6875. Move the decimal two points to the right and we have 68.75%. Finally, the right hand section. 100 (target) divided by 960 (context) gives us .104166667. Move the decimal point and we have 10.4166667%. That's as difficult as it gets. Say it with me: target, divided by context, equals result.

To prove the point, let's quickly build that basic layout as blocks in the browser. You can view the layout as `example_03-01`. Here is the HTML:

```
<div class="Wrap">
    <div class="Header"></div>
    <div class="WrapMiddle">
        <div class="Left"></div>
        <div class="Middle"></div>
        <div class="Right"></div>
    </div>
    <div class="Footer"></div>
</div>
```

And here is the CSS:

```
html,
body {
    margin: 0;
    padding: 0;
}

.Wrap {
    max-width: 1400px;
    margin: 0 auto;
}

.Header {
    width: 100%;
    height: 130px;
    background-color: #038C5A;
}

.WrapMiddle {
    width: 100%;
    font-size: 0;
}

.Left {
    height: 625px;
    width: 20.8333333%;
    background-color: #03A66A;
    display: inline-block;
}

.Middle {
```

```
        height: 625px;
        width: 68.75%;
        background-color: #bbbf90;
        display: inline-block;
}

.Right {
        height: 625px;
        width: 10.4166667%;
        background-color: #03A66A;
        display: inline-block;
}

.Footer {
        height: 200px;
        width: 100%;
        background-color: #025059;
}
```

If you open the example code in a browser and resize the page you will see the dimensions of the middle sections remain proportional to one another. You can also play around with the max-width of the .Wrap values to make the bounding dimensions for the layout bigger or smaller (it's set in the example to 1400px).

 If you're looking at the markup and wondering why I haven't used semantic elements like header, footer, and aside, then worry not. *Chapter 4, HTML5 for Responsive Web Designs*, deals with those semantic HTML5 elements in detail.

Now, let's consider how we would have the same content on a smaller screen that flexes to a point and then changes to the layout we have already seen. You can view the final code of this layout in example_03-02.

The idea is that for smaller screens we will have a single 'tube' of content. The left hand side area will only be viewable as an 'off canvas' area; typically an area for a menu area or similar, that sits off the viewable screen area and slides in when a menu button is pressed. The main content sits below the header, then the right hand section below that, and finally the footer area. In our example, we can expose the left hand menu area by clicking anywhere on the header. Typically, when making this kind of design pattern for real, a menu button would be used to activate the side menu.

To switch the class on the body of the document, I've employed a little JavaScript. This isn't 'production ready' though as we are using 'click' as the event handler in JavaScript, when ideally we would have some provision for touch (to remove the 300ms delay still present on iOS devices).

As you would expect, when combining this with our newly mastered media query skills we can adjust the viewport and the design just 'responds'—effortlessly moving from one layout to another and stretching between the two.

I'm not going to list out all the CSS here, it's all in example_03-02. However, here's an example—the left hand section:

```
.Left {
    height: 625px;
    background-color: #03A66A;
    display: inline-block;
    position: absolute;
    left: -200px;
    width: 200px;
    font-size: .9rem;
    transition: transform .3s;
}

@media (min-width: 40rem) {
    .Left {
        width: 20.8333333%;
        left: 0;
        position: relative;
    }
}
```

You can see that up first, without a media query, is the small screen layout. Then, at larger screen sizes, the width becomes proportional, the positioning relative and the left value is set to zero. We don't need to re-write properties such as the height, display, or background-color as we aren't changing them.

This is progress. We have combined two of the core responsive web design techniques we have covered; converting fixed dimensions to proportions and using media queries to target CSS rules relevant to the viewport size.

There are two important things to note in our prior example. Firstly, you may be wondering if it's strictly necessary to include all the digits after the decimal point. While the widths themselves will ultimately be converted to pixels by the browser, their values are retained for future calculations (for example, more accurately computing the width of nested elements). Subsequently, I always recommend leaving the numbers after the decimals in.

Secondly, in a real project we should be making some provision for if JavaScript isn't available and we need to view the content of the menu. We deal with this scenario in detail in *Chapter 8, Transitions, Transformations, and Animations*.

Why do we need Flexbox?

We are now going to get into the detail of using CSS Flexible Box Layouts, or Flexbox as it is more commonly known.

However, before we do that, I think it will be prudent to first consider the shortfalls of existing layout techniques such as inline-block, floats and tables.

Inline block and whitespace

The biggest issue with using inline-block as a layout mechanism is that it renders space in-between HTML elements. This is not a bug (although most developers would welcome a sane way to remove the space) but it does mean a few hacks to remove the space when it's unwanted, which for me is about 95% of the time. There are a bunch of ways to do this, in the previous example we used the 'font-size zero' approach; an approach not without its own problems and limitations. However, rather than list each possible workaround for removing the whitespace when using inline-block, check out this article by the irrepressible Chris Coyier: `http://css-tricks.com/fighting-the-space-between-inline-block-elements/`.

It's also worth pointing out that there no simple way to vertically center content within an inline-block. Using inline-blocks, there is also no way of having two sibling elements where one has a fixed width and another fluidly fills the remaining space.

Floats

I hate floats. There I said it. In their favor they work everywhere fairly consistently. However, there are two major irritations.

Firstly, when specifying the width of floated elements in percentages, their computed widths don't get rounded consistently across browsers (some browsers round up, some down). This means that sometimes sections will drop down below others when it isn't intended and other times they can leave an irritating gap at one side.

Secondly you usually have to 'clear' the floats so that parent boxes/elements don't collapse. It's easy enough to do this but it's a constant reminder that floats were never intended to be used as a robust layout mechanism.

Table and table-cell

Don't confuse `display: table` and `display: table-cell` with the equivalent HTML elements. These CSS properties merely mimic the layout of their HTML based brethren. They in no way affect the structure of the HTML.

I've found enormous utility in using CSS table layouts. For one, they enable consistent and robust vertical centring of elements within one another. Also, elements set to be `display: table-cell` inside an element set as `display: table` space themselves perfectly; they don't suffer rounding issues like floated elements. You also get support all the way back to Internet Explorer 7!

However, there are limitations. Generally, it's necessary to wrap an extra element around items (to get the joys of perfect vertical centring, a table-cell must live inside an element set as a table). It's also not possible to wrap items set as `display: table-cell` onto multiple lines.

In conclusion, all of the existing layout methods have severe limitations. Thankfully, there is a new CSS layout method that addresses these issues and much more. Cue the trumpets, roll out the red carpet. Here comes Flexbox.

Introducing Flexbox

Flexbox addresses the shortfalls in each of the aforementioned display mechanisms. Here's a brief overview of its super powers:

- It can easily vertically center contents
- It can change the visual order of elements
- It can automatically space and align elements within a box, automatically assigning available space between them
- It can make you look 10 years younger (probably not, but in low numbers of empirical tests (me) it has been proven to reduce stress)

The bumpy path to Flexbox

Flexbox has been through a few major iterations before arriving at the relatively stable version we have today. For example, consider the changes from the 2009 version (`http://www.w3.org/TR/2009/WD-css3-flexbox-20090723/`), the 2011 version (`http://www.w3.org/TR/2011/WD-css3-flexbox-20111129/`), and the 2014 version we are basing our examples on (`http://www.w3.org/TR/css-flexbox-1/`). The syntax differences are marked.

These differing specifications mean there are three major implementation versions. How many of these you need to concern yourself with depends on the level of browser support you need.

Browser support for Flexbox

Let's get this out of the way up front: there is no Flexbox support in Internet Explorer 9, 8, or below.

For everything else you'd likely want to support (and virtually all mobile browsers), there is a way to enjoy most (if not all) of Flexbox's features. You can check the support information at `http://caniuse.com/`.

Before we get stuck into Flexbox, we need to take a brief but essential tangent.

Leave prefixing to someone else

It's my hope that once you have seen a few examples of Flexbox, you will appreciate its utility and feel empowered to use it. However, manually writing all the necessary code to support each of the different Flexbox specifications is a tough task. Here's an example. I'm going to set three Flexbox related properties and values. Consider this:

```
.flex {
    display: flex;
    flex: 1;
    justify-content: space-between;
}
```

That's how the properties and values would look in the most recent syntax. However, if we want support for Android browsers (v4 and below) and IE 10, here is what would actually be needed:

```
.flex {
    display: -webkit-box;
    display: -webkit-flex;
    display: -ms-flexbox;
```

```
    display: flex;
    -webkit-box-flex: 1;
    -webkit-flex: 1;
        -ms-flex: 1;
            flex: 1;
    -webkit-box-pack: justify;
    -webkit-justify-content: space-between;
        -ms-flex-pack: justify;
            justify-content: space-between;
}
```

It's necessary to write all that because in the last few years, as browsers made experimental versions of new functionality available, they did so with a 'vendor prefix'. Each vendor had their own prefix. For example `-ms-` for Microsoft, `-webkit-` for WebKit, `-moz-` for Mozilla, and so on. For every new feature this meant it was necessary to write multiple versions of the same property; the vendor prefixed versions first, and the official W3C version at the bottom.

The result of this spell in web history is CSS that looks like the previous example. It's the only way to get the feature working across the widest number of devices. Nowadays, vendors rarely add prefixes but for the foreseeable future we must live with the reality of many existing browsers still requiring prefixes to enable certain features. This brings us back to Flexbox, an extreme example of vendor prefixing thanks to not just multiple vendor versions but also different specifications of the feature. And understanding and remembering everything you need to write in the current format and each previous format is not a whole lot of fun.

I don't know about you, but I'd rather spend my time doing something more productive than writing out that little lot each time! In short, if you intend to use Flexbox in anger, take the time to setup an auto-prefixing solution.

Choosing your auto-prefixing solution

For the sake of your sanity, to accurately and easily add vendor-prefixes to CSS, use some form of automatic prefixing solution. Right now, I favor Autoprefixer (`https://github.com/postcss/autoprefixer`). It's fast, easy to setup and very accurate.

There are versions of Autoprefixer for most setups; you don't necessarily need a command line based build tool (for example, Gulp or Grunt). For example, if you use Sublime Text, there is a version that will work straight from the command palette: `https://github.com/sindresorhus/sublime-autoprefixer`. There are also versions of Autoprefixer for Atom, Brackets, and Visual Studio.

From this point on, unless essential to illustrate a point, there will be no more vendor prefixes in the code samples.

Getting Flexy

Flexbox has four key characteristics: **direction**, **alignment**, **ordering**, and **flexibility**. We'll cover all these characteristics and how they relate by way of a few examples.

The examples are deliberately simplistic; just moving some boxes and their content around so we can understand the principals of how Flexbox works.

Perfect vertically centered text

Note that this first Flexbox example is `example_03-03`:

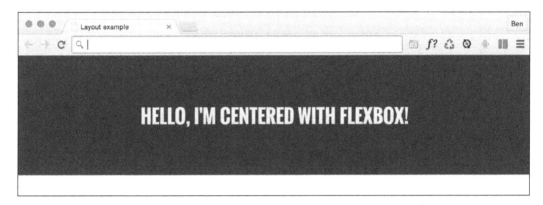

Here's the markup:

```
<div class="CenterMe">
    Hello, I'm centered with Flexbox!
</div>
```

Here is the entire CSS rule that's styling that markup:

```
.CenterMe {
    background-color: indigo;
    color: #ebebeb;
    font-family: 'Oswald', sans-serif;
    font-size: 2rem;
    text-transform: uppercase;
    height: 200px;
    display: flex;
    align-items: center;
    justify-content: center;
}
```

The majority of the property/value pairs in that rule are merely setting colors and font sizing. The three properties we are interested in are:

```
.CenterMe {
    /* other properties */
    display: flex;
    align-items: center;
    justify-content: center;
}
```

If you have not used Flexbox or any of the properties in the related Box Alignment specification (http://www.w3.org/TR/css3-align/) these properties probably seem a little alien. Let's consider what each one does:

- `display: flex`: This is the bread and butter of Flexbox. This merely sets the item to be a Flexbox (as opposed to a block, inline-block, and so on).

- `align-items`: This aligns the items within a Flexbox in the cross axis (vertically centering the text in our example).

- `justify-content`: This sets the main axis centring of the content. With a Flexbox row, you can think of it like the button in a word processor that sets the text to the left, right, or center (although there are additional `justify-content` values we will look at shortly).

OK, before we get further into the properties of Flexbox, we will consider a few more examples.

In some of these examples I'm making use of the Google hosted font 'Oswald' (with a fallback to a sans-serif font). In *Chapter 5, CSS3 – Selectors, Typography, Color Modes, and New Features*, we will look at how we can use the `@font-face` rule to link to custom font files.

Offset items

How about a simple list of navigation items, but with one offset to one side?

Here's what it looks like:

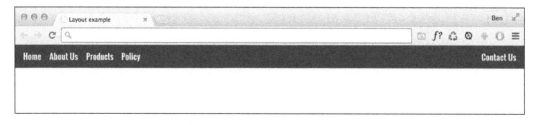

Here's the markup:

```
<div class="MenuWrap">
    <a href="#" class="ListItem">Home</a>
    <a href="#" class="ListItem">About Us</a>
    <a href="#" class="ListItem">Products</a>
    <a href="#" class="ListItem">Policy</a>
    <a href="#" class="LastItem">Contact Us</a>
</div>
```

And here is the CSS:

```
.MenuWrap {
    background-color: indigo;
    font-family: 'Oswald', sans-serif;
    font-size: 1rem;
    min-height: 2.75rem;
    display: flex;
    align-items: center;
    padding: 0 1rem;
}

.ListItem,
.LastItem {
    color: #ebebeb;
    text-decoration: none;
}

.ListItem {
    margin-right: 1rem;
}

.LastItem {
    margin-left: auto;
}
```

How about that—not a single float, inline-block, or table-cell needed! When you set
`display: flex;` on a wrapping element, the children of that element become flex-
items which then get laid out using the flex layout model. The magic property here is
`margin-left: auto` which makes that item use all available margin on that side.

Reverse the order of items

Want to reverse the order of the items?

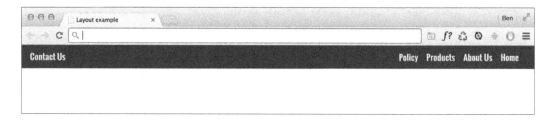

It's as easy as adding `flex-direction: row-reverse;` to the wrapping element and changing `margin-left: auto` to `margin-right: auto` on the offset item:

```
.MenuWrap {
    background-color: indigo;
    font-family: 'Oswald', sans-serif;
    font-size: 1rem;
    min-height: 2.75rem;
    display: flex;
    flex-direction: row-reverse;
    align-items: center;
    padding: 0 1rem;
}

.ListItem,
.LastItem {
    color: #ebebeb;
    text-decoration: none;
}

.ListItem {
    margin-right: 1rem;
}

.LastItem {
    margin-right: auto;
}
```

How about if we want them laid out vertically instead?

Simple. Change to `flex-direction: column;` on the wrapping element and remove the auto margin:

```css
.MenuWrap {
    background-color: indigo;
    font-family: 'Oswald', sans-serif;
    font-size: 1rem;
    min-height: 2.75rem;
    display: flex;
    flex-direction: column;
    align-items: center;
    padding: 0 1rem;
}

.ListItem,
.LastItem {
    color: #ebebeb;
    text-decoration: none;
}
```

Column reverse

Want them stacked in the opposite direction? Just change to `flex-direction: column-reverse;` and you're done.

You should be aware that there is a `flex-flow` property that is shorthand for setting `flex-direction` and `flex-wrap` in one. For example, `flex-flow: row wrap;` would set the direction to a row and set wrapping on. However, at least initially, I find it easier to specify the two settings separately. The `flex-wrap` property is also absent from the oldest Flexbox implementations so can render the whole declaration void in certain browsers.

Different Flexbox layouts inside different media queries

As the name suggests, Flexbox is inherently flexible so how about we go for a column list of items at smaller viewports and a row style layout when space allows. It's a piece of cake with Flexbox:

```css
.MenuWrap {
    background-color: indigo;
```

```
        font-family: 'Oswald', sans-serif;
        font-size: 1rem;
        min-height: 2.75rem;
        display: flex;
        flex-direction: column;
        align-items: center;
        padding: 0 1rem;
    }

    @media (min-width: 31.25em) {
        .MenuWrap {
            flex-direction: row;
        }
    }

    .ListItem,
    .LastItem {
        color: #ebebeb;
        text-decoration: none;
    }

    @media (min-width: 31.25em) {
        .ListItem {
            margin-right: 1rem;
        }
        .LastItem {
            margin-left: auto;
        }
    }
```

You can view that as example_03-05. Be sure to resize the browser window to see the different layouts.

Inline-flex

Flexbox has an inline variant to complement inline-block and inline-table. As you might have guessed it is display: inline-flex;. Thanks to its beautiful centering abilities you can do some wacky things with very little effort.

Here's the markup:

```
<p>Here is a sentence with a <a href="http://www.w3.org/TR/css-
flexbox-1/#flex-containers" class="InlineFlex">inline-flex link</a>.</
p>
```

And here is the CSS for that:

```
.InlineFlex {
    display: inline-flex;
    align-items: center;
    height: 120px;
    padding: 0 4px;
    background-color: indigo;
    text-decoration: none;
    border-radius: 3px;
    color: #ddd;
}
```

When items are set as `inline-flex` anonymously (for example, their parent element is not set to `display: flex;`) then they retain whitespace between elements, just like inline-block or inline-table do. However, if they are within a flex container, then whitespace is removed, much as it is with table-cell items within a table.

Of course, you don't always have to center items within a Flexbox. There are a number of different options. Let's look at those now.

Flexbox alignment properties

If you want to play with this example, you can find it at `example_03-07`. Remember the example code you download will be at the point where we finish this section so if you want to 'work along' you may prefer to delete the CSS in the example file and start again.

The important thing to understand with Flexbox alignment is the concept of axis. There are two axis to consider, the 'main axis' and the 'cross axis'. What each of these represents depends upon the direction the Flexbox is heading. For example, if the direction of your Flexbox is set to `row`, the main axis will be the horizontal axis and the cross axis will be the vertical axis.

Conversely, if your Flexbox direction is set to `column`, the main axis will be the vertical axis and the cross axis will be the horizontal.

The specification (`http://www.w3.org/TR/css-flexbox-1/#justify-content-property`) provides the following illustration to aid authors:

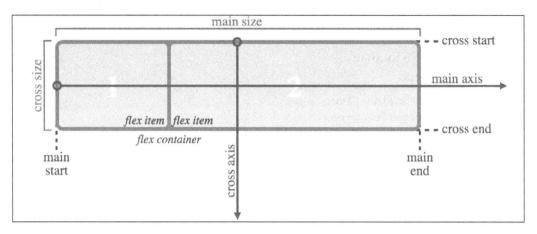

Here's the basic markup of our example:

```
<div class="FlexWrapper">
    <div class="FlexInner">I am content in the inner Flexbox.</div>
</div>
```

Let's set basic Flexbox related styles:

```
.FlexWrapper {
    background-color: indigo;
    display: flex;
    height: 200px;
    width: 400px;
}

.FlexInner {
    background-color: #34005B;
    display: flex;
    height: 100px;
    width: 200px;
}
```

In the browser, that produces this:

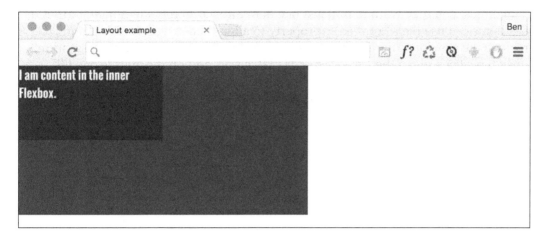

Right, let's test drive the effects of some of these properties.

The align-items property

The `align-items` property positions items in the cross axis. If we apply this property to our wrapping element like so:

```
.FlexWrapper {
    background-color: indigo;
    display: flex;
    height: 200px;
    width: 400px;
    align-items: center;
}
```

As you would imagine, the item within that box gets centered vertically:

The same effect would be applied to any number of children within.

The align-self property

Sometimes, you may want to pull just one item into a different alignment. Individual flex items can use the `align-self` property to align themselves. At this point, I'll remove the previous alignment properties, add another two items into the markup (they have been given the `.FlexInner` HTML class), and on the middle one I'll add another HTML class (`.AlignSelf`) and use it to add the `align-self` property. Viewing the CSS at this point may be more illustrative:

```
.FlexWrapper {
    background-color: indigo;
    display: flex;
    height: 200px;
    width: 400px;
}
.FlexInner {
    background-color: #34005B;
    display: flex;
    height: 100px;
    width: 200px;
}

.AlignSelf {
    align-self: flex-end;
}
```

Here is the effect in the browser:

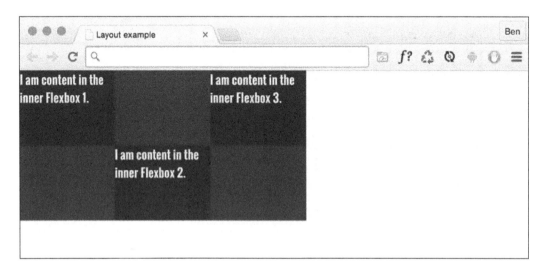

Wow! Flexbox really makes these kinds of changes trivial. In that example the value of `align-self` was set to `flex-end`. Let's consider the possible values we could use on the cross axis before looking at alignment in the main axis.

Possible alignment values

For cross axis alignment, Flexbox has the following possible values:

- `flex-start`: Setting an element to `flex-start` would make it begin at the 'starting' edge of its flex container

- `flex-end`: Setting to `flex-end` would align the element at the end of the flex container

- `center`: Puts it in the middle of the flex container

- `baseline`: Sets all flex items in the container so that their baselines align

- `stretch`: Makes the items stretch to the size of their flex container (in the cross axis)

 There are some particulars inherent to using these properties, so if something isn't playing happily, always refer to the specification for any edge case scenarios: `http://www.w3.org/TR/css-flexbox-1/`.

The justify-content property

Alignment in the main axis is controlled with `justify-content` (for non Flexbox/block-level items, the `justify-self` property has also been proposed (`http://www.w3.org/TR/css3-align/`). Possible values for `justify-content` are:

- `flex-start`
- `flex-end`
- `center`
- `space-between`
- `space-around`

The first three do exactly what you would now expect. However, let's take a look what `space-between` and `space-around` do. Consider this markup:

```
<div class="FlexWrapper">
    <div class="FlexInner">I am content in the inner Flexbox 1.</div>
    <div class="FlexInner">I am content in the inner Flexbox 2.</div>
    <div class="FlexInner">I am content in the inner Flexbox 3.</div>
</div>
```

And then consider this CSS. We are setting the three flex-items (`FlexInner`) to each be 25% width, wrapped by a flex container (`FlexWrapper`) set to be 100% width.

```css
.FlexWrapper {
    background-color: indigo;
    display: flex;
    justify-content: space-between;
    height: 200px;
    width: 100%;
}
.FlexInner {
background-color: #34005B;
display: flex;
height: 100px;
width: 25%;
}
```

As the three items will only take up 75% of the available space, `justify-content` explains what we would like the browser to do with the remaining space. A value of `space-between` puts equal amount of space between the items and `space-around` puts it around. Perhaps a screenshot here will help: This is `space-between`.

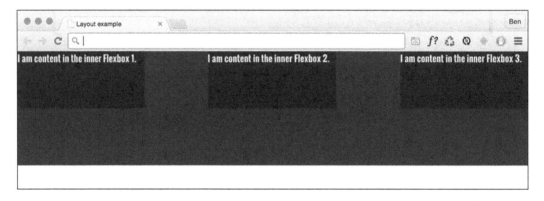

And here is what happens if we switch to `space-around`.

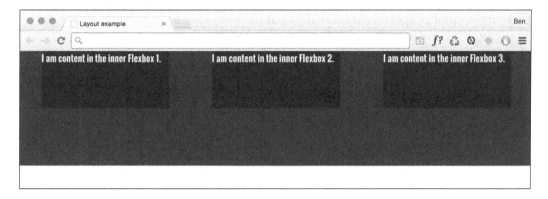

Those two values are pretty handy I think you will agree.

The various alignment properties of Flexbox are currently being specified into the CSS Box Alignment Module Level 3. This should give the same fundamental alignment powers to other display properties, such as `display: block;` and `display: table;`. The specification is still being worked upon so check the status at `http://www.w3.org/TR/css3-align/`.

The flex property

We've used the `width` property on those flex-items but it's also possible to define the width, or 'flexiness' if you will, with the `flex` property. To illustrate, consider another example; same markup, but amended CSS for the items:

```
.FlexItems {
    border: 1px solid #ebebeb;
    background-color: #34005B;
    display: flex;
    height: 100px;
    flex: 1;
}
```

The `flex` property is actually a shorthand way of specifying three separate properties: `flex-grow`, `flex-shrink`, and `flex-basis`. The specification covers these individual properties in more detail at `http://www.w3.org/TR/css-flexbox-1/`. However, the specification recommends that authors use the `flex` shorthand property, so that's what we're rolling with here, capiche?

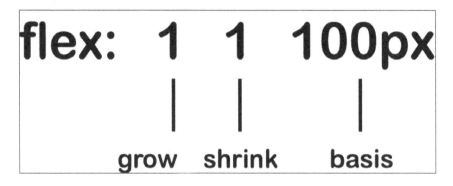

For flex-items, if a `flex` property is present (and the browser supports it), it is used to size the item rather than a width or height value (if present). Even if the width or height value is specified after the `flex` property, it will still have no effect. Let's look at what each of these values do.

- `flex-grow` (the first value you can pass to flex) is the amount, relevant to the other flex items, the flex-item can grow when free space is available

- `flex-shrink` is the amount the flex-item can shrink relevant to the other flex-items when there is not enough space available

- `flex-basis` (the final value you can pass to Flex) is the basis size the flex-item is sized to

Although it's possible to just write `flex: 1`, I recommend writing all the values into a `flex` property. I think it's clearer what you intend to happen. For example: `flex: 1 1 auto` means that the item will grow into 1 part of the available space, it will also shrink 1 part when space is lacking and the basis size for the flexing is the intrinsic width of the content (the size the content would be if flex wasn't involved).

Let's try another: `flex: 0 0 50px` means this item will neither grow nor shrink and it's basis is 50px (so it will be 50px regardless of any free space). How about flex: 2 0 50% — that's going to take two 'lots' of available space, it won't shrink and its basis size is 50%. Hopefully, these brief examples have demystified the flex property a little.

[If you set the `flex-shrink` value to zero, then the flex basis effectively behaves like a minimum width.]

You can think of the `flex` property as a way to set ratios. With each flex-item set to 1, they each take an equal amount of space:

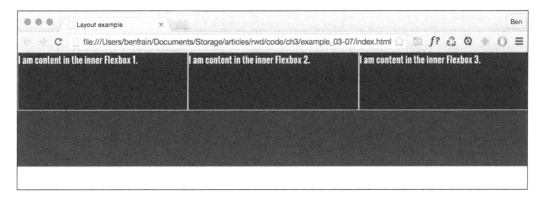

Right, so to test the theory, let's amend the HTML classes in the markup:

```
<div class="FlexWrapper">
    <div class="FlexItems FlexOne">I am content in the inner Flexbox
1.</div>
        <div class="FlexItems FlexTwo">I am content in the inner Flexbox
2.</div>
        <div class="FlexItems FlexThree">I am content in the inner Flexbox
3.</div>
</div>
```

And then here is the amended CSS:

```
.FlexItems {
    border: 1px solid #ebebeb;
    background-color: #34005B;
    display: flex;
    height: 100px;
}

.FlexOne {
    flex: 1.5 0 auto;
}

.FlexTwo,
.FlexThree {
    flex: 1 0 auto;
}
```

In this instance, FlexOne takes up 1.5 the amount of space that FlexTwo and FlexThree take up.

This shorthand syntax really becomes useful for quickly bashing out relationships between items. For example, if the request comes in, "that needs to be 1.8 times wider than the others", you could easily facilitate that request with the flex property.

Hopefully, the incredibly powerful flex property is starting to make a little sense now?

I could write chapters and chapters on Flexbox! There are so many examples we could look at. However, before we move on to the other main topic of this chapter (responsive images) there are just two more things I would like to share with you.

Simple sticky footer

Suppose you want a footer to sit at the bottom of the viewport when there is not enough content to push it there. This has always been a pain to achieve but with Flexbox it's simple. Consider this markup (which can be viewed in example_03-08):

```
<body>
    <div class="MainContent">
        Here is a bunch of text up at the top. But there isn't enough
content to push the footer to the bottom of the page.
    </div>
    <div class="Footer">
        However, thanks to flexbox, I've been put in my place.
    </div>
</body>
```

And here's the CSS:

```
html,
body {
    margin: 0;
    padding: 0;
}

html {
    height: 100%;
}

body {
    font-family: 'Oswald', sans-serif;
    color: #ebebeb;
    display: flex;
```

```
    flex-direction: column;
    min-height: 100%;
}

.MainContent {
    flex: 1;
    color: #333;
    padding: .5rem;
}

.Footer {
    background-color: violet;
    padding: .5rem;
}
```

Take a look at that in the browser and test adding more content into `.MainContentdiv`. You'll see that when there is not enough content, the footer is stuck to the bottom of the viewport. When there is, it sits below the content.

This works because our `flex` property is set to grow where space is available. As our body is a flex container of 100% minimum height, the main content can grow into all that available space. Beautiful.

Changing source order

Since the dawn of CSS, there has only been one way to switch the visual ordering of HTML elements in a web page. That was achieved by wrapping elements in something set to `display: table` and then switching the `display` property on the items within, between `display: table-caption` (puts it on top), `display: table-footer-group` (sends it to the bottom), and `display: table-header-group` (sends it to just below the item set to `display: table-caption`). However, as robust as this technique is, it was a happy accident, rather than the true intention of these settings.

However, Flexbox has visual source re-ordering built in. Let's have a look at how it works.

Consider this markup:

```
<div class="FlexWrapper">
    <div class="FlexItems FlexHeader">I am content in the Header.</
div>
    <div class="FlexItems FlexSideOne">I am content in the SideOne.</
div>
    <div class="FlexItems FlexContent">I am content in the Content.</
div>
```

```
    <div class="FlexItems FlexSideTwo">I am content in the SideTwo.</
div>
    <div class="FlexItems FlexFooter">I am content in the Footer.</
div>
</div>
```

You can see here that the third item within the wrapper has a HTML class of FlexContent — imagine that this div is going to hold the main content for the page.

OK, let's keep things simple. We will add some simple colors to more easily differentiate the sections and just get these items one under another in the same order they appear in the markup.

```
.FlexWrapper {
    background-color: indigo;
    display: flex;
    flex-direction: column;
}

.FlexItems {
    display: flex;
    align-items: center;
    min-height: 6.25rem;
    padding: 1rem;
}

.FlexHeader {
    background-color: #105B63;
}

.FlexContent {
    background-color: #FFFAD5;
}

.FlexSideOne {
    background-color: #FFD34E;
}

.FlexSideTwo {
    background-color: #DB9E36;
}

.FlexFooter {
    background-color: #BD4932;
}
```

That renders in the browser like this:

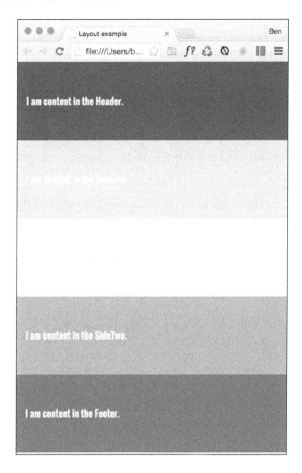

Now, suppose we want to switch the order of .FlexContent to be the first item, without touching the markup. With Flexbox it's as simple as adding a single property/value pair:

```
.FlexContent {
    background-color: #FFFAD5;
    order: -1;
}
```

The order property lets us revise the order of items within a Flexbox simply and sanely. In this example, a value of -1 means that we want it to be before all the others.

If you want to switch items around quite a bit, I'd recommend being a little more declarative and add an order number for each. This makes things a little easier to understand when you combine them with media queries.

Let's combine our new source order changing powers with some media queries to produce not just a different layout at different sizes but different ordering.

Note: you can view this finished example at example_03-09.

As it's generally considered wise to have your main content at the beginning of a document, let's revise our markup to this:

```
<div class="FlexWrapper">
    <div class="FlexItems FlexContent">I am content in the Content.</
div>
    <div class="FlexItems FlexSideOne">I am content in the SideOne.</
div>
    <div class="FlexItems FlexSideTwo">I am content in the SideTwo.</
div>
    <div class="FlexItems FlexHeader">I am content in the Header.</
div>
    <div class="FlexItems FlexFooter">I am content in the Footer.</
div>
</div>
```

First the page content, then our two sidebar areas, then the header and finally the footer. As I'll be using Flexbox, we can structure the HTML in the order that makes sense for the document, regardless of how things need to be laid out visually.

For the smallest screens (outside of any media query), I'll go with this ordering:

```
.FlexHeader {
    background-color: #105B63;
    order: 1;
}

.FlexContent {
    background-color: #FFFAD5;
    order: 2;
}

.FlexSideOne {
```

```css
    background-color: #FFD34E;
    order: 3;
}

.FlexSideTwo {
    background-color: #DB9E36;
    order: 4;
}

.FlexFooter {
    background-color: #BD4932;
    order: 5;
}
```

Which gives us this in the browser:

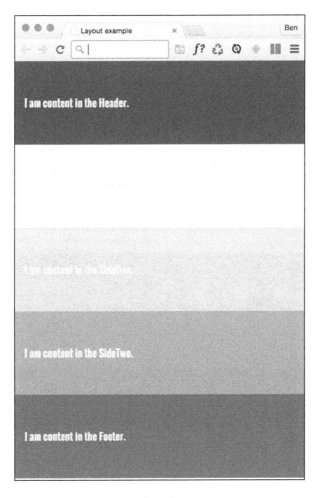

And then, at a breakpoint, I'm switching to this:

```
@media (min-width: 30rem) {
    .FlexWrapper {
        flex-flow: row wrap;
    }
    .FlexHeader {
        width: 100%;
    }
    .FlexContent {
        flex: 1;
        order: 3;
    }
    .FlexSideOne {
        width: 150px;
        order: 2;
    }
    .FlexSideTwo {
        width: 150px;
        order: 4;
    }
    .FlexFooter {
        width: 100%;
    }
}
```

Which gives us this in the browser:

In that example, the shortcut `flex-flow: row wrap` has been used. That allows the flex items to wrap onto multiple lines. It's one of the poorer supported properties, so depending upon how far back support is needed, it might be necessary to wrap the content and two side bars in another element.

Wrapping up Flexbox

There are near endless possibilities when using the Flexbox layout system and due to its inherent 'flexiness', it's a perfect match for responsive design. If you've never built anything with Flexbox before, all the new properties and values can seem a little odd and it's sometimes disconcertingly easy to achieve layouts that have previously taken far more work. To double-check implementation details against the latest version of the specification, make sure you check out `http://www.w3.org/TR/css-flexbox-1/`.

I think you'll love building things with Flexbox.

Hot on the heels of the Flexible Box Layout Module is the Grid Layout Module Level 1: `http://www.w3.org/TR/css3-grid-layout/`.

It's relatively immature compared to Flexbox (much like the early history of Flexbox, grid layout has already been through some major changes) and as such we aren't looking at it in detail here. However, it's definitely one to keep an eye on as it promises us even more layout powers.

Responsive images

Serving the appropriate image to users based upon the particulars of their device and environment has always been a tricky problem. This problem was highlighted with the advent of responsive web design, the very nature of which is to serve a single code base to each and every device.

The intrinsic problem of responsive images

As an author, you cannot know or plan for every possible device that may visit your site now or in the future. Only a browser knows the particulars of the device using it (screen size and device capabilities for example) at the moment it serves up and renders the content.

Conversely only the author (you and I) know what versions of an image we have at our disposal. For example, we may have three versions of the same image. A small, medium, and large: each with increasing dimensions to cover off a host of screen size and density eventualities. The browser does not know this. We have to tell it.

To summarize the conundrum, we have halve of the solution in that we know what images we have, and the browser has the other halve of the solution in that the browser knows what device is visiting the site and what the most appropriate image dimensions and resolution would be.

How can we tell the browser what images we have at our disposal so that it may chose the most appropriate one for the user?

In the first few years of responsive web design, there was no specified way. Thankfully, now we have the Embedded Content specification: `https://html.spec.whatwg.org/multipage/embedded-content.html`.

The Embedded Content specification describes ways to deal with the simple resolution switching of images (to facilitate a user on a higher resolution screen receiving a higher resolution version of images) and 'art direction' situations, for when authors want users to see a totally different image, depending upon a number of device characteristics (think media queries).

Demonstrating responsive image examples is tricky. It's not possible to appreciate on a single screen the different images that could be loaded with a particular syntax or technique. Therefore, the examples that follow will be mainly code and you'll just have to trust me that's it's going to produce the result you need in supporting browsers.

Let's look at the two most common scenarios you likely need responsive images for. These are switching an image when a different resolution is needed, and changing an image entirely depending upon the available viewport space.

Simple resolution switching with srcset

Let's suppose you have three versions of an image. They all look the same except one is a smaller size or resolution intended for smaller viewports, another caters for medium size viewports, and finally a larger version covers off every other viewport. Here is how we can let the browser know we have these three versions available.

```
<img src="scones_small.jpg" srcset="scones_medium.jpg 1.5x, scones_
large.jpg 2x" alt="Scones taste amazing">
```

This is about as simple as things get with responsive images, so let's ensure that syntax makes perfect sense.

First of all, the `src` attribute, which you will already be familiar with, has a dual role here; it's specifying the small 1x version of the image and it also acts as a fallback image if the browser doesn't support the `srcset` attribute. That's why we are using it for the small image. This way, older browsers that will ignore the `srcset` information will get the smallest and best performing image possible.

For browsers that understand `srcset`, with that attribute, we provide a comma-separated list of images that the browser can choose from. After the image name (such as `scones_medium.jpg`) we issue a simple resolution hint. In this example 1.5x and 2x have been used but any integer would be valid. For example, 3x or 4x would work too (providing you can find a suitably high resolution screen).

However, there is an issue here; a device with a 1440px wide, 1x screen will get the same image as a 480px wide, 3x screen. That may or may not be the desired effect.

Advanced switching with srcset and sizes

Let's consider another situation. In a responsive web design, it wouldn't be uncommon for an image to be the full viewport width on smaller viewports, but only half the width of the viewport at larger sizes. The main example in *Chapter 1*, *The Essentials of Responsive Web Design*, was a typical example of this. Here's how we can communicate these intentions to the browser:

```
<img srcset="scones-small.jpg 450w, scones-medium.jpg 900w"
sizes="(min-width: 17em) 100vw, (min-width: 40em) 50vw" src="scones-
small.jpg" alt="Scones">
```

Inside the image tag we are utilizing `srcset` again. However, this time, after specifying the images we are adding a value with a w suffix. This tells the browser how wide the image is. In our example we have a 450px wide image (called `scones-small.jpg`) and a 900px wide image (called `scones-medium.jpg`). It's important to note this w suffixed value isn't a 'real' size. It's merely an indication to the browser, roughly equivalent to the width in 'CSS pixels'.

 What exactly defines a pixel in CSS? I wondered that myself. Then I found the explanation at http://www.w3.org/TR/ css3-values/ and wished I hadn't wondered.

This w suffixed value makes more sense when we factor in the `sizes` attribute. The `sizes` attribute allows us to communicate the intentions for our images to the browser. In our preceding example, the first value is equivalent to, "for devices that are at least 17em wide, I intend the image to be shown around 100vw wide".

If some of the units used, such as vh (where 1vh is equal to 1% of the viewport height) and vw (where 1vw is equal to 1% of the viewport width) don't make sense, be sure to read *Chapter 5, CSS3 – Selectors, Typography, Color Modes, and New Features.*

The second part is effectively, "Hi browser, for devices that are at least 40em wide, I only intend the image to be shown at 50vw". That may seem a little redundant until you factor in DPI (or DPR for Device Pixel Ratio). For example, on a 320px wide device with a 2x resolution (effectively requiring a 640px wide image if shown at full width) the browser might decide the 900px wide image is actually a better match as it's the first option it has for an image that would be big enough to fulfill the required size.

Did you say the browser 'might' pick one image over another?

An important thing to remember is that the `sizes` attributes are merely hints to the browser. That doesn't necessarily ensure that the browser will always obey. This is a good thing. Trust me, it really is. It means that in future, if there is a reliable way for browsers to ascertain network conditions, it may choose to serve one image over another because it knows things at that point that we can't possibly know at this point as the author. Perhaps a user has a setting on their device to 'only download 1x images' or 'only download 2x images'; in these scenarios the browser can make the best call.

The alternative to the browser deciding is to use the `picture` element. Using this element ensures that the browser serves up the exact image you asked for. Let's take a look at how it works.

Art direction with the picture element

The final scenario you may find yourself in is one in which you have different images that are applicable at different viewport sizes. For example, consider our cake based example again from *Chapter 1, The Essentials of Responsive Web Design*. Maybe on the smallest screens we would like a close up of the scone with a generous helping of jam and cream on top. For larger screens, perhaps we have a wider image we would like to use. Perhaps it's a wide shot of a table loaded up with all manner of cakes. Finally, for larger viewports still, perhaps we want to see the exterior of a cake shop on a village street with people sat outside eating cakes and drinking tea (I know, sounds like nirvana, right?). We need three different images that are most appropriate at different viewport ranges. Here is how we could solve this with `picture`:

```
<picture>
    <source media="(min-width: 30em)" srcset="cake-table.jpg">
```

```
    <source media="(min-width: 60em)" srcset="cake-shop.jpg">
    <img src="scones.jpg" alt="One way or another, you WILL get
cake.">
</picture>
```

First of all, be aware that when you use the `picture` element, it is merely a wrapper to facilitate other images making their way to the `img` tag within. If you want to style the images in any way, it's the `img` that should get your attention.

Secondly, the `srcset` attribute here works exactly the same as the previous example.

Thirdly, the `img` tag provides your fallback image and also the image that will be displayed if a browser understands picture but none of the media definitions match. Just to be crystal clear; do not omit the `img` tag from within a `picture` element or things won't end well.

The key difference with picture is that we have a `source` tag. Here we can use media query style expressions to explicitly tell the browser which asset to use in a matching situation. For example, our first one in the preceding example is telling the browser, "Hey you, if the screen is at least 30em wide, load in the `cake-table.jpg` image instead". As long as conditions match, the browser will dutifully obey.

Facilitate new-fangled image formats

As a bonus, `picture` also facilitates us providing alternate formats of an image. 'WebP' (more info at `https://developers.google.com/speed/webp/`) is a newer format that plenty of browsers lack support for (`http://caniuse.com/`). For those that do, we can offer a file in that format and a more common format for those that don't:

```
<picture>
    <source type="image/webp" srcset="scones-baby-yeah.webp">
    <img src="scones-baby-yeah.jpg" alt="Again, you WILL eat cake.">
</picture>
```

Hopefully this is now a little more straightforward. Instead of the `media` attribute, we are using `type` (we will do more with the type attribute in *Chapter 4*, *HTML5 for Responsive Web Designs*), which, although more typically used to specify video sources (possible video source types can be found at `https://html.spec.whatwg. org/multipage/embedded-content.html`), allows us here to define WebP as the preferred image format. If the browser can display it, it will, otherwise it will grab the default one in the `img` tag.

There are plenty of older browsers that will never be able to make use of the official W3C responsive images. Unless there is a specific reason not to, my advice would be to allow the built-in fallback capabilities do their thing. Use a sensibly sized fallback image to provide them with a good experience and allow more capable devices to enjoy an enhanced experience.

Summary

We've covered a lot of ground in this chapter. We have spent considerable time getting acquainted with Flexbox, the most recent, powerful, and now well-supported layout technique. We have also covered how we can serve up any number of alternative images to our users depending upon the problems we need to solve. By making use of `srcset`, `sizes`, and `picture`, our users should always get the most appropriate image for their needs, both now and in the future.

So far we've looked at lots of CSS and some of its emerging possibilities and capabilities, but only with responsive images have we looked at more modern markup. Let's address that issue next.

The next chapter is going to be all about HTML5. What it offers, what's changed from the previous version, and for the most part, how we can make best use of its new semantic elements to create cleaner, more meaningful HTML documents.

4

HTML5 for Responsive Web Designs

If you are looking for guidance on using the HTML5 **application programming interfaces** (**APIs**), I'm going to paraphrase a line from a great Western movie and say, "I'm not your Huckleberry".

What I would like to look at with you is the 'vocabulary' part of HTML5; its semantics. More succinctly, the way we can use the new elements of HTML5 to describe the content we place in markup. The majority of content in this chapter is not specific to a responsive web design. However, HTML is the very foundation upon which all web-based designs and applications are built. Who doesn't want to build upon the strongest possible foundation?

You might be wondering 'what is HTML5 anyway?' In which case I would tell you that HTML5 is simply the description given to the latest version of HTML, the language of tags we use to build web pages. HTML itself is a constantly evolving standard, with the prior major version being 4.01.

For a little more background on the versions and timeline of HTML's evolution, you can read the Wikipedia entry at `http://en.wikipedia.org/wiki/HTML#HTML_versions_timeline`.

 HTML5 is now a recommendation from the W3C. You can read the specification at `http://www.w3.org/TR/html5/`.

The topics we will cover in this chapter are:

- How well supported is HTML5?
- Starting an HTML5 page the right way
- Easy-going HTML5
- New semantic elements
- Text-level semantics
- Obsolete features
- Putting the new elements to use
- **Web Content Accessibility Guidelines** (**WCAG**) accessibility conformance and **Web Accessibility Initiative-Accessible Rich Internet Applications** (**WAI-ARIA**) for more accessible web applications
- Embedding media
- Responsive video and iFrames
- A note about 'offline first'

 HTML5 also provides specific tools for handling forms and user input. This set of features takes much of the burden away from more resource heavy technologies like JavaScript for things like form validation. However, we're going to look at HTML5 forms separately in *Chapter 9, Conquer Forms with HTML5 and CSS3*.

HTML5 markup – understood by all modern browsers

Nowadays, the majority of websites I see (and all of those I make myself) are written using HTML5, rather than the older HTML 4.01 standard.

All modern browsers understand the new semantic elements of HTML5 (the new structural elements, video, and audio tags) and even older versions of Internet Explorer (versions before Internet Explorer 9) can be served a tiny 'polyfill' to allow it to render these new elements.

What is a polyfill?

The term **polyfill** was originated by Remy Sharp as an allusion to filling the cracks in older browsers with Polyfilla (known as **Spackling Paste** in the US). Therefore, a polyfill is a JavaScript 'shim' to effectively replicate newer features in older browsers. However, it's important to be aware that polyfills add extra flab to your code. Therefore, even if you could add 15 polyfill scripts to make Internet Explorer 6 render a site identically to every other browser, it doesn't mean you necessarily should.

If you need to enable HTML5 structural elements, I'd look at Remy Sharp's original script (http://remysharp.com/2009/01/07/html5-enabling-script/) or create a custom build of Modernizr (http://modernizr.com). If Modernizr is a tool you've not come across or used, there is a whole section on it in the next chapter.

With that in mind, let's consider the start of an HTML5 page. Let's get a handle on all the opening tags and what they do.

Starting an HTML5 page the right way

Let's start right at the beginning of an HTML5 document. Screw this part up and you could spend a long time wondering why your page doesn't behave as it should. The first few lines should look something like this:

```
<!DOCTYPE html>
<html lang="en">
<head>
<meta charset=utf-8>
```

Let's go through these tags one by one. Generally, they will be the same every time you create a web page but trust me, it's worth understanding what they do.

The doctype

The doctype is a means of communicating to the browser the type of document we have. Otherwise, it wouldn't necessarily know how to use the content within it.

We opened our document with the HTML5 doctype declaration:

```
<!DOCTYPE html>
```

If you're a fan of lowercase, then `<!doctype html>` is just as good. It makes no difference.

This is a welcome change from HTML 4.01 pages. They used to start something like this:

```
<!DOCTYPE html PUBLIC "-//W3C//DTD XHTML 1.0 Transitional//EN"
"http://www.w3.org/TR/xhtml1/DTD/xhtml1-transitional.dtd">
```

What an enormous pain in the pimply rear! No wonder I used to copy and paste it!

The HTML5 `doctype` on the other hand is nice and short, just `<!DOCTYPE html>`. Interesting fact (to me anyway): it actually ended up this way as it was determined that this was the shortest method of telling a browser to render the page in "standards mode".

 Want a history lesson in what 'quirks' and 'standards' mode were? Wikipedia has you covered: `http://en.wikipedia.org/wiki/Quirks_mode`

The HTML tag and lang attribute

After the `doctype` declaration, we open the `html` tag; the root tag for our document. We also use the `lang` attribute to specify the language for the document, and then we open the `<head>` section:

```
<html lang="en">
<head>
```

Specifying alternate languages

According to the W3C specifications (`http://www.w3.org/TR/html5/dom.html#the-lang-and-xml:lang-attributes`), the `lang` attribute specifies the primary language for the element's contents and for any of the element's attributes that contain text. If you're not writing pages in English, you'd best specify the correct language code. For example, for Japanese, the HTML tag would be `<html lang="ja">`. For a full list of languages take a look at `http://www.iana.org/assignments/language-subtag-registry`.

Character encoding

Finally, we specify the character encoding. As it's a void element (cannot contain anything) it doesn't require a closing tag:

```
<meta charset="utf-8">
```

Unless you have a good reason to specify otherwise, the value for the charset is almost always utf-8. For the curious, more information on the subject can be found at http://www.w3.org/International/questions/qa-html-encoding-declarations#html5charset.

Easy-going HTML5

I remember, back in school, every so often our super-mean (but actually very good) math teacher would be away. The class would breathe a collective sigh of relief as, rather than "Mr. Mean" (names have been changed to protect the innocent), the replacement teacher was usually an easy-going and amiable man. He sat quietly and left us to get on without shouting or constant needling. He didn't insist on silence whilst we worked, he didn't much care if we adhered to the way he worked out problems, all that mattered was the answers and that we could articulate how we came to them. If HTML5 were a math teacher, it would be that easy-going supply teacher. I'll now qualify this bizarre analogy.

If you pay attention to how you write code, you'll typically use lower-case for the most part, wrap attribute values in quotation marks, and declare a "type" for scripts and style sheets. For example, perhaps you link to a style sheet like this:

```
<link href="CSS/main.css" rel="stylesheet" type="text/css" />
```

HTML5 doesn't require such precision, it's just as happy to see this:

```
<link href=CSS/main.css rel=stylesheet >
```

Did you notice that? There's no end tag/slash, there are no quotation marks around the attribute values, and there is no type declaration. However, easy going HTML5 doesn't care. The second example is just as valid as the first.

This more lax syntax applies across the whole document, not just linked assets. For example, specify a div like this if you like:

```
<div id=wrapper>
```

That's perfectly valid HTML5. The same goes for inserting an image:

```
<img SRC=frontCarousel.png aLt=frontCarousel>
```

That's also valid HTML5. No end tag/slash, no quotes, and a mix of capitalization and lower case characters. You can even omit things such as the opening `<head>` tag and the page still validates. What would XHTML 1.0 say about this?

Want a short-cut to great HTML5 code? Consider the HTML5 Boilerplate (`http://html5boilerplate.com/`). It's a pre-made "best practice" HTML5 file, including essential styles, polyfills, and optional tools such as Modernizr. You can pick up lots of great tips just by viewing the code and it's also possible to custom build the template to match your specific needs. Highly recommended!

A sensible approach to HTML5 markup

Personally, I like writing my markup 'XHTML' style. That means closing tags, quoting attribute values, and adhering to a consistent letter case. One could argue that ditching some of these practices would save a few bytes of data but that's what tools are for (any needless characters/data could be stripped if needed). I want my markup to be as legible as possible and I would encourage others to do the same. I'm of the opinion that clarity in code should trump brevity.

When writing HTML5 documents therefore, I think you can write clean and legible code while still embracing the economies afforded by HTML5. To exemplify, for a CSS link, I'd go with the following:

```
<link href="CSS/main.css" rel="stylesheet"/>
```

I've kept the closing tag and the quotation marks but omitted the `type` attribute. The point to make here is that you can find a level you're happy with yourself. HTML5 won't be shouting at you, flagging up your markup in front of the class and standing you in a corner with a dunces hat on for not validating (was it just my school that did that?). However you want to write your markup is just fine.

Who am I kidding? I want you to know right now that if you're writing your code without quoting attribute values and closing your tags, I am silently judging you.

Despite HTML5's looser syntax, it's always worth checking whether your markup is valid. Valid markup is more accessible markup. The W3C validator was created for just this reason: `http://validator.w3.org/`

Enough of me berating writers of 'hipster' style markup. Let's look at some more benefits of HTML5.

All hail the mighty `<a>` tag

A huge economy in HTML5 is that we can now wrap multiple elements in an `<a>` tag (woohoo! About time, right?). Previously, if you wanted your markup to validate, it was necessary to wrap each element in its own `<a>` tag. For example, look at the following HTML 4.01 code:

```
<h2><a href="index.html">The home page</a></h2>
<p><a href="index.html">This paragraph also links to the home page</a></p>
<a href="index.html"><img src="home-image.png" alt="home-slice" /></a>
```

With HTML5, we can ditch all the individual `<a>` tags and instead wrap the group with one:

```
<a href="index.html">
  <h2>The home page</h2>
  <p>This paragraph also links to the home page</p>
  <img src="home-image.png" alt="home-slice" />
</a>
```

The only limitations to keep in mind are that, understandably, you can't wrap one `<a>` tag within another `<a>` tag (because, like, duh) or another interactive element such as a `button` (because like, double duh!) and you can't wrap a form in an `<a>` tag either (because like, oh, you get the idea).

New semantic elements in HTML5

If I check the definition of the word 'semantics' in the dictionary of OS X, it is defined as:

> *"the branch of linguistics and logic concerned with meaning"*.

For our purposes, semantics is the process of giving our markup meaning. Why is this important? Glad you asked.

Most websites follow fairly standard structural conventions; typical areas include a header, a footer, a sidebar, a navigation bar, and so on. As web authors we will often name the divs we use to more clearly designate these areas (for example, `class="Header"`). However, as far as the code itself goes, any user agent (web browser, screen reader, search engine crawler, and so on) looking at it couldn't say for sure what the purpose of each of these `div` elements is. Users of assistive technology would also find it difficult to differentiate one `div` from another. HTML5 aims to solve that problem with new semantic elements.

For the full list of HTML5 elements, get yourself (very) comfy and point your browser at `http://www.w3.org/TR/html5/semantics.html#semantics`.

We won't cover every one of the new elements here, merely those I feel are the most beneficial or interesting in day-to-day responsive web design use. Let's dig in.

The <main> element

For a long time, HTML5 had no element to demarcate the main content of a page. Within the body of a web page, this would be the element that contains the main block of content.

At first, it was argued that the content that wasn't inside one of the other new semantic HTML5 elements would, by negation, be the main content. Thankfully, the spec changed and we now have a more declarative way to group the main content; the aptly named `<main>` tag.

Whether you're wrapping the main content of a page or the main section of a web-based application, the `main` element is what you should be grouping it all with. Here's a particularly useful line from the specification:

> *"The main content area of a document includes content that is unique to that document and excludes content that is repeated across a set of documents such as site navigation links, copyright information, site logos and banners and search forms (unless the document or applications main function is that of a search form)."*

It's also worth noting that there shouldn't be more than one main on each page (after all, you can't have two main pieces of content) and it shouldn't be used as a descendent as some of the other semantic HTML5 elements such as `article`, `aside`, `header`, `footer`, `nav`, or `header`. They can live within a main element however.

Read the official line on the main element at: `http://www.w3.org/TR/html5/grouping-content.html#the-main-element`

The \<section> element

The \<section> element is used to define a generic section of a document or application. For example, you may choose to create sections round your content; one section for contact information, another section for news feeds, and so on. It's important to understand that it isn't intended for styling purposes. If you need to wrap an element merely to style it, you should continue to use a div as you would have before.

When working on web-based applications I tend to use section as the wrapping element for visual components. It provides a simple way to see the beginning and end of components in the markup.

You can also qualify for yourself whether you should be using a section based upon whether the content you are sectioning has a natural heading within it (for example an h1). If it doesn't, it's likely you'd be better off opting for a div.

To find out what the W3C HTML5 specification says about \<section> go to the following URL:

http://www.w3.org/TR/html5/sections.html#the-section-element

The \<nav> element

The \<nav> element is used to wrap major navigational links to other pages or parts within the same page. It isn't strictly intended for use in footers (although it can be) and the like, where groups of links to other pages are common.

If you usually markup your navigational elements with an un-ordered list (\<ul>) and a bunch of list tags (li), you may be better served with a nav and a number of nested a tags instead.

To find out what the W3C HTML5 specification says about \<nav> go to the following URL:

http://www.w3.org/TR/html5/sections.html#the-nav-element

The <article> element

The <article> element, alongside <section> can easily lead to confusion. I certainly had to read and re-read the specifications of each before it sank in. Here's my re-iteration of the specification. The <article> element is used to wrap a self-contained piece of content. When structuring a page, ask whether the content you're intending to use within a <article> tag could be taken as a whole lump and pasted onto a different site and still make complete sense? Another way to think about it is, would the content that you are considering wrapping in an <article> actually constitute a separate article in a RSS feed? Obvious examples of content that should be wrapped with an <article> element would be blog posts or news stories. Be aware that if nesting <article> elements, it is presumed that the nested <article> elements are principally related to the outer article.

 To see what the W3C HTML5 specification says about <article> visit http://www.w3.org/TR/html5/sections.html#the-article-element.

The <aside> element

The <aside> element is used for content that is tangentially related to the content around it. In practical terms, I often use it for sidebars (when it contains suitable content). It's also considered suitable for pull quotes, advertising, and groups of navigation elements. Basically anything not directly related to the main content would work well in an aside. If it was an e-commerce site, I'd consider areas like 'customers who bought this also bought' as prime candidates for an <aside>.

 For more on what the W3C HTML5 specification says about <aside> visit http://www.w3.org/TR/html5/sections.html#the-aside-element.

The <figure> and <figcaption> elements

The specification relates that the figure element:

> "...can thus be used to annotate illustrations, diagrams, photos, code listings, etc."

Here's how we could use it to revise a portion of markup from the first chapter:

```
<figure class="MoneyShot">
    <img class="MoneyShotImg" src="img/scones.jpg" alt="Incredible
scones" />
    <figcaption class="ImageCaption">Incredible scones, picture from
Wikipedia</figcaption>
</figure>
```

You can see that the `<figure>` element is used to wrap this little self-contained block. Inside, the `<figcaption>` is used to provide a caption for the parent `<figure>` element.

It's perfect when images or code need a little caption alongside (that wouldn't be suitable in the main text of the content).

> The specification for the `figure` element can be found at `http://www.w3.org/TR/html5/grouping-content.html#the-figure-element`.
>
> The specification for the `figcaption` is at `http://www.w3.org/TR/html5/grouping-content.html#the-figcaption-element`.

The <details> and <summary> elements

How many times have you wanted to create a simple open and close 'widget' on your page? A piece of summary text that when clicked, opens a panel with additional information. HTML5 facilitates this pattern with the `details` and `summary` elements. Consider this markup (you can open `example3.html` from this chapter's code to play with it for yourself):

```
<details>
    <summary>I ate 15 scones in one day</summary>
    <p>Of course I didn't. It would probably kill me if I did. What a
way to go. Mmmmmm, scones!</p>
</details>
```

Opening this in Chrome, with no added styling, shows only the summary text by default:

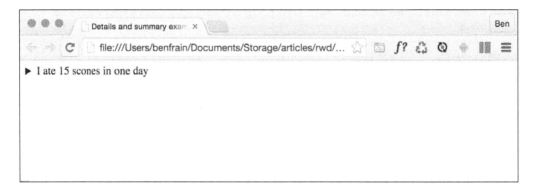

Clicking anywhere on the summary text opens the panel. Clicking it again toggles it shut. If you want the panel open by default you can add the open attribute to the details element:

```
<details open>
    <summary>I ate 15 scones in one day</summary>
    <p>Of course I didn't. It would probably kill me if I did. What a
way to go. Mmmmmm, scones!</p>
</details>
```

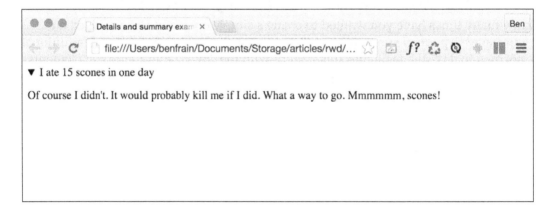

Supporting browsers typically add some default styling to indicate the panel can be opened. Here in Chrome (and also Safari) that's a dark disclosure triangle. To disable this, you need to use a WebKit specific proprietary pseudo selector:

```
summary::-webkit-details-marker {
    display: none;
}
```

You can of course use that same selector to style the marker differently.

Currently, there is no way of animating the open and close. Neither is there a (non JavaScript) way of toggling other details panels closed (at the same level) when a different one is open. I'm not sure either of these desires will (or should) ever be addressed. You should think of it more as a way to facilitate what you would have done with a `display: none;` toggle with the help of JavaScript.

Sadly, as I write this (mid 2015), there is no support for this element in Firefox or Internet Explorer (they just render the two elements as inline elements). Polyfills exist (`https://mathiasbynens.be/notes/html5-details-jquery`) and hopefully will be fully implemented soon.

The <header> element

Practically, the `<header>` element can be used for the "masthead" area of a site's header. It can also be used as an introduction to other content such as a section within an `<article>` element. You can use it as many times on the same page as needed (you could have a `<header>` inside every `<section>` on your page for example).

> This is what the W3C HTML5 specification says about `<header>`:
> `http://www.w3.org/TR/html5/sections.html#the-header-element`

The <footer> element

The `<footer>` element should be used to contain information about the section it sits within. It might contain links to other documents or copyright information for example. Like the `<header>` it can be used multiple times within a page if needed. For example, it could be used for the footer of a blog but also a `footer` section within a blog post article. However, the specification explains that contact information for the author of a blog post should instead be wrapped by an `<address>` element.

> See what the W3C HTML5 specification says about `<footer>`:
> `http://www.w3.org/TR/html5/sections.html#the-footer-element`

The <address> element

The <address> element is to be used explicitly for marking up contact information for its nearest <article> or <body> ancestor. To confuse matters, keep in mind that it isn't to be used for postal addresses and the like (unless they are indeed the contact addresses for the content in question). Instead postal addresses and other arbitrary contact information should be wrapped in good ol' <p> tags.

I'm not a fan of the <address> element as in my experience it would be far more useful to markup a physical address in its own element, but that's a personal gripe. Hopefully it makes more sense to you.

For more on what the W3C HTML5 specification says about <address> check out:

http://www.w3.org/TR/html5/sections.html#the-address-element

A note on h1-h6 elements

Something that I hadn't realized until very recently is that using h1-h6 tags to markup headings and sub-headings is discouraged. I'm talking about this kind of thing:

```
<h1>Scones:</h1>
<h2>The most resplendent of snacks</h2>
```

Here's a quote from the HTML5 specification:

h1–h6 elements must not be used to markup subheadings, subtitles, alternative titles and taglines unless intended to be the heading for a new section or subsection.

That's certainly one of the less ambiguous sentences in the specification! Ooops!

So, how should we author such eventualities? The specification actually has a whole section, (http://www.w3.org/TR/html5/common-idioms.html#common-idioms) dedicated to this. Personally, I preferred the old <hgroup> element but sadly that ship has sailed (more information in the *Obsolete HTML features* section). So, to follow the advice of the specification, our prior example could be rewritten as:

```
<h1>Scones:</h1>
<p>The most resplendent of snacks</p>
```

HTML5 text-level semantics

Besides the structural and grouping elements we've looked at, HTML5 also revises a few tags that used to be referred to as inline elements. The HTML5 specification now refers to these tags as text-level semantics (`http://www.w3.org/TR/html5/text-level-semantics.html#text-level-semantics`). Let's take a look at a few common examples.

The <b> element

Historically, the `<b>` element meant "make this bold" (`http://www.w3.org/TR/html4/present/graphics.html#edef-B`). This was from back in the day when stylistic choices were part of the markup. However, you can now officially use it merely as a styling hook in CSS as the HTML5 specification now declares that `<b>` is:

> *"The b element represents a span of text to which attention is being drawn for utilitarian purposes without conveying any extra importance and with no implication of an alternate voice or mood, such as key words in a document abstract, product names in a review, actionable words in interactive text-driven software, or an article lede."*

Although no specific meaning is now attached to it, as it's text level, it's not intended to be used to surround large groups of markup, use a `div` for that. You should also be aware that because it was historically used to bold text, you'll typically have to reset the font-weight in CSS if you want content within a `<b>` tag to not appear bold.

The <em> element

OK, hands up, I've often used `<em>` merely as a styling hook too. I need to mend my ways, as in HTML5:

The `em` element represents stress emphasis of its contents.

Therefore, unless you actually want the enclosed contents to be emphasized, consider using a `<b>` tag or, where relevant, an `<i>` tag instead.

The <i> element

The HTML5 specification describes the `<i>` as:

> *"...a span of text in an alternate voice or mood, or otherwise offset from the normal prose in a manner indicating a different quality of text."*

Suffice it to say, it's not to be used to merely italicize something. For example, we could use it to markup the odd name in this line of text:

```
<p>However, discussion on the hgroup element is now frustraneous as
it's now gone the way of the <i>Raphus cucullatus</i>.</p>
```

 There are plenty of other text-level semantic tags in HTML5. For the full run down, take a look at the relevant section of the specification at the following URL:

```
http://www.w3.org/TR/html5/text-level-semantics.
html#text-level-semantics
```

Obsolete HTML features

Besides things such as the language attributes in script links, there are some further parts of HTML you may be used to using that are now considered "obsolete" in HTML5. It's important to be aware that there are two camps of obsolete features in HTML5 — conforming and non-conforming. Conforming features will still work but will generate warnings in validators. Realistically, avoid them if you can but they aren't going to make the sky fall down if you do use them. Non-conforming features might still render in certain browsers but if you use them, you are considered very, very naughty and you might not get a treat at the weekend!

In terms of obsolete and non-conforming features, there is quite a raft. I'll confess that many I have never used (some I've never even seen!). It's possible you may experience a similar reaction. However, if you're curious, you can find the full list of obsolete and non-conforming features at `http://www.w3.org/TR/html5/obsolete.html`. Notable obsolete and non-conforming features are `strike`, `center`, `font`, `acronym`, `frame`, and `frameset`.

There are also features that were present in earlier drafts of HTML5 which have now been dropped. `hgroup` is one such example. The tag was originally proposed to wrap groups of headings; an `h1` for a title and a `h2` for a sub-title might have been wrapped in a `hgroup` element. However, discussion on the `hgroup` element is now frustraneous as it's now gone the way of the Raphus cucullatus (go on, Google it, you know you want to).

Putting HTML5 elements to use

It's time to practice using some of the elements we have just looked at. Let's revisit the example from *Chapter 1*, *The Essentials of Responsive Web Design*. If we compare the markup below to the original markup in *Chapter 1*, *The Essentials of Responsive Web Design*, (remember, you can download all the examples from the `http://rwd.education` website, or from the GitHub repo) you can see where the new elements we've looked at have been employed below.

```
<article>
  <header class="Header">
    <a href="/" class="LogoWrapper"><img src="img/SOC-Logo.png"
alt="Scone O'Clock logo" /></a>
    <h1 class="Strap">Scones: the most resplendent of snacks</h1>
  </header>
  <section class="IntroWrapper">
    <p class="IntroText">Occasionally maligned and misunderstood; the
scone is a quintessentially British classic.</p>
    <figure class="MoneyShot">
      <img class="MoneyShotImg" src="img/scones.jpg" alt="Incredible
scones" />
      <figcaption class="ImageCaption">Incredible scones, picture from
Wikipedia</figcaption>
    </figure>
  </section>
  <p>Recipe and serving suggestions follow.</p>
  <section class="Ingredients">
    <h3 class="SubHeader">Ingredients</h3>
  </section>
  <section class="HowToMake">
    <h3 class="SubHeader">Method</h3>
  </section>
  <footer>
    Made for the book, <a href="http://rwd.education">'Resonsive
web design with HTML5 and CSS3'</a> by <address><a href="http://
benfrain">Ben Frain</a></address>
  </footer>
</article>
```

Applying common sense to your element selection

I've removed a good portion of the inner content so we can concentrate on the structure. Hopefully you will agree that it's easy to discern different sections of markup from one another. However, at this point I'd also like to offer some pragmatic advice; it isn't the end of the world if you don't always pick the correct element for every single given situation. For example, whether or not I used a <section> or <div> in the preceding example is of little real consequence. If we use an <em> when we should actually be using an <i>, I certainly don't feel it's a crime against humanity; the folks at the W3C won't hunt you down and feather and tar you for making the wrong choice. Just apply a little common sense. That said, if you can use elements like the <header> and <footer> when relevant, there are inherent accessibility benefits in doing so.

WCAG and WAI-ARIA for more accessible web applications

Even since writing *Responsive Web Design with HTML5 and CSS3 - First Edition, Packt Publishing* from 2011 to 2012, the W3C has made strides in making it easier for authors to write more accessible web pages.

WCAG

The WCAG exists to provide:

> *"a single shared standard for web content accessibility that meets the needs of individuals, organizations, and governments internationally."*

When it comes to more pedestrian web pages (as opposed to single page web applications and the like) it makes sense to concentrate on the WCAG guidelines. They offer a number of (mostly common sense) guidelines for how to ensure your web content is accessible. Each recommendation is rated as a conformance level: A, AA, or AAA. For more on these conformance levels look at http://www.w3.org/TR/UNDERSTANDING-WCAG20/conformance.html#uc-levels-head.

You'll probably find that you are already adhering to many of the guidelines, like providing alternative text for images for example. However, you can get a brief run-down of the guidelines at http://www.w3.org/WAI/WCAG20/glance/Overview.html and then build your own custom quick reference list of checks at http://www.w3.org/WAI/WCAG20/quickref/.

I'd encourage everyone to spend an hour or two looking down the list. Many of the guidelines are simple to implement and offer real benefits to users.

WAI-ARIA

The aim of WAI-ARIA is principally to solve the problem of making dynamic content on a web page accessible. It provides a means of describing roles, states, and properties for custom widgets (dynamic sections in web applications) so that they are recognizable and usable by assistive technology users.

For example, if an on-screen widget displays a constantly updating stock price, how would a blind user accessing the page know that? WAI-ARIA attempts to solve these very problems.

Don't use roles for semantic elements

It used to be advisable to add 'landmark' roles to headers and footers like this:

```
<header role="banner">A header with ARIA landmark banner role</header>
```

However, this is now considered surplus to requirements. If you look at the specifications for any of the elements listed earlier there is a dedicated *Allowed ARIA role attributes* section. Here is the relevant explanation from the section element as an example:

"Allowed ARIA role attribute values:

region role (default - do not set), alert, alertdialog, application, contentinfo, dialog, document, log, main, marquee, presentation, search or status."

The key part there being 'role (default - do not set)'. This means that explicitly adding an ARIA role to the element is pointless as it is implied by the element itself. A note in the specification now makes this clear:

"In the majority of cases setting an ARIA role and/or aria- attribute that matches the default implicit ARIA semantics is unnecessary and not recommended as these properties are already set by the browser."*

If you only remember one thing

The easiest thing you can do to aid assistive technologies is to use the correct elements where possible. A `header` element is going to be far more useful than `div class="Header"`. Similarly, if you have a button on your page, use the `<button>` element (rather than a `span` or other element styled to look like a `button`). I accept that the `button` element doesn't always allow exact styling (it doesn't like being set to `display: table-cell` or `display: flex` for example) and in those instances at least choose the next best thing; usually an `<a>` tag.

Taking ARIA further

ARIA isn't limited to landmark roles only. To take things further, a full list of the roles and a succinct description of their usage suitability is available at `http://www.w3.org/TR/wai-aria/roles`.

For a lighter take on the subject, I'd also recommend Heydon Pickering's book, *Apps For All: Coding Accessible Web Applications* (available at `https://shop.smashingmagazine.com/products/apps-for-all-coding-accessible-web-applications`).

Test your designs for free with non-visual desktop access (NVDA)

If you develop on the Windows platform and you'd like to test your ARIA enhanced designs on a screen reader, you can do so for free with NVDA. You can get it at the following URL:

`http://www.nvda-project.org/`

Google now also ships the free 'Accessibility Developer Tools' for the Chrome browser (available cross-platform); well worth checking out.

There's also a growing number of tools that help quickly test your own designs against things like color blindness. For example, `https://michelf.ca/projects/sim-daltonism/` is a Mac app that lets you switch color blindness types and see a preview in a floating palette.

Finally, OS X also includes VoiceOver utility for testing your web pages.

Hopefully, this brief introduction to WAI-ARIA and WCAG has given you enough information to think a little more about how to approach supporting assistive technologies. Perhaps adding assistive technology support to your next HTML5 project will be easier than you think.

As a final resource for all things accessibility, there are handy links and advice galore on the A11Y project home page at `http://a11yproject.com/`.

Embedding media in HTML5

For many, HTML5 first entered their vocabulary when Apple refused to add support for Flash in their iOS devices. Flash had gained market dominance (some would argue market stranglehold) as the plugin of choice to serve up video through a web browser. However, rather than using Adobe's proprietary technology, Apple decided to rely on HTML5 instead to handle rich media rendering. While HTML5 was making good headway in this area anyway, Apple's public support of HTML5 gave it a major leg up and helped its media tools gain greater traction in the wider community.

As you might imagine, Internet Explorer 8 and lower versions don't support HTML5 video and audio. Most other modern browsers (Firefox 3.5+, Chrome 4+, Safari 4, Opera 10.5+, Internet Explorer 9+, iOS 3.2+, Opera Mobile 11+, Android 2.3+) handle it just fine.

Adding video and audio the HTML5 way

Video and audio in HTML5 is easy. The only real difficulty with HTML5 media used to be listing out alternate source formats for media (as different browsers supported different file formats). Nowadays, MP4 is ubiquitous across desktop and mobile platforms, making the inclusion of media in your web pages via HTML5 a breeze. Here's a 'simple as can be' example of how to link to a video file in your page:

```
<video src="myVideo.mp4"></video>
```

HTML5 allows a single `<video></video>` tag (or `<audio></audio>` for audio) to do all the heavy lifting. It's also possible to insert text between the opening and closing tag to inform users when there is a problem. There are also additional attributes you'd ordinarily want to add, such as the `height` and `width`. Let's add these in:

```
<video src="myVideo.mp4" width="640" height="480">What, do you mean
you don't understand HTML5?</video>
```

Now, if we add the preceding code snippet into our page and look at it in Safari, it will appear but there will be no controls for playback. To get the default playback controls we need to add the `controls` attribute. We could also add the `autoplay` attribute (not recommended — it's common knowledge that everyone hates videos that auto-play). This is demonstrated in the following code snippet:

```
<video src="myVideo.mp4" width="640" height="480" controls autoplay>
What, do you mean you don't understand HTML5?</video>
```

The result of the preceding code snippet is shown in the following screenshot:

Further attributes include `preload` to control pre-loading of media (early HTML5 adopters should note that preload replaces autobuffer), `loop` to repeat the video, and `poster` to define a poster frame for the video. This is useful if there's likely to be a delay in the video playing (or buffering is likely to take some time). To use an attribute, simply add it to the tag. Here's an example including all these attributes:

```
<video src="myVideo.mp4" width="640" height="480" controls autoplay
preload="auto" loop poster="myVideoPoster.png">What, do you mean you
don't understand HTML5?</video>
```

Fallback capability for older browsers

The `<source>` tag enables us to provide fallbacks, as needed. For example, alongside providing an MP4 version of the video, if we wanted to ensure a suitable fallback for Internet Explorer 8 and lower versions, we could add a Flash fallback. Further still, if the user didn't have any suitable playback technology in the browser, we could provide download links to the files themselves. Here's an example:

```
<video width="640" height="480" controls preload="auto" loop
poster="myVideoPoster.png">
    <source src="video/myVideo.mp4" type="video/mp4">
    <object width="640" height="480" type="application/x-shockwave-
flash" data="myFlashVideo.SWF">
        <param name="movie" value="myFlashVideo.swf" />
        <param name="flashvars" value="controlbar=over&amp;image=myVideo
Poster.jpg&amp;file=myVideo.mp4" />
        <img src="myVideoPoster.png" width="640" height="480" alt="__
TITLE__"
            title="No video playback capabilities, please download the
video below" />
    </object>
    <p><b>Download Video:</b>
  MP4 Format:  <a href="myVideo.mp4">"MP4"</a>
    </p>
</video>
```

That code example and the sample video file (me appearing in the UK soap Coronation Street, back when I had hair and hopes of staring alongside DeNiro) in MP4 format are in `example2.html` of the chapter code.

Audio and video tags work almost identically

The `<audio>` tag works on the same principles with the same attributes (excluding `width`, `height`, and `poster`). The main difference between the two being the fact that `<audio>` has no playback area for visible content.

Responsive HTML5 video and iFrames

We have seen that, as ever, supporting older browsers leads to code bloat. What began with the `<video>` tag being one or two lines ended up being 10 or more lines (and an extra Flash file) just to make older versions of Internet Explorer happy! For my own part, I'm usually happy to forego the Flash fallback in pursuit of a smaller code footprint but each use-case differs.

Now, the only problem with our lovely HTML5 video implementation is it's not responsive. That's right, an example in a responsive web design with HTML5 and CSS3 book that doesn't 'respond'.

Thankfully, for HTML5 embedded video, the fix is easy. Simply remove any height and width attributes in the markup (for example, remove `width="640"` `height="480"`) and add the following in the CSS:

```
video { max-width: 100%; height: auto; }
```

However, while that works fine for files that we might be hosting locally, it doesn't solve the problem of videos embedded within an iFrame (take a bow YouTube, Vimeo, and others). The following code will add a film trailer for Midnight Run from YouTube:

```
<iframe width="960" height="720" src="https://www.youtube.com/
watch?v=B1_N28DA3gY" frameborder="0" allowfullscreen></iframe>
```

However, if you add that to a page as is, even if adding that earlier CSS rule, if the viewport is less than 960px wide, things will start to get clipped.

The easiest way to solve this problem is with a little CSS trick pioneered by Gallic CSS maestro Thierry Koblentz; essentially creating a box of the correct aspect ratio for the video it contains. I won't spoil the magician's own explanation, go take a read at http://alistapart.com/article/creating-intrinsic-ratios-for-video.

If you're feeling lazy, you don't even need to work out the aspect ratio and plug it in yourself, there's an online service that can do it for you. Just head to http://embedresponsively.com/ and paste your iFrame URL in. It will spit you out a simple chunk of code you can paste into your page. For example, our Midnight Run trailer results in this:

```
<style>.embed-container { position: relative; padding-bottom: 56.25%;
height: 0; overflow: hidden; max-width: 100%; height: auto; } .embed-
container iframe, .embed-container object, .embed-container embed {
position: absolute; top: 0; left: 0; width: 100%; height: 100%; }</
style><div class='embed-container'><iframe src='http://www.youtube.
com/embed/B1_N28DA3gY' frameborder='0' allowfullscreen></iframe></div>
```

That's all there is to it, simply add to your page and you're done: we now have a fully responsive YouTube video (note: kids, don't pay any attention to Mr. DeNiro; smoking is bad)!

A note about 'offline first'

I believe that the ideal way to build responsive web pages and web-based applications is 'offline first'. This approach means that websites and applications will continue to work and load, even without an Internet connection.

HTML5 offline web applications (`http://www.w3.org/TR/2011/WD-html5-20110525/offline.html`) were specified to meet this aim.

Although support for offline web applications is good (`http://caniuse.com/#feat=offline-apps`), sadly, it's an imperfect solution. Although it's relatively simple to set up, there are a number of limitations and pitfalls. Documenting them all here is beyond the scope of this module. Instead I would recommend reading the humorous and thorough post by Jake Archibald on the subject at `http://alistapart.com/article/application-cache-is-a-douchebag`.

I'm therefore of the opinion that while it's possible to achieve offline first experiences using offline web applications (a good tutorial of how to do so is at `http://diveintohtml5.info/offline.html`) and LocalStorage (or some combination of the two), a better solution will be with us before too long. I'm pinning my hopes on 'Service Workers' (`http://www.w3.org/TR/service-workers/`).

At the time of writing, Service Workers is still a relatively new specification but for a good overview I'd encourage you to watch this 15-minute introduction: `https://www.youtube.com/watch?v=4uQM17mFB6g`. Read this introduction `http://www.html5rocks.com/en/tutorials/service-worker/introduction/` and check for support at `https://jakearchibald.github.io/isserviceworkerready/`

I'm hopeful that if and when I come to write a newer edition of this module, we will be able to consider a full overview and implementation of this technique. Fingers crossed.

Summary

We've covered a lot in this chapter. Everything from the basics of creating a page that validates as HTML5, through to embedding rich media (video) into our markup and ensuring it behaves responsively.

Although not specific to responsive designs, we've also covered how we can write semantically rich and meaningful code and considered how we might ensure pages are meaningful and usable for users that are relying on assistive technology.

By necessity, it's been a very markup heavy chapter so let's change tack now. In the next couple of chapters we're going to embrace the power and flexibility of CSS. First up, let's look at the power of CSS level 3 and 4 selectors, new viewport relative CSS units, and capabilities such as calc and HSL color. They will all enable us to create faster, more capable, and maintainable responsive designs.

5
CSS3 – Selectors, Typography, Color Modes, and New Features

In the last few years, CSS has enjoyed a raft of new features. Some enable us to animate and transform elements, others allow us to create background images, gradients, mask and filter effects, and others still allow us to bring SVG elements to life.

We will get to all those capabilities in the next few chapters. Firstly I think it will be useful to look at some of the fundamentals that have changed in CSS in the last few years: how we select elements on the page, the units we can use to style and size our elements, and how existing (and future) pseudo-classes and pseudo-elements make CSS ever more powerful. We will also look at how we can create forks in our CSS code to facilitate the features supported in different browsers.

In this chapter, we will learn the following:

- The anatomy of a CSS rule (what defines a rule, declaration and property, and value pairs)

- Quick and handy CSS tricks for responsive designs (multiple columns, word wraps, truncation/text ellipsis, scrolling areas)

- Facilitating feature forks in CSS (how to have some rules apply to some browsers and other rules apply to others)

- How to use sub-string attribute selectors to select HTML elements

- What nth-based selectors are and how we can use them

- What pseudo classes and pseudo elements are (`:empty`, `::before`, `::after`, `:target`, `:scope`)

- The new selectors in CSS Level 4 Selectors module (`:has`)
- What CSS variables and custom properties are and how to write them
- What the CSS `calc` function is and how to use it
- Making use of viewport related units (`vh`, `vw`, `vmin`, and `vmax`)
- How to make use of web typography with `@font-face`
- RGB and HSL color modes with Alpha transparency

No one knows it all

No one can know everything. I've been working with CSS for over a decade and on a weekly basis I still discover something new in CSS (or rediscover something I'd forgotten). As such, I don't feel that trying to know every possible CSS property and value permutation is actually a worthy pursuit. Instead, I think it's more sensible to develop a good grasp of what's possible.

As such, we are going to concentrate in this chapter on some of the techniques, units, and selectors I have found most useful when building responsive web designs. I'm hoping you'll then have the requisite knowledge to solve most problems that come your way when developing a responsive web design.

Anatomy of a CSS rule

Before exploring some of what CSS3 has to offer, to prevent confusion, let's establish the terminology we use to describe a CSS rule. Consider the following example:

```
.round { /* selector */
  border-radius: 10px; /* declaration */
}
```

This rule is made up of the selector (`.round`) and then the declaration (`border-radius: 10px;`). The declaration is further defined by the property (`border-radius:`) and the value (`10px;`). Happy we're on the same page? Great, let's press on.

Remember to check support for your users

As we delve into CSS3 more and more, don't forget to visit `http://caniuse.com/`, if you ever want to know what the current level of browser support is available for a particular CSS3 or HTML5 feature. Alongside showing browser version support (searchable by feature), it also provides the most recent set of global usage statistics from `http://gs.statcounter.com/`.

Quick and useful CSS tricks

In my day-to-day work, I've found I use some CSS3 features constantly and others hardly ever. I thought it might be useful to share those I've used most often. These are CSS3 goodies that can make life easier, especially in responsive designs. They solve problems that used to be minor headaches with relative ease.

CSS multi-column layouts for responsive designs

Ever needed to make a single piece of text appear in multiple columns? You could solve the problem by splitting the content into different markup elements and then styling accordingly. However, altering markup for purely stylistic purposes is never ideal. The CSS multi-column layout specification describes how we can span one or more pieces of content across multiple columns with ease. Consider the following markup:

```
<main>
    <p>lloremipsimLoremipsum dolor sit amet, consectetur
<!-- LOTS MORE TEXT -->
</p>
    <p>lloremipsimLoremipsum dolor sit amet, consectetur
<!-- LOTS MORE TEXT -->
</p>
</main>
```

With CSS multi-columns you can make all that content flow across multiple columns in a number of ways. You could make the columns a certain column width (for example, 12em) or instead you could specify that the content needs to span a certain number of columns (for example, 3).

Let's look at the code needed to achieve each of those scenarios. For columns of a set width, use the following syntax:

```
main {
  column-width: 12em;
}
```

This will mean, no matter the viewport size, the content will span across columns that are 12em in width. Altering the viewport will adjust the number of columns displayed dynamically. You can view this in the browser by looking at example_05-01 (or at the GitHub repository: https://github.com/benfrain/rwd).

Consider how the page renders on an iPad in portrait orientation (768px wide viewport):

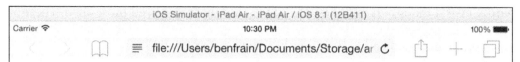

Lorem ipsum dolor sit amet, consectetur adipisicing elit, sed do eiusmod tempor incididunt ut labore et dolore magna aliqua. Ut enim ad minim veniam, quis nostrud exercitation ullamco laboris nisi ut aliquip ex ea commodo consequat. Duis aute irure dolor in reprehenderit in voluptate velit esse cillum dolore eu fugiat nulla pariatur. Excepteur sint occaecat cupidatat non proident, sunt in culpa qui officia deserunt mollit anim id est laborum. Lorem ipsum dolor sit amet, consectetur adipisicing elit, sed do eiusmod tempor incididunt ut labore et dolore magna aliqua. Ut enim ad minim veniam, quis nostrud exercitation ullamco laboris nisi ut aliquip ex ea commodo consequat. Duis aute irure dolor in reprehenderit in voluptate velit esse cillum dolore eu fugiat nulla pariatur. Excepteur sint occaecat cupidatat non proident, sunt in culpa qui officia deserunt mollit anim id est laborum. Lorem ipsum dolor sit amet, consectetur adipisicing elit, sed do eiusmod tempor ncididunt ut labore et dolore magna aliqua. Ut enim ad minim veniam, quis nostrud exercitation ullamco laboris nisi ut aliquip ex ea commodo consequat. Duis aute irure dolor in reprehenderit in voluptate velit esse cillum dolore eu fugiat nulla pariatur.Lorem ipsum dolor sit

amet, consectetur adipisicing elit, sed do eiusmod tempor incididunt ut labore et dolore magna aliqua. Ut enim ad minim veniam, quis nostrud exercitation ullamco laboris nisi ut aliquip ex ea commodo consequat. Duis aute irure dolor in reprehenderit in voluptate velit esse cillum dolore eu fugiat nulla pariatur. Excepteur sint occaecat cupidatat non proident, sunt in culpa qui officia deserunt mollit anim id est laborum. Lorem ipsum dolor sit amet, consectetur adipisicing elit, sed do eiusmod tempor incididunt ut labore et dolore magna aliqua. Ut enim ad minim veniam, quis nostrud exercitation ullamco laboris nisi ut aliquip ex ea commodo consequat. Duis aute irure dolor in reprehenderit in voluptate velit esse cillum dolore eu fugiat nulla pariatur. Excepteur sint occaecat cupidatat non proident, sunt in culpa qui officia deserunt mollit anim id est laborum. Lorem ipsum dolor sit amet, consectetur adipisicing elit, sed do eiusmod tempor ncididunt ut labore et dolore magna aliqua. Ut enim ad minim veniam, quis nostrud exercitation ullamco laboris nisi ut aliquip ex ea commodo consequat. Duis aute irure dolor in reprehenderit in voluptate velit esse cillum dolore eu fugiat nulla pariatur.Lorem ipsum dolor sit amet, consectetur adipisicing elit, sed

do eiusmod tempor incididunt ut labore et dolore magna aliqua. Ut enim ad minim veniam, quis nostrud exercitation ullamco laboris nisi ut aliquip ex ea commodo consequat. Duis aute irure dolor in reprehenderit in voluptate velit esse cillum dolore eu fugiat nulla pariatur. Excepteur sint occaecat cupidatat non proident, sunt in culpa qui officia deserunt mollit anim id est laborum. Lorem ipsum dolor sit amet, consectetur adipisicing elit, sed do eiusmod tempor incididunt ut labore et dolore magna aliqua. Ut enim ad minim veniam, quis nostrud exercitation ullamco laboris nisi ut aliquip ex ea commodo consequat. Duis aute irure dolor in reprehenderit in voluptate velit esse cillum dolore eu fugiat nulla pariatur. Excepteur sint occaecat cupidatat non proident, sunt in culpa qui officia deserunt mollit anim id est laborum. Lorem ipsum dolor sit amet, consectetur adipisicing elit, sed do eiusmod tempor ncididunt ut labore et dolore magna aliqua. Ut enim ad minim veniam, quis nostrud exercitation ullamco laboris nisi ut aliquip ex ea commodo consequat. Duis aute irure dolor in reprehenderit in voluptate velit esse cillum dolore eu fugiat nulla pariatur.

And then on Chrome in the desktop (approximately 1100px wide viewport):

Simple responsive text columns with minimum work; I like it!

Fixed columns, variable width

If you'd rather keep a fixed number of columns and vary the width, you can write a rule like the following:

```
main {
  column-count: 4;
}
```

Adding a gap and column divider

We can take things even further by adding a specified gap for the columns and a divider:

```
main {
  column-gap: 2em;
  column-rule: thin dotted #999;
  column-width: 12em;
}
```

This gives us a result like the following:

To read the specification on the CSS3 Multi-column Layout Module, visit `http://www.w3.org/TR/css3-multicol/`.

For the time being, despite being at CR status at the W3C, you'll likely still need vendor prefixes on the column declarations for maximum compatibility.

The only caveat I would place on using CSS multi-column is that for longer spans of text it can lead to a flawed user experience. In these instances the user will have to scroll up and down the page to read the columns of text, which can become a little laborious.

Word wrapping

How many times have you had to add a big URL into a tiny space and, well, despaired? Take a look at `rwd.education/code/example_05-04`. The problem can also be seen in the following screenshot; notice that the URL is breaking out of its allocated space.

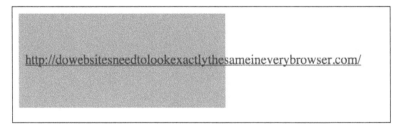

It's easy to fix this issue with a simple CSS3 declaration, which as chance would have it, also works in older versions of Internet Explorer as far back as 5.5! Just add:

```
word-wrap: break-word;
```

to the containing element, which gives an effect as shown in the following screenshot.

Hey presto, the long URL now wraps perfectly!

Text ellipsis

Text truncation used to be the sole domain of server side technology. Nowadays we can do text ellipsis/truncation with CSS alone. Let's consider how.

Consider this markup (you can view this example online at rwd.education/code/ch5/example_05-03/):

```
<p class="truncate">OK, listen up, I've figured out the key eternal
happiness. All you need to do is eat lots of scones.</p>
```

But we actually want to truncate the text at 520px wide. So it looks like this:

OK, listen up, I've figured out the key eternal happiness. All you need to do is …

Here is the CSS to make that happen:

```
.truncate {
  width: 520px;
  overflow: hidden;
  text-overflow: ellipsis;
  white-space: no-wrap;
}
```

 You can read the specification for the text-overflow property at http://dev.w3.org/csswg/css-ui-3/.

Whenever the width of the content exceeds the width defined (the width can just as happily be set as a percentage such as 100% if it's inside a flexible container) it will be truncated. The `white-space: no-wrap` property/value pair is used to ensure that the content doesn't wrap inside the surrounding element.

Creating horizontal scrolling panels

Hopefully you know the kind of thing I mean? Horizontal scrolling panels are common on the iTunes store and Apple TV for showing panels of related content (movies, albums, and so on). Where there is enough horizontal space, all the items are viewable. When space is limited (think mobile devices) the panel is scrollable from side to side.

The scrolling panels work particularly well on modern Android and iOS devices. If you have a modern iOS or Android device to hand, take a look at this next example on that, alongside a desktop browser like Safari or Chrome: `rwd.education/code/ch5/example_05-02/`.

I've created a scrolling panel of the top-grossing films of 2014. It looks something like this on an iPhone:

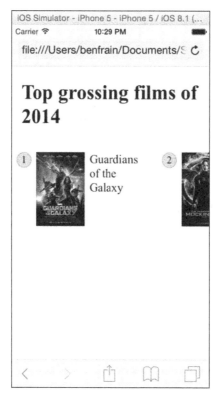

I'm actually cheating a little. The key to this technique is the `white-space` property, which has actually been around since CSS 2.1 (`http://www.w3.org/TR/CSS2/text.html`). However, I'm going to use it alongside the new Flexbox layout mechanism, so hopefully you'll indulge me regardless?

To get the basics of this technique working we just need a wrapper narrower than the sum of its contents and to set it's width to auto in the *x* axis. This way, it won't scroll if there is enough space but it will if there isn't.

```
.Scroll_Wrapper {
  width: 100%;
  white-space: nowrap;
  overflow-x: auto;
  overflow-y: hidden;
}

.Item {
  display: inline-flex;
}
```

By using `white-space: nowrap` we are saying 'do not wrap these elements when you find white space'. Then to keep everything in a single line, we set all the first children of that container to display inline. We're using `inline-flex` here but it could just as easily be inline, `inline-block`, or `inline-table`.

::before and ::after pseudo-elements

If viewing the sample code you will notice that the `::before` pseudo element is used to display the number of the item. If using pseudo-elements, remember that for `::before` or `::after` to display, they must have a content value, even if just whitespace. When these pseudo-elements are displayed, they then behave like the first and last child of that element respectively.

To make things a little more aesthetically pleasing I'm going to hide the scroll bar where I can. Unfortunately these are browser specific so you will need to add these by hand (an Autoprefixer tool won't add them as they are proprietary properties). I'm also going to add touch style inertia scrolling for WebKit browsers (typically iOS devices). Now the updated `.Scroll_Wrapper` rule looks like this:

```
.Scroll_Wrapper {
  width: 100%;
  white-space: nowrap;
  overflow-x: auto;
  overflow-y: hidden;
```

```
    /*Give us inertia style scrolling on WebKit based touch devices*/
    -webkit-overflow-scrolling: touch;
    /*Remove the scrollbars in supporting versions of IE*/
    -ms-overflow-style: none;
}

/*Stops the scrollbar appearing in WebKit browsers*/
.Scroll_Wrapper::-webkit-scrollbar {
    display: none;
}
```

Where space is limited, we get a nice scrollable horizontal panel. Otherwise, the content just fits.

There are, however, a couple of caveats to this pattern. Firstly, at the time of writing, Firefox has no property that allows you to hide the scroll bars. Secondly, older Android devices can't perform horizontal scrolling (no, really). I therefore tend to qualify this pattern with the help of feature detection. We'll look at how that works next.

Facilitating feature forks in CSS

When you're building out a responsive web design, attempting to provide a single design that works everywhere, on every device, it's a simple fact that you'll frequently encounter situations when features or techniques are not supported on certain devices. In these instances you'll likely want to create a fork in your CSS; if the browser supports a feature, provide one chunk of code, if they don't, they get different code. It's the kind of situation that gets handled by if/else or switch statements in JavaScript.

We currently have two possible approaches. One is entirely CSS based but with fewer browser implementations, and the other is only made possible with the help of a JavaScript library but enjoys far broader support. Let's consider each in turn.

Feature queries

The native solution to forking code in CSS is to use 'Feature Queries', part of the CSS Conditional Rules Module Level 3 (http://www.w3.org/TR/css3-conditional/). However, right now, CSS Conditional Rules lack support in Internet Explorer (as of version 11) and Safari (including iOS devices up to iOS 8.1) so support is hardly ubiquitous.

Feature queries follow a similar syntax to media queries. Consider this:

```
@supports (flashing-sausages: lincolnshire) {
  body {
    sausage-sound: sizzling;
    sausage-color: slighty-burnt;
    background-color: brown;
  }
}
```

Here the styles will only get applied if the browser supports the `flashing-sausages` property. I'm quite confident that no browser is ever going to support a `flashing-sausages` feature (and if they do, I want full credit) so none of the styles inside the `@supports` block will be applied.

Let's consider a more practical example. How about we use Flexbox for when browsers support it, and fallback to another layout technique when they don't. Consider this example:

```
@supports (display: flex) {
  .Item {
    display: inline-flex;
  }
}


@supports not (display: flex) {
  .Item {
    display: inline-block;
  }
}
```

Here we are defining one block of code for when the browser supports a feature, and another lot for when it doesn't. This pattern is fine if the browser supports `@supports` (yes, I realise that is confusing) but if it doesn't, it won't apply any of those styles.

If you want to cover off devices that don't support `@supports`, you're better off writing your default declarations first and then your `@supports` specific one after, so that the prior rule will be overruled if support for `@support` exists, and the `@support` block will be ignored if the browser doesn't support it. Our prior example could therefore be reworked to:

```
.Item {
  display: inline-block;
}
```

```
@supports (display: flex) {
  .Item {
    display: inline-flex;
  }
}
```

Combining conditionals

You can also combine conditionals. Let's suppose we only wanted to apply some rules if both Flexbox and `pointer: coarse` were supported (in case you missed it, we covered the 'pointer' interaction media feature back in *Chapter 2*, *Media Queries – Supporting Differing Viewports*). Here is what that might look like:

```
@supports ((display: flex) and (pointer: coarse)) {
  .Item {
    display: inline-flex;
  }
}
```

Here we have used the `and` keyword but we could use `or` as well as, or instead of it. For example, if we were happy to apply styles if those two prior property/value combinations were supported, or 3D transforms were supported:

```
@supports ((display: flex) and (pointer: coarse)) or (transform:
translate3d(0, 0, 0)) {
  .Item {
    display: inline-flex;
  }
}
```

Note in that prior example, the extra set of parenthesis that separates the flex and pointer conditional from the transform conditional.

Sadly, as I already mentioned, support for `@support` is far from universal. Boohoo! What's a responsive web designer to do? Fear not, there's a great JavaScript tool that is more than capable of rising to this challenge.

Modernizr

Until `@supports` is more widely implemented in browsers, we can use a JavaScript tool called Modernizr. At present, it's simply the most robust manner in which to facilitate forks in your code.

When forks are needed in CSS, I try and adopt a progressive enhancement approach. Progressive enhancement means starting with simple accessible code; code that will provide, at the very least, a functional design for less capable devices. Then that code is progressively enhanced for more capable devices.

 We'll talk a lot more about progressive enhancement in *Chapter 10, Approaching a Responsive Web Design.*

Let's look how we can facilitate progressive enhancement and forking our CSS code with Modernizr.

Feature detection with Modernizr

If you're a web developer, it's likely you have heard of Modernizr, even if you have perhaps not used it. It's a JavaScript library that you include in your page that feature tests the browser. To start using Modernizr, it's as simple as including a link to the downloaded file in the `head` section of your pages:

```
<script src="/js/libs/modernizr-2.8.3-custom.min.js"></script>
```

With that in place, when the browser loads the page, any of the included tests are run. If the browser passes the test, Modernizr handily (for our purposes) adds a relevant class to the root HTML tag.

For example, after Mondernizr has done its thing, the classes on the HTML tag for a page might look like this:

```
<html class="js no-touch cssanimations csstransforms csstransforms3d
csstransitions svg inlinesvg" lang="en">
```

In that instance just a few features have been tested: animations, transforms, SVG, inline SVG, and support for touch. With those classes in place, the code can be forked like this:

```
.widget {
  height: 1rem;
}

.touch .widget {
  height: 2rem;
}
```

In the preceding example, the widget item is just 1rem high ordinarily, but if the touch class is present on the HTML (thanks to Modernizr), then the widget would be 2rem high.

We could flip the logic too:

```
.widget {
  height: 2rem;
}

.no-touch .widget {
  height: 1rem;
}
```

This way we would default to the item being 2rem high, and adjust down if the no-touch class was present.

Whichever way you want to structure things, Modernizr provides a widely supported way to fork features. You'll find it especially useful when you want to use features like transform3d but still provide a working substitute for browsers that can't make use of it.

Modernizr can provide accurate tests for most things you'll likely need to fork code on, but not all. For example, overflow-scrolling is notoriously difficult to accurately test for. In situations where a class of devices isn't playing happily, it may make more sense to fork your code on a different feature. For example, as older Android versions have difficulty with horizontal scrolling you might fork with no-svg (as Android 2-2.3 doesn't support SVG either).

Finally, you may wish to combine tests to make your own custom test. That's a little outside the scope here but if that's something that interests you, take a look at http://benfrain. com/combining-modernizr-tests-create-custom-convenience-forks/.

New CSS3 selectors and how to use them

CSS3 gives incredible power for selecting elements within a page. You may not think this sounds very glitzy but trust me, it will make your life easier and you'll love CSS3 for it! I'd better qualify that bold claim.

CSS3 attribute selectors

You've probably used CSS attribute selectors to create rules. For example, consider the following rule:

```
img[alt] {
  border: 3px dashed #e15f5f;
}
```

This would target any image tags in the markup which have an `alt` attribute. Or, let's say we wanted to select all elements with a `data-sausage` attribute:

```
[data-sausage] {
  /* styles */
}
```

All you need is to specify the attribute in squared brackets.

The `data-*` type attribute was introduced in HTML5 to provide a place for custom data that can't be stored sensibly by any other existing mechanism. The specification description for these can be found at `http://www.w3.org/TR/2010/WD-html5-20101019/elements.html`.

You can also narrow things down by specifying what the attribute value is. For example, consider the following rule:

```
img[alt="sausages"] {
  /* Styles */
}
```

This would only target images which have an `alt` attribute of `sausages`. For example:

```
<img class="oscarMain" src="img/sausages.png" alt="sausages" />
```

So far, so 'big deal we could do that in CSS2'. What does CSS3 bring to the party?

CSS3 substring matching attribute selectors

CSS3 lets us select elements based upon the substring of their attribute selector. That sounds complicated. It isn't! The three options are whether the attribute is:

- Beginning with the prefix
- Contains an instance of
- Ends with the suffix

Let's see what they look like.

The 'beginning with' substring matching attribute selector

Consider the following markup:

```
<img src="img/ace-film.jpg" alt="film-ace">
<img src="img/rubbish-film.jpg" alt="film-rubbish">
```

We can use the 'beginning with' substring matching attribute selector to select both of those images like this:

```
img[alt^="film"] {
    /* Styles */
}
```

The key character in all this is the ^ symbol (the symbol is called the **caret**, although it is often referred to as the 'hat' symbol too) which means "begins with". Because both `alt` tags begin with `film` our selector selects them.

The 'contains an instance of' substring matching attribute selector

The 'contains an instance of' substring matching attribute selector has the following syntax:

```
[attribute*="value"] {
  /* Styles */
}
```

Like all attribute selectors, you can combine them with a type selector (one that references the actual HTML element used) if needed, although personally I would only do that if I had to (in case you want to change the type of element used).

Let's try an example. Consider this markup:

```
<p data-ingredients="scones cream jam">Will I get selected?</p>
We can select that element like this:
[data-ingredients*="cream"] {
  color: red;
}
```

The key character in all this is the * symbol that in this context means "contains".

The 'begins with' selector would not have worked in with this markup as the string inside the attribute didn't *begin with* 'cream'. It did however *contain* 'cream' so the 'contains an instance of' substring attribute selector finds it.

The 'ends with' substring matching attribute selector

The "ends with" substring matching attribute selector has the following syntax:

```
[attribute$="value"] {
  /* Styles */
}
```

An example should help. Consider this markup:

```
<p data-ingredients="scones cream jam">Will I get selected?</p>
<p data-ingredients="toast jam butter">Will I get selected?</p>
<p data-ingredients="jam toast butter">Will I get selected?</p>
```

Suppose we only want to select the element with scones, cream, and jam in the `data-ingredients` attribute (the first element). We can't use the 'contains an instance of' (it will select all three) or 'begins with' (it will only select the last one) substring attribute selector. However, we can use the 'ends with' substring attribute selector.

```
[data-ingredients$="jam"] {
color: red;
}
```

The key character in all this is the `$` (dollar) symbol which means "ends with".

Gotchas with attribute selection

There is a 'gotcha' with attribute selection that's it's important to grasp: attributes are seen as a single string. Consider this CSS rule:

```
[data-film^="film"] {
  color: red;
}
```

It might surprise you to know that it would not select this, even though one of the words inside the attribute begins with `film`:

```
<span data-film="awful moulin-rouge film">Moulin Rouge is dreadful</span>
```

That's because the `data-film` attribute here doesn't begin with `film`, in this case it begins with awful (and if you've seen *Moulin Rouge* you'll know that it begins awfully too—and never improves).

There are a couple of ways around this, in addition to the substring matching selectors we looked at a moment ago. You could use the whitespace separated selector (note the tilde symbol), which has support all the way back to Internet Explorer 7:

```
[data-film~="film"] {
  color: red;
}
```

You could select the entire attribute:

```
[data-film="awful moulin-rouge film"] {
  color: red;
}
```

Or, if you only wanted to select based upon the presence of a couple of strings inside an attribute, you could join a couple (or as many as were needed) of 'contains an instance of' substring attribute selectors:

```
[data-film*="awful"] [data-film*="moulin-rouge"] {
  color: red;
}
```

There's no 'right' thing to do, it really just depends on the complexity of the string you are trying to select.

Attribute selectors allow you to select IDs and classes that start with numbers

Before HTML5, it wasn't valid markup to start IDs or class names with a number. HTML5 removes that restriction. When it comes to IDs, there are still some things to remember. There should be no spaces in the ID name and it must be unique on the page. For more information visit http://www.w3.org/html/wg/drafts/html/master/dom.html.

Now, although you can start ID and class values with numbers in HTML5, CSS still restricts you from using ID and class selectors that start with a number (http://www.w3.org/TR/CSS21/syndata.html).

Lucky for us, we can easily workaround this by using an attribute selector. For example, [id="10"].

CSS3 structural pseudo-classes

CSS3 gives us more power to select elements based upon where they sit in the structure of the DOM.

Let's consider a common design treatment; we're working on the navigation bar for a larger viewport and we want to have all but the last link over on the left.

Historically, we would have needed to solve this problem by adding a class name to the last link so that we could select it, like this:

```
<nav class="nav-Wrapper">
  <a href="/home" class="nav-Link">Home</a>
  <a href="/About" class="nav-Link">About</a>
  <a href="/Films" class="nav-Link">Films</a>
  <a href="/Forum" class="nav-Link">Forum</a>
  <a href="/Contact-Us" class="nav-Link nav-LinkLast">Contact Us</a>
</nav>
```

This in itself can be problematic. For example, sometimes, just getting a content management system to add a class to a final list item can be frustratingly difficult. Thankfully, in those eventualities, it's no longer a concern. We can solve this problem and many more with CSS3 structural pseudo-classes.

The :last-child selector

CSS 2.1 already had a selector applicable for the first item in a list:

```
div:first-child {
  /* Styles */
}
```

However, CSS3 adds a selector that can also match the last:

```
div:last-child {
  /* Styles */
}
```

Let's look how that selector could fix our prior problem:

```
@media (min-width: 60rem) {
  .nav-Wrapper {
    display: flex;
  }
  .nav-Link:last-child {
    margin-left: auto;
  }
}
```

There are also useful selectors for when something is the only item: `:only-child` and the only item of a type: `:only-of-type`.

The nth-child selectors

The `nth-child` selectors let us solve even more difficult problems. With the same markup as before, let's consider how nth-child selectors allow us to select any link(s) within the list.

Firstly, what about selecting every other list item? We could select the odd ones like this:

```
.nav-Link:nth-child(odd) {
  /* Styles */
}
```

Or, if you wanted to select the even ones:

```
.nav-Link:nth-child(even) {
  /* Styles */
}
```

Understanding what nth rules do

For the uninitiated, nth-based selectors can look pretty intimidating. However, once you've mastered the logic and syntax you'll be amazed what you can do with them. Let's take a look.

CSS3 gives us incredible flexibility with a few nth-based rules:

- `nth-child(n)`
- `nth-last-child(n)`
- `nth-of-type(n)`
- `nth-last-of-type(n)`

We've seen that we can use (odd) or (even) values already in an nth-based expression but the (n) parameter can be used in another couple of ways:

As an integer; for example, `:nth-child(2)` would select the second item

As a numeric expression; for example, `:nth-child(3n+1)` would start at 1 and then select every third element

The integer based property is easy enough to understand, just enter the element number you want to select.

The numeric expression version of the selector is the part that can be a little baffling for mere mortals. If math is easy for you, I apologize for this next section. For everyone else, let's break it down.

Breaking down the math

Let's consider 10 spans on a page (you can play about with these by looking at `example_05-05`):

```
<span></span>
<span></span>
<span></span>
<span></span>
<span></span>
<span></span>
<span></span>
<span></span>
<span></span>
<span></span>
```

By default they will be styled like this:

```
span {
  height: 2rem;
  width: 2rem;
  background-color: blue;
  display: inline-block;
}
```

As you might imagine, this gives us 10 squares in a line:

OK, let's look at how we can select different ones with nth-based selections.

For practicality, when considering the expression within the parenthesis, I start from the right. So, for example, if I want to figure out what (2n+3) will select, I start with the right-most number (the three here indicates the third item from the left) and know it will select every second element from that point on. So adding this rule:

```
span:nth-child(2n+3) {
  color: #f90;
  border-radius: 50%;
}
```

Results in this in the browser:

As you can see, our nth selector targets the third list item and then every subsequent second one after that too (if there were 100 list items, it would continue selecting every second one).

How about selecting everything from the second item onwards? Well, although you could write `:nth-child(1n+2)`, you don't actually need the first number 1 as unless otherwise stated, n is equal to 1. We can therefore just write `:nth-child(n+2)`. Likewise, if we wanted to select every third element, rather than write `:nth-child(3n+3)`, we can just write `:nth-child(3n)` as every third item would begin at the third item anyway, without needing to explicitly state it. The expression can also use negative numbers, for example, `:nth-child(3n-2)` starts at -2 and then selects every third item.

You can also change the direction. By default, once the first part of the selection is found, the subsequent ones go down the elements in the DOM (and therefore from left to right in our example). However, you can reverse that with a minus. For example:

```css
span:nth-child(-2n+3) {
  background-color: #f90;
  border-radius: 50%;
}
```

This example finds the third item again, but then goes in the opposite direction to select every two elements (up the DOM tree and therefore from right to left in our example):

Hopefully, the nth-based expressions are making perfect sense now?

The `nth-child` and `nth-last-child` differ in that the `nth-last-child` variant works from the opposite end of the document tree. For example, `:nth-last-child(-n+3)` starts at 3 from the end and then selects all the items after it. Here's what that rule gives us in the browser:

Finally, let's consider :nth-of-type and :nth-last-of-type. While the previous examples count any children regardless of type (always remember the nth-child selector targets all children at the same DOM level, regardless of classes), :nth-of-type and :nth-last-of-type let you be specific about the type of item you want to select. Consider the following markup (example_05-06):

```
<span class="span-class"></span>
<span class="span-class"></span>
<span class="span-class"></span>
<span class="span-class"></span>
<span class="span-class"></span>
<div class="span-class"></div>
<div class="span-class"></div>
<div class="span-class"></div>
<div class="span-class"></div>
<div class="span-class"></div>
```

If we used the selector:

```
.span-class:nth-of-type(-2n+3) {
  background-color: #f90;
  border-radius: 50%;
}
```

Even though all the elements have the same span-class, we will only actually be targeting the span elements (as they are the first type selected). Here is what gets selected:

We will see how CSS4 selectors can solve this issue shortly.

CSS3 doesn't count like JavaScript and jQuery!

If you're used to using JavaScript and jQuery you'll know that it counts from 0 upwards (zero index based). For example, if selecting an element in JavaScript or jQuery, an integer value of 1 would actually be the second element. CSS3 however, starts at 1 so that a value of 1 is the first item it matches.

nth-based selection in responsive web designs

Just to close out this little section I want to illustrate a real life responsive web design problem and how we can use nth-based selection to solve it.

Remember the horizontal scrolling panel from `example_05-02`? Let's consider how that might look in a situation where horizontal scrolling isn't possible. So, using the same markup, let's turn the top 10 grossing films of 2014 into a grid. For some viewports the grid will only be two items wide, as the viewport increases we show three items and at larger sizes still we show four. Here is the problem though. Regardless of the viewport size, we want to prevent any items on the bottom row having a border on the bottom. You can view this code at `example_05-09`.

Here is how it looks with four items wide:

See that pesky border below the bottom two items? That's what we need to remove. However, I want a robust solution so that if there were another item on the bottom row, the border would also be removed on that too. Now, because there are a different number of items on each row at different viewports, we will also need to change the nth-based selection at different viewports. For the sake of brevity, I'll show you the selection that matches four items per row (the larger of the viewports). You can view the code sample to see the amended selection at the different viewports.

```
@media (min-width: 55rem) {
  .Item {
    width: 25%;
```

```
    }
    /*  Get me every fourth item and of those, only ones that are in the
last four items */
    .Item:nth-child(4n+1):nth-last-child(-n+4),
    /* Now get me every one after that same collection too. */
    .Item:nth-child(4n+1):nth-last-child(-n+4) ~ .Item {
      border-bottom: 0;
    }
}
```

> You'll notice here that we are chaining the nth-based pseudo-class selectors. It's important to understand that the first doesn't filter the selection for the next, rather the element has to match each of the selections. For our preceding example, the first element has to be the first item of four and also be one of the last four.

Nice! Thanks to nth-based selections we have a defensive set of rules to remove the bottom border regardless of the viewport size or number of items we are showing.

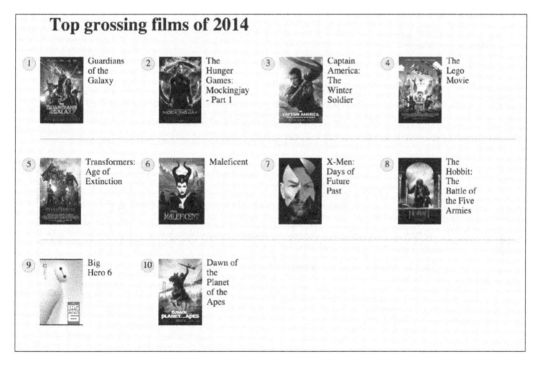

The negation (:not) selector

Another handy selector is the negation pseudo-class selector. This is used to select everything that isn't something else. Consider this:

```
<div class="a-div"></div>
<div class="a-div"></div>
<div class="a-div"></div>
<div class="a-div not-me"></div>
<div class="a-div"></div>
```

And then these styles:

```
div {
  display: inline-block;
  height: 2rem;
  width: 2rem;
  background-color: blue;
}

.a-div:not(.not-me) {
  background-color: orange;
  border-radius: 50%;
}
```

Our final rule will make every element with a class of .a-div orange and round, with the exception the div that also has the .not-me class. You can find that code in the example_05-07 folder of the code samples (remember, you can grab them all at http://rwd.education/).

So far we have looked primarily at what's known as structural pseudo-classes (full information on this is available at http://www.w3.org/TR/selectors/). However, CSS3 has many more selectors. If you're working on a web application, it's worth looking at the full list of UI element states pseudo-classes (http://www.w3.org/TR/selectors/), as they can, for example, help you target rules based on whether something is selected or not.

The empty (:empty) selector

I've encountered situations where I have an element that includes some padding on the inside and gets content dynamically inserted. Sometimes it gets content, sometimes it doesn't. The trouble is, when it doesn't include content, I still see the padding. Consider the HTML and CSS in `example_05-08`:

```
<div class="thing"></div>
.thing {
  padding: 1rem;
  background-color: violet;
}
```

Without anything content in that `div` I still see the `background-color`. Thankfully, we can easily hide it like this:

```
.thing:empty {
  display: none;
}
```

However, just be careful with the `:empty` selector. For example, you might think this is empty:

```
<div class="thing"> </div>
```

It isn't! Look at the whitespace in there. Whitespace is not no space!

However, just to confuse matters, be aware that a comment doesn't affect whether an element has whitespace or not. For example, this is still considered empty:

```
<div class="thing"><!--I'm empty, honest I am--></div>
```

Amendments to pseudo-elements

Pseudo-elements have been around since CSS2 but the CSS3 specification revises the syntax of their use very slightly. To refresh your memory, until now, `p:first-line` would target the first line in a `<p>` tag. Or `p:first-letter` would target the first letter. Well, CSS3 asks us to separate these pseudo-elements with a double colon to differentiate them from pseudo-classes (such as `nth-child()`). Therefore, we should write `p::first-letter` instead. Note, however, that Internet Explorer 8 and lower versions don't understand the double colon syntax, they only understand the single colon syntax.

Do something with the :first-line regardless of viewport

One thing that you may find particularly handy about the `:first-line` pseudo-element is that it is specific to the viewport. For example, if we write the following rule:

```
p::first-line {
  color: #ff0cff;
}
```

As you might expect, the first line is rendered in an awful shade of pink. However, on a different viewport, it renders a different selection of text.

So, without needing to alter the markup, with a responsive design, there's a handy way of having the first visual line of text (as the browser renders it, not as it appears in the markup) appear differently than the others.

CSS custom properties and variables

Thanks to the popularity of CSS pre-processors, CSS is starting to gain some more 'programmatic' features. The first of which is custom properties. They are more often referred to as variables although that is not necessarily their only use case. You can find the full specification at `http://dev.w3.org/csswg/css-variables/`. Be warned, as of early 2015, browser implementations are few and far between (only Firefox).

CSS custom properties allow us to store information in our style sheets that can then be utilized in that style sheet or perhaps acted upon with JavaScript. An obvious use case would be to store a font-family name and then reference it. Here is how we create a custom property:

```
:root {
  --MainFont: 'Helvetica Neue', Helvetica, Arial, sans-serif;
}
```

Here, we are using the `:root` pseudo-class to store the custom property in the document root (although you can store them inside any rule you like).

The `:root` pseudo-class always references the top-most parent element in a document structure. In an HTML document this would always be the HTML tag but for an SVG document (we look at SVG in *Chapter 7, Using SVGs for Resolution Independence*), it would reference a different element.

A custom property always begins with two dashes, then the custom name, and then its end, signified like every other property in CSS; with a colon.

We can reference that value with the `var()` notation. Like so:

```
.Title {
  font-family: var(--MainFont);
}
```

You could obviously store as many custom properties as you need in this manner. The main benefit of this approach is that you can change the value inside the variable and every rule that makes use of the variable gets the new value without having to amend them directly.

It's envisaged that in future these properties might be parsed and utilized by JavaScript. For more on that kind of craziness, you might be interested in the new CSS Extensions module:

`http://dev.w3.org/csswg/css-extensions/`

CSS calc

How many times have you been trying to code out a layout and thought something like, "it needs to half the width of the parent element minus exactly 10px"? This is particularly useful with responsive web design, as we never know the size of the screen that will be viewing our web pages. Thankfully CSS now has a way to do this. It's called the `calc()` function. Here's that example in CSS:

```
.thing {
  width: calc(50% - 10px);
}
```

Addition, subtraction, division, and multiplication are supported so it's possible to solve a bunch of problems that have been impossible without JavaScript in the past.

Browser support is quite good, but a notable exception is Android 4.3 and below. Read the specification at `http://www.w3.org/TR/css3-values/`.

CSS Level 4 selectors

There are a number of new selector types being specified for CSS Selectors Level 4 (the latest version available was the Editor's Draft dated December 14, 2014, (`http://dev.w3.org/csswg/selectors-4/`). However, as I write this, there are no implementations of them in browsers. As such we will just look at one example as they are liable/probable to change.

The Relational Pseudo-class selector is from the 'Logical Combinations' (`http://dev.w3.org/csswg/selectors-4/`) section of the latest draft.

The :has pseudo class

This selector takes this format:

```
a:has(figcaption) {
  padding: 1rem;
}
```

This would add padding to any item `a` tag that contains a `figcaption`. You could invert the selection in combination with the negation pseudo class too:

```
a:not(:has(figcaption)) {
  padding: 1rem;
}
```

This would add the padding if the `a` tag did not contain a `figcaption` element.

I'll be honest and say that right now, there aren't many new selectors in that draft that get me excited. But who knows what they'll come up with by the time they start being available to use in browsers?

Responsive viewport-percentage lengths (vmax, vmin, vh, vw)

Let's change tack now. We've looked at how we can select items in our responsive world. But how about how we size them? The CSS Values and Units Module Level 3 (`http://www.w3.org/TR/css3-values/`), ushered in viewport relative units. These are great for responsive web design as each unit is a percentage length of the viewport:

- The vw unit (for viewport width)
- vh unit (for viewport height)
- vmin unit (for viewport minimum; equal to the smaller of either vw or vh)
- vmax (viewport maximum; equal to the larger of either vw or vh)

Browser support isn't bad either (`http://caniuse.com/`).

Want a modal window that's 90% of the browser height? It's as easy as:

```
.modal {
  height: 90vh;
}
```

As useful as viewport relative units are, some browsers have curious implementations. Safari in iOS 8, for example, changes the viewable screen area as you scroll from the top of a page (it shrinks the address bar) but doesn't make any changes to the reported viewport height.

However, you can perhaps find more utility for these units when coupled with fonts. For example, it's now trivially easy to create text that scales in size depending upon the viewport.

Now, I could show you that right now. However, I'd like to use a distinct font, so that regardless of whether you are viewing the example on a Windows, Mac, or Linux box we will all see the same thing.

OK, I'll be honest, this is a cheap ploy to allow me to document how we can use web fonts with CSS3.

Web typography

For years the web has had to make do with a boring selection of 'web safe' fonts. When some fancy typography was essential for a design, it was necessary to substitute a graphical element for it and used a text-indent rule to shift the actual text from the viewport. Oh, the joy!

There were also a few inventive methods for adding fancy typography to a page along the way. sIFR (http://www.mikeindustries.com/blog/sifr/) and Cufón (http://cufon.shoqolate.com/generate/) used Flash and JavaScript respectively to re-make text elements appear as the fonts they were intended to be. Thankfully, CSS3 provides a means of custom web typography that is now ready for the big time.

The @font-face CSS rule

The @font-face CSS rule has been around since CSS2 (but subsequently absent in CSS 2.1). It was even supported partially by Internet Explorer 4 (no, really)! So what's it doing here, when we're supposed to be talking about CSS3?

Well, as it turns out, @font-face was re-introduced for the CSS3 Fonts module (http://www.w3.org/TR/css3-fonts). Due to the historic legal quagmire of using fonts on the web, it's only in recent years that it has started to gain serious traction as the de facto solution for web typography.

Like anything on the web that involves assets, there is no single file format. Just as images can come in JPG, PNG, GIF, and other formats, fonts have their own set of formats to choose from. The Embedded OpenType (files with an `.eot` extension) font was Internet Explorer's (and not anyone else's) preferred choice. Others favor the more common TrueType (`.ttf` file extension), whilst there is also SVGs and Web Open Font Format (`.woff` / `.woff2` extension).

Right now, it's necessary to serve multiple file versions of the same font to cover the different browser implementations.

However, the good news is that adding each custom font format for every browser is easy. Let's see how!

Implementing web fonts with @font-face

CSS provides a `@font-face` 'at-rule' to reference online fonts that can then be used to display text.

There are now a number of great sources for viewing and acquiring web fonts; both free and paid. My personal favorite for free fonts is Font Squirrel (`http://www.fontsquirrel.com/`) although Google also offers free web fonts, ultimately served with the `@font-face` rule (`http://www.google.com/webfonts`). There are also great, paid services from Typekit (`http://www.typekit.com/`) and Font Deck (`http://www.fontdeck.com/`).

For this exercise, I'm going to download Roboto. It's the Font used for later Android handsets so if you have one of those it will be familiar. Otherwise, all you need to know is that it's a lovely interface font designed to be highly legible on small screens. You can grab it yourself at `http://www.fontsquirrel.com/fonts/roboto`.

 If you can download a 'subset' of your font, specific to the language you intend to use, do so. It means, the resultant file size will be much smaller as it won't contain glyphs for languages you have no intention of using.

Having downloaded the `@font-face` kit, a look inside the ZIP file reveals folders of the different Roboto fonts. I'm choosing the Roboto Regular version and inside that folder the font exists in various file formats (WOFF, TTF, EOT, and SVG), plus a `stylesheet.css` file containing a font stack. For example, the rule for Roboto Regular looks like this:

```
@font-face {
    font-family: 'robotoregular';
    src: url('Roboto-Regular-webfont.eot');
```

```
    src: url('Roboto-Regular-webfont.eot?#iefix') format('embedded-
opentype'),
          url('Roboto-Regular-webfont.woff') format('woff'),
          url('Roboto-Regular-webfont.ttf') format('truetype'),
          url('Roboto-Regular-webfont.svg#robotoregular')
format('svg');
    font-weight: normal;
    font-style: normal;
}
```

Much like the way vendor prefixes work, the browser will apply styles from that list of properties (with the lower properties, if applicable, taking precedence) and ignore ones it doesn't understand. That way, no matter what the browser, there should be a font that it can use.

Now, although this block of code is great for fans of copy and paste, it's important to pay attention to the paths the fonts are stored in. For example, I tend to copy the fonts from the ZIP file and store them in a folder inventively called `fonts` on the same level as my `css` folder. Therefore, as I'm usually copying this font stack rule into my main style sheet, I need to amend the paths. So, my rule becomes:

```
@font-face {
    font-family: 'robotoregular';
    src: url('../fonts/Roboto-Regular-webfont.eot');
    src: url('../fonts/Roboto-Regular-webfont.eot?#iefix')
format('embedded-opentype'),
          url('../fonts/Roboto-Regular-webfont.woff') format('woff'),
          url('../fonts/Roboto-Regular-webfont.ttf')
format('truetype'),
          url('../fonts/Roboto-Regular-webfont.svg#robotoregular')
format('svg');
    font-weight: normal;
    font-style: normal;
}
```

It's then just a case of setting the correct font and weight (if needed) for the relevant style rule. Look at `example_05-10`, it's the same markup as `example_05-09`, we are merely declaring this `font-family` as the default:

```
body {
  font-family: robotoregular;
}
```

An added bonus with web fonts is that, if the composite uses the same fonts you are using in the code, you can plug the sizes in direct from the composite file. For example, if the font is 24px in Photoshop, we either plug that value straight in or convert it to a more flexible unit such as REM (assuming a root font-size of 16px, 24 / 16 = 1.5rem).

However, as I mentioned before, we now have viewport relative sizes at our disposal. We can use them here to scale the text relative to the amount of viewport space.

```
body {
  font-family: robotoregular;
  font-size: 2.1vw;
}

@media (min-width: 45rem) {
  html,
  body {
    max-width: 50.75rem;
    font-size: 1.8vw;
  }
}

@media (min-width: 55rem) {
  html,
  body {
    max-width: 78.75rem;
    font-size: 1.7vw;
  }
}
```

If you open that example in the browser and resize the viewport you will see that with just a few lines of CSS we have text that scales to the available space. Beautiful!

A note about custom @font-face typography and responsive designs

The @font-face method of web typography is, on the whole, great. The only caveats to be aware of when using the technique with responsive designs are in relation to the font file size. By way of an example, if the device rendering our example required the SVG font format of Roboto Regular, it would need to fetch an extra 34 KB, compared with using the standard web-safe fonts such as Arial. We have used an English subset in our example which reduces the file size but that isn't always an option. Be sure to check the size of custom fonts and be judicious with their use if you want the best possible site performance.

New CSS3 color formats and alpha transparency

So far in this chapter, we have looked at how CSS3 has given us new powers of selection and the ability to add custom typography to our designs. Now, we'll look at ways that CSS3 allows us to work with color that were simply not possible before.

Firstly, CSS3 provides two new ways to declare color: RGB and HSL. In addition, these two formats enable us to use an alpha channel alongside them (RGBA and HSLA respectively).

RGB color

Red, Green, and Blue (RGB) is a coloring system that's been around for decades. It works by defining different values for the red, green, and blue components of a color. For example, a red color might be defined in CSS as a HEX (hexadecimal) value, #fe0208:

```
.redness {
  color: #fe0208;
}
```

 For a great post describing how to understand HEX values more intuitively, I can recommend this blog post at Smashing Magazine: http://www.smashingmagazine.com/2012/10/04/the-code-side-of-color/

However, with CSS3, that color can equally be described by an RGB value:

```
.redness {
  color: rgb(254, 2, 8);
}
```

Most image editing applications show colors as both HEX and RGB values in their color picker. The Photoshop color picker, has R, G, and B boxes showing the values for each channel. For example, the R value might be 254, the G value 2, and the B value 8. This is easily transferable to the CSS `color` property value. In the CSS, after defining the color mode (for example, RGB) the values for red, green, and blue colors are comma separated in that order within parenthesis (as we have in the previous code).

HSL color

Besides RGB, CSS3 also allows us to declare color values as **Hue, Saturation, and Lightness (HSL)**.

HSL isn't the same as HSB!

Don't make the mistake of thinking that the **Hue, Saturation, and Brightness (HSB)** value shown in the color picker of image editing applications such as Photoshop is the same as HSL—it isn't!

What makes HSL such a joy to use is that it's relatively simple to understand the color that will be represented based on the values given. For example, unless you're some sort of color picking ninja, I'd wager you couldn't instantly tell me what color rgb(255, 51, 204) is? Any takers? No, me neither. However, show me the HSL value of hsl(315, 100%, 60%) and I could take a guess that it is somewhere between Magenta and Red color (it's actually a festive pink color). How do I know this? Simple.

HSL works on a 360° degree color wheel. It looks like this:

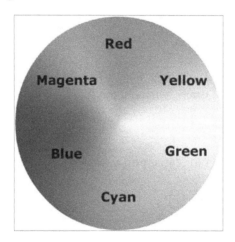

The first figure in a HSL color definition represents Hue. Looking at our wheel we can see that Yellow is at 60°, Green at 120°, Cyan at 180°, Blue at 240°, Magenta at 300°, and finally Red at 360°. So as the aforementioned HSL color had a hue of 315, it's easy to know that it will be between Magenta (at 300°) and Red (at 360°).

The following two values in an HSL definition are for saturation and lightness, specified as percentages. These merely alter the base hue. For a more saturated or 'colorful' appearance, use a higher percentage in the second value. The final value, controlling the Lightness, can vary between 0 percent for black and 100 percent for white.

So, once you've defined a color as an HSL value, it's also easy to create variations on it, merely by altering the saturation and lightness percentages. For example, our red color can be defined in HSL values as follows:

```
.redness {
  color: hsl(359, 99%, 50%);
}
```

If we wanted to make a slightly darker color, we could use the same HSL value and merely alter the lightness (the final value) percentage value only:

```
.darker-red {
  color: hsl(359, 99%, 40%);
}
```

In conclusion, if you can remember the mnemonic 'Young Guys Can Be Messy Rascals' (or any other mnemonic you care to memorize) for the HSL color wheel, you'll be able to approximately write HSL color values without resorting to a color picker, and also create variations upon it. Show that trick to the savant Ruby, Node, and .NET guys and gals at the office party and earn some quick kudos!

Alpha channels

So far you'd be forgiven for wondering why on earth we'd bother using HSL or RGB instead of our trusty HEX values we've been using for years. Where HSL and RGB differ from HEX is that they allow the use of an alpha transparency channel so something beneath an element can 'show through'.

An HSLA color declaration is similar in syntax to a standard HSL rule. However, in addition, you must declare the value as hsla (rather than merely hsl) and add an additional opacity value, given as a decimal value between 0 (completely transparent) and 1 (completely opaque). For example:

```
.redness-alpha {
  color: hsla(359, 99%, 50%, .5);
}
```

The RGBA syntax follows the same convention as the HSLA equivalent:

```
.redness-alpha-rgba {
  color: rgba(255, 255, 255, 0.8);
}
```

Why not just use opacity?

CSS3 also allows elements to have opacity set with the opacity declaration. A value is set between 0 and 1 in decimal increments (for example, opacity set to .1 is 10 percent). However, this differs from RGBA and HSLA in that setting an opacity value on an element effects the entire element. Whereas, setting a value with HSLA or RGBA meanwhile allows particular parts of an element to have an alpha layer. For example, an element could have an HSLA value for the background but a solid color for the text within it.

Color manipulation with CSS Color Module Level 4

Although in the very early specification stages, it should be possible in the not too distant future to enjoy color manipulations in CSS using the `color()` function.

Until there is wide browser support, this kind of thing is best handled by CSS pre/post processors (do yourself a favor and buy yourself a book on the subject right now; I recommend *Sass and Compass for Designers* by that wonderful chap, Ben Frain).

You can follow the progress of the CSS Color Module Level 4 at `http://dev.w3.org/csswg/css-color-4/`.

Summary

In this chapter, we've learned how to easily select almost anything we need on the page with CSS3's new selectors. We've also looked at how we can make responsive columns and scrolling panels for content in record time and solve common and annoying problems such as long URL wrapping. We now also have an understanding of CSS3's new color module and how we can apply colors with RGB and HSL complete with transparent alpha layers for great aesthetic effects.

In this chapter, we've also learned how to add web typography to a design with the `@font-face` rule, finally freeing us from the shackles of the humdrum selection of web-safe fonts. Despite all these great new features and techniques, we've only picked at the surface of what we can do with CSS3. Let's move on now and look at even more ways CSS3 can make a responsive design as fast, efficient, and maintainable as possible with CSS3 text shadows, box shadows, gradients, and multiple backgrounds.

6
Stunning Aesthetics
with CSS3

The aesthetically focused features of CSS3 are so useful in responsive design because using CSS3 lets us replace images in many situations. This saves you time, makes your code more maintainable and flexible and results in less page 'weight' for the end user. Those benefits would be useful even on a typical fixed-width desktop design but it's even more important with a responsive design as using CSS in these situations makes it trivial to create different aesthetic effects at different viewports.

In this chapter we will cover:

- How to create text shadows with CSS3
- How to create box shadows with CSS3
- How to make gradient backgrounds with CSS3
- How to use multiple backgrounds with CSS3
- Using CSS3 background gradients to make patterns
- How to implement high-resolution background images with media queries
- How to use CSS filters (and their performance implications)

Let's dig in.

Vendor prefixes

When implementing experimental CSS, just remember to add relevant vendor prefixes via a tool, rather than by hand. This ensures the broadest cross-browser compatibility and also negates you adding in prefixes that are no longer required. I'm mentioning Autoprefixer (`https://github.com/postcss/autoprefixer`) in most chapters as, at the time of writing, I think it's the best tool for the job.

Text shadows with CSS3

One of the most widely implemented CSS3 features is `text-shadow`. Like `@font-face`, it had a previous life but was dropped in CSS 2.1. Thankfully it's back and widely supported (for all modern browsers and Internet Explorer 9 onwards). Let's look at the basic syntax:

```
.element {
    text-shadow: 1px 1px 1px #ccc;
}
```

Remember, the values in shorthand rules always go right and then down (or think of it as clockwise if you prefer). Therefore, the first value is the amount of shadow to the right, the second is the amount down, the third value is the amount of blur (the distance the shadow travels before fading to nothing), and the final value is the color.

Shadows to the left and above can be achieved using negative values. For example:

```
.text {
    text-shadow: -4px -4px 0px #dad7d7;
}
```

The color value doesn't need to be defined as a HEX value. It can just as easily be HSL(A) or RGB(A):

```
text-shadow: 4px 4px 0px hsla(140, 3%, 26%, 0.4);
```

However, keep in mind that the browser must then also support HSL/RGB color modes along with `text-shadow` in order to render the effect.

You can also set the shadow values in any other valid CSS length units such as em, rem, ch, rem, and so on. Personally, I rarely use em or rem units for `text-shadow` values. As the values are always really low, using 1px or 2px generally looks good across all viewports.

Thanks to media queries, we can easily remove text shadows at different viewport sizes too. The key here is the none value:

```css
.text {
    text-shadow: .0625rem .0625rem 0 #bfbfbf;
}
@media (min-width: 30rem) {
    .text {
        text-shadow: none;
    }
}
```

 As an aside, it's worth knowing that in CSS, where a value starts with a zero, such as 0.14s, there is no need to write the leading zero: .14s is exactly the same.

Omitting the blur value when not needed

If there is no blur to be added to a `text-shadow` the value can be omitted from the declaration, for example:

```css
.text {
    text-shadow: -4px -4px #dad7d7;
}
```

That is perfectly valid. The browser assumes that the first two values are for the offsets if no third value is declared.

Multiple text shadows

It's possible to add multiple text shadows by comma separating two or more shadows. For example:

```css
.multiple {
    text-shadow: 0px 1px #fff,4px 4px 0px #dad7d7;
}
```

Also, as CSS is forgiving of whitespace, you can lay out the values like this if it helps with readability:

```css
.text {
    font-size: calc(100vmax / 40); /* 100 of vh or vw, whichever is
larger divided by 40 */
    text-shadow:
```

```
    3px 3px #bbb, /* right and down */
    -3px -3px #999; /* left and up */
}
```

> You can read the W3C specification for the `text-shadow` property at `http://www.w3.org/TR/css3-text/`.

Box shadows

Box shadows allow you to create a box-shaped shadow around the outside or inside of the element it is applied to. Once text shadows are understood, box shadows are a piece of cake; principally, they follow the same syntax: horizontal offset, vertical offset, blur, spread (we will get to spread in a moment), and color.

Only two of the possible four length values are required (in the absence of the last two, the value of color defines the shadow color and a value of zero is used for the blur radius). Let's look at a simple example:

```
.shadow {
    box-shadow: 0px 3px 5px #444;
}
```

The default `box-shadow` is set on the outside of the element. Another optional keyword, `inset` allows the `box-shadow` to be applied inside the element.

An inset shadow

The `box-shadow` property can also be used to create an `inset` shadow. The syntax is identical to a normal box shadow except that the value starts with the keyword `inset`:

```
.inset {
    box-shadow: inset 0 0 40px #000;
}
```

Everything functions as before but the `inset` part of the declaration instructs the browser to set the effect on the inside. If you look at `example_06-01` you'll see an example of each type:

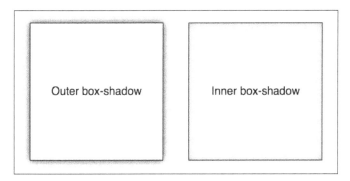

Multiple shadows

Like `text-shadow`, you can apply multiple `box-shadow`. Separate the `box-shadow` with a comma and they are applied bottom to top (last to first) as they are listed. Remind yourself of the order by thinking that the declaration nearest to the top in the rule (in the code) appears nearest to the 'top' of the order when displayed in the browser. As with `text-shadow`, you may find it useful to use whitespace to visually stack the different `box-shadow`:

```
box-shadow: inset 0 0 30px hsl(0, 0%, 0%),
            inset 0 0 70px hsla(0, 97%, 53%, 1);
```

Stacking longer, multiple values, one under the other in the code, has an added benefit when using version control systems; it makes it easy to spot differences when you 'diff' two versions of a file. That's the primary reason I stack groups of selectors one under the other too.

Understanding spread

I'll be honest, for literally years I didn't truly understand what the spread value of a `box-shadow` actually did. I don't think the name 'spread' is useful. Think of it more as an offset. Let me explain.

Look at the box on the left in `example_06-02`. This has a standard `box-shadow` applied. The one on the right has a negative spread value applied. It's set with the fourth value. Here is the relevant code:

```css
.no-spread {
  box-shadow: 0 10px 10px;
}

.spread {
  box-shadow: 0 10px 10px -10px;
}
```

Here is the effect of each (element with spread value on the right):

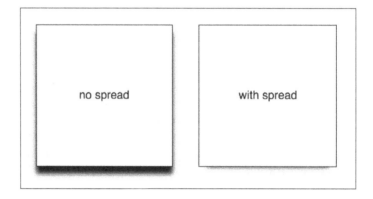

The spread value lets you extend or contract the shadow in all directions by the amount specified. In this example, a negative value is pulling the shadow back in all directions. The result being that we see the shadow at the bottom, only instead of seeing the blur 'leak' out on all sides (as the blur is being counter-balanced by the negative spread value).

You can read the W3C specification for the `box-shadow` property at `http://www.w3.org/TR/css3-background/`.

Background gradients

In days gone by, to achieve a background gradient on an element, it was necessary to tile a thin graphical slice of the gradient. As graphics resources go, it's quite an economical trade-off. An image, only a pixel or two wide, isn't going to break the bandwidth bank and on a single site it can be used on multiple elements.

However, if we need to tweak the gradient it still requires round-trips to the graphics editor. Plus, occasionally, content might 'break out' of the gradient background, extending beyond the images' fixed size limitations. This problem is compounded with a responsive design, as sections of a page may increase at different viewports.

With a CSS `background-image` gradient however, things are far more flexible. As part of the CSS Image Values and Replaced Content Module Level 3, CSS enables us to create linear and radial background gradients. Let's look how we can define them.

 The specification for CSS Image Values and Replaced Content Module Level 3 can be found at `http://www.w3.org/TR/css3-images/`.

The linear-gradient notation

The `linear-gradient` notation, in its simplest form, looks like this:

```
.linear-gradient {
    background: linear-gradient(red, blue);
}
```

This will create a linear gradient that starts at red (the gradient starts from the top by default) and fades to blue.

Specifying gradient direction

Now, if you want to specify a direction for the gradient, there are a couple of ways. The gradient will always begin in the opposite direction to where you are sending it. However, when no direction is set, a gradient will always default to a top to bottom direction. For example:

```
.linear-gradient {
    background: linear-gradient(to top right, red, blue);
}
```

In this instance, the gradient heads to the top right. It starts red in the bottom-left corner and fades to blue at the top right.

If you're more mathematically minded, you may believe it would be comparable to write the gradient like this:

```
.linear-gradient {
    background: linear-gradient(45deg, red, blue);
}
```

However, keep in mind that on a rectangular box, a gradient that heads 'to top right' (always the top right of the element it's applied to) will end in a slightly different position than `45deg` (always 45 degrees from its starting point).

It's worth knowing you can also start gradients before they are visible within a box. For example:

```
.linear-gradient {
    background: linear-gradient(red -50%, blue);
}
```

This would render a gradient as if it had started before it is even visible inside the box.

We've actually used a color stop in that last example to define a place where a color should begin and end so let's look at those more fully.

Color stops

Perhaps the handiest thing about background gradients is color stops. They provide the means to set which color is used at which point in a gradient. With color stops you can specify something as complex as you are likely to need. Consider this example:

```
.linear-gradient {
  margin: 1rem;
  width: 400px;
  height: 200px;
  background: linear-gradient(#f90 0, #f90 2%, #555 2%, #eee 50%, #555
98%, #f90 98%, #f90 100%);
}
```

Here's how that `linear-gradient` renders:

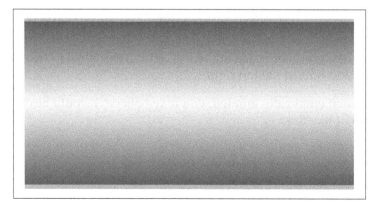

In this example (`example_06-03`), a direction has not been specified so the default top to bottom direction applies.

Color stops inside a gradient are written comma separated and defined by giving first the color, and then the position of the stop. It's generally advisable not to mix units in one notation but you can. You can have as many color stops as you like and colors can be written as a keyword, HEX, RGBA, or HSLA value.

Note that there have been a number of different background gradient syntaxes over the years so this is one area that is particularly difficult to write fallbacks for by hand. At the risk of sounding like a broken record (kids, if you don't know what a 'record' is, ask mom or dad), make your life easier with a tool such as Autoprefixer. This lets you write the current W3C standard syntax (as detailed earlier) and it will automatically create the prior versions for you.

Read the W3C specification for linear background gradients at `http://www.w3.org/TR/css3-images/`.

Adding fallback for older browsers

As a simple fallback for older browsers that don't support background gradients, just define a solid background color first. That way older browsers will at least render a solid background if they don't understand the gradient that's defined afterwards. For example:

```
.thing {
  background: red;
  background: linear-gradient(45deg, red, blue);
}
```

Radial background gradients

It's equally simple to create a radial gradient in CSS. These typically begin from a central point and spread out smoothly in an elliptical or circular shape.

Here's the syntax for a radial background gradient (you can play with it in `example_06-04`):

```
.radial-gradient {
    margin: 1rem;
    width: 400px;
    height: 200px;
```

```
        background: radial-gradient(12rem circle at bottom,  yellow,
    orange, red);
    }
```

Breakdown of the radial-gradient syntax

After specifying the property (`background:`) we begin the `radial-gradient` notation. To start with, before the first comma, we define the shape or size of the gradient and the position. We have used 12rem circle for the shape and size above but consider some other examples:

- `5em` would be a circle 5em in size. It's possible to omit the 'circle' part if giving just a size.
- `circle` would be a circle the full size of the container (the size of a radial gradient defaults to 'farthest corner' if omitted — more on sizing keywords shortly)
- `40px 30px` would be a ellipse as if drawn inside a box 40px wide by 30px tall
- `ellipse` would create an ellipse shape that would fit within the element

Next, after the size and/or shape, we define the position. The default position is center but let's look at some other possibilities and how they can be defined:

- **at top right** starts the radial gradient from the top right
- **at right 100px top 20px** starts the gradient 100px from the right edge and 20px from the top edge
- **at center left** starts it halfway down the left side of the element

We end our size, shape, and position 'parameters' with a comma and then define any color stops; which work in exactly the same manner as they do with `linear-gradient`.

To simplify the notation: size, shape, and position before the first comma, then as many color stops as needed after it (with each stop separated with commas).

Handy 'extent' keywords for responsive sizing

For responsive work, you may find it advantageous to size gradients proportionally rather than using fixed pixel dimensions. That way you know you are covered (both literally and figuratively) when the size of elements change. There are some handy sizing keywords that can be applied to gradients. You would write them like this, in place of any size value:

```
    background: radial-gradient(closest-side circle at center, #333,
    blue);
```

Here is what each of them does:

- `closest-side`: The shape meets the side of the box nearest to the center (in the case of circles), or meets both the horizontal and vertical sides that are closest to the center (in the case of ellipses)
- `closest-corner`: The shape meets exactly the closest corner of the box from its center
- `farthest-side`: The opposite of `closest-side`, in that rather than the shape meeting the nearest size, it's sized to meet the one farthest from its center (or both the furthest vertical and horizontal side in the case of an ellipse)
- `farthest-corner`: The shape expands to the farthest corner of the box from the center
- `cover`: Identical to `farthest-corner`
- `contain`: Identical to `closest-side`

Read the W3C specification for radial background gradients at `http://www.w3.org/TR/css3-images/`.

The cheat's way to perfect CSS3 linear and radial gradients

If defining gradients by hand seems like hard work, there are some great online gradient generators. My personal favorite is `http://www.colorzilla.com/gradient-editor/`. It uses a graphics editor style GUI, allowing you to pick your colors, stops, gradient style (linear and radial gradients are supported), and even the color space (HEX, RGB(A), HSL(A)) you'd like the final gradient in. There are also loads of preset gradients to use as starting points. If that wasn't enough, it even gives you optional code for fixing up Internet Explorer 9 to show the gradient and a fallback flat color for older browsers. Still not convinced? How about the ability to generate a CSS gradient based on upon the gradient values in an existing image? Thought that might swing it for you.

Repeating gradients

CSS3 also gives us the ability to create repeating background gradients. Let's take a look at how it's done:

```
.repeating-radial-gradient {
    background: repeating-radial-gradient(black 0px, orange 5px, red 10px);
}
```

Here's how that looks (don't look for long, may cause nausea):

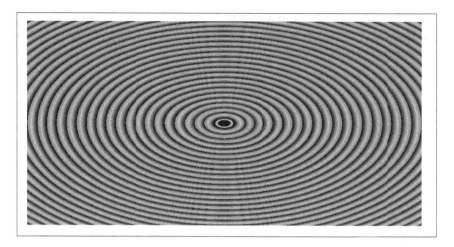

Firstly, prefix the `linear-gradient` or `radial-gradient` with repeating, then it follows the same syntax as a normal gradient. Here I've used pixel distances between the black, orange, and red colors (0px, 5px, and 10px respectively) but you could also choose to use percentages. For best results, it's recommended to stick to the same measurement units (such as pixels or percentages) within a gradient.

Read the W3C information on repeating gradients at `http://www.w3.org/TR/css3-images/`.

There's one more way of using background gradients I'd like to share with you.

Background gradient patterns

Although I've often used subtle linear gradients in designs, I've found less practical use for radial gradients and repeating gradients. However, clever folks out there have harnessed the power of gradients to create background gradient patterns. Let's look at an example from CSS Ninja, Lea Verou's collection of CSS3 background patterns, available at `http://lea.verou.me/css3patterns/`:

```
.carbon-fibre {
    margin: 1rem;
    width: 400px;
    height: 200px;
    background:
    radial-gradient(black 15%, transparent 16%) 0 0,
    radial-gradient(black 15%, transparent 16%) 8px 8px,
```

```
    radial-gradient(rgba(255,255,255,.1) 15%, transparent 20%) 0 1px,
    radial-gradient(rgba(255,255,255,.1) 15%, transparent 20%) 8px
9px;
    background-color:#282828;
    background-size:16px 16px;
}
```

Here's what that gives us in the browser, a `carbon-fibre` background effect:

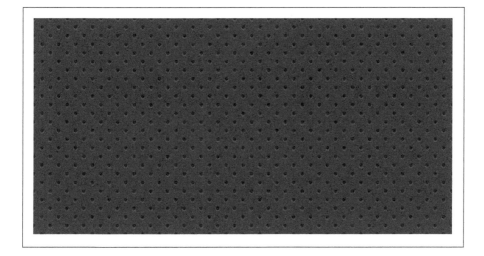

How about that? Just a few lines of CSS3 and we have an easily editable, responsive, and scalable background pattern.

 You might find it useful to add `background-repeat:` `no-repeat` at the end of the rule to better understand how it works.

As ever, thanks to media queries, different declarations can be used for different responsive scenarios. For example, although a gradient pattern might work well at smaller viewports, it might be better to go with a plain background at larger ones:

```
@media (min-width: 45rem) {
    .carbon-fibre {
        background: #333;
    }
}
```

You can view this example at `example_06-05`.

Multiple background images

Although a little out of fashion at the moment, it used to be a fairly common design requirement to build a page with a different background image at the top of the page than at the bottom. Or perhaps to use different background images for the top and bottom of a content section within a page. Back in the day, with CSS2.1, achieving the effect typically required additional markup (one element for the header background and another for the footer background).

With CSS3 you can stack as many background images as you need on an element.

Here's the syntax:

```
.bg {
    background:
        url('../img/1.png'),
        url('../img/2.png'),
        url('../img/3.png');
}
```

As with the stacking order of multiple shadows, the image listed first appears nearest to the top in the browser. You can also add a general color for the background in the same declaration if you wish, like this:

```
.bg {
    background:
    url('../img/1.png'),
    url('../img/2.png'),
    url('../img/3.png') left bottom, black;
}
```

Specify the color last and this will show below every image specified above.

 When specifying multiple background elements, you don't have to stack the different images on different lines; I just find it easier to read code when written this way.

Browsers that don't understand the multiple backgrounds rule (such as Internet Explorer 8 and below) will ignore the rule altogether, so you may wish to declare a 'normal' background property immediately before a CSS3 multiple background rule as a fallback for really old browsers.

With the multiple background images, as long as you're using PNG files with transparency, any partially transparent background images that sit on top of another will show through below. However, background images don't have to sit on top of one another, nor do they all have to be the same size.

Background size

To set different sizes for each image, use the `background-size` property. When multiple images have been used, the syntax works like this:

```
.bg {
    background-size: 100% 50%, 300px 400px, auto;
}
```

The size values (first width, then height) for each image are declared, separated by commas, in the order they are listed in the background property. As in the example above, you can use percentage or pixel values for each image alongside the following:

- `auto`: Which sets the element at its native size
- `cover`: Which expands the image, preserving its aspect ratio, to cover the area of the element
- `contain`: Which expands the image to fit its longest side within the element while preserving the aspect ratio

Background position

If you have different background images, at different sizes, the next thing you'll want is the ability to position them differently. Thankfully, the `background-position` property facilitates that too.

Let's put all this background image capability together, alongside some of the responsive units we have looked at in previous chapters.

Let's create a simple space scene, made with a single element and three background images, set at three different sizes, and positioned in three different ways:

```
.bg-multi {
    height: 100vh;
    width: 100vw;
    background:
        url('rosetta.png'),
        url('moon.png'),
        url('stars.jpg');
    background-size: 75vmax, 50vw, cover;
    background-position: top 50px right 80px, 40px 40px, top center;
    background-repeat: no-repeat;
}
```

You'll see something like this in the browser:

We have the stars image at the bottom, then the moon on top, and finally an image of the Rosetta space probe on top. View this for yourself in `example_06-06`. Notice that if you adjust the browser window, the responsive length units work well (vmax, vh, and vw) and retain proportion, while pixel based ones do not.

 Where no `background-position` is declared, the default position of top left is applied.

Background shorthand

There is a shorthand method of combining the different background properties together. You can read the specification for it at `http://www.w3.org/TR/css3-background/`. However, my experience so far has been that it produces erratic results. Therefore, I recommend the longhand method and declare the multiple images first, then the size, and then the position.

 Read the W3C documentation on multiple background elements at `http://www.w3.org/TR/css3-background/`.

High-resolution background images

Thanks to media queries, we have the ability to load in different background images, not just at different viewport sizes but also different viewport resolutions.

For example, here is the official way of specifying a background image for a 'normal' and a high DPI screen. You can find this in `example_06-07`:

```
.bg {
    background-image: url('bg.jpg');
}
@media (min-resolution: 1.5dppx) {
    .bg {
        background-image: url('bg@1_5x.jpg');
    }
}
```

The media query is written exactly as it is with width, height, or any of the other capability tests. In this example, we are defining the minimum resolution that `bg@1_5x.jpg` should use as 1.5dppx (device pixels per CSS pixel). We could also use **dpi (dots per inch)** or **dpcm (dots per centimeter)** units if preferable. However, despite the poorer support, I find dppx the easiest unit to think about; as 2dppx is twice the resolution, 3dppx would be three times the resolution. Thinking about that in dpi is trickier. 'Standard' resolution would be 96dpi, twice that resolution would be 192dpi and so on.

Support for the 'dppx' unit isn't great right now (check your target browsers at `http://caniuse.com/`) so to get this working everywhere smoothly, you'll need to write a few versions of the media query resolution or, as ever, rely on a tool to do the prefixing for you.

A brief note on performance

Just remember that large images can potentially slow down the feel of your site and lead to a poor experience for users. While a background image won't block the rendering of the page (you'll still see the rest of the site drawn to the page while you wait for the background image), it will add to the total weight of the page, which is important if users are paying for data.

CSS filters

There is a glaring problem with box-shadow. As the name implies, it is limited to the rectangular CSS box shape of the element it is applied to. Here's a screen grab of a triangle shape made with CSS (you can view the code in example_06-08) with a box shadow applied:

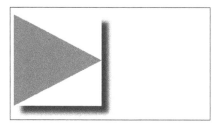

Not exactly what I was hoping for. Thankfully, we can overcome this issue with CSS filters, part of the Filter Effects Module Level 1 (http://www.w3.org/TR/filter-effects/). They are not as widely supported as box-shadow, but work great with a progressive enhancement approach. If a browser doesn't understand what to do with the filter it simply ignores it. For supporting browsers, the fancy effects are rendered.

Here is that same element with a CSS drop-shadow filter applied instead of a box-shadow:

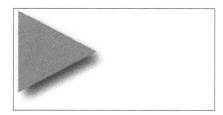

Here is the format for CSS filters:

```
.filter-drop-shadow {
    filter: drop-shadow(8px 8px 6px #333);
}
```

After the filter property we specify the filter we want to use, drop-shadow in this example, and then pass in the arguments for the filter. The drop-shadow follows a similar syntax to box-shadow so this one is easy; x and y offset, blur, then spread radius (both optional), and finally color (also optional, although I recommend specifying a color for consistency).

CSS filters are actually based upon SVG filters which have a wider support. We'll look at the SVG based equivalent in *Chapter 7, Using SVGs for Resolution Independence*.

Available CSS filters

There are a few filters to choose from. We will look at each. While images of most of the filters follow, readers reading a hard copy of this module (with monochrome images) may struggle to notice the differences. If you're in that situation, remember you can still view the various filters in the browser by opening `example_06-08`. I'm going to list each out now with a suitable value specified. As you might imagine, more of a value means more of the filter applied. Where images are used, the image is shown after the relevant code.

- `filter: url ('./img/filters.svg#filterRed')`: Lets you specify an SVG filter to use.

- `filter: blur(3px)`: Use a single length value (but not as a percentage).

- `filter: brightness(2)`: Use a value from 0 to 1 or 0% to 100%. 0/0% is black, 1/100% is 'normal,' and anything beyond brightens the element further.

- `filter: contrast(2)`: Use a value from 0 to 1 or 0% to 100%. 0/0% is black, 1/100% is 'normal,' and anything beyond raises the color contrast.

- `filter: drop-shadow(4px 4px 6px #333)`: We looked at `drop-shadow` in detail earlier.
- `filter: grayscale(.8)`: Use a value from 0 to 1, or 0% to 100% to apply varying amounts of grayscale to the element. A value of 0 would be no grayscale while a value of 1 would be fully grayscale.

- `filter: hue-rotate(25deg)`: Use a value between 0 and 360 degrees to adjust the colors around the color wheel.

- `filter: invert(75%)`: Use a value from 0 to 1, or 0% to 100% to define the amount the element has its colors inverted.

- `filter: opacity(50%)`: Use a value from 0 to 1, or 0% to 100% to alter the opacity of the element. This is similar to the `opacity` property you will already be familiar with. However, filters, as we shall see, can be combined and this allows opacity to be combined with other filters in one go.

- `filter: saturate(15%)`: Use a value from 0 to 1, or 0% to 100% to de-saturate an image and anything above 1/100% to add extra saturation.

- `filter: sepia(.75)`: Use a value from 0 to 1, or 0% to 100% to make the element appear with a more sepia color. 0/0% leaves the element 'as is' while anything above that applies greater amounts of sepia up to a maximum of 1/100%.

Combining CSS filters

You can also combine filters easily; simply space separate them. For example, here is how you would apply `opacity`, `blur`, and `sepia` filters at once:

```
.MultipleFilters {
    filter: opacity(10%) blur(2px) sepia(35%);
}
```

 Note: Apart from `hue-rotate`, when using filters, negative values are not allowed.

I think you'll agree, CSS filters offer some pretty powerful effects. They are also effects we can transition and transform from situation to situation. We'll look at how to do that in *Chapter 8, Transitions, Transformations, and Animations*.

However, before you go crazy with these new toys, we need to have a grown up conversation about performance.

A warning on CSS performance

When it comes to CSS performance, I would like you to remember this one thing:

> *"Architecture is outside the braces, performance is inside."*

> – Ben Frain

Let me expand on my little maxim:

As far as I am able to prove, worrying about whether a CSS selector (the part outside the curly braces), is fast or slow is pointless. I set out to prove this at `http://benfrain.com/css-performance-revisited-selectors-bloat-expensive-styles/`.

However, one thing that really can grind a page to a halt, CSS wise, is 'expensive' properties (the parts inside the curly braces). When we use the term 'expensive', in relation to certain styles, it simply means it costs the browser a lot of overhead. It's something that the browser finds overly taxing to do.

It's possible to take a common sense guess about what will likely cause the browser extra work. It's basically anything it would have to compute before it can paint things to the screen. For example, compare a standard div with a flat solid background, against a semi-opaque image, on top of a background made up of multiple gradients, with rounded corners and a `drop-shadow`. The latter is more expensive; it will result in far more computational work for the browser and subsequently cause more overhead.

Therefore, when you apply effects like filters, do so judiciously and, if possible, test whether the page speed suffers on the lowest powered devices you are hoping to support. At the least, switch on development tool features such as continuous page repainting in Chrome and toggle any affects you think may cause problems. This will provide you with data (in the form of a millisecond reading of how long the current viewport is taking to paint) to make a more educated decision on which effects to apply. The lower the figure, the faster the page will perform (although be aware that browsers/platforms vary so, as ever, test on real devices where possible).

For more on this subject I recommend the following resource:

`https://developers.google.com/web/fundamentals/performance/rendering/`

A note on CSS masks and clipping

In the near future, CSS will be able to offer masks and clipping as part of the CSS Masking Module Level 1. These features will enable us to clip an image with a shape or arbitrary path (specified via SVG or a number of polygon points). Sadly, despite the specification being at the more advanced CR stage, as I write this, the browser implementations are just too buggy to recommend. However, it's a fluid situation so by the time you are reading this, there's every chance the implementations will be solid. For the curious, I'll therefore refer you to the specification at `http://www.w3.org/TR/css-masking/`.

I also think Chris Coyier does a great job of explaining where things are at support wise in this post:

`http://css-tricks.com/clipping-masking-css/`

Finally, a good overview and explanation of what will be possible is offered by Sara Soueidan in this post:

`http://alistapart.com/article/css-shapes-101`

Summary

In this chapter we've looked at a selection of the most useful CSS features for creating lightweight aesthetics in responsive web designs. CSS3's background gradients curb our reliance on images for background effects. We have even considered how they can be used to create infinitely repeating background patterns. We've also learned how to use text-shadows to create simple text enhancements and box-shadows to add shadows to the outside and inside of elements. We've also looked at CSS filters. They allow us to achieve even more impressive visual effects with CSS alone and can be combined for truly impressive results.

In the next chapter we're going to turn our attention to creating and using SVGs as they are more simply called. While it's a very mature technology, it is only in the current climate of responsive, and high-performing websites that it has really come of age.

7
Using SVGs for Resolution Independence

Scalable Vector Graphics (SVG) is an important technology for responsive web design as it provides pin-sharp and future-proof graphical assets for all screen resolutions.

Images on the web, with formats such as JPEG, GIF, or PNG have their visual data saved as set pixels. If you save a graphic in any of those formats with a set width and height, and zoom the image to twice its original size or more, their limitations can be easily exposed.

Here's a screen grab of just that. A PNG image I've zoomed into in the browser:

Can you see how the image looks obviously pixelated? Here is the exact same image saved as a vector image, in SVG format, and zoomed to a similar level:

Hopefully the difference is obvious.

Beyond the smallest graphical assets, where at all possible, using SVG rather than JPEG, GIF, or PNG will produce resolution independent graphics that require far smaller file sizes compared to bitmap images.

While we will touch upon many aspects of SVG in this chapter, the focus will be on how to integrate them into your workflow, while also providing an overview of what is possible with SVG.

In this chapter we will cover:

- SVG, a brief history, and an anatomy of a basic SVG document
- Creating SVGs with popular image editing packages and services
- Inserting SVGs into a page with `img` and `object` tags
- Inserting SVGs as background images
- Inserting SVGs directly (inline) into HTML
- Re-using SVG symbols
- Referencing external SVG symbols
- What capabilities are possible with each insertion method
- Animating SVGs with SMIL
- Styling SVGs with an external style sheet
- Styling SVGs with internal styles
- Amending and animating SVGs with CSS
- Media queries and SVGs
- Optimizing SVGs
- Using SVGs to define filters for CSS

- Manipulating SVGs with JavaScript and JavaScript libraries
- Implementation tips
- Further resources

SVG is a dense subject. Which portions of this chapter are most relevant to your needs will depend on what you actually need from SVG. Hopefully, I can offer a few shortcuts right up front.

If you simply want to replace static graphical assets on a website with SVG versions, for sharper images and/or smaller file sizes, then look at the shorter sections on using SVG as background images and within `img` tags.

If you're curious about what applications and services can help you generate and manage SVG assets, skip down to the section, *Creating SVGs with popular image editing packages and services*, for some useful links and pointers.

If you want to understand SVG more fully, or animate and manipulate SVG, you had better get yourself comfy and get a double size of your favorite beverage as this is quite a long one.

To begin our journey of understanding, step with me back into 2001.

A brief history of SVG

The first release of SVG was in 2001. That was not a typo. SVG has been 'a thing' since 2001. While it gained traction along the way, it's only since the advent of high-resolution devices that they have received widespread interest and adoption. Here is the introduction to SVGs from the 1.1 specification (`http://www.w3.org/TR/SVG11/intro.html`):

SVG is a language for describing two-dimensional graphics in XML [XML10]. SVG allows for three types of graphic objects: vector graphic shapes (for example, paths consisting of straight lines and curves), images, and text.

As the name implies, SVGs allow two-dimensional images to be described in code as vector points. This makes them a great candidate for icons, line drawings, and charts.

As vectors describe relative points, they can scale to any size, without loss of fidelity. Furthermore, in terms of data, as SVG are described as vector points, it tends to make them tiny, compared to a comparably sized JPEG, GIF, or PNG file.

Browser support for SVG is now also very good. Android 2.3 and above, and Internet Explorer 9 and above, support them (`http://caniuse.com/#search=svg`).

The graphic that is a document

Ordinarily, if you try and view the code of a graphics file in a text editor the resultant text is completely unintelligible.

Where SVG graphics differ is that they are actually described in a markup style language. SVG is written in **Extensible Markup Language** (**XML**), a close relative of HTML. Although you may not realize it, XML is actually everywhere on the Internet. Do you use an RSS reader? That's XML right there. XML is the language that wraps up the content of an RSS feed and makes it easily consumable to a variety of tools and services.

So not only can machines read and understand SVG graphics, but we can too.

Let me give you an example. Take a look at this star graphic:

This is an SVG graphic, called `Star.svg` inside `example_07-01`. You can either open this example in the browser where it will appear as the star or you can open it in a text editor and you can see the code that generates it. Consider this:

```
<?xml version="1.0" encoding="UTF-8" standalone="no"?>
<svg width="198px" height="188px" viewBox="0 0 198 188" version="1.1"
xmlns="http://www.w3.org/2000/svg" xmlns:xlink="http://www.
w3.org/1999/xlink" xmlns:sketch="http://www.bohemiancoding.com/sketch/
ns">
    <!-- Generator: Sketch 3.2.2 (9983) - http://www.bohemiancoding.
com/sketch -->
    <title>Star 1</title>
    <desc>Created with Sketch.</desc>
    <defs></defs>
    <g id="Page-1" stroke="none" stroke-width="1" fill="none" fill-
rule="evenodd" sketch:type="MSPage">
        <polygon id="Star-1" stroke="#979797" stroke-width="3"
fill="#F8E81C" sketch:type="MSShapeGroup" points="99 154 40.2214748
184.901699 51.4471742 119.45085 3.89434837 73.0983006 69.6107374
63.5491503 99 4 128.389263 63.5491503 194.105652 73.0983006 146.552826
119.45085 157.778525 184.901699 "></polygon>
    </g>
</svg>
```

That is the entirety of the code needed to generate that star as an SVG graphic.

Now, ordinarily, if you've never looked at the code of an SVG graphic before, you may be wondering why you would ever want to. If all you want is vector graphics displayed on the web, you certainly don't need to. Just find a graphics application that will save your vector artwork as an SVG and you're done. We will list a few of those packages in the coming pages.

However, although it's certainly common and possible to only work with SVG graphics from within a graphics editing application, understanding exactly how an SVG fits together and how you can tweak it to your exact will can become very useful if you need to start manipulating and animating an SVG.

So, let's take a closer look at that SVG markup and get an appreciation of what exactly is going on in there. I'd like to draw your attention to a few key things.

The root SVG element

The root SVG element here has attributes for `width`, `height`, and `viewbox`.

```
<svg width="198px" height="188px" viewBox="0 0 198 188"
```

Each of these plays an important role in how an SVG is displayed.

Hopefully at this point you understand the term 'viewport'. It's been used in most chapters of this module to describe the area of a device through which content is viewed. For example, a mobile device might have a 320px by 480px viewport. A desktop computer might have a 1920px by 1080px viewport.

The `width` and `height` attributes of the SVG effectively create a viewport. Through this defined viewport we can peek in to see the shapes defined inside the SVG. Just like a web page, the contents of the SVG may be bigger than the viewport but that doesn't mean the rest isn't there, it's merely hidden from our current view.

The viewbox on the other hand defines the coordinate system in which all the shapes of the SVG are governed.

You can think of the viewbox values 0 0 198 188 as describing the top left and bottom right area of a rectangle. The first two values, known technically as **min-x** and **min-y**, describe the top left corner, while the second two, known technically as width and height, describe the bottom right corner.

Having the `viewbox` attribute allows you to do things like zoom an image in or out. For example, if you halve the width and height in the `viewbox` attribute like this:

```
<svg width="198px" height="188px" viewBox="0 0 99 94"
```

The shape will 'zoom' to fill the size of the SVG width and height.

To really understand the viewbox and SVG coordinate system and the opportunities it presents, I recommend this post by Sara Soueidan: `http://sarasoueidan.com/blog/svg-coordinate-systems/` and this post by Jakob Jenkov: `http://tutorials.jenkov.com/svg/svg-viewport-view-box.html`

Namespace

This SVG has an additional namespace defined for the Sketch graphics program that generated it (`xmlns` is short for XML namespace).

```
xmlns:sketch="http://www.bohemiancoding.com/sketch/ns"
```

These namespace references tend to only be used by the program that generated the SVG, so they are often unneeded when the SVGs are bound for the web. Optimization processes for reducing the size of SVGs will often strip them out.

The title and desc tags

There are `title` and `desc` tags which make an SVG document highly accessible:

```
<title>Star 1</title>
    <desc>Created with Sketch.</desc>
```

These tags can be used to describe the contents of the graphics when they cannot be seen. However, when SVG graphics are used for background graphics, these tags can be stripped to further reduce file size.

The defs tag

There is an empty `defs` tag in our example code:

```
<defs></defs>
```

Despite being empty in our example, this is an important element. It is used to store definitions of all manner of reusable content such as gradients, symbols, paths, and more.

The g element

The g element is used to group other elements together. For example, if you were drawing an SVG of a car, you might group the shapes that make up an entire wheel inside a g tag.

```
<g id="Page-1" stroke="none" stroke-width="1" fill="none" fill-
rule="evenodd" sketch:type="MSPage">
```

In our g tag we can see the earlier namespace of sketch reused here. This will help that graphics application open this graphic again but it serves no further purpose should this image be bound elsewhere.

SVG shapes

The innermost node in this example is a polygon.

```
<polygon id="Star-1" stroke="#979797" stroke-width="3" fill="#F8E81C"
sketch:type="MSShapeGroup" points="99 154 40.2214748 184.901699
51.4471742 119.45085 3.89434837 73.0983006 69.6107374 63.5491503 99
4 128.389263 63.5491503 194.105652 73.0983006 146.552826 119.45085
157.778525 184.901699 "></polygon>
```

SVGs have a number of readymade shapes available (path, rect, circle, ellipse, line, polyline, and polygon).

SVG paths

SVG paths differ from the other shapes of SVG as they are composed of any number of connected points (giving you the freedom to create any shape you like).

So that's the guts of an SVG file, and hopefully now you have a high-level understanding of what's going on. While some will relish the opportunity to hand write or edit SVG files in code, a great many more would rather generate SVGs with a graphics package. Let's consider some of the more popular choices.

Creating SVGs with popular image editing packages and services

While SVGs can be opened, edited, and written in a text editor, there are plenty of applications offering a **graphical user interface** (GUI) that make authoring complex SVG graphics easier if you come from a graphics editing background. Perhaps the most obvious choice is Adobe's Illustrator (PC/Mac). However, it is expensive for casual users so my own preference is Bohemian Coding's Sketch (Mac only: http://bohemiancoding.com/sketch/). That itself isn't cheap (currently at $99), but it's still the option I would recommend if you use a Mac.

If you use Windows/Linux or are looking for a cheaper option, consider the free and open-source, Inkscape (https://inkscape.org/en/). It's by no means the prettiest tool to work with but it is very capable (if you want any proof, view the Inkscape gallery at https://inkscape.org/en/community/gallery/).

Finally, there are a few online editors. Google has SVG-edit (http://svg-edit. googlecode.com/svn/branches/stable/editor/svg-editor.html). There is also Draw SVG (http://www.drawsvg.org), and Method Draw, an arguably better looking fork of SVG-edit (http://editor.method.ac/).

Save time with SVG icon services

The aforementioned applications all give you the capability to create SVG graphics from scratch. However, if it's icons you're after, you can probably save a lot of time (and for me, get better results) by downloading SVG versions of icons from an online icon service. My personal favorite is http://icomoon.io/ is also great.

To quickly illustrate the benefits of an online icon service, loading the icomoon.io application gives you a searchable library of icons (some free, some paid):

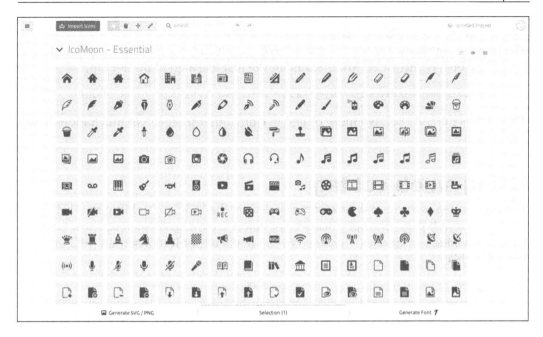

You select the ones you want and then click download. The resultant file contains the icons as SVGs, PNGs, and also SVG symbols for placement in the `defs` element (remember the `defs` element is a container element for referenced elements).

To see for yourself, open `example_07-02` and you can see the resultant download files after I'd chosen five icons from `http://icomoon.io/`.

Inserting SVGs into your web pages

There are a number of things that you can do (browser dependent) with SVG images that you can't do with normal image formats (JPEG, GIF, PNG). The range of what's possible is largely dependent upon the way that the SVG is inserted into the page. So, before we get to what we can actually do with SVGs, we'll consider the various ways we can actually get them on the page in the first place.

Using an img tag

The most straightforward way to use an SVG graphic is exactly how you would insert any image into an HTML document. We just use a good ol' `img` tag:

```
<img src="mySconeVector.svg" alt="Amazing line art of a scone" />
```

This makes the SVG behave more or less like any other image. Not much more to say about that.

Using an object tag

The `object` tag is the container recommended by the W3C for holding non-HTML content in a web page (the specification for object is at `http://www.w3.org/TR/html5/embedded-content-0.html`). We can make use of it to insert an SVG into our page like this:

```
<object data="img/svgfile.svg" type="image/svg+xml">
    <span class="fallback-info">Your browser doesn't support SVG</span>
</object>
```

Either a `data` or `type` attribute is required, although I would always recommend adding both. The `data` attribute is where you link out to the SVG asset in the same manner you would link to any other asset. The `type` attribute describes the MIME type relevant for the content. In this instance, `image/svg+xml` is the MIME (Internet media type) type to indicate the data is SVG. You can also add a `width` and `height` attribute too if you want to constrain the size of the SVG with this container.

An SVG inserted into the page via an `object` tag is also accessible with JavaScript so that's one reason to insert them this way. However, an additional bonus of using the `object` tag is that it provides a simple mechanism for when a browser doesn't understand the data type. For example, if that prior `object` element was viewed in Internet Explorer 8 (which has no support for SVG), it would simply see the message 'Your browser doesn't support SVG'. You can use this space to provide a fallback image in an `img` tag. However, be warned that from my cursory testing, the browser will always download the fallback image, regardless of whether it actually needs it. Therefore, if you want your site to load in the shortest possible time (you do, trust me) this might not actually be the best choice.

 If you want to manipulate an SVG inserted via an `object` tag with jQuery, you'll need to use the native `.contentDocument` JavaScript property. You can then use the jQuery `.attr` to change things like `fill`.

An alternative approach to providing a fallback would be to add a `background-image` via the CSS. For example, in our example above, our fallback span has a class of `.fallback-info`. We could make use of this in CSS to link to a suitable `background-image`. That way the `background-image` will only be downloaded if required.

Insert an SVG as a background image

SVGs can be used as a background image in CSS, much the same way as any other image format (PNG, JPG, GIF). There's nothing special about the way you reference them:

```
.item {
    background-image: url('image.svg');
}
```

For older browsers that don't support SVG, you might want to include a 'fallback' image in a more widely supported format (typically PNG). Here's one way to do that for Internet Explorer 8 and Android 2, as IE8 doesn't support SVG or `background-size`, and Android 2.3 doesn't support SVG and requires a vendor prefix for `background-size`:

```
.item {
    background: url('image.png') no-repeat;
    background: url('image.svg') left top / auto auto no-repeat;
}
```

In CSS, where two equivalent properties are applied, the one further down the style sheet will always overrule those above. In CSS, a browser will always disregard a property/value pair in a rule it cannot make sense of. Therefore, in this case the older browsers get the PNG, as they cannot make use of the SVG or understand an un-prefixed `background-size` property, while newer browsers that could actually use either, take the bottom one as it supersedes the first.

You can also provide fallbacks with the aid of Modernizr; the JavaScript tool for feature testing the browser (Modernizr is discussed more fully in *Chapter 5, CSS3 – Selectors, Typography, Color Modes, and New Features*). Modernizr has individual tests for some of the different SVG insertion methods, and the next version of Modernizr (unreleased at the time of writing) may have something more specific for SVG in CSS. For now however, you can do this:

```
.item {
    background-image: url('image.png');
}
.svg .item {
    background-image: url('image.svg');
}
```

Or invert the logic if preferred:

```css
.item {
    background-image: url('image.svg');
}
.no-svg .item {
    background-image: url('image.png');
}
```

When Feature Queries are more fully supported, you could also do this:

```css
.item {
    background-image: url('image.png');
}

@supports (fill: black) {
    .item {
        background-image: url('image.svg');
    }
}
```

The `@supports` rule works here because `fill` is a SVG property so if the browser understands that, it would take the lower rule over the first.

If your needs for SVG are primarily static background images, perhaps for icons and the like, I highly recommend implementing SVGs as background images. That's because there are a number of tools that will automatically create image sprites or style sheet assets (which means including the SVGs as data URIs), fallback PNG assets, and requisite style sheets from any individual SVGs you create. Using SVGs this way is very well supported, the images themselves cache well (so performance wise they work very well), and it's simple to implement.

A brief aside on data URIs

If you're reading that prior section and wondering what on earth a data **Uniform Resource Identifier (URI)** is, in relation to CSS, it's a means of including what would ordinarily be an external asset, such as an image, within the CSS file itself. Therefore, where we might do this to link at an external image file:

```css
.external {
  background-image: url('Star.svg');
}
```

We could simply include the image inside our style sheet with a data URI like this:

```
.data-uri {
  background-image: url(data:image/svg+xml,%3C%3Fxml%20
version%3D%221.0%22%20encoding%3D%22UTF-8%22%20standalone%3D%22
no%22%3F%3E%0A%3Csvg%20width%3D%22198px%22%20height%3D%22188px-
%22%20viewBox%3D%220%200%20198%20188%22%20version%3D%221.1%22%20
xmlns%3D%22http%3A%2F%2Fwww.w3.org%2F2000%2Fsvg%22%20xmlns%3Axlink
%3D%22http%3A%2F%2Fwww.w3.org%2F1999%2Fxlink%22%20xmlns%3Asketch%3
D%22http%3A%2F%2Fwww.bohemiancoding.com%2Fsketch%2Fns%22%3E%0A%20
%20%20%20%3C%21--%20Generator%3A%20Sketch%203.2.2%20%289983%29%20
-%20http%3A%2F%2Fwww.bohemiancoding.com%2Fsketch%20--%3E%0A%20
%20%20%20%3Ctitle%3EStar%201%3C%2Ftitle%3E%0A%20%20%20%20
%3Cdesc%3ECreated%20with%20Sketch.%3C%2Fdesc%3E%0A%20%20%20%20-
%3Cdefs%3E%3C%2Fdefs%3E%0A%20%20%20%20%3Cg%20id%3D%22Page-1%22%20
stroke%3D%22none%22%20stroke-width%3D%221%22%20fill%3D%22none%22%20
fill-rule%3D%22evenodd%22%20sketch%3Atype%3D%22MSPage%22%3E%
0A%20%20%20%20%20%20%20%20%3Cpolygon%20id%3D%22Star-1%22%20
stroke%3D%22%23979797%22%20stroke-width%3D%223%22%20
fill%3D%22%23F8E81C%22%20sketch%3Atype%3D%22MSShapeGroup%22%20
points%3D%2299%20154%2040.2214748%20184.901699%2051.4471742%20
119.45085%203.89434837%2073.0983006%2069.6107374%2063.5491503%2099%20
4%20128.389263%2063.5491503%20194.105652%2073.0983006%20146.552826%20
119.45085%20157.778525%20184.901699%20%22%3E%3C%2Fpolygon%3E%0A%20%20
%20%20%3C%2Fg%3E%0A%3C%2Fsvg%3E);
}
```

It's not pretty but it provides a way to negate a separate request over the network. There are different encoding methods for data URIs and plenty of tools available to create data URIs from your assets.

If encoding SVGs in this manner, I would suggest avoiding the base64 method as it doesn't compress as well as text for SVG content.

Generating image sprites

My personal recommendation, tool wise, for generating image sprites or data URI assets, is Iconizr (`http://iconizr.com/`). It gives you complete control over how you would like your resultant SVG and fallback PNG assets. You can have the SVGs and fallback PNG files output as data URIs or image sprites and it even includes the requisite JavaScript snippet for loading the correct asset if you opt for data URIs; highly recommended.

Also, if you are wondering whether to choose data URIs or image sprites for your projects, I did further research on the pros and cons of data URIs or image sprites that you may be interested in should you be facing the same choice: `http://benfrain.com/image-sprites-data-uris-icon-fonts-v-svgs/`

While I'm a big fan of SVGs as background images, if you want to animate them dynamically, or inject values into them via JavaScript, then it will be best to opt for inserting SVG data 'inline' into the HTML.

Inserting an SVG inline

As SVG is merely an XML document, you can insert it directly into the HTML. For example:

```
<div>
    <h3>Inserted 'inline':</h3>
    <span class="inlineSVG">
        <svg id="svgInline" width="198" height="188" viewBox="0 0
198 188" xmlns="http://www.w3.org/2000/svg" xmlns:xlink="http://www.
w3.org/1999/xlink">
        <title>Star 1</title>
            <g class="star_Wrapper" fill="none" fill-rule="evenodd">
                <path id="star_Path" stroke="#979797" stroke-
width="3" fill="#F8E81C" d="M99 154l-58.78 30.902 11.227-65.45L3.894
73.097l65.717-9.55L99 4l29.39 59.55 65.716 9.548-47.553 46.353 11.226
65.452z" />
            </g>
        </svg>
    </span>
</div>
```

There is no special wrapping element needed, you literally just insert the SVG markup inside the HTML markup. It's also worth knowing that if you remove any width and height attributes on the svg element, the SVG will scale fluidly to fit the containing element.

Inserting SVGs into your documents is probably the most versatile in terms of SVG features.

Re-using graphical objects from symbols

Earlier in the chapter I mentioned that I had picked and downloaded some icons from IcoMoon (`http://icomoon.io`). They were icons depicting touch gesture: swipe, pinch, drag, and so on. Suppose in a website you are building you need to make use of them multiple times. Remember I mentioned that there was a version of those icons as SVG symbol definitions? That's what we will make use of now.

In `example_07-09` we will insert the various symbol definitions inside the `defs` element of an SVG in the page. You'll notice that on the SVG element, an inline style is used: `display:none` and the `height` and `width` attributes have both been set to zero (those styles could be set in CSS if you would rather). This is so that this SVG takes up no space. We are only using this SVG to house symbols of the graphical objects we want to use elsewhere.

So, our markup starts like this:

```
<body>
    <svg display="none" width="0" height="0" version="1.1"
xmlns="http://www.w3.org/2000/svg" xmlns:xlink="http://www.
w3.org/1999/xlink">
    <defs>
    <symbol id="icon-drag-left-right" viewBox="0 0 1344 1024">
        <title>drag-left-right</title>
        <path class="path1" d="M256 192v-160l-224 224 224
224v-160h256v-128z"></path>
```

Notice the `symbol` element inside the `defs` element? This is the element to use when we want to define a shape for later reuse.

After the SVG defining all necessary symbols for our work, we have all our 'normal' HTML markup. Then, when we want to make use of one of those symbols, we can do this:

```
<svg class="icon-drag-left-right">
  <use xlink:href="#icon-drag-left-right"></use>
</svg>
```

That will display the drag left and right icon:

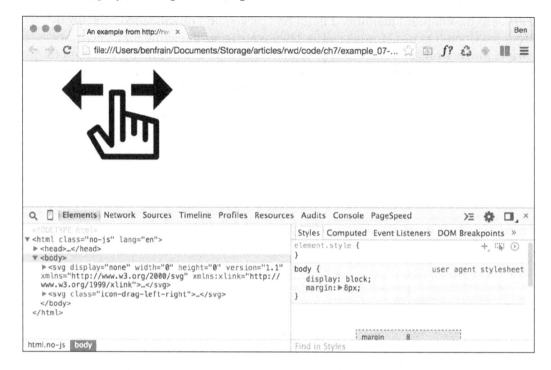

The magic here is the use element. As you might have guessed from the name, it's used to make use of existing graphical objects that have already been defined elsewhere. The mechanism for choosing what to reference is the xlink attribute that in this case is referencing the symbol ID of the 'drag left and right' icon (#icon-drag-left-right) we have inline at the beginning of the markup.

When you re-use a symbol, unless you explicitly set a size (either with attributes on the element itself or with CSS) the use will be set to width and height 100%. So, to re-size our icon we could do this:

```
.icon-drag-left-right {
    width: 2.5rem;
    height: 2.5rem;
}
```

The use element can be used to re-use all sorts of SVG content: gradients, shapes, symbols, and more.

Inline SVGs allow different colors in different contexts

With inline SVGs you can also do useful things like change colors based on context, and that's great when you need multiple versions of the same icon in different colors:

```
.icon-drag-left-right {
    fill: #f90;
}

.different-context .icon-drag-left-right {
    fill: #ddd;
}
```

Make dual-tone icons that inherit the color of their parent

With inline SVGs you can also have some fun and create a two-tone effects from a single color icon (as long as the SVG is made up of more than one path) with the use of `currentColor`, the oldest CSS variable. To do this, inside the SVG symbol, set the `fill` of the path you want to be one color as `currentColor`. Then use the color value in your CSS to color the element. For the paths in the SVG symbol without the fill, set as `currentColor`, they will receive the fill value. To exemplify:

```
.icon-drag-left-right {
    width: 2.5rem;
    height: 2.5rem;
    fill: #f90;
    color: #ccc; /* this gets applied to the path that has it's fill
attribute set to currentColor in the symbol */
}
```

Here's that same symbol re-used three times, each with different colors and sizes:

Remember you can dig around the code in example_07-09. It's also worth knowing that the color doesn't have to be set on that element itself, it can be on any parent element; the currentColor will inherit a value from up the DOM tree to the nearest parent with a color value set.

There are a lot of positives to using SVG in this way. The only downside being that it's necessary to include the same SVG data on every page you want to use the icons. Sadly, this is bad for performance, as the assets (the SVG data) isn't going to be cached easily. However, there is another option (if you are happy to add a script to support Internet Explorer).

Re-using graphical objects from external sources

Rather than paste in an enormous set of SVG symbols in each page, while still using the use element, it's possible to link out to external SVG files and grab the portion of the document you want to use. Take a look at example-07-10 and the same three icons as we had in example_07-09 are put on the page in this manner:

```
<svg class="icon-drag-left-right">
    <use xlink:href="defs.svg#icon-drag-left-right"></use>
</svg>
```

The important part to understand is the href. We are linking to an external SVG file (the defs.svg part) and then specifying the ID of the symbol within that file we want to use (the #icon-drag-left-right part).

The benefits of this approach are that the asset is cached by the browser (just like any other external image would/could be) and it saves littering our markup with an SVG full of symbol definitions. The downside is that, unlike when the defs are placed inline, any dynamic changes made to the defs.svg (for example, if a path was being manipulated by JavaScript) won't be updated in the use tags.

Sadly, Internet Explorer does not allow referencing symbols from external assets. However, there's a polyfill script for IE9-11, called **SVG For Everybody** that allows us to use this technique regardless. Head over to https://github.com/jonathantneal/svg4everybody for more information.

When using that piece of JavaScript, you can happily reference external assets and the polyfill will insert the SVG data directly into the body of the document for Internet Explorer.

What you can do with each SVG insertion method (inline, object, background-image, and img)

As mentioned previously, SVGs differ from other graphical assets. They can behave differently, depending upon the way they are inserted into a page. As we have seen, there are four main ways in which to place SVG onto the page:

- Inside an `img` tag
- Inside an `object` tag
- As a background image
- Inline

And depending upon the insertion method, certain capabilities will or will not be available to you.

To understand what should be possible with each insertion method, it might be simpler to consider this table.

Feature	img	object	inline	bg image
SMIL	Y	Y	Y	Y
External CSS	N	*1	Y	N
Internal CSS	Y	Y	Y	Y
Access via JS	N	Y	Y	N
Cacheable	Y	Y	*2	Y
MQ in SVG	Y	Y	*3	Y
Use possible	N	Y	Y	N

Now there are caveats to consider, marked within numbers:

- ***1**: When using an SVG inside an object you can use an external style sheet to style the SVG but you have to link to that style sheet from within the SVG
- ***2**: You can use SVGs in an external asset (which is cacheable) but it doesn't work by default in Internet Explorer
- ***3**: A media query inside the styles section of an 'inlined' SVG works on the size of the document it lives in (not the size of the SVG itself)

Browser schisms

Be aware that browser implementations of SVG also vary. Therefore, just because those things should be possible (as indicated above), doesn't mean they actually will be in every browser, or that they will behave consistently!

For example, the results in the preceding table are based upon the test page in `example_07-03`.

The behavior of the test page is comparable in the latest version of Firefox, Chrome, and Safari. However, Internet Explorer sometimes does things a little differently.

For example, in all the SVG capable versions of Internet Explorer (at this point, that's 9, 10, and 11), as we have already seen, it is not possible to reference external SVG sources. Furthermore, Internet Explorer applies the styles from the external style sheet onto the SVGs regardless of how they have been inserted (all the other browsers only apply styles from external style sheets if the SVGs have been inserted via an `object` or inline). Internet Explorer also doesn't allow any animation of SVG via CSS; animation of SVG in Internet Explorer has to be done via JavaScript. I'll say that one again for the folks at the back in the cheap seats: you cannot animate SVGs in Internet Explorer by any means other than JavaScript.

Extra SVG capabilities and oddities

Let's put aside the foibles of browsers for a moment and consider what some of these features in the table actually allow and why you may or may not want to make use of them.

SVGs will always render as sharp as the viewing device will allow and regardless of the manner of insertion. For most practical situations, resolution independence is usually reason enough to use SVG. It's then just a question of choosing whichever insertion method suits your workflow and the task at hand.

However, there are other capabilities and oddities that are worth knowing about such as SMIL animation, different ways to link to external style sheets, marking internal styles with character data delimiters, amending an SVG with JavaScript, and making use of media queries within an SVG. Let's cover those next.

SMIL animation

SMIL animations (`http://www.w3.org/TR/smil-animation/`) are a way to define animations for an SVG within the SVG document itself.

SMIL (pronounced 'smile' in case you were wondering) stands for synchronized multimedia integration language and was developed as a method of defining animations inside an XML document (remember, SVG is XML based).

Here's an example of how to define a SMIL based animation:

```
<g class="star_Wrapper" fill="none" fill-rule="evenodd">
    <animate xlink:href="#star_Path" attributeName="fill"
attributeType="XML" begin="0s" dur="2s" fill="freeze" from="#F8E81C"
to="#14805e" />

    <path id="star_Path" stroke="#979797" stroke-width="3"
fill="#F8E81C" d="M99 154l-58.78 30.902 11.227-65.45L3.894
73.097l65.717-9.55L99 4l29.39 59.55 65.716 9.548-47.553 46.353 11.226
65.452z" />
</g>
```

I've grabbed a section of the earlier SVG we looked at. The `g` is a grouping element in SVG, and this one includes both a star shape (the `path` element with the `id="star_Path"`) and the SMIL animation within the `animate` element. That simple animation tweens the fill color of the star from yellow to green over two seconds. What's more, it does that whether the SVG is put on the page in an `img`, `object`, `background-image`, or inline (no, honestly, open up `example_07-03` in any recent browser other than Internet Explorer to see).

> **Tweening**
>
> In case you didn't already know (I didn't), 'tweening' as a term is simply a shortening of 'inbetweening' as it merely indicates all the inbetween stages from one animation point to another.

Wow! Great, right? Well, it could have been. Despite being a standard for some time, it looks like SMILs days are numbered.

The end of SMIL

SMIL has no support in Internet Explorer. None. Nada. Zip. Zilch. I could go on with other words that amount to very little but I trust you understand there's not much support for SMIL in Internet Explorer at this point.

Worse still (I know, I'm giving you both barrels here) Microsoft have no plans to introduce it either. Take a look at the platform status: `https://status.modern.ie/svgsmilanimation?term=SMIL`

Plus Chrome have now indicated an intent to deprecate SMIL in the Chrome browser: `https://groups.google.com/a/chromium.org/forum/#!topic/blink-dev/5o0yiO440LM`

Mic. Dropped.

 If you still have a need to use SMIL, Sara Soueidan wrote an excellent, in-depth article about SMIL animations at `http://css-tricks.com/guide-svg-animations-smil/`.

Thankfully, there are plenty of other ways we can animate SVGs, which we will come to shortly. So if you have to support Internet Explorer hang on in there.

Styling an SVG with an external style sheet

It's possible to style an SVG with CSS. This can be CSS enclosed in the SVG itself, or in the CSS style sheets you would write all your 'normal' CSS in.

Now, if you refer back to our features table from earlier in the chapter, you can see that styling SVG with external CSS isn't possible when the SVG is included via an `img` tag or as a background-image (apart from Internet Explorer). It's only possible when SVGs are inserted via an `object` tag or `inline`.

There are two syntaxes for linking to an external style sheet from an SVG. The most straightforward way is like this (you would typically add this in the `defs` section):

```
<link href="styles.css" type="text/css" rel="stylesheet"/>
```

It's akin to the way we used to link to style sheets prior to HTML5 (for example, note the `type` attribute is no longer necessary in HTML5). However, despite this working in many browsers, it isn't the way the specifications define how external style sheets should be linked in SVG (`http://www.w3.org/TR/SVG/styling.html`). Here is the correct/official way, actually defined for XML back in 1999 (`http://www.w3.org/1999/06/REC-xml-stylesheet-19990629/`):

```
<?xml-stylesheet href="styles.css" type="text/css"?>
```

You need to add that above the opening SVG element in your file. For example:

```
<?xml-stylesheet href="styles.css" type="text/css"?>
<svg width="198" height="188" viewBox="0 0 198 188" xmlns="http://www.w3.org/2000/svg" xmlns:xlink="http://www.w3.org/1999/xlink">
```

Interestingly, the latter syntax is the only one that works in Internet Explorer. So, when you need to link out to a style sheet from your SVG, I'd recommend using this second syntax for wider support.

You don't have to use an external style sheet; you can use inline styles directly in the SVG itself if you would rather.

Styling an SVG with internal styles

You can place styles for an SVG within the SVG itself. They should be placed within the `defs` element. As SVG is XML based, it's safest to include the **Character Data (CDATA)** marker. The CDATA marker simply tells the browser that the information within the character data delimited section could possibly be interpreted as XML markup but should not be. The syntax is like this:

```
<defs>
    <style type="text/css">
        <![CDATA[
            #star_Path {
                stroke: red;
            }
        ]]>
    </style>
</defs>
```

SVG properties and values within CSS

Notice that `stroke` property in that prior code block. That isn't a CSS property, it's an SVG property. There are quite a few specific SVG properties you can use in styles (regardless of whether they are declared inline or via an external style sheet). For example, with an SVG, you don't specify a `background-color`, instead you specify a `fill`. You don't specify a `border`, you specify a `stroke-width`. For the full list of SVG specific properties, take a look at the specification here: `http://www.w3.org/TR/SVG/styling.html`

With either inline or external CSS, it's possible to do all the 'normal' CSS things you would expect; change an elements appearance, animate, transform elements, and so on.

Animate an SVG with CSS

Let's consider a quick example of adding a CSS animation inside an SVG (remember, these styles could just as easily be in an external style sheet too).

Let's take the star example we have looked at throughout this chapter and make it spin. You can look at the finished example in example_07-07:

```html
<div class="wrapper">
    <svg width="198" height="188" viewBox="0 0 220 200" xmlns="http://
www.w3.org/2000/svg" xmlns:xlink="http://www.w3.org/1999/xlink">
        <title>Star 1</title>
        <defs>
            <style type="text/css">
                <![CDATA[
                @keyframes spin {
                    0% {
                        transform: rotate(0deg);
                    }
                    100% {
                        transform: rotate(360deg);
                    }
                }
                .star_Wrapper {
                    animation: spin 2s 1s;
                    transform-origin: 50% 50%;
                }
                .wrapper {
                    padding: 2rem;
                    margin: 2rem;
                }
                ]]>
            </style>
            <g id="shape">
                <path fill="#14805e" d="M50 50h50v50H50z"/>
                <circle fill="#ebebeb" cx="50" cy="50" r="50"/>
            </g>
        </defs>
        <g class="star_Wrapper" fill="none" fill-rule="evenodd">
            <path id="star_Path" stroke="#333" stroke-width="3"
fill="#F8E81C" d="M99 154l-58.78 30.902 11.227-65.45L3.894
73.097l65.717-9.55L99 4l29.39 59.55 65.716 9.548-47.553 46.353 11.226
65.453z"/>
        </g>
    </svg>
</div>
```

If you load that example in the browser, after a 1 second delay, the star will spin a full circle over the course of 2 seconds.

 Notice how a transform origin of `50% 50%` has been set on the SVG? That's because, unlike CSS, the default `transform-origin` of an SVG is not 50% 50% (center in both axis), it's actually 0 0 (top left). Without that property set, the star would rotate around the top left point.

You can get quite far animating SVGs with CSS animations alone (well, assuming you don't need to worry about Internet Explorer). However, when you want to add interactivity, support Internet Explorer, or synchronize a number of events, it's generally best to lean on JavaScript. And the good news is that there are great libraries that make animating SVGs really easy. Let's look at an example of that now.

Animating SVG with JavaScript

With an SVG inserted into the page via an `object` tag or inline, it's possible to manipulate the SVG directly or indirectly with JavaScript.

By indirectly, I mean it's possible with JavaScript to change a class on or above the SVG that would cause an CSS animation to start. For example:

```
svg {
    /* no animation */
}

.added-with-js svg {
    /* animation */
}
```

However, it's also possible to animate an SVG via JavaScript directly.

If animating just one or two things independently, it's probable things would be lighter, code wise, by writing the JavaScript by hand. However, if you need to animate lots of elements or synchronize the animation of elements as if on a timeline, JavaScript libraries can really help. Ultimately, you will need to judge whether the weight of including the library in your page can be justified for the goal you are trying to achieve.

My recommendation for animating SVGs via JavaScript is the GreenSock animation platform (`http://greensock.com`), Velocity.js (`http://julian.com/research/velocity/`), or Snap.svg (`http://snapsvg.io/`). For the next example, we'll cover a very simple example using GreenSock.

A simple example of animating an SVG with GreenSock

Suppose we want to make an interface dial, that animates around when we click a button from zero to whatever value we input. We want not only the stroke of the dial to animate in both length and color, but also the number from zero to the value we input. You can view the completed implementation in `example_07-08`.

So, if we entered a value of 75, and clicked animate, it would fill around to look like this:

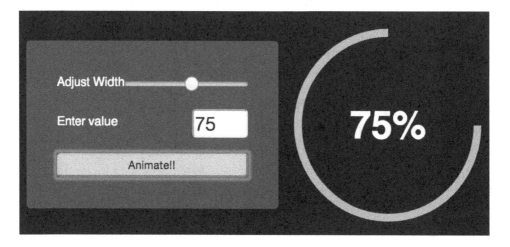

Instead of listing out the entire JavaScript file (which is heavily commented so should make some sense to read in isolation), for brevity's sake, we'll just consider the key points.

The basic idea is that we have made a circle as an SVG `<path>` (rather than a `<circle>` element). As it's a path it means we can animate the path as if it were being drawn using the `stroke-dashoffset` technique. There's more info on this technique in the boxed out section below but briefly, we use JavaScript to measure the length of the path and then use the `stroke-dasharray` attribute to specify the length of the rendered part of the line and the length of the gap. Then we use `stroke-dashoffset` to change where that `dasharray` starts. This means you can effectively start the stroke 'off' the path and animate it in. This gives the illusion that the path is being drawn.

If the value to animate the `dasharray` to was a static, known value, this effect would be relatively simple to achieve with a CSS animation and a little trial and error (more on CSS animations in the next chapter).

However, besides a dynamic value, at the same time as we are 'drawing' the line we want to fade in the stroke color from one value to another and visually count up to the input value in the text node. This is an animation equivalent of patting our heads, rubbing our tummy, and counting backwards from 10,000. GreenSock makes those things trivially easy (the animation part; it won't rub your tummy or pat your head, although it can count back from 10,000 should you need to). Here are the lines of JavaScript needed to make GreenSock do all three:

```
// Animate the drawing of the line and color change
TweenLite.to(circlePath, 1.5, {'stroke-dashoffset': "-"+amount,
stroke: strokeEndColour});
// Set a counter to zero and animate to the input value
var counter = { var: 0 };
TweenLite.to(counter, 1.5, {
    var: inputValue,
    onUpdate: function () {
        text.textContent = Math.ceil(counter.var) + "%";
    },
    ease:Circ.easeOut
});
```

In essence, with the `TweenLite.to()` function you pass in the thing you want to animate, the time over which the animation should occur, and then the values you want to change (and what you want them to change to).

The GreenSock site has excellent documentation and support forums so if you find yourself needing to synchronize a number of animations at once, be sure to clear a day from your diary and familiarize yourself with GreenSock.

In case you haven't come across the SVG 'line drawing' technique before it was popularized by Polygon magazine when Vox Media animated a couple of line drawings of the Xbox One and Playstation 4 games consoles. You can read the original post at `http://product.voxmedia.com/2013/11/25/5426880/polygon-feature-design-svg-animations-for-fun-and-profit`

There's also an excellent and more thorough explanation of the technique by Jake Archibald at `http://jakearchibald.com/2013/animated-line-drawing-svg/`.

Optimising SVGs

As conscientious developers, we want to ensure that assets are as small as possible. The easiest way to do this with SVGs is to make use of automation tools that can optimize various particulars of SVG documents. Besides obvious economies such as removing elements (for example, stripping the title and description elements) it's also possible to perform a raft of micro-optimizations that, when added up, make for far leaner SVG assets.

Presently, for this task I would recommend SVGO (`https://github.com/svg/svgo`). If you have never used SVGO before I would recommend starting with SVGOMG (`https://jakearchibald.github.io/svgomg/`). It's a browser-based version of SVGO that enables you to toggle the various optimization plugins and get instant feedback on the file savings.

Remember our example star SVG markup from the beginning of the chapter? By default, that simple SVG is 489 bytes in size. By passing that through SVGO, it's possible to get the size down to just 218 bytes, and that's leaving the `viewBox` in. That's a saving of 55.42%. If you're using a raft of SVG images, these savings can really add up. Here's what the optimized SVG markup looks like:

```
<svg width="198" height="188" viewBox="0 0 198 188" xmlns="http://
www.w3.org/2000/svg"><path stroke="#979797" stroke-width="3"
fill="#F8E81C" d="M99 154l-58.78 30.902 11.227-65.45L3.894
73.097l65.717-9.55L99 4l29.39 59.55 65.716 9.548-47.553 46.353 11.226
65.454z"/></svg>
```

Before you spend too long with SVGO, be aware that such is the popularity of SVGO, plenty of other SVG tools also make use of it. For example, the aforementioned Iconizr (`http://iconizr.com/`) tool runs your SVG files through SVGO by default anyway, before creating your assets so ensure you aren't unnecessarily double-optimizing.

Using SVGs as filters

In *Chapter 6*, *Stunning Aesthetics with CSS3*, we looked at the CSS filter effects. However, they are not currently supported in Internet Explorer 10 or 11. That can be frustrating if you want to enjoy filter effects in those browsers. Luckily, with help from SVG, we can create filters that work in Internet Explorer 10 and 11 too but as ever, it's perhaps not as straight forward as you might imagine. For example, in `example_07-05`, we have a page with the following markup inside the `body`:

```
<img class="HRH" src="queen@2x-1024x747.png"/>
```

It's an image of the Queen of England. Ordinarily, it looks like this:

Now, also in that example folder, is an SVG with a filter defined in the `defs` elements. The SVG markup looks like this:

```
<svg xmlns="http://www.w3.org/2000/svg" version="1.1">
    <defs>
        <filter id="myfilter" x="0" y="0">
            <feColorMatrix in="SourceGraphic" type="hueRotate"
values="90" result="A"/>
            <feGaussianBlur in="A" stdDeviation="6"/>
        </filter>
    </defs>
</svg>
```

Within the filter, we are first defining a hue rotation of 90 (using the `feColorMatrix`, and then passing that effect, via the `result` attribute, to the next filter (the `feGaussianBlur`) with a blur value of 6. Be aware that I've been deliberately heavy handed here. This doesn't produce a nice aesthetic, but it should leave you in no doubt that the effect has worked!

Now, rather than add that SVG markup to the HTML, we can leave it where it is and reference it using the same CSS filter syntax we saw in the last chapter.

```
.HRH {
    filter: url('.filter.svg#myfilter');
}
```

In most evergreen browsers (Chrome, Safari, Firefox) this is the effect:

Sadly, this method doesn't work in IE 10 or 11. However, there is another way to achieve our goal, and that's using SVGs own image tag to include the image within the SVG. Inside `example_07-06`, we have the following markup:

```
<svg height="747px" width="1024px" viewbox="0 0 1024 747"
xmlns="http://www.w3.org/2000/svg" version="1.1">
    <defs>
        <filter id="myfilter" x="0" y="0">
            <feColorMatrix in="SourceGraphic" type="hueRotate"
values="90" result="A"/>
            <feGaussianBlur in="A" stdDeviation="6"/>
```

```
        </filter>
    </defs>
    <image x="0" y="0" height="747px" width="1024px"
xmlns:xlink="http://www.w3.org/1999/xlink" xlink:href="queen@2x-
1024x747.png" filter="url(#myfilter)"></image>
</svg>
```

The SVG markup here is very similar to the external `filter.svg` filter we used in the previous example but `height`, `width`, and `viewbox` attributes have been added. In addition, the image we want to apply the filter to is the only content in the SVG outside of the `defs` element. To link to the filter, we are using the `filter` attribute and passing the ID of the filter we want to use (in this case from within the `defs` element above).

Although this approach is a little more involved, it means you can get the many and varied filter effects that SVG affords, even in versions 10 and 11 of Internet Explorer.

A note on media queries inside SVGs

All browsers that understand SVG should respect the CSS media queries defined inside. However, when it comes to media queries inside SVGs there are a few things to remember.

For example, suppose you insert a media query inside an SVG like this:

```
<style type="text/css"><![CDATA[
    #star_Path {
        stroke: red;
    }
    @media (min-width: 800px) {
        #star_Path {
            stroke: violet;
        }
    }
]]></style>
```

And that SVG is displayed on the page at a width of 200px while the viewport is 1200px wide.

We might expect the stroke of the star to be violet when the screen is 800px and above. After all, that's what we have our media query set to. However, when the SVG is placed in the page via an `img` tag, as a background image or inside an `object` tag, it is has no knowledge of the outer HTML document. Hence, in this situation, `min-width` means the min-width of the SVG itself. So, unless the SVG itself was displaying on the page at a width of 800px or more, the stroke wouldn't be violet.

Conversely, when you insert an SVG inline, it merges, (in a manner of speaking), with the outer HTML document. The `min-width` media query here is looking to the viewport (as is the HTML) to decide when the media query matches.

To solve this particular problem and make the same media query behave consistently, we could amend our media query to this:

```
@media (min-device-width: 800px) {
    #star_Path {
        stroke: violet;
    }
}
```

That way, regardless of the SVG size or how it is embedded it is looking to the device width (effectively the viewport).

Implementation tips

We're almost at the end of the chapter now and there is still so much we could talk about regarding SVG. Therefore, at this point I'll just list a few unrelated considerations. They aren't necessarily worthy of protracted explanations but I'll list them here in note form in case they save you from an hour of Googling:

- If you have no need to animate your SVGs, opt for an image sprite of your assets or a data URI style sheet. It's far easier to provide fallback assets and they almost always perform better from a performance perspective.

- Automate as many steps in the asset creation process as possible; it reduces human error and produces predictable results faster.

- To insert static SVGs in a project, try and pick a single delivery mechanism and stick to it (image sprite, data URI, or inline). It can become a burden to produce some assets one way and some another and maintain the various implementations.

- There is no easy 'one size fits all' choice with SVG animation. For occasional and simple animations, use CSS. For complex interactive or timeline style animations, that will also work in Internet Explorer, lean on a proven library such as Greensock, Velocity.js, or Snap.svg.

Further resources

As I mentioned at the start of this chapter, I have neither the space, nor the knowledge, to impart all there is to know about SVG. Therefore, I'd like to make you aware of the following excellent resources which provide additional depth and range on the subject:

- *SVG Essentials, 2nd Edition* by J. David Eisenberg, Amelia Bellamy-Royds (`http://shop.oreilly.com/product/0636920032335.do`)

- *A Guide to SVG Animations (SMIL)* by Sara Soueidan (`http://css-tricks.com/guide-svg-animations-smil/`)

- *Media Queries inside SVGs Test* by Jeremie Patonnier (`http://jeremie.patonnier.net/experiences/svg/media-queries/test.html`)

- *An SVG Primer for Today's Browsers* (`http://www.w3.org/Graphics/SVG/IG/resources/svgprimer.html`)

- *Understanding SVG Coordinate Systems and Transformations (Part 1)* by Sara Soueidan (`http://sarasoueidan.com/blog/svg-coordinate-systems/`)

- *Hands On: SVG Filter Effects* (`http://ie.microsoft.com/testdrive/graphics/hands-on-css3/hands-on_svg-filter-effects.htm`)

- Full set of SVG tutorials by Jakob Jenkov (`http://tutorials.jenkov.com/svg/index.html`)

Summary

In this chapter we have covered a lot of the essential information needed to start making sense of, and implementing, SVGs in a responsive project. We have considered the different graphics applications and online solutions available to create SVG assets, then the various insertion methods possible and the capabilities each allows, along with the various browser peculiarities to be aware of.

We've also considered how to link to external style sheets and re-use SVG symbols from within the same page and when referenced externally. We even looked at how we can make filters with SVG that can be referenced and used in CSS for wider support than CSS filters.

Finally, we considered how to make use of JavaScript libraries to aid animating SVGs and also how to optimize SVGs with the aid of the SVGO tool.

In the next chapter, we'll be looking at CSS transitions, transforms and animations. It's also worth reading that chapter in relation to SVG, as many of the syntaxes and techniques can be used and applied in SVG documents too. So grab yourself a hot beverage (you're worth it) and I'll see you again in a moment.

8
Transitions, Transformations, and Animations

Historically, whenever elements needed to be moved or animated around the screen, it was the sole domain of JavaScript. Nowadays, CSS can handle the majority of motion jobs via three principal agents: CSS transitions, CSS transforms, and CSS animations. In fact, only transitions and animations are directly related to motion, transforms simply allow us to change elements, but as we shall see, they are often integral to successful motion effects.

To clearly understand what each of these things is responsible for, I will offer this, perhaps overly simplistic summary:

- Use a CSS transition when you already have the beginning and end state of the things you want to apply motion to, and need a simple way to 'tween' from one state to another.

- Use a CSS transform if you need to visually transform an item, without affecting the layout of the page.

- Use a CSS animation if you want to perform a series of changes to an element at various key points over time.

Right, so we had better crack on and get our heads around how we can wield all these capabilities. In this chapter, we'll cover:

- What CSS3 transitions are and how we can use them

- How to write a CSS3 transition and its shorthand syntax

- CSS3 transition timing functions (`ease`, `cubic-bezier`, and so on)

- Fun transitions for responsive websites

- What CSS3 transforms are and how we can use them

- Understanding different 2D transforms (`scale`, `rotate`, `skew`, `translate`, and so on)
- Understanding 3D transforms
- How to animate with CSS3 using `keyframes`

What CSS3 transitions are and how we can use them

Transitions are the simplest way to create some visual 'effect' between one state and another with CSS. Let's consider a simple example, an element that transitions from one state to another when hovered over.

When styling hyperlinks in CSS, it's common practice to create a hover state; an obvious way to make users aware that the item they are hovering over is a link. Hover states are of little relevance to the growing number of touch screen devices but for mouse users, they're a great and simple interaction between website and user. They're also handy for illustrating transitions, so that's what we will start with.

Traditionally, using only CSS, hover states are an on/off affair. There is one set of properties and values on an element as the default, and when a pointer is hovered over that element, the properties and values are instantly changed. However, CSS3 transitions, as the name implies, allow us to transition between one or more properties and values to other properties and values.

A couple of important things to know up front. Firstly, you can't transition from `display: none;`. When something is set to `display: none;` it isn't actually 'painted' on the screen so has no existing state you can transition from. In order to create the effect of something fading in, you would have to transition opacity or position values. Secondly, not all properties can be transitioned. To ensure you're not attempting the impossible, here is the list of transitionable (I know, it's not even a word) properties: `http://www.w3.org/TR/css3-transitions/`

If you open up `example_08-01` you'll see a few links in a `nav`. Here's the relevant markup:

```
<nav>
    <a href="#">link1</a>
    <a href="#">link2</a>
    <a href="#">link3</a>
```

```
    <a href="#">link4</a>
    <a href="#">link5</a>
</nav>
```

And here's the relevant CSS:

```
a {
    font-family: sans-serif;
    color: #fff;
    text-indent: 1rem;
    background-color: #ccc;
    display: inline-flex;
    flex: 1 1 20%;
    align-self: stretch;
    align-items: center;
    text-decoration: none;
    transition: box-shadow 1s;
}

a + a {
    border-left: 1px solid #aaa;
}

a:hover {
    box-shadow: inset 0 -3px 0 #CC3232;
}
```

And here are the two states, first the default:

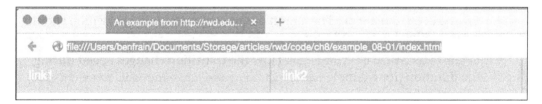

And then here's the hover state:

In this example, when the link is hovered over, we add a red box-shadow at the bottom (I chose a box-shadow as it won't affect the layout of the link like a border might). Ordinarily, hovering over the link snaps from the first state (no red line) to the second (red line); it's an on/off affair. However, this line:

```
transition: box-shadow 1s;
```

Adds a transition to the `box-shadow` from the existing state to the hover state over 1 second.

 You'll notice in the CSS of the preceding example we're using the adjacent sibling selector +. This means if a selector (an anchor tag in our example) directly follows another selector (another anchor tag) then apply the enclosed styles. It's useful here as we don't want a left border on the first element.

Note that the transition property is applied in the CSS to the original state of the element, not the state the element ends up as. More succinctly, apply the transition declaration on the 'from' state, not the 'to' state. This is so that different states such as `:active` can also have different styles set and enjoy the same transition.

The properties of a transition

A transition can be declared using up to four properties:

- `transition-property`: The name of the CSS property to be transitioned (such as `background-color`, `text-shadow`, or `all` to transition every possible property).

- `transition-duration`: The length of time over which the transition should occur (defined in seconds, for example `.3s`, `2s`, or `1.5s`).

- `transition-timing-function`: How the transition changes speed during the duration (for example `ease`, `linear`, `ease-in`, `ease-out`, `ease-in-out`, or `cubic-bezier`).

- `transition-delay`: An optional value to determine a delay before the transition commences. Alternatively, a negative value can be used to commence a transition immediately but part way through its transition 'journey'. It's defined in seconds, for example, `.3s`, `1s`, or `2.5s`.

Used separately, the various transition properties can be used to create a transition like this:

```
.style {
    /*...(more styles)...*/
    transition-property: all;
    transition-duration: 1s;
    transition-timing-function: ease;
    transition-delay: 0s;
}
```

The transition shorthand property

We can roll these individual declarations into a single, shorthand version:

```
transition: all 1s ease 0s;
```

One important point to note when writing the shorthand version is that the first time related value is given is always taken to be the `transition-duration`. The second time related value is taken to be the `transition-delay`. The shorthand version is the one I tend to favor as I generally only need to define the duration of the transition and the properties that should be transitioned.

It's a minor point, but only define the property or properties you actually need to transition. It's really handy to just set `all` but if you only need to transition the opacity, then only define the opacity as the transition property. Otherwise you're making the browser work harder than necessary. In most cases this isn't a big deal but if you're hoping to have the best performing site possible, especially on older devices, then every little helps.

Transitions are very well supported but, as ever, ensure you have a tool like Autoprefixer set up to add any vendor prefixes relevant to the browsers you need to support. You can also check which browsers support the various capabilities at `caniuse.com`.

The short version:

Transitions and 2D transforms work everywhere apart from IE9 and below, 3D transforms work everywhere except IE9 and below, Android 2.3 and below, and Safari 3.2 and below.

Transition different properties over different periods of time

Where a rule has multiple properties declared you don't have to transition all of them in the same way. Consider this rule:

```
.style {
    /* ...(more styles)... */
    transition-property: border, color, text-shadow;
    transition-duration: 2s, 3s, 8s;
}
```

Here we have specified with the `transition-property` that we'd like to transition the `border`, `color`, and `text-shadow`. Then with the `transition-duration` declaration, we are stating that the border should transition over 2 seconds, the color over 3 seconds, and the text-shadow over 8 seconds. The comma-separated durations match the comma-separated order of the transition properties.

Understanding timing functions

When you declare a transition, the properties, durations, and delays are relatively simple to understand. However, understanding what each timing function does can be a little trickier. Just what do `ease`, `linear`, `ease-in`, `ease-out`, `ease-in-out`, and `cubic-bezier` actually do? Each of them is actually a pre-defined cubic-bezier curve, essentially the same as an easing function. Or, more simplistically, a mathematical description of how the transition should look. It's generally easier to visualize these curves so I recommend you head over to `http://cubic-bezier.com/` and `http://easings.net/`.

Both these sites let you compare timing functions and see the difference each one makes. Here is a screenshot of http://easings.net — you can hover over each line for a demonstration of the easing function.

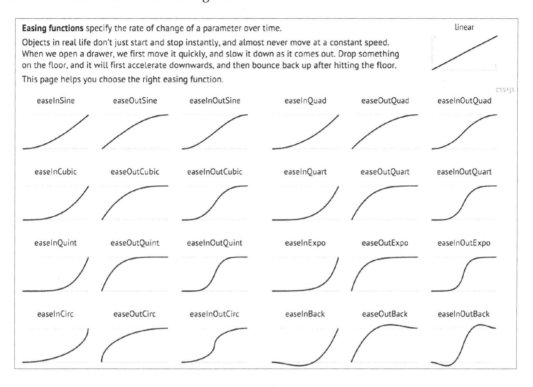

However, even if you can write your own cubic-bezier curves blindfolded, the likelihood is, for most practical situations, it makes little difference. The reason being that, like any enhancement, it's necessary to employ transition effects subtly. For 'real world' implementations, transitions that occur over too great a period of time tend to make a site feel slow. For example, navigation links that take 5 seconds to transition are going to frustrate, rather than wow your users. The perception of speed is incredibly important for our users and you and I must concentrate on making websites and applications feel as fast as possible.

Therefore, unless there is a compelling reason to do so, using the default transition (ease) over a short interval is often best; a maximum of 1 second is my own preference.

Fun transitions for responsive websites

Did you ever have one of those occasions growing up when one parent was out for the day and the other parent said something to the effect of, "OK, while your mom/dad are out we're going to put sugar all over your breakfast cereal but you have to promise not to tell them when they come back"? I'm certainly guilty of that with my little ankle biters. So here's the thing. While no one is looking, let's have a bit of fun. I don't recommend this for production, but try adding this to your responsive project.

```
* {
    transition: all 1s;
}
```

Here, we are using the CSS universal selector * to select everything and then setting a transition on all properties for 1 second (1s). As we have omitted to specify the timing function, ease will be used by default and there will be no delay as again, a default of 0 is assumed if an alternative value is not added. The effect? Well, try resizing your browser window and most things (links, hover states, and the like) behave as you would expect. However, because everything transitions, it also includes any rules within media queries, so as the browser window is resized, elements sort of flow from one state to the next. Is it essential? Absolutely not! Is it fun to watch and play around with? Certainly! Now, remove that rule before your mom sees it!

CSS3 2D transforms

Despite sounding similar, CSS transforms are entirely different to CSS transitions. Think of it like this: transitions smooth the change from one state to another, while transforms are defining what the element will actually become. My own (admittedly childish) way of remembering the difference is like this: imagine a transformer robot such as Optimus Prime. When he has changed into a truck he has transformed. However, the period between robot and truck is a transition (he's transitioning from one state to another).

Obviously, if you have no idea who or what Optimus Prime even is, feel free to mentally discard the last few sentences. Hopefully all will become clear momentarily.

There are two groups of CSS3 transforms available: 2D and 3D. 2D variants are far more widely implemented, browser wise, and certainly easier to write so let's look at those first. The CSS3 2D Transforms Module allows us to use the following transforms:

- `scale`: Used to scale an element (larger or smaller)
- `translate`: Move an element on the screen (up, down, left, and right)
- `rotate`: Rotate the element by a specified amount (defined in degrees)
- `skew`: Used to skew an element with its x and y co-ordinates
- `matrix`: Allows you to move and shape transformations with pixel precision

 It's important to remember that transforms occur outside of the document flow. Any element that is transformed will not affect the position of an element nearby that is not being transformed.

Let's try out the various 2D transitions. You can test each of these out by opening `example_08-02` in the browser. There's a transition applied to all of the transforms so you get a better idea of what's happening.

Scale

Here's the syntax for `scale`:

```
.scale:hover {
    transform: scale(1.4);
}
```

Hovering over the 'scale' link in our example produces this effect:

We've told the browser that when this element is hovered over, we want the element to scale to 1.4 times its original value.

Besides the values we've already used to enlarge elements, by using values below 1, we can shrink elements; the following will shrink the element to half its size:

```
transform: scale(0.5);
```

Translate

Here's the syntax for `translate`:

```
.translate:hover {
    transform: translate(-20px, -20px);
}
```

Here's the effect that rule has in our example:

The `translate` property tells the browser to move an element by an amount, defined in either pixels or percentages. The first value is the x axis and the second value is the y axis. Positive values given within parentheses move the element right or down; negative values move it left or up.

If you only pass one value then it is applied to the x axis. If you want to specify just one axis to translate an element you can also use `translateX` or `translateY`.

Using translate to center absolutely positioned elements

The `translate` provides a really useful way to center absolutely positioned elements within a relatively positioned container. You can view this example at `example_08-03`.

Consider this markup:

```
<div class="outer">
    <div class="inner"></div>
</div>
```

And then this CSS:

```
.outer {
    position: relative;
    height: 400px;
    background-color: #f90;
}

.inner {
    position: absolute;
```

```
    height: 200px;
    width: 200px;
    margin-top: -100px;
    margin-left: -100px;
    top: 50%;
    left: 50%;
}
```

You've perhaps done something similar to this yourself. When the dimensions of the absolutely positioned element are known (200px x 200px in this case) we can use negative margins to 'pull' the item back to the center. However, what happens when you want to include content and have no way of knowing how tall it will be? Transform to the rescue.

Let's add some random content into the inner box:

Yes, that problem! Right, let's use `transform` to sort this mess out.

```
.inner {
    position: absolute;
    width: 200px;
    background-color: #999;
    top: 50%;
    left: 50%;
    transform: translate(-50%, -50%);
}
```

And here is the result:

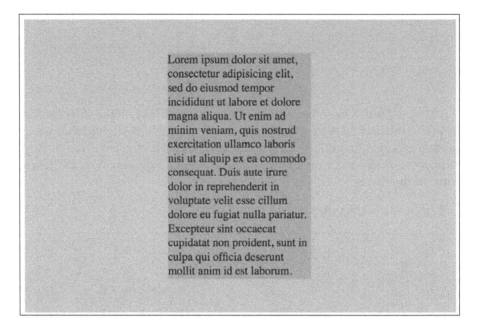

Here, `top` and `left` are positioning the inner box inside its container so that the top left corner of the inner box starts at a point 50% along and 50% down the outer. Then the `transform` is working on the inner element and positioning it negatively in those axis by half (-50%) of its own width and height. Nice!

Rotate

The `rotate` transform allows you to rotate an element. Here's the syntax:

```
.rotate:hover {
    transform: rotate(30deg);
}
```

In the browser, here's what happens:

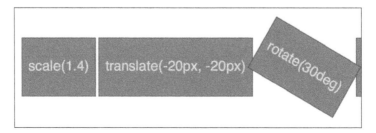

The value in parentheses should always be in degrees (for example, 90deg). While positive values always apply clockwise, using negative values will rotate the element counter-clockwise. You can also go crazy and make elements spin by specifying a value like the following:

```
transform: rotate(3600deg);
```

This will rotate the element 10 times in a complete circle. Practical uses for this particular value are few and far between but you know, if you ever find yourself designing websites for a windmill company, it may come in handy.

Skew

If you've spent any time working in Photoshop, you'll have a good idea what `skew` will do. It allows an element to be skewed on either or both of its axes. Here's the code for our example:

```
.skew:hover {
    transform: skew(40deg, 12deg);
}
```

Setting this on the hover link produces the following effect on hover:

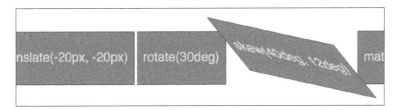

The first value is the `skew` applied to the *x* axis (in our example, 40deg), while the second (12deg) is for the *y* axis. Omitting the second value means any value will merely be applied to the *x* axis (horizontal). For example:

```
transform: skew(10deg);
```

Matrix

Did somebody mention a completely over-rated film? No? What's that? You want to know about the CSS3 matrix, not the film? Oh, okay.

I'm not going to lie. I think the matrix transform syntax looks scary. Here's our example code:

```
.matrix:hover {
    transform: matrix(1.678, -0.256, 1.522, 2.333, -51.533, -1.989);
}
```

It essentially allows you to combine a number of other transforms (`scale`, `rotate`, `skew`, and so on) into a single declaration. The preceding declaration results in the following effect in the browser:

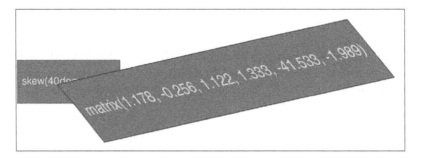

Now, I like a challenge like the best of them (unless, you know, it's sitting through the *Twilight* films) but I'm sure we can agree that syntax is a bit testing. For me, things got worse when I looked at the specification and realized that it involved mathematics knowledge beyond my rudimentary level to fully understand: `http://www.w3.org/TR/css3-2d-transforms/`

If you find yourself doing work with animations in JavaScript without the help of an animation library, you'll probably need to become a little more acquainted with the matrix. It's the syntax all the other transforms get computed into so if you're grabbing the current state of an animation with JavaScript, it will be the matrix value you will need to inspect and understand.

Matrix transformations for cheats and dunces

I'm not a mathematician by any stretch of the imagination, so when faced with the need to create a matrix-based transformation, I cheat. If your mathematical skills are also found wanting, I'd suggest heading over to `http://www.useragentman.com/matrix/`.

The Matrix Construction Set website allows you to drag and drop the element exactly where you want it and then includes good ol' copy and paste code (including vendor-prefixes) for your CSS file.

The transform-origin property

Notice how with CSS, the default transform origin (the point at which the browser uses as the center for the transform) is in the middle: 50% along the *x* axis and 50% along the *y* axis of the element. This differs from SVG which defaults to top left (or 0 0).

Using the `transform-origin` property we can amend the point from which transforms originate.

Consider our earlier matrix transform. The default `transform-origin` is '50% 50%' (the center of the element). The Firefox developer tools show how the `transform` is applied:

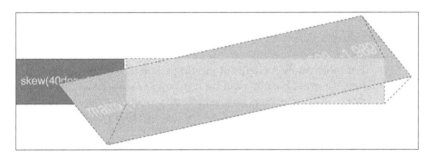

Now, if we adjust the `transform-origin` like this:

```
.matrix:hover {
    transform: matrix(1.678, -0.256, 1.522, 2.333, -51.533, -1.989);
    transform-origin: 270px 20px;
}
```

Then you can see the effect this has:

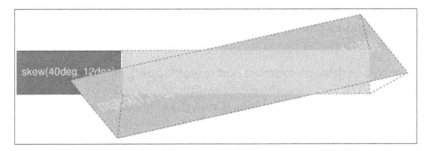

The first value is the horizontal offset and the second value is the vertical offset. You can use keywords. For example, left is equal to 0% horizontal, right is equal to 100% horizontal, top is equal to 0% vertical, and bottom is equal to 100% vertical. Alternatively, you can use a length, using any of the CSS length units.

If you use a percentage for the `transform-origin` values, then the horizontal/vertical offset is relative to the height/width of the elements bounding box.

If you use a length, then the values are measured from the top-left corner of the elements bounding box.

Full information on the `transform-origin` property can be found at `http://www.w3.org/TR/css3-2d-transforms/`.

That covers the essentials of 2D transforms. They are far more widely implemented than their 3D brethren and provide a far better means to move elements around the screen than older methods such as absolute positioning.

Read the full specification on CSS3 2D Transforms Module Level 3 at `http://www.w3.org/TR/css3-2d-transforms/`.

For more on the benefits of moving element with `transform`, here's a great post by Paul Irish (`http://www.paulirish.com/2012/why-moving-elements-with-translate-is-better-than-posabs-topleft/`) that provides some good data.

And, for a fantastic overview of how browsers actually deal with transitions and animations, and why transforms can be so effective, I highly recommend the following blog post: `http://blogs.adobe.com/webplatform/2014/03/18/css-animations-and-transitions-performance/`

CSS3 3D transformations

Let's look at our first example. An element that flips when we hover over it. I've used hover here to invoke the change as it's simple for the sake of illustration, however the flipping action could just as easily be initiated with a class change (via JavaScript) or when an element received focus.

We will have two of these elements; a horizontal flipping element and a vertical flipping element. You can view the final example at `example_08-04`. Images fail to fully convey this technique but the idea is that the element flips from the green 'face' to the red 'face' and gives the illusion of doing so through 3D space with the aid of perspective. Here's a grab partway through the transition from green to red which hopefully conveys some of the effect.

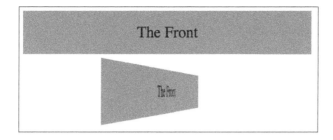

 It's also worth knowing that while positioning an element absolutely with top/left/bottom/right values operates pixel by pixel, a transform can interpolate at sub-pixel positions.

Here's the markup for the flipping element:

```
<div class="flipper">
    <span class="flipper-object flipper-vertical">
        <span class="panel front">The Front</span>
        <span class="panel back">The Back</span>
    </span>
</div>
```

The only difference with the horizontal one, markup wise is the `flipper-horizontal` class instead of `flipper-vertical`.

As the majority of the styles relate to aesthetics, we'll merely look at the essential ingredients in our styles to make the flipping effect possible. Refer to the full style sheet in the example for the aesthetic styles.

First of all, we need to set some perspective for the `.flipper-object` to flip within. For that we use the `perspective` property. This takes a length attempting to simulate the distance from the viewer's screen to the edge of the elements 3D space.

If you set a low number like 20px for the perspective value, the 3D space of the element will extend right out to only 20px from your screen; the result being a very pronounced 3D effect. Setting a high number on the other hand, will mean the edge of that imaginary 3D space will be further away, and therefore produce a less pronounced 3D effect.

```
.flipper {
    perspective: 400px;
    position: relative;
}
```

We are positioning the outer element relatively to create a context for the `flipper-object` to be positioned within:

```
.flipper-object {
    position: absolute;
    transition: transform 1s;
    transform-style: preserve-3d;
}
```

Besides positioning the `.flipper-object` absolutely at the top left of its closest relatively positioned parent (the default position for absolutely positioned elements), we have set a transition for the transform. The key thing here, 3D wise, though is the `transform-styles: preserve-3d`. This tells the browser that when we transform this element, we want any children elements to preserve the 3D effect.

If we didn't set `preserve-3d` on the `.flipper-object`, we would never get to see the back (the red part) of the flipping element. You can read the specification for this property at `http://www.w3.org/TR/2009/WD-css3-3d-transforms-20090320/`.

Each 'panel' in our flipping element needs positioning at the top of its container but we also want to make sure that if rotated, we don't see the 'rear' of it (otherwise we would never see the green panel as it sits 'behind' the red one). To do that we use the `backface-visibility` property. We set this to hidden so that the back face of the element is, you guessed it, hidden:

```
.panel {
    top: 0;
    position: absolute;
    backface-visibility: hidden;
}
```

 I've found that `backface-visibility` actually has a few surprising side effects in some browsers. It's particularly useful for improving the performance of fixed position elements on older Android devices. For more on this and why it does what it does, take a look at this post: `http://benfrain.com/easy-css-fix-fixed-positioning-android-2-2-2-3/` and this one: `http://benfrain.com/improving-css-performance-fixed-position-elements/`

Next we want to make our back panel flipped by default (so that when we flip the whole thing it will actually be in the correct position). To do that we apply a `rotate` transform:

```
.flipper-vertical .back {
    transform: rotateX(180deg);
```

```
    }

    .flipper-horizontal .back {
        transform: rotateY(180deg);
    }
```

Now everything is in place, now all we want to do is flip the entire inner element when the outer one is hovered over:

```
    .flipper:hover .flipper-vertical {
        transform: rotateX(180deg);
    }

    .flipper:hover .flipper-horizontal {
        transform: rotateY(180deg);
    }
```

As you can imagine there are a bazillion (by the way, that's definitely not a real amount, I just checked) ways you can use these principals. If you're wondering what a fancy navigation effect, or off-canvas menu, might look like with a spot of perspective, I highly recommend paying Codrops a visit: `http://tympanus.net/Development/PerspectivePageViewNavigation/index.html`.

Read about the latest W3C developments on CSS Transforms Module Level 1 at `http://dev.w3.org/csswg/css-transforms/`.

The transform3d property

In addition to using perspective, I've also found great utility in the `transform3d` value. With a single property and value, this allows you to move an element in the X (left/right), Y (up/down), and Z (forwards/backwards) axis. Let's amend our last example and make use of the `translate3d` transform. You can view this example at `example_08-06`.

Besides setting the elements in with a little padding, the only changes from our previous example can be seen here:

```
    .flipper:hover .flipper-vertical {
        transform: rotateX(180deg) translate3d(0, 0, -120px);
        animation: pulse 1s 1s infinite alternate both;
    }

    .flipper:hover .flipper-horizontal {
        transform: rotateY(180deg) translate3d(0, 0, 120px);
        animation: pulse 1s 1s infinite alternate both;
    }
```

We're still applying a transform but this time, in addition to our rotate we have also added a `translate3d`. The syntax for the comma-separated 'arguments' you can pass into `translate3d` are *x* axis movement, *y* axis movement, and *z* axis movement.

In our two examples I'm not moving the element in the *x* or *y* axis (left to right, and up and down) instead I'm moving towards or further away from you as you look at it.

If you look at the top example you will see it flip behind the bottom button and end 120px closer to the screen (minus values effectively pull it backwards towards you).

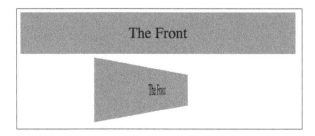

On the other hand, the bottom button flips around horizontally and ends with the button 120px further away from you.

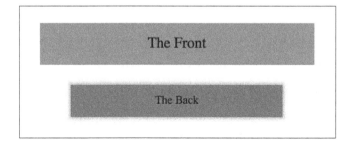

 You can read the specification for `translate3d` at http://www.w3.org/TR/css3-3d-transforms/.

Use transforms with progressive enhancement

The area I have found the greatest utility for `transform3d` is in sliding panels on and off the screen, particularly 'off-canvas' navigation patterns. If you open `example_08-07` you'll see I have created a basic, progressively enhanced off-canvas pattern.

Whenever you create interaction with JavaScript and modern CSS features like transforms it makes sense to try and consider things from the lowest possible device you want to support. What about the two people that don't have JavaScript (yes, those guys) or if there is a problem with the JavaScript loading or executing? What if somebody's device doesn't support transform (Opera Mini for example)? Don't worry, it's possible, with a little effort, to ensure a working interface for every eventuality.

When building these kind of interface patterns I find it most useful to start with the lowest set of features and enhance from there. So, first establish what someone sees if they don't have JavaScript available. After all, it's no use parking a menu off-screen if the method for displaying the menu relies upon JavaScript. In this case, we are relying upon markup to place the navigation area in the normal document flow. Worst case, whatever the viewport width, they can merely scroll down the page and click a link:

If JavaScript is available, for smaller screens we 'pull' the menu off to the left. When the menu button is clicked, we add a class onto the `body` tag (with JavaScript) and use this class as a hook to move the navigation back into view with CSS.

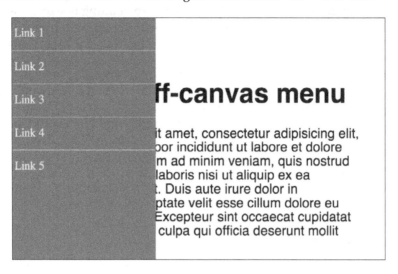

For larger viewports we hide the menu button and merely position the navigation to the left and move the main content over to accommodate.

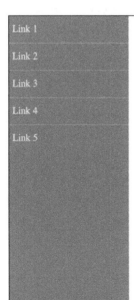

We then progressively enhance the navigation show/hide effect. This is where a tool like Modernizr really earns its place; adding classes to the HTML tag we can use as styling hooks (Modernizr is discussed in greater detail in *Chapter 5, CSS3 – Selectors, Typography, Color Modes, and New Features*).

First, for browsers that only support translate transforms (old Android for example), a simple `translateX`:

```
.js .csstransforms .navigation-menu {
    left: auto;
    transform: translateX(-200px);
}
```

For browsers that support `translate3d` we use `translate3d` instead. This will perform far better, where supported, thanks to being offloaded to the graphics processors on most devices:

```
.js .csstransforms3d .navigation-menu {
    left: auto;
    transform: translate3d(-200px, 0, 0);
}
```

Embracing a progressive enhancement approach ensures the widest possible audience will get a workable experience from your design. Remember, your users don't need visual parity but they might appreciate capability parity.

Animating with CSS3

If you've worked with applications like Flash, Final Cut Pro or After Effects, you'll have an instant advantage when working with CSS3 animations. CSS3 employs animation keyframing conventions found in timeline-based applications.

Animations are widely implemented; supported in Firefox 5+, Chrome, Safari 4+, Android (all versions), iOS (all versions), and Internet Explorer 10+. There are two components to a CSS3 animation; firstly a `keyframes` declaration and then employing that `keyframes` declaration in an `animation` property. Let's take a look.

In a previous example, we made a simple flip effect on elements that combined transforms and transitions. Let's bring together all the techniques we have learned in this chapter and add an animation to that previous example. In this next example, `example_08-05`, let's add a pulsing animation effect once the element has flipped.

Firstly we will create a `keyframes` at-rule:

```
@keyframes pulse {
  100% {
    text-shadow: 0 0 5px #bbb;
    box-shadow: 0 0 3px 4px #bbb;
  }
}
```

As you can see, after writing at `@keyframes` to define a new `keyframes` at-rule we name this particular animation (pulse in this instance).

It's generally best to use a name that represents what the animation does, not where you intend to use the animation, as a single `@keyframes` rule can be used as many times as you need throughout a project.

We have used a single keyframe selector here: 100%. However, you can set as many keyframe selectors (defined as percentage points) as you like within a `keyframes` rule. Think of these as points along a timeline. For example, at 10%, make the background blue, at 30% make the background purple, at 60%, make the element semi-opaque. On and on as you need. There is also the keyword from which is equivalent to 0% and to which is equivalent to100%. You can use them like this:

```
@keyframes pulse {
  to {
    text-shadow: 0 0 5px #bbb;
    box-shadow: 0 0 3px 4px #bbb;
  }
}
```

Be warned, however, that WebKit browsers (iOS, Safari) don't always play happily with from and to values (preferring 0% and 100%) so I'd recommend sticking with percentage keyframe selectors.

You'll notice here that we haven't bothered to define a starting point. That's because the starting point is the state each of those properties is already at. Here's the part of the specification that explains that: `http://www.w3.org/TR/css3-animations/`

If a `0%` or `from` keyframe is not specified, then the user agent constructs a `0%` keyframe using the computed values of the properties being animated. If a `100%` or `to` keyframe is not specified, then the user agent constructs a `100%` keyframe using the computed values of the properties being animated. If a keyframe selector specifies negative percentage values or values higher than `100%`, then the keyframe will be ignored.

In this `keyframes` at-rule we've added a text-shadow and box-shadow at 100%. We can then expect the `keyframes`, when applied to an element to animate the text-shadow and box-shadow to the defined amount. But how long does the animation last? How do we make it repeat, reverse, and other eventualities I hope to have the answer for? This is how we actually apply a `keyframes` animation:

```
.flipper:hover .flipper-horizontal {
    transform: rotateY(180deg);
    animation: pulse 1s 1s infinite alternate both;
}
```

The `animation` property here is being used as a shorthand for a number of animation related properties. In this example, we are actually declaring (in order), the name of the `keyframes` declaration to use (pulse), the `animation-duration` (1 second), the delay before the animation begins (1 second, to allow time for our button to first flip), the amount of times the animation will run (infinitely), the direction of the animation (alternate, so it animates first one way and then back the other) and that we want the `animation-fill-mode` to retain the values that are defined in the `keyframes` whether going forwards or backwards (both).

The shorthand property can actually accept all seven animation properties. In addition to those used in the preceding example, it's also possible to specify `animation-play-state`. This can be set to running or paused to effectively play and pause an animation. Of course, you don't need to use the shorthand property; sometimes it can make more sense (and help when you revisit the code in the future) to set each property separately. Below are the individual properties and where appropriate, alternate values separated with the pipe symbol:

```
.animation-properties {
    animation-name: warning;
    animation-duration: 1.5s;
    animation-timing-function: ease-in-out;
    animation-iteration-count: infinite;
    animation-play-state: running | paused;
    animation-delay: 0s;
    animation-fill-mode: none | forwards | backwards | both;
    animation-direction: normal | reverse | alternate | alternate-
reverse;
}
```

 You can read the full definition for each of these animation properties at `http://www.w3.org/TR/css3-animations/`.

As mentioned previously, it's simple to reuse a declared `keyframes` on other elements and with completely different settings:

```
.flipper:hover .flipper-vertical {
    transform: rotateX(180deg);
    animation: pulse 2s 1s cubic-bezier(0.68, -0.55, 0.265, 1.55) 5
alternate both;
}
```

Here the `pulse` animation would run over 2 seconds and uses an ease-in-out-back timing function (defined as a cubic-bezier curve). It runs five times in both directions. This declaration has been applied to the vertically flipping element in the example file.

This is just one very simple example of using CSS animations. As virtually anything can be key-framed, the possibilities are pretty endless. Read about the latest developments on CSS3 animations at `http://dev.w3.org/csswg/css3-animations/`.

The animation-fill-mode property

The `animation-fill-mode` property is worthy of a special mention. Consider an animation that starts with a yellow background and animates to a red background over 3 seconds. You can view this in `example_08-08`.

We apply the animation like this:

```
.background-change {
  animation: fillBg 3s;
  height: 200px;
  width: 400px;
  border: 1px solid #ccc;
}

@keyframes fillBg {
  0% {
    background-color: yellow;
  }
  100% {
    background-color: red;
  }
}
```

However, once the animation completes, the background of the `div` will return to nothing. That's because by default 'what happens outside of animations, stays outside of animations'! In order to override this behavior, we have the `animation-fill-mode` property. In this instance we could apply this:

```
animation-fill-mode: forwards;
```

This makes the item retain any values that have been applied at the animation end. In our case, the `div` would retain the red background color that the animation ended on. More on the `animation-fill-mode property` here: `http://www.w3.org/TR/css3-animations/#animation-fill-mode-property`

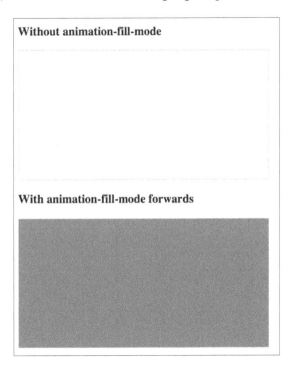

Summary

It would be entirely possible to fill multiple modules covering the possibilities of CSS transforms, transitions, and animations. However, hopefully, by dipping your toe in the water with this chapter you'll be able to pick up the basics and run with them. Ultimately, by embracing these newer features and techniques of CSS, the aim is to make a responsive design even leaner and richer than ever by using CSS, rather than JavaScript, for some of the fancier aesthetic enhancements.

In this chapter we've learned what CSS3 transitions are and how to write them. We've got a handle on timing functions like ease and linear, and then used them to create simple but fun effects. We then learned all about 2D transforms such as scale and skew and then how to use them in tandem with transitions. We also looked briefly at 3D transformations before learning all about the power and relative simplicity of CSS animations. You'd better believe our CSS3 muscles are growing!

However, if there's one area of site design that I always avoid where possible, it's making forms. I don't know why, I've just always found making them a tedious and largely frustrating task. Imagine my joy when I learned that HTML5 and CSS3 can make the whole form building, styling, and even validating (yes, validating!), process easier than ever before. I was quite joyous. As joyous as you can be about building web forms that is. In the next chapter I'd like to share this knowledge with you.

9
Conquer Forms with HTML5 and CSS3

Before HTML5, adding things such as date pickers, placeholder text, and range sliders into forms has always needed JavaScript. Similarly, there has been no easy way to tell users what we expect them to input into certain input fields, for example, whether we want users to input telephone numbers, e-mail addresses, or URLs. The good news is that HTML5 largely solves these common problems.

We have two main aims in this chapter. Firstly, to understand HTML5 form features and secondly, to understand how we can lay out forms more simply for multiple devices with the latest CSS features.

In this chapter, we will learn how to:

- Easily add placeholder text into relevant form input fields
- Disable auto-completion of form fields where necessary
- Set certain fields to be required before submission
- Specify different input types such as e-mail, telephone number, and URL
- Create number range sliders for easy value selection
- Place date and color pickers into a form
- Learn how we can use a regular expression to define an allowed form value
- How to style forms using Flexbox

HTML5 forms

I think the easiest way to get to grips with HTML5 forms is to work our way through an example form. From the finest of daytime TV examples, I have one I made earlier. A minor introduction is needed.

Two facts: firstly, I love films. Secondly, I'm very opinionated on what is a good film and what is not.

Every year, when the Oscar nominations are announced, I can't help feeling the wrong films have got 'the nod' from the Academy. Therefore, we will start with an HTML5 form that enables fellow cinephiles to vent their frustrations at the continual travesties of the Oscar nominations.

It's made up of a few `fieldset` elements, within which we are including a raft of the HTML5 form input types and attributes. Besides standard form input fields and text areas, we have a number spinner, a range slider, and placeholder text for many of the fields.

Here's how it looks with no styles applied in Chrome:

Oscar Redemption

Here's your chance to set the record straight: tell us what year the wrong film got nominated, and which film should have received a nod...

About the offending film (part 1 of 3)

The film in question? e.g. King Kong
Year Of Crime 1929
Award Won

Tell us why that's wrong? I fell asleep within 20 minutes...
How you rate it (1 is woeful, 10 is awesome-sauce) 7

What should have won? (part 2 of 3)

The film that should have won? e.g. Cable Guy

Tell us why it should have won? Hello? CAABBLLLLE GUUUY!!!!
How you rate it (1 is woeful, 10 is awesomesauce) 5

About you? (part 3 of 3)

Your Name Dwight Schultz
Your favorite color
Date/Time dd/mm/yyyy
Telephone (so we can berate you if you're wrong) 1-234-546758
Your Email address dwight.schultz@gmail.c
Your Web address www.mysite.com

Submit Redemption

If we 'focus' on the first field and start inputting text, the placeholder text is removed. If we blur focus without entering anything (by clicking outside of the input box again) the placeholder text re-appears. If we submit the form (without entering anything), the following happens:

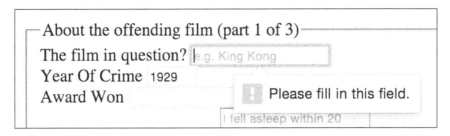

The great news is that all these user interface elements, including the aforementioned slider, placeholder text, and spinner, and the input validation, are all being handled natively by the browser via HTML5, and no JavaScript. Now, the form validation isn't entirely cross browser compatible, but we will get to that shortly. First of all, let's get a handle on all the new capabilities of HTML5 that relate to forms and make all this possible. Once we understand all the mechanics, we can get to work styling it up.

Understanding the component parts of HTML5 forms

There's a lot going on in our HTML5 powered form, so let's break it down. The three sections of the form are each wrapped in a `fieldset` with a legend:

```
<fieldset>
<legend>About the offending film (part 1 of 3)</legend>
<div>
  <label for="film">The film in question?</label>
  <input id="film" name="film" type="text" placeholder="e.g. King
Kong" required>
</div>
```

You can see from the previous code snippet that each input element of the form is also wrapped in a `div` with a label associated with each input (we could have wrapped the input with the label element if we wanted to too). So far, so normal. However, within this first input we've just stumbled upon our first HTML5 form feature. After common attributes of ID, name, and type, we have `placeholder`.

placeholder

The `placeholder` attribute looks like this:

```
placeholder="e.g. King Kong"
```

Placeholder text within form fields is such a common requirement that the folks creating HTML5 decided it should be a standard feature of HTML. Simply include the `placeholder` attribute within your input and the value will be displayed by default until the field gains focus. When it loses focus, if a value has not been entered it will re-display the placeholder text.

Styling the placeholder text

You can style the `placeholder` attribute with the `:placeholder-shown` pseudo selector. Be aware that this selector has been through a number of iterations so ensure you have the prefixer tool set up to provide the fallback selectors for already implemented versions.

```
input:placeholder-shown {
  color: #333;
}
```

After the `placeholder` attribute, in the previous code snippet, the next HTML5 form feature is the `required` attribute.

required

The `required` attribute looks like this:

```
required
```

In supporting HTML5 capable browsers, by adding the Boolean (meaning you simply include the attribute or not) attribute `required` within the `input` element, it indicates that a value is required. If the form is submitted without the field containing the requisite information, a warning message should be displayed. The message displayed is specific (both in content and styling) to both the browser and the input type used.

We've already seen what the `required` field browser message looks like in Chrome. The following screenshot shows the same message in Firefox:

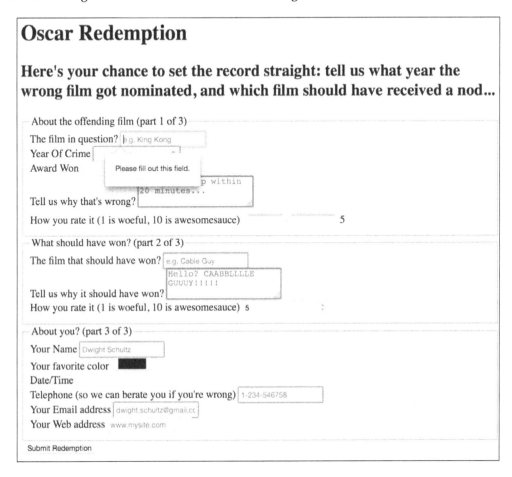

The `required` value can be used alongside many input types to ensure a value is entered. Notable exceptions are the `range`, `color`, `button`, and `hidden` input types as they almost always have a default value.

autofocus

The HTML5 `autofocus` attribute allows a form to have a field already focused, ready for user input. The following code is an example of an `input` field wrapped in a `div` with the `autofocus` attribute added at the end:

```
<div>
  <label for="search">Search the site...</label>
  <input id="search" name="search" type="search" placeholder="Wyatt
Earp" autofocus>
</div>
```

Be careful when using this attribute. Cross browser confusion can reign if multiple fields have the `autofocus` attribute added. For example, if multiple fields have `autofocus` added, in Safari, the last field with the `autofocus` attributed is focused on page load. However, Firefox and Chrome do the opposite with the first `autofocus` field selected.

It's also worth considering that some users use the spacebar to quickly skip down the content of a web page once it's loaded. On a page where a form has an autofocused input field, it prevents this capability; instead it adds a space into the focused input field. It's easy to see how that could be a source of frustration for users.

If using the `autofocus` attribute, be certain it's only used once in a form and be sure you understand the implications for those who scroll with the spacebar.

autocomplete

By default, most browsers aid user input by auto-completing the value of form fields where possible. While the user can turn this preference on and off within the browser, we can now also indicate to the browser when we don't want a form or field to allow auto-completion. This is useful not just for sensitive data (bank account numbers for example) but also if you want to ensure users pay attention and enter something by hand. For example, for many forms I complete, if a telephone number is required, I enter a 'spoof' telephone number. I know I'm not the only one that does that (doesn't everyone?) but I can ensure that users don't enter an autocompleted spoof number by setting the `autocomplete` attribute to off on the relevant input field. The following is a code example of a field with the `autocomplete` attribute set to `off`:

```
<div>
  <label for="tel">Telephone (so we can berate you if you're wrong)</
label>
```

```
<input id="tel" name="tel" type="tel" placeholder="1-234-546758"
autocomplete="off" required>
</div>
```

We can also set entire forms (but not fieldsets) to not autocomplete by using the attribute on the form itself. The following is a code example:

```
<form id="redemption" method="post" autocomplete="off">
```

List and the associated datalist element

This `list` attribute and the associated `datalist` element allow a number of selections to be presented to a user once they start entering a value in the field. The following is a code example of the `list` attribute in use with an associated `datalist`, all wrapped in a `div`:

```
<div>
  <label for="awardWon">Award Won</label>
  <input id="awardWon" name="awardWon" type="text" list="awards">
  <datalist id="awards">
    <select>
      <option value="Best Picture"></option>
      <option value="Best Director"></option>
      <option value="Best Adapted Screenplay"></option>
      <option value="Best Original Screenplay"></option>
    </select>
  </datalist>
</div>
```

The value given in the `list` attribute (`awards`) refers to the ID of the `datalist`. Doing this associates the `datalist` with the input field. Although wrapping the options with a `<select>` element isn't strictly necessary, it helps when applying polyfills for browsers that haven't implemented the feature.

Amazingly, in mid-2015, the `datalist` element still isn't supported natively in iOS, Safari, or Android 4.4 and below (http://caniuse.com/)

You can read the specification for `datalist` at http://www.w3.org/TR/html5/forms.html.

While the input field seems to be just a normal text input field, when typing in the field, a selection box appears below it (in supporting browsers) with matching results from the datalist. In the following screenshot, we can see the list in action (Firefox). In this instance, as B is present in all options within the datalist, all the values are shown for the user to select from:

However, when typing D instead, only the matching suggestions appear as shown in the following screenshot:

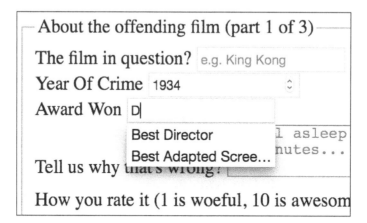

The list and datalist don't prevent a user entering different text in the input box but they do provide another great way of adding common functionality and user enhancement through HTML5 markup alone.

HTML5 input types

HTML5 adds a number of extra input types, which amongst other things, enable us to limit the data that users input without the need for extraneous JavaScript code. The most comforting thing about these new input types is that by default, where browsers don't support the feature, they degrade to a standard text input box. Furthermore, there are great polyfills available to bring older browsers up to speed, which we will look at shortly. In the meantime, let's look at these new HTML5 input types and the benefits they provide.

email

You can set an input to the `email` type like this:

```
type="email"
```

Supporting browsers will expect a user input that matches the syntax of an e-mail address. In the following code example `type="email"` is used alongside `required` and `placeholder`:

```
<div>
  <label for="email">Your Email address</label>
  <input id="email" name="email" type="email" placeholder="dwight.
schultz@gmail.com" required>
</div>
```

When used in conjunction with required, submitting a non-conforming input will generate a warning message:

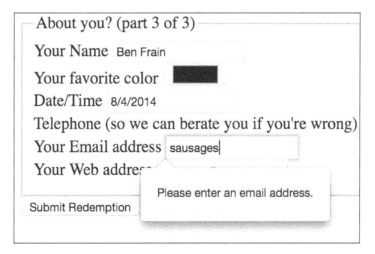

Furthermore, many touch screen devices (for example, Android, iPhone, and so on) change the input display based upon this input type. The following screenshot shows how an input `type="email"` screen looks on the iPad. Notice the @ symbol for been added to the software keyboard for easy email address completion:

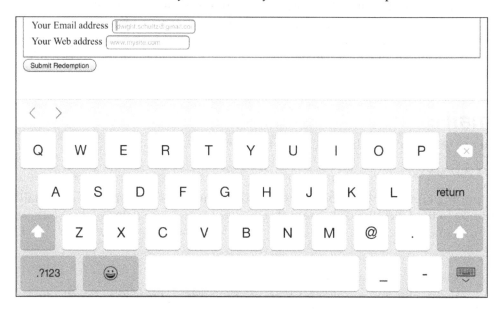

number

You can set an input field to a type of number like this:

```
type="number"
```

A supporting browser expects a number to be entered here. Supporting browsers also provide what's called **spinner controls**. These are tiny pieces of user interface that allow users to easily click up or down to alter the value input. The following is a code example:

```
<div>
  <label for="yearOfCrime">Year Of Crime</label>
  <input id="yearOfCrime" name="yearOfCrime" type="number"
min="1929"  max="2015" required>
</div>
```

And the following screenshot shows how it looks in a supporting browser (Chrome):

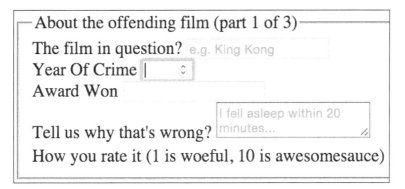

Implementation of what happens if you don't enter a number varies. For example, Chrome and Firefox do nothing until the form is submitted, at which point they pop up a warning above the field. Safari on the other hand, simply does nothing, and merely lets the form be submitted. Internet Explorer 11 simply empties the field as soon as focus leaves it.

min and max ranges

You'll notice in the previous code example, we have also set a minimum and maximum allowed range, similar to the following code:

```
type="number" min="1929" max="2015"
```

Numbers outside of this range (should) get special treatment.

You probably won't be surprised to learn that browser implementation of min and max ranges is varied. For example, Internet Explorer 11, Chrome, and Firefox, display a warning while Safari does nothing.

Changing the step increments

You can alter the step increments (granularity) for the spinner controls of various input types with the use of the step attribute. For example, to step 10 units at a time:

```
<input type="number" step="10">
```

url

You can set an input field to expect a URL like this:

```
type="url"
```

As you might expect, the `url` input type is for URL values. Similar to the `tel` and `email` input types; it behaves almost identically to a standard text input. However, some browsers add specific information to the warning message provided when submitted with incorrect values. The following is a code example including the `placeholder` attribute:

```
<div>
  <label for="web">Your Web address</label>
  <input id="web" name="web" type="url" placeholder="www.mysite.com">
</div>
```

The following screenshot shows what happens when an incorrectly entered URL field is submitted in Chrome:

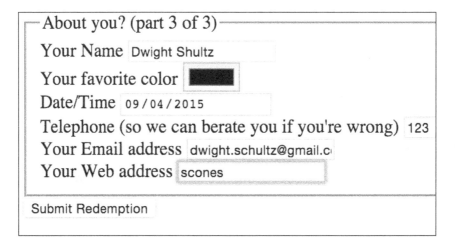

Like `type="email"`, touch screen devices often amend the input display based upon this input type. The following screenshot shows how an input `type="url"` screen looks on the iPad:

Notice the *.com* key? Because we've used a URL input type they are presented by the device for easy URL completion (on iOS, if you're not going to a .com site you can press and hold for a few other popular top level domains).

tel

Set an input field to expect a telephone number like this:

```
type="tel"
```

Here's a more complete example:

```
<div>
  <label for="tel">Telephone (so we can berate you if you're wrong)</label>
  <input id="tel" name="tel" type="tel" placeholder="1-234-546758" autocomplete="off" required>
</div>
```

Although, a number format is expected on many browsers, even modern evergreen ones such as Internet Explorer 11, Chrome, and Firefox, it merely behaves like a text input field. When an incorrect value is input, they fail to provide a suitable warning message when the field loses focus or on form submission.

However, better news is that, like the `email` and `url` input types, touch screen devices often thoughtfully accommodate this kind of input with an amended input display for easy completion; here's the `tel` input when accessed with an iPad (running iOS 8.2):

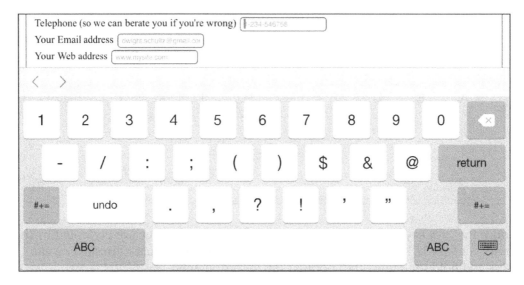

Notice the lack of alphabet characters in the keyboard area? This makes it much faster for users to enter a value in the correct format.

> **Quick tip**
>
> If the default blue color of telephone numbers in iOS Safari annoys you when you use a `tel` input, you can amend it with the following selector:
>
> ```
> a[href^=tel] { color: inherit; }
> ```

search

You can set an input as a search type like this:

```
type="search"
```

The `search` input type works like a standard text input. Here's an example:

```
<div>
  <label for="search">Search the site...</label>
  <input id="search" name="search" type="search" placeholder= "Wyatt
Earp">
</div>
```

However, software keyboards (such as those found on mobile devices) often provided a more tailored keyboard. Here's the iOS 8.2 keyboard that appears when a `search` input type gets focus:

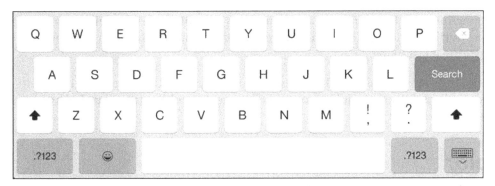

pattern

You can set an input to expect a certain pattern input like this:

```
pattern=""
```

The `pattern` attribute allows you to specify, via a regular expression, the syntax of data that should be allowed in a given input field.

Learn about regular expressions

If you've never encountered regular expressions before, I'd suggest starting here: `http://en.wikipedia.org/wiki/Regular_expressions`

Regular expressions are used across many programming languages as a means of matching possible strings. While the format is intimidating at first, they are incredibly powerful and flexible. For example, you could build a regular expression to match a password format, or select a certain style CSS class naming pattern. To help build up your own regex pattern and get a visual understanding of how they work, I'd recommend starting with a browser based tool like `http://www.regexr.com/`.

The following code is an example:

```
<div>
  <label for="name">Your Name (first and last)</label>
  <input id="name" name="name" pattern="([a-zA-Z]{3,30}\s*)+[a-zA- Z]
{3,30}" placeholder="Dwight Schultz" required>
</div>
```

Such is my commitment to this module, I searched the Internet for approximately 458 seconds to find a regular expression that would match a first and last name syntax. By entering the regular expression value within the `pattern` attribute, it makes supporting browsers expect a matching input syntax. Then, when used in conjunction with the `required` attribute, incorrect entries get the following treatment in supporting browsers. In this instance, I tried submitting the form without providing a last name.

Again, browsers do things differently. Internet Explorer 11 requests that the field is entered correctly, Safari, Firefox, and Chrome do nothing (they just behave like a standard text input).

color

Want to set an input field to receive a hexadecimal color value? You can do this:

```
type="color"
```

The `color` input type invokes a color picker in supporting browsers (currently just Chrome and Firefox), allowing users to select a color value in a hexadecimal value. The following code is an example:

```
<div>
  <label for="color">Your favorite color</label>
  <input id="color" name="color" type="color">
</div>
```

Date and time inputs

The thinking behind the new `date` and `time` input types is to provide a consistent user experience for choosing dates and times. If you've ever bought tickets to an event online, chances are that you have used a date picker of one sort or another. This functionality is almost always provided via JavaScript (typically jQuery UI library) but the hope is to make this common necessity possible merely with HTML5 markup.

date

The following code is an example:

```
<input id="date" type="date" name="date">
```

Similar to the `color` input type, native browser support is thin on the ground, defaulting on most browsers to a standard text input box. Chrome and Opera are the only two of the modern browsers to have implemented this functionality. That's not surprising as they both use the same engine (known as **Blink** in case you were interested).

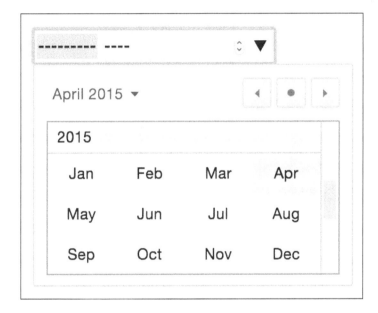

There are a variety of different `date` and `time` related input types available. What follows is a brief overview of the others.

month

The following code is an example:

```
<input id="month" type="month" name="month">
```

The interface allows the user to select a single month and provides the input as a year and month for example 2012-06. The following screenshot shows how it looks in the browser:

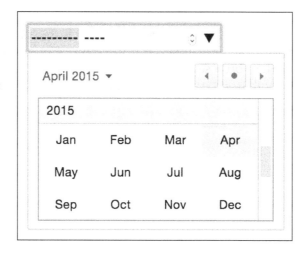

week

The following code is an example:

```
<input id="week" type="week" name="week">
```

When the week input type is used, the picker allows the user to select a single week within a year and provides the input in the 2012-W47 format.

The following screenshot shows how it looks in the browser:

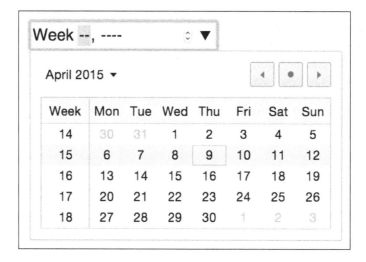

time

The following code is an example:

```
<input id="time" type="time" name="time">
```

The `time` input type allows a value in the 24-hour format, for example 23:50.

It displays in supporting browsers with spinner controls but only allows relevant time values.

range

The `range` input type creates a slider interface element. Here's an example:

```
<input type="range" min="1" max="10" value="5">
```

And the following screenshot shows how it looks in Firefox:

The default range is from 0 to 100. However, by specifying a `min` and `max` value in our example we have limited it to between 1 and 10.

One big problem I've encountered with the `range` input type is that the current value is never displayed to the user. Although the range slider is only intended for vague number selections, I've often wanted to display the value as it changes. Currently, there is no way to do this using HTML5. However, if you absolutely must display the current value of the slider, it can be achieved easily with some simple JavaScript. Amend the previous example to the following code:

```
<input id="howYouRateIt" name="howYouRateIt" type="range" min="1"
max="10" value="5" onchange="showValue(this.value)"><span
id="range">5</span>
```

We've added two things, an `onchange` attribute and also a `span` element with the ID of range. Now, we'll add the following tiny piece of JavaScript:

```
<script>
  function showValue(newValue)
  {
    document.getElementById("range").innerHTML=newValue;
  }
</script>
```

All this does is get the current value of the range slider and display it in the element with an ID of range (our `span` tag). You can then use whatever CSS you deem appropriate to change the appearance of the value.

There are a few other form related features that are new in HTML5. You can read the full specification at `http://www.w3.org/TR/html5/forms.html`.

How to polyfill non-supporting browsers

All this HTML5 form malarkey is all well and good. There seems however, to be two things that put a serious dent in our ability to use them: disparity between how supporting browsers implement the features, and how to deal with browsers that don't support the features at all.

If you need to support some of these features in older or non-supporting browsers then consider Webshims Lib, which you can download at `http://afarkas.github.com/webshim/demos/`. It is a polyfill library written by Alexander Farkas that can load form polyfills to make non-supporting browsers handle HTML5 based form features.

Exercise caution with polyfills

Whenever you reach for a polyfill script remember to consider carefully. While they can be very handy, they add weight to your project. For example, Webshims also requires jQuery so there's yet another dependency needed if you weren't using jQuery before. Unless polyfilling older browsers is essential, I steer clear.

The handy thing about Webshims is that it only adds polyfills as needed. If being viewed by a browser that supports these HTML5 features natively it adds very little. Older browsers, although they need to load more code (as they are less capable by default), get a similar user experience, albeit with the relevant functionality created with the help of JavaScript.

But it isn't just older browsers that benefit. As we've seen, many modern browsers haven't implemented the HTML5 form features fully. Employing Webshims lib to the page also fills any gaps in their capability. For example, Safari doesn't offer any warning when a HTML5 form is submitted with required fields empty. No feedback is given to the user as to what the problem is: hardly ideal. With Webshims lib added to the page, the following happens in the aforementioned scenario.

So when Firefox isn't able to provide a spinner for a `type="number"` attribute, Webshims lib provides a suitable, jQuery powered, fallback. In short, it's a great tool, so let's get this beautiful little package installed and hooked up and then we can carry on writing forms with HTML5, safe in the knowledge that all users will see what they need to use our form (except those two people using IE6 with JavaScript turned off—you know who you are—now pack it in!).

First download Webshims lib (`http://github.com/aFarkas/webshim/downloads`) and extract the package. Now copy the `js-webshim` folder to a relevant section of your web page. For simplicity, for this example I've copied it into the website root.

Now add the following code into the section of your page:

```
<script src="js/jquery-2.1.3.min.js"></script>
<script src="js-webshim/minified/polyfiller.js"></script>
<script>
  //request the features you need:
  webshim.polyfill('forms');
</script>
```

Let's go through this a section at a time. Firstly, we link to a local copy of the jQuery library (get the latest version at `www.jquery.com`) and the Webshim script:

```
<script src="js/jquery-2.1.3.min.js"></script>
<script src="js-webshim/minified/polyfiller.js"></script>
```

Finally, I'm telling the script to load all needed polyfills:

```
<script>
  //request the features you need:
  webshim.polyfill('forms');
</script>
```

And that's all there is to it. Now, missing functionality is automatically added by the relevant polyfill. Excellent!

Styling HTML5 forms with CSS3

Our form is now fully functional across browsers so now we need to make it a little more appealing across different viewport sizes. Now, I don't consider myself a designer, but by applying some of the techniques we've learned throughout the previous chapters, I still think we can improve the aesthetics of our form.

You can view the styled form at `example_09-02`, and remember, if you don't already have the example code, you can grab it at `http://rwd.education`.

In this example, I've also included two versions of the style sheet: `styles.css` is the version that includes vendor prefixes (added via Autoprefixer) and `styles-unprefixed.css` is the CSS as written. The latter is probably easier to look at if you want to see how anything is being applied.

Here's how the form looks in a small viewport with some basic styling applied:

And here it is at a larger viewport:

Oscar Redemption

Here's your chance to set the record straight: tell us what year the wrong film got nominated, and which film **should** have received a nod...

About the offending film (part 1 of 3)	
The film in question?	e.g. King Kong
Year Of Crime	1954
Award Won	jdhbdfhb
Tell us why that's wrong?	I fell asleep within 20 minutes...
How you rate it (1 is woeful, 10 is great)	⑤

What should have won? (part 2 of 3)	
The film that should have won?	Cable Guy
Tell us why it should have won?	Hello? CAABBLLLLE GUUUY!!!!!

About you? (part 3 of 3)	
Your Name	Dwight Schultz
Your favorite color	
Date/Time	
Telephone (so we can berate you if you're wrong)	1-234-546758
Your Email address	dwight.schultz@gmail.com
Your Web address	www.mysite.com

Ready?

If you look at the CSS you'll see many of the techniques we've looked at throughout previous chapters applied. For example, Flexbox (*Chapter 3, Fluid Layouts and Responsive Images*) has been used to create uniform spacing and flexibility for elements; transforms and transitions (*Chapter 8, Transitions, Transformations, and Animations*) so that the focused input fields grow and the ready/submit button flips vertically when it gains focus. Box-shadows and gradients (*Chapter 6, Stunning Aesthetics with CSS3*) are used to emphasize different areas of the form. Media queries (*Chapter 2, Media Queries – Supporting Differing Viewports*) are being used to switch the Flexbox direction for different viewport sizes and CSS Level 3 selectors (*Chapter 5, CSS3 – Selectors, Typography, Color Modes, and New Features*) are being used for selector negation.

We won't go over those techniques in detail here again. Instead, we will focus on a couple of peculiarities. Firstly, how to visually indicate required fields (and for bonus points indicate a value has been entered) and secondly, how to create a 'fill' effect when a field gets user focus.

Indicating required fields

We can indicate required input fields to a user using CSS alone. For example:

```
input:required {
  /* styles */
}
```

With that selector we could add a border or outline to the required fields or add a `background-image` inside the field. Basically the sky's the limit! We could also use a specific selector to target an input field that is required, only when it gains focus. For example:

```
input:focus:required {
  /* styles */
}
```

However, that would apply styles to the input box itself. What if we want to amend styles on the associated `label` element? I've decided I'd like to indicate required fields with a little asterisk symbol to the side of the label. But this presents a problem. Generally, CSS only lets us affect a change on elements if they are children of an element, the element itself, or a general or adjacent sibling of an element that receives 'state' (when I say state I'm talking about `hover`, `focus`, `active`, `checked`, and so on). In the following examples I'm using `:hover` but that would obviously be problematic for touch based devices.

```
.item:hover .item-child {}
```

With the preceding selector, styles are applied to `item-child` when item is hovered over.

```
.item:hover ~ .item-general-sibling {}
```

With this selector, when the item is hovered over, styles are applied to `item-general-sibling` if it is at the same DOM level as item and follows it.

```
.item:hover + .item-adjacent-sibling {}
```

Here, when the item is hovered over, styles are applied to `item-adjacent-sibling` if it is the adjacent sibling element of item (straight after it in the DOM).

So, back to our issue. If we have a form with labels and fields like this, with the label above the input (to give us the requisite basic layout), it leaves us a little stuck:

```
<div class="form-Input_Wrapper">
  <label for="film">The film in question?</label>
  <input id="film" name="film" type="text" placeholder="e.g. King
Kong" required/>
</div>
```

In this situation, using just CSS, there is no way to change the style of the label based upon whether the input is required or not (as it comes after the label in the markup). We could switch the order of those two elements in the markup but then we would end up with the label underneath the input.

However, Flexbox gives us the ability to visually reverse the order of elements (read all about that in *Chapter 3*, *Fluid Layouts and Responsive Images*, if you haven't already) with ease. That allows us to use this markup:

```
<div class="form-Input_Wrapper">
  <input id="film" name="film" type="text" placeholder="e.g. King
Kong" required/>
  <label for="film">The film in question?</label>
</div>
```

And then simply apply `flex-direction: row-reverse` or `flex-direction: column-reverse` to the parent. These declarations reverse the visual order of their child elements, allowing the desired aesthetic of the label above (smaller viewports), or to the left (larger viewports) of the input. Now we can get on with actually providing some indication of required fields and when they have received input.

Thanks to our revised markup, the adjacent sibling selector now makes this possible.

```
input:required + label:after { }
```

This selector essentially says, for every label that follows an input with a `required` attribute, apply the enclosed rules. Here is the CSS for that section:

```
input:required + label:after {
  content: "*";
  font-size: 2.1em;
  position: relative;
  top: 6px;
  display: inline-flex;
  margin-left: .2ch;
  transition: color, 1s;
}
```

```
input:required:invalid + label:after {
  color: red;
}

input:required:valid + label:after {
  color: green;
}
```

Then, if you focus on a required input and enter a relevant value, the asterisk changes color to green. It's a subtle but helpful touch.

 There are more selectors (both implemented and being specified) alongside all the ones we have already looked at. For the most up to date list, take a look at the latest editors draft of the Selectors Level 4 specification: `http://dev.w3.org/csswg/selectors-4/`

Creating a background fill effect

Back in *Chapter 6, Stunning Aesthetics with CSS3*, we learned how to generate linear and radial gradients as background-images. Sadly, it isn't possible to transition between two background-images (which makes sense as the browser effectively rasterizes the declaration into an image). However, we can transition between values of associated properties like background-position and background-size. We'll use this factor to create a fill effect when an input or textarea receives focus.

Here are the properties and values added to the input:

```
input:not([type="range"]),
textarea {
  min-height: 30px;
  padding: 2px;
  font-size: 17px;
  border: 1px solid #ebebeb;
  outline: none;
  transition: transform .4s, box-shadow .4s, background-position .2s;
  background: radial-gradient(400px circle,  #fff 99%, transparent
99%), #f1f1f1;
  background-position: -400px 90px, 0 0;
  background-repeat: no-repeat, no-repeat;
  border-radius: 0;
  position: relative;
}
```

```
input:not([type="range"]):focus,
textarea:focus {
  background-position: 0 0, 0 0;
}
```

In the first rule, a solid white radial gradient is being generated but positioned offset out of view. The background color that sits behind (the HEX value after the `radial-gradient`) is not offset and so provides a default color. When the input gains focus, the background position on the `radial-gradient` is set back to the default and because we have a transition on the background-image set, we get a nice transition between the two. The result being the appearance that the input is 'filled' with a different color when it gains focus.

 Different browsers each have their own proprietary selectors and capabilities when it comes to styling parts of the native UI. For a handy list of lots of the specific selectors, Aurelius Wendelken compiled an impressive list. I made my own copy of it (or 'fork' in Git version control speak) for prosperity, which you can find at `https://gist.github.com/benfrain/403d3d3a8e2b6198e395`

Summary

In this chapter, we have learned how to use a host of new HTML5 form attributes. They enable us to make forms more usable than ever before and the data they capture more relevant. Furthermore, we can future-proof this new markup when needed with JavaScript polyfill scripts so that all users experience similar form features, regardless of the capability of their browser.

We're nearing the end of our responsive HTML5 and CSS3 journey. While we have covered an enormous amount in our time together, I'm conscious I'll never manage to impart all the information for every eventuality you'll encounter. Therefore, in the last chapter I'd like to take a higher level look at approaching a responsive web design and try and relate some solid best practices for getting your next/first responsive project off on the right footing.

10
Approaching a Responsive Web Design

In my favorite stories and films, there's usually a scene where a mentor passes on valuable advice and some magical items to the hero. You know those items will prove useful; you just don't know when or how.

Well, I'd like to assume the role of the mentor in this final chapter (plus my hair has waned, and I don't have the looks for the hero role). I would like you, my fine apprentice, to spare me just a few more moments of your time while I offer up some final words of advice before you set forth on your responsive quest.

This chapter will be half philosophical musings and guidance, and half grab-bag of unrelated tips and techniques. I hope at some point in your responsive adventures, these tips will prove useful. Here's what we'll cover:

- Getting designs in the browser and on real devices as soon as possible
- Letting the design dictate the breakpoints
- Embracing progressive enhancement
- Defining a browser support matrix
- Progressive enhancement in practice
- Linking CSS breakpoints to JavaScript
- Avoiding CSS frameworks in production
- Developing pragmatic solutions
- Writing the simplest possible code
- Hiding, showing, and loading content across viewports
- Letting CSS do the (visual) heavy lifting

- Using validators and linting tools
- Analyzing and testing web page performance (`webpagetest.org`)
- Embracing faster and more effective techniques
- Keeping an eye out for the next 'big' things

Get designs in the browser as soon as possible

The more responsive design work I have done, the more important I have found it to get designs up and running in a browser environment as soon as possible. If you are a designer as well as a developer, that simplifies matters. As soon as you have enough of a feel, visually, for what you need, you can get it prototyped in a browser and develop the idea further in a browser environment. This approach can be embraced more fully by letting go of high-fidelity full-page mock-ups altogether. Instead, consider things like Style Tiles—positioned between a moodboard and full mockup. The introduction to Style Tiles (`http://styletil.es/`) describes them as:

> *"Style Tiles are a design deliverable consisting of fonts, colors and interface elements that communicate the essence of a visual brand for the web."*

I've found graphical deliverables of this nature can be useful for presenting and communicating look and feel between stakeholders without resorting to the endless rounds of composites.

Let the design dictate the breakpoints

I'd like to reiterate a point made in previous chapters. Let the design define where breakpoints should be set. With a design in the browser, it makes this process far easier. You should always start amending the design from the smallest screen sizes upwards, so as the viewport size increases, you can see how far your design works before you need to introduce a breakpoint.

You'll also find that coding the design will be easier this way. Write the CSS for the smallest viewport first and then add any changes to different elements within media queries afterwards. For example:

```
.rule {
  /* Smallest viewport size styles */
}

@media (min-width: 40em) {
  .rule {
    /* Medium viewport size changes */
  }
}

@media (min-width: 70em) {
  .rule {
    /* Larger viewport size changes */
  }
}
```

View and use the design on real devices

If you can, start to build up a 'device lab' of older devices (phones/tablets) to view your work on. Having a number of varied devices is hugely beneficial. Not only does it let you feel how a design actually works across different devices, it also exposes layout/rendering peculiarities earlier in the process. After all, no one enjoys believing they have finished on a project to be told it doesn't work properly in a certain environment. Test early, test often! It need not cost the earth. For example, you can pick up older phone and tablet models on eBay, or buy them from friends/ relatives as they upgrade.

Use tools such as BrowserSync to synchronize your work

One of the biggest time-saving tools I've used lately is **BrowserSync**. Once configured, as you save your work, any changes to things like CSS are injected into the browser without you needing to constantly refresh your screen. If that wasn't good enough, any other browser windows on devices you have on the same WiFi refresh too. This saves having to pick up each of your testing devices and clicking refresh with each change. It even synchronizes scrolling and clicks too. Highly recommended: `http://browsersync.io/`

Embracing progressive enhancement

In previous chapters, we have considered briefly the notion of progressive enhancement. It's an approach to development that I have found so useful in practice I think it bears repeating. The fundamental idea with progressive enhancement is that you begin all your front-end code (HTML, CSS, JavaScript) with the lowest common denominator in mind. Then, you progressively enhance the code for more capable devices and browsers. That may seem simplistic and it is, but if you are used to working the other way around; designing the optimum experience and then figuring out a way of making that thing work on lesser devices/browsers, you'll find progressive enhancement an easier approach.

Imagine a low powered, poorly featured device. No JavaScript, no Flexbox support, no CSS3/CSS4 support. In that instance what can you do to provide a usable experience?

Most importantly, you should write meaningful HTML5 markup that accurately describes the content. This is an easier task if you're building text and content-based websites. In that instance, concentrate on using elements such as `main`, `header`, `footer`, `article`, `section`, and `aside` correctly. Not only will it help you discern different sections of your code, it will also provide greater accessibility for your users at no extra cost.

If you're building something like a web-based application or visual UI components (carousels, tabs, accordions, and the like) you'll need to think about how to distil the visual pattern down into accessible markup.

The reason good markup is so crucial is that it provides a base level experience for all users. The more you can achieve with HTML, the less you have to do in CSS and JavaScript to support older browsers. And nobody, and I really mean nobody, likes writing the code to support older browsers.

 For further reading and great practical examples on the subject, I would recommend the following two articles. They provide great insight into how fairly complex interactions can be handled with the constructs of HTML and CSS:

- `http://www.cssmojo.com/how-to-style-a-carousel/`
- `http://www.cssmojo.com/use-radio-buttons-for-single-option/`

It's by no means a simple feat to start thinking in this manner. It is however, an approach that is likely to serve you well in your quest to do as little as possible to support ailing browsers.

Now, about those browsers.

Defining a browser support matrix

Knowing the browsers and devices a web project needs to support up front can be crucial to developing a successful responsive web design. We've already considered why progressive enhancement is so useful in this respect; if done correctly, it means that the vast majority of your site will be functional on even the oldest browsers.

However, there may also be times when you need to start your experience with a higher set of prerequisites. Perhaps you are working on a project where JavaScript is essential, not an uncommon scenario. In that instance, you can still progressively enhance. Instead, you are merely enhancing from a different start point.

Whatever your starting point, the key thing is establishing what it is. Then, and only then, can you define and agree upon what visual and functional experiences the different browsers and devices that you intend to support will get.

Functional parity, not aesthetic parity

It's both unrealistic and undesirable to try and get any website looking and working the same in every browser. Besides quirks specific to certain browsers, there are essential functional considerations. For example, we have to consider things like touch targets for buttons and links on touch screens that aren't relevant on mouse-based devices.

Therefore, some part of your role as a responsive web developer is educating whoever you are answerable to (boss, client, shareholders) that 'supporting older browsers' does not mean 'looks the same in older browsers'. The line I tend to run with is that all browsers in the support matrix will get task parity, not visual parity. This means that if you have a checkout to build, all users will be able to get through the checkout and purchase goods. There may visual and interaction flourishes afforded to the users of more modern browsers, but the core task will be achievable by all.

Choosing the browsers to support

Typically, when we talk about which browsers to support, we're talking about how far back we need to look. Here are a couple of possibilities to consider, depending upon the situation.

If it's an existing website, look at visitor statistics (Google Analytics or similar). Armed with some figures you can likely do some rough calculations. For example: if cost of supporting browser X is less than the value produced by supporting browser X, then support browser X!

Also, consider that if there are browsers in the statistics that represent less than 10% of users, look further back and consider trends. How has usage changed over the last 3, 6, and 12 months? If it's currently 6% and that value has halved over the last 12 months you have a more compelling argument to consider ruling that browser out for specific enhancements.

If it's a new project and statistics are unavailable, I usually opt for a 'previous two' policy. This would be the current version plus the previous two versions of each browser. For example, if Internet Explorer 12 was the current version, look to offer your enhancements for that version plus IE10 and IE11 (the previous two). This choice is easier with the 'evergreen' browsers, the term given to browsers that continually update on a rapid release cycle (Firefox and Chrome for example).

Tiering the user experience

At this point, let's assume shareholders are educated and on board. Let's also assume you have a clear set of browsers that you would like to add enhanced experiences for. We can now set about tiering the experience. I like to keep things simple, so where possible I opt to define a simple 'base' tier and a more 'enhanced' tier.

The base experience being the minimal viable version of the site and the enhanced version being the most fully-featured and aesthetically pleasing version. You might need to accommodate more granularity in your tiers, for example, forking the experience in relation to browser features; support for Flexbox or support for `translate3d` for example. Regardless of how the tiers are defined, ensure you define them and what you expect to deliver with each. Then you can actually go about coding those tiers.

Practically delivering experience tiers

Right now, Modernizr facilitates the most robust manner to enhance and fork experiences based upon device capabilities. While it means adding a JavaScript dependency to your project, I think it is worthwhile.

Remember, that when writing CSS, the code outside of media queries and without selectors that require classes added by Modernizr should make up our 'base' experience.

Then thanks to Modernizr, we can layer on ever more enhanced experiences based upon the browser capabilities. If you refer back to `example_08-07` you can see this mind-set and code pattern applied to an off-canvas menu pattern.

Linking CSS breakpoints to JavaScript

Typically, with something web-based involving any sort of interaction, JavaScript will be involved. When you're developing a responsive project, it's likely you will want to do different things at different viewport sizes. Not just in CSS but also in JavaScript.

Let's suppose we want to invoke a certain JavaScript function when we reach a certain breakpoint in the CSS (remember that 'breakpoint' is the term used to define the point in which a responsive design should change significantly). Let's suppose that breakpoint is 47.5rem (with a 16px root font size that would equate to 760px) and we only want to run the function at that size. The obvious solution would be to simply measure the screen width and invoke the function if the value matched the same value you had decided for your CSS breakpoint.

JavaScript will always return the value of widths as pixels rather than REM values so that's the first complication. However, even if we set the breakpoints in CSS as pixel values, it would still mean two places to update and change those values when we are changing viewport sizes.

Thankfully, there is a better way. I first came across this technique on Jeremy Keith's website: `http://adactio.com/journal/5429/`

You can find the full code for this at `example_10-01`. However, the basic idea is that in CSS we insert something that can be easily read and understood by JavaScript.

Consider this in the CSS:

```css
@media (min-width: 20rem) {
    body::after {
        content: "Splus";
        font-size: 0;
    }
}
@media (min-width: 47.5rem) {
    body::after {
        content: "Mplus";
        font-size: 0;
    }
}
@media (min-width: 62.5rem) {
    body::after {
        content: "Lplus";
        font-size: 0;
    }
}
```

For each breakpoint that we want to communicate to JavaScript, we use the `after` pseudo element (you could use before too, either is just as good) and set the content of that pseudo element to be the name of our breakpoint. In our preceding example, I am using `Splus` for small screens and above, `Mplus` for medium screens and above, and `Lplus` for large screens and above. You can use whatever name makes sense to you and change the value whenever it makes sense to you (different orientations, different heights, different widths, and so on).

> The `::before` and `::after` pseudo elements are inserted into the DOM as shadow DOM elements. The `::before` pseudo element is inserted as the first child of its parent, and `::after` gets inserted as the last child. You can confirm this point in the developer tools of your browser.

With that CSS set, we can browse the DOM tree and see our `::after` pseudo element.

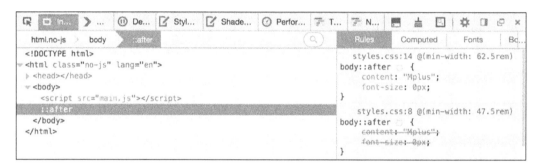

Then in our JavaScript, we can read this value. Firstly, we assign the value to a variable:

```
var size = window.getComputedStyle(document.body,':after).
getPropertyValue('content');
```

And then once we have it we can do something with it. To prove this concept I have made a simple self-invoking function (self-invoking simply means it is executed as soon as the browser parses it) that alerts a different message on page load depending upon the viewport size:

```
;(function alertSize() {
    if (size.indexOf("Splus") !=-1) {
        alert('I will run functions for small screens');
    }
    if (size.indexOf("Mplus") !=-1) {
```

```
        alert('At medium sizes, a different function could run');
    }
    if (size.indexOf("Lplus") !=-1) {
        alert('Large screen here, different functions if needed');
    }
})();
```

I'd hope you do something a little more interesting than alert a message in your projects but I think you will find great benefit in approaching the problem this way. You'll never be in danger of your CSS media queries and your width dependent JavaScript functions getting out of sync again.

Avoid CSS frameworks in production

There are a plethora of free frameworks available that aim to aid in the rapid prototyping and building of responsive websites. The two most common examples being Bootstrap (`http://getbootstrap.com/`) and Foundation (`http://foundation.zurb.com/`). While they are great projects, particularly for learning how to build responsive visual patterns, I think they should be avoided in production.

I've spoken to plenty of developers who start all projects with one of these frameworks and then amend them to fit their needs. This approach can be incredibly advantageous for rapid prototyping (for example, to illustrate some interaction to clients) but I think it's the wrong thing to do for projects you intend to take through to production.

Firstly, from a technical perspective, it's likely that starting with a framework will result in your project having more code than it actually needs. Secondly, from an aesthetic perspective, due to the popularity of these frameworks, it's likely your project will end up looking very similar to countless others.

Finally, if you only copy and paste code into your project and tweak it to your needs, you'll be unlikely to fully appreciate what's going on 'under the hood'. It's only by defining and solving the problems you have that you can master the code you place into your projects.

Coding pragmatic solutions

When it comes to front-end web development, 'ivory towered idealism' is a particular bugbear of mine. While we should always endeavor try to do things 'the right way', pragmatism must always win out. Let me give you an example (the finished code is `example_10-02`). Suppose we have a button to style that opens an off-canvas menu. Our natural inclination might be to mark it up something like this:

```
<button class="menu-toggle js-activate-off-canvas-menu">
    <span aria-label="site navigation">&#9776;</span> menu
</button>
```

Nice and simple. It's a button so we have used the `button` element. We have used two different HTML classes on the button, one will be a hook for CSS styling (`menu-toggle`), and the other as a JavaScript hook (`js-activate-off-canvas-menu`). In addition, we are using the `aria-label` attribute (ARIA is covered in more detail in *Chapter 4, HTML5 for Responsive Web Designs*) to communicate to screen readers the meaning of the character inside the `span`. In this example, we have used the HTML entity `&#9776;` which is the Unicode character 'Trigram for Heaven'. It's used here merely because it looks like the 'Hamburger icon' often used to symbolize a menu.

 If you'd like some solid advice on when and how to use the `aria-label` attribute I thoroughly recommend the following post on the Opera developer site by Heydon Pickering: `https://dev.opera.com/articles/ux-accessibility-aria-label/`

At this point, we seem to be in good shape. Semantic, highly accessible markup and classes to separate concerns. Great. Let's add some styling:

```
.menu-toggle {
    appearance: none;
    display: inline-flex;
    padding: 0 10px;
    font-size: 17px;
    align-items: center;
    justify-content: center;
    border-radius: 8px;
    border: 1px solid #ebebeb;
    min-height: 44px;
    text-decoration: none;
    color: #777;
}
```

```
[aria-label="site navigation"] {
    margin-right: 1ch;
    font-size: 24px;
}
```

Open this up in Firefox and this is what we see:

Not exactly what we were hoping for. In this case, the browser has decided we've gone too far; Firefox simply won't allow us to use a button element as a Flex container. This is a very real conflict for a developer. Do we choose the right element or the right aesthetic? Given that ideally, we would like to have the menu 'hamburger icon' on the left and the word 'menu' on the right.

You can see in the prior code we have used the `appearance` property. It's used to remove the browsers default styling for form elements, and has had a potted history. It was specified by the W3C for some time and then later dropped, leaving behind vendor-prefixed versions of the property in both Mozilla and WebKit browsers. Thankfully, it's now back on the standards track: `http://dev.w3.org/csswg/css-ui-4/#appearance-switching`

When a link becomes a button

I won't lie. Given this conundrum, I usually opt for the latter. Then I try and make up for the fact I'll be using the wrong element by choosing the next best element and changing the ARIA role where possible. In this case, while our menu button is certainly not a link (after all, it doesn't take the user anywhere), it's an `a` tag that I will be using. I've decided it's the next best thing—more like a button than any other element. And by using a link we can achieve the desired aesthetic. Here's the markup I'd go with. Note the added ARIA role on the `a` tag to indicate its role as a button (and not a link which is the default) to assistive technology:

```
<a class="menu-toggle js-activate-off-canvas-menu" role="button">
    <span aria-label="site navigation">&#9776;</span> menu
</a>
```

It's not perfect but it's a pragmatic solution. Here's the two (button element on the left, a tag on the right) next to each other in Firefox (version 39.0a2 if you're curious):

Of course, for this simplistic example, we could change the display from flex to block and play around with the padding until our desired aesthetic was achieved. Or, we could keep the button element and nest another semantically meaningless element (span) and make that a Flex container. There are trade-offs whichever approach you favor.

Ultimately, it's up to us to markup documents as sensibly as possible. At one end of the scale, there are developers that only markup with divs and spans to ensure no unwanted styles from the browser. The cost being no inherent meaning from their elements and in turn, no 'free' accessibility. At the other end of the scale are markup purists, who will only ever markup content in what they consider to be the correct element, regardless of how 'off' the visuals might end up as a result. There is a middle ground. I feel that's the sensible and most productive place to be.

Use the simplest code possible

It's easy to get drunk on the power that new techniques afford us. With this in mind, aim to solve your responsive problems in the simplest manner possible. For example, if you need to style the fifth item in a list of items and you have access to the markup, don't use an nth-child selector like this:

```
.list-item:nth-child(5) {
    /* Styles */
}
```

If you have access to the markup, make life easier by adding an HTML class to the item:

```
<li class="list-item specific-class">Item</li>
```

And then style the item with that simple class:

```
.specific-class {
    /* Styles */
}
```

Not only is this easier to understand, it gets you wider support for free (older versions of Internet Explorer don't support nth-child selectors).

Hiding, showing, and loading content across viewports

One of the commonly touted maxims regarding responsive web design is: if you don't have something on the screen at smaller viewports, you shouldn't have it there at larger ones either.

This means users should be able to accomplish all the same goals (buy a product, read an article, accomplish an interface task) at every viewport size. This is common sense. After all, as users ourselves, we've all felt the frustration of going to a website to accomplish a goal and being unable to, simply because we're using a smaller screen.

It also means that as screen real estate is more plentiful, we shouldn't feel compelled to add extra things just to fill the space (widgets, adverts, or links for example). If the user could live without those extras at smaller screen sizes, they'll manage just fine at bigger ones. Displaying extra content at larger viewport sizes also means that either the content was there at smaller viewports and was merely hidden (typically using display: none; in CSS) or it's being loaded in at a particular viewport size (with the help of JavaScript). Succinctly: either the content is loaded but not viewable, or it's viewable yet probably superfluous.

In broad terms I think the above maxim is sound advice. If nothing else, it makes designers and developers question more thoroughly the content they display on screen. However, as ever in web design, there are always going to be exceptions.

As far as possible, I resist loading in new markup for different viewports but occasionally it's a necessity. I've worked on complex user interfaces that rightfully required different markup and designs at wider viewports.

In this instance, JavaScript was used to replace one area of markup with another. It wasn't the ideal scenario but it was the most pragmatic. If, for whatever reason, the JavaScript failed, users got the smallest screen layout. They could accomplish all the same goals, just the layout was sub-optimal for achieving the task at hand.

These are the kind of choices you will likely face as you code more and more complex responsive web designs, and you'll need to use your own judgment as to what the best choice is in any given scenario. However, it's not a cardinal sin if you toggle the visibility of the odd bit of markup with `display: none` to achieve your goal.

Let CSS do the (visual) heavy lifting

It's a fact that JavaScript provides a level of interactivity on webpages that simply cannot be achieved with CSS alone. However, where possible, when it comes to visuals, we should still do all the heavy lifting with CSS. In practicality, this means not animating menus in, out, on and off, with JavaScript alone (I'm looking at you jQuery `show` and `hide` methods). Instead, use JavaScript to perform simple class changes on the relevant section of the markup. Then let that class change trigger the menu being shown/animated in CSS.

For the best performance, when toggling classes in the HTML, ensure you add a class as close as possible to the item you want to effect. For example, if you want a pop-up box to appear over another element, add the class on the closest shared parent element. This will ensure that, for the sake of optimal performance, only that particular section of the page is made 'dirty' and the browser shouldn't have to paint vast areas of the page again. For a great, free, course on performance, take a look at Paul Lewis's 'Browser Rendering Optimization' course: `https://www.udacity.com/course/browser-rendering-optimization--ud860`

Validators and linting tools

Generally speaking, writing HTML and CSS is pretty forgiving. You can nest the odd thing incorrectly, miss the occasional quotation mark or self-closing tag and not always notice a problem. Despite this, on an almost weekly basis I manage to befuddle myself with incorrect markup. Sometimes it's a slip-up like accidentally typing an errant character. Other times it's school-boy errors like nesting a `div` inside a `span` (invalid markup as a `span` is an inline element and a `div` is a block level element—leading to unpredictable results). Thankfully, there are great tools to help out. At worst, if you're encountering a weird issue, head over to `http://validator.w3.org/` and paste your markup in there. It will point out all errors along with line numbers, helping you to easily fix things up.

Better still, install and configure 'linting' tools for your HTML, CSS, and JavaScript. Or, choose a text editor with some degree of sanity-checking built in. Then problem areas are flagged up in your code as you go. Here's an example of a simple spelling error in CSS flagged up by Microsoft's 'Code' editor:

Like a clown, I've clumsily typed `widthh` instead of `width`. The editor has spotted this fact and pointed out the error of my ways and offered some sensible alternatives. Embrace these tools where possible. There are better uses of your time than tracking down simple syntax errors in your code.

Performance

Considering the performance of your responsive web designs is as important as the aesthetics. However, performance presents something of a moving target. For example, browsers update and improve the way they handle assets, new techniques are discovered that supersede existing 'best practices', technologies eventually get enough browser support that they become viable for widespread adoption. The list goes on.

There are however, some basic implementation details that are pretty solid (well, until HTTP2 is common place, more of which shortly). These are:

1. Minimize the number of assets (for example, don't load 15 JavaScript files if you concatenate them into one).

2. Minimize the page weight (if you can compress images to a fraction of their original size you should).

3. Defer non-essential assets (if you can put off loading CSS and JavaScript until the page has rendered it can greatly reduce the perceived load time).

4. Ensure the page is usable as soon as possible (usually a by-product of doing all the preceding steps).

There are a number of great tools available to measure and optimize performance too. My personal favorite being `http://webpagetest.org/`. At its simplest, you pick a URL and click on **START TEST**. It will show you a complete analysis of the page but even more usefully, it shows a 'filmstrip' view of the page as it has loaded, allowing you to concentrate on getting the rendered page complete sooner. Here's an example of the filmstrip view of the BBC home page:

Whenever trying to optimize performance, ensure you take measurements before you begin (otherwise, you have no idea how effective your performance work has been). Then make amendments, test, and repeat.

The next big things

One of the things that make front-end web development interesting, is that things change rapidly. There is always something new to learn and the web community is always figuring out better, faster, and more effective ways of solving problems.

For example, three years before writing this module responsive images (`srcset` and the `picture` element that are detailed in *Chapter 3*, *Fluid Layouts and Responsive Images*) simply didn't exist. Back then, we had to use clever third party workarounds to serve up more appropriate images to different viewport sizes. Now that common need has been rationalized into a W3C standard we can all now use and enjoy.

Similarly, not long ago, Flexbox was just a twinkle in a specification writer's eyes. Even when the specification evolved it was still difficult to implement until Andrey Sitnik and those clever folks at Evil Martians (`https://evilmartians.com/`) created Autoprefixer and we are subsequently able to use it cross-browser with relative ease.

The future holds yet more exciting capabilities for us to understand and implement. We've already mentioned Service Workers in *Chapter 4*, *HTML5 for Responsive Web Designs*, for example (`http://www.w3.org/TR/service-workers/`); a better way to create offline capable web-based applications.

There is also 'Web Components' a collection of standards made up of Shadow DOM (`http://w3c.github.io/webcomponents/spec/shadow/`), Custom Elements (`http://w3c.github.io/webcomponents/spec/custom/`) and HTML Imports (`http://w3c.github.io/webcomponents/spec/imports/`) that will allow us to create entirely bespoke and re-usable components.

Then there are the other forthcoming enhancements such as CSS Level 4 Selectors (`http://dev.w3.org/csswg/selectors-4/`) and CSS Level 4 Media Queries, which we covered in some detail in *Chapter 2*, *Media Queries – Supporting Differing Viewports*.

Finally, another big change looming on the horizon is HTTP2. It promises to make many of our current best practices, bad practices. For a good in-depth primer I'd suggest reading *http2 explained* by Daniel Stenberg (it's a free PDF). Alternatively, for a lighter summary, read Matt Wilcox's excellent post, *HTTP2 for front-end web developers* (`https://mattwilcox.net/web-development/http2-for-front-end-web-developers`).

Summary

As we reach the end of our time together, your humble author hopes to have related all the techniques and tools you'll need to start building your next website or web application responsively.

It's my conviction that by approaching web projects with a little forethought and by making a few modifications to existing workflows, practices, and techniques, it's possible to create responsive web designs that provide fast, flexible, and maintainable websites that can look incredible regardless of the device used to visit them.

We've covered a wealth of information in our time together; techniques, technologies, performance optimizations, specifications, workflow, tooling, and more. I wouldn't expect anybody to take it all in in one read. Therefore, next time you need to remember this or that syntax, or refresh your mind about one of the responsive related subjects we've covered, I hope you'll dip back in to these pages. I'll be right here waiting for you.

Until then, I wish you good fortunes in your responsive web design quests.

See you again sometime.

Module 3

HTML5 and CSS3 Responsive Web Design Cookbook

Learn the secrets of developing responsive websites capable of interfacing with today's mobile internet devices

1
Responsive Elements and Media

In this chapter, you will learn about:

- ▸ Resizing an image using percent width
- ▸ Responsive images using the cookie and JavaScript
- ▸ Making your video respond to your screen width
- ▸ Resizing an image using media queries
- ▸ Changing your navigation with media queries
- ▸ Making a responsive padding based on size
- ▸ Making a CSS3 button glow for a loading element

Introduction

The responsiveness website design and media is one of the most exciting things to happen to web development since ASCII art appeared on bulletin boards back when I was a school boy. The new cool features of HTML5, CSS3, and jQuery have brought new life to the old web in ways that have brought back the fun and really gets the Web audiences excited for using your applications. This chapter contains several recipes that will help you create responsive HTML elements and different media.

Some recipes are easy and some are more challenging. All of the code used for the **responsive web design** elements is provided with the module, therefore nothing inside will be impossible to accomplish. Each and all of the responsive web design recipes will help you optimize your website's presentation to create an amazing responsive web experience for your audience no matter what device type or size you are using.

In this chapter, if examples don't work on a real device, the issue can be fixed if you add the following code:

```
<meta name="viewport"
content="width=device-width, initial-scale=1">
```

Resizing an image using percent width

This method relies on client-side coding for resizing a large image. It serves only one image to the client and asks it to render the image according to the size of the browser's window. This is usually the preferable method when you are confident that the clients have the bandwidth to download the image without causing the page to load slowly.

Getting ready

First you will need an image. To find a high-quality image, use Google Image Search. A search for `robots`, for example, the search gives me 158,000,000 results, which is pretty good. However, what I really want is a large image, so I click on **Search tools**, and then click on **Any Size**, which I change to **Large**. I still have 4,960,000 images to choose from.

The image should be resized to match the largest scale viewable. Open it in your image-editing software. If you don't have an image-editing software already, there are many free ones, go get one. Gimp is a powerful image-editing software and it's open source, or free to download. Go to `http://www.gimp.org` to get this powerful open source image-editing software.

How to do it...

Once you have your image-editing software, open the image in it and change the image's width to 300px. Save your new image and then move or upload the image to your web directory.

Your HTML should contain your image and some text to demonstrate the responsive effect. If you do not have time to write your life story, you can go back to the Internet and get some sample text from an Ipsum generator. Go to `http://www.lipsum.com` and generate a paragraph of Ipsum text.

```
<p class="text">Loremipsum dolor sit amet…</p>
<div class="img-wrap" >
    <img alt="robots image" class="responsive" src="robots.jpg" >
    <p>Loremipsum dolor sit amet</p>
</div>
```

Your CSS should include a class for your paragraph and one for your image and an image wrapper. Float the paragraph to the left and give it a width of 60%, and the image wrapper with a width of `40%`.

```
p.text {
    float:left;
    width:60%;
}
div.img-wrap{
    float:right;
    width:40%;
}
```

This creates a fluid layout, but does not yet do anything to create a responsive image. The image will stay at a static width of 300px until you add the following CSS. Then, add a new class to the CSS for the image. Assign it a `max-width` value of `100%`. This allows the width to adjust to the browser width changes. Next, add a dynamic `height` property to the class.

```
img.responsive {
    max-width: 100%;
    height: auto;
}
```

This creates an image that responds to the browser window's width with an optimized version of that image for the audience.

How it works...

The `responsive` property of the image CSS forces it to take 100 percent of its parent element. When the parent element's width changes, the image changes to fill in that width. The `height: auto` property acts to preserve the aspect ratio of the image.

See also

- ▶ The *Responsive images using the cookie and JavaScript* recipe
- ▶ The *Making a responsive padding based on size* recipe

Responsive images using the cookie and JavaScript

A responsive image's width can be delivered through complicated server logic. Sometimes because of the requirements you cannot achieve the desired results through the easiest method. The percent-width method relies on the client side for image resizing of a large image file. This method provides a server-side delivery of the properly sized image you request. It may reduce the server load and bandwidth and help you with long loading, if you are concerned with slow loading affecting the performance of your website.

Getting ready

These methods require your server to perform some sort of logic function on it. Firstly, it requires PHP on your server. It also requires you to create three different sized versions of the image and serve them to the client as requested.

How to do it...

The JavaScript is simple. It creates a cookie based on your device's screen dimensions. When the client makes a request to the server for an image, it fires the PHP code to deliver the appropriate image.

```
<script >
    document.cookie = "screen_dimensions=" + screen.width + "x" +
screen.height;
</script>
```

Now, on your server, create an `images` folder in the web directory and create a PHP file (`index.php`) with the following code in it:

```php
<?php
 $screen_w = 0;
 $screen_h = 0;
 $img = $_SERVER['QUERY_STRING'];

 if (file_exists($img)) {

   // Get screen dimensions from the cookie
   if (isset($_COOKIE['screen_dimensions'])) {
     $screen = explode('x', $_COOKIE['screen_dimensions']);
     if (count($screen)==2) {
       $screen_w = intval($screen[0]);
       $screen_h = intval($screen[1]);
     }
   }
 }
```

```php
    if ($screen_w > 0) {
    $theExt = pathinfo($img, PATHINFO_EXTENSION);

    // for Low resolution screen
    if ($screen_w <= 800) {
        $output = substr_replace($img, '-low', -strlen($theExt) - 1,
0);
    }
    // for Medium resolution screen
    else if ($screen_w <= 1024) {
        $output = substr_replace($img, '-med', -strlen($theExt) - 1,
0);
    }

    // check if file exists
    if (isset($output) && file_exists($output)) {
        $img = $output;
    }
    }

    // return the image file;
    readfile($img);
    }

?>
```

Now with your image-editing software, open your large image and create two smaller versions of it. If the original version is 300px, then make the next two copies 200px and 100px. Then, name them `robot.png`, `robot-med.png`, and `robot-low.png` respectively. Upload these three images into the `images` folder.

Last, but not least, put the following HTML file in your server's document root:

```html
<!doctype html>

<html>

<head>

<title>Responsive Images</title>

<meta charset="utf-8">

<script>

document.cookie = "screen_dimensions=" + screen.width + "x" + screen.
height;

</script>

</head>
```

```
<body>

<img alt="robot image" src="images/index.php?robot.png">

</body>

</html>
```

You can see the recipe in action in the following screenshot:

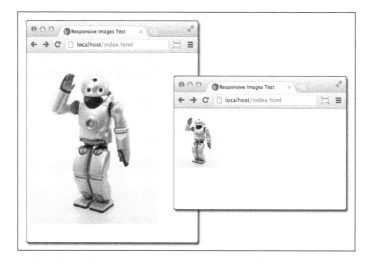

While this method is limited to delivering a specific image for each screen size, and is not fluidly dynamic, it does provide the same functionality on the server side as a CSS media query. You can style the served image with CSS or animate it with JavaScript. It can be used with a combination of methods to provide responsive content.

The code for this recipe was originally created by the clever folks at `http://www.html.it/articoli/responsive-images-con-i-cookie/`.

How it works...

The HTML file first creates a cookie describing your device's screen dimensions. When the image element calls the PHP file it works like an `include` statement in PHP. The PHP file first checks for the file to exist, then reads the cookie for the screen width, and delivers the appropriate-sized version of the image.

Making your video respond to your screen width

The streaming of video can also be responsive. You can easily embed an HTML5 video in your page and make it responsive. The `video` tag easily supports using a percent width. However, it requires that you have the video source on your website's host. If you have this available, this is easy.

```
<style>
video {
    max-width: 100%;
    height: auto;
}
</style>

<video width="320" height="240" controls="controls">
    <source src="movie.mp4" type="video/mp4">
    <source src="movie.ogg" type="video/ogg">
    Your browser does not support the video tag.
</video>
```

However, using a video-hosting site, such as YouTube or Vimeo, has many advantages over hosting it yourself. First, there is the bandwidth issue, you may have bandwidth or disk space limits on your hosting server. Additionally, video-hosting sites make the upload conversion to a usable web video surprisingly easy, compared to using only your own resources.

Getting ready

The video-hosting sites allow you to embed an iFrame or object code snippet in your page to stream the video on your site. This won't work inside the `video` tag. So, to make it responsive, there is a more complex, but still easy method.

How to do it...

Wrap the video-source snippet in an HTML containing the `div` element and give it a 50 to 60 percent padding on the bottom and relative positions. Then give its child element, the video iFrame object, a `100%` width and `100%` height, and an `absolute` position. This makes the iFrame object completely fill in the parent element.

The following is the HTML code that uses an `iframe` tag to get a video from Vimeo:

```
<div class="video-wrap">
    <iframe src="http://player.vimeo.com/video/52948373?badge=0"
width = "800" height= "450" frameborder="0"></iframe>
```

```
    </div>
```

The following is the HTML code using the older YouTube object with markup:

```
<div class="video-wrap">
    <object width="800" height="450">
        <param name="movie" value="http://www.youtube.com/v/
b803LeMGkCA?version=3&amp;hl=en_US">
            </param>
        <param name="allowFullScreen" value="true"></param>
        <param name="allowscriptaccess" value="always"></param>
        <embed src="http://www.youtube.com/v/
b803LeMGkCA?version=3&amp;hl=en_US" type="application/x-shockwave-
flash" width="560" height="315" allowscriptaccess="always"
allowfullscreen="true">
            </embed>
    </object>
</div>
```

Both video types use the same CSS:

```
.video-wrap {
    position:relative;
    padding-bottom: 55%;
    padding-top: 30px;
    height: 0;
    overflow:hidden;
}
.video-wrap iframe,
.video-wrap object,
.video-wrap embed {
    position:absolute;
    top:0;
    width:100%;
    height:100%;
}
```

You might not want the video to take up the entire width of the page. In this case, you can limit the width of the video using width and max-width. Then, wrap the video-wrap element with the another div element and assign a fixed width value and max-width:100%.

```
<div class="video-outer-wrap">
    <div class="video-wrap">
        <iframe src="http://player.vimeo.com/video/6284199?title=0&b
yline=0&portrait=0" width="800" height="450" frameborder="0">
        </iframe>
    </div>
```

```
</div>

.video-outer-wrap {
    width: 500px;
    max-width:100%;
}
```

This recipe will work on all modern browsers.

How it works...

This method is called Intrinsic Ratios for Videos, created by Thierry Koblentz on A List Apart. You wrap the video inside an element that has an intrinsic aspect ratio, and then give the video an absolute position. This locks the aspect ratio, while allowing the size to be fluid.

Resizing an image using media queries

The media query is another useful and highly customizable method for responsive images. This is different than responsive fluid width achieved by the percent-width method. Your design may require some specific image widths for different screen size ranges and a fluid width would break your design.

Getting ready

This method only requires one image, and makes the client's browser resize the image instead of the server.

How to do it...

The HTML code is simple, using the standard image tag, create an image element, as follows:

```
<img alt="robot image" src="robot.png">
```

To start with a simple version, create a media query that will detect the browser window's size and deliver a larger image for browser screens larger than `1024px`, and a smaller image for smaller browser windows. First the media query, it looks for the media type `screen`, and then the screen size. When the media query is satisfied the browser will render the CSS inside the brackets.

```
@media screen and ( max-width: 1024px ) {…}
@media screen and ( min-width: 1025px ) {…}
```

Now, add a class to your image tag. The class will respond differently in different media queries, as shown in the following code line:

```
img alt="robot image" src="robot.png" class="responsive"/>
```

Adding the CSS class to each media query with a different size will make the browser render the desired image size to each differently sized browser window. The media query can coexist with other CSS classes. Then, outside of the media queries, add a CSS class for the image with `height:auto`. This will work for both media queries with only adding one line of CSS.

```
@media screen and ( max-width: 1024px ) {
img.responsive { width: 200px; }
}
@media screen and ( min-width: 1025px) {
img.responsive { width: 300px;}
}
img.responsive { height: auto; }
```

To make the image respond to multiple ranges you can combine the `max-width` and `min-width` media queries. To specify an image size for browser windows, sized between `1024px` and `1280px`, add a media query for screen, `1024px` as `min-width`, and `1280px` as `max-width`.

```
@media screen and ( max-width: 1024px ) {
img.responsive { width: 200px; }
}
@media screen and ( min-width:1025px ) and ( max-width: 1280px ) {
img.responsive { width: 300px; }
}
@media screen and ( min-width: 1081px ) {
img.responsive { width: 400px; }
}
img.responsive { height: auto; }
```

You can specify many different image sizes for many different browser window sizes with the media query method.

How it works...

The media query of CSS3 gives your CSS logical conditions based on the browser's viewport properties, and can render different styles based on the browser's window properties. This recipe takes advantage of this by setting a different image width for many different browser's window sizes. Thus delivering a responsive image size, you can control with a high degree of granularity.

Changing your navigation with media queries

The media query can do more than just resizing images. You can use the media query to deliver a much more dynamic web page to your viewers. You can display a responsive menu based on different screen sizes using media queries.

Getting ready

To make a responsive menu system, using two different menus we will display a dynamic menu for three different browser window sizes.

How to do it...

For the smaller browser windows, and especially for mobile devices and tablets, create a simple `select` menu that only takes up a small amount of vertical space. This menu uses an HTML `form` element for the navigation options that fires a JavaScript code to load the new page on selection.

```
<div class="small-menu">
    <form>
        <select name="URL" onchange="window.location.href=this.form.
URL.options[this.form.URL.selectedIndex].value">
            <option value="blog.html">My Blog</option>
            <option value="home.html">My Home Page</option>
            <option value="tutorials.html">My Tutorials</option>
        </select>
    <form>
</div>
```

For the larger browser window sizes, create a simple `ul` list element that can be styled through CSS. This menu will receive a different layout and look from the different media queries. This menu is added to the same page following the `select` menu:

```
<div class="large-menu">
    <ul>
        <li>
            <a href="blog.html">My Blog</a>
        </li>
        <li>
            <a href="home.html">My Home Page</a>
        </li>
        <li>
            <a href="tutorials.html">My Tutorials</a>
        </li>
```

```
        </ul>
    </div>
```

To make the menu responsive, create a media query for the target browser window sizes. For browser windows smaller than `800px`, the CSS will display only the `select` form inside the `div` element with the `small-menu` class, for all larger browser windows, the CSS will display the `ul` list inside the `div` element with the `large-menu` class. This creates an effect where the page will shift between menus when the browser window crosses width of `801px`.

```css
@media screen and ( max-width: 800px ) {
.small-menu { display:inline; }
.large-menu { display:none; }
}
@media screen and ( min-width: 801px ) and ( max-width: 1024px ) {
.small-menu { display:none; }.
.large-menu { display:inline; }
}
@media screen and ( min-width: 1025px ) {
.small-menu { display:none; }
.large-menu { display:inline; }
}
```

For the larger screen sizes, you can use the same `ul` list and use the media query even further to deliver a different menu by simply switching out the CSS and using the same HTML.

For the medium-sized menu, use CSS to display the list items as a horizontal list, as shown in the following code snippet:

```css
.large-menu ul{
    list-style-type:none;
}
.large-menu ul li {
    display:inline;
}
```

This turns the list into a horizontal list. We want this version of the navigation to appear on the medium-sized browser windows. Place it inside the media query ranging between `801px` and `1024px`, as shown in the following code snippet:

```css
@media screen and ( min-width: 801px ) and (max-width: 1024px ) {
    .small-menu {
        display:none;
    }
.large-menu {
        display:inline;
    }
    .large-menu ul {
```

```
                list-style-type:none;
        }
    .large-menu ul li {
            display:inline;
        }
    }
    @media screen and (min-width: 1025px ) {
    .small-menu {
            display:none;
        }
        .large-menu {
            display:inline;
        }
    }
```

To further utilize the responsive navigation elements in the best way possible, we want the menu list version to move to a different layout location when the screen's width changes. For the middle width, 801px to 1024px, the menu stays on top of the page and has a 100% width. When the screen is wider than 1025px, the menu will float to the left-hand side of its parent element. Add to the 801px to 1024px media query a 100% width to the large-menu class, and to the 1025px media query, add a 20% width and a float:left value to the large-menu class.

To fill out the page we will also add a paragraph of text wrapped in a div element. You can go back to the Lorem Ipsum text generator to create filler text (http://lipsum.com/). In the medium-width media query give the element containing the paragraph a 100% width. In the largest media query, give the element containing the paragraph a width of 80% and float it to the right-hand side of its parent element.

```
    <div class="small-menu">
        <form>
            <select name="URL" onchange="window.location.href=this.form.
    URL.options[this.form.URL.selectedIndex].value">
                <option value="blog.html">My Blog</option>
                <option value="home.html">My Home Page</option>
                <option value="tutorials.html">My Tutorials</option>
            </select>
        <form>
    </div>

    <div class="large-menu">
        <ul>
            <li>
                <a href="blog.html">My Blog</a>
            </li>
            <li>
                <a href="home.html">My Home Page</a>
```

```
                </li>
                <li>
                        <a href="tutorials.html">My Tutorials</a>
                </li>
        </ul>
</div>

<div class="content">
        <p>Loremipsum dolor sitamet, consecteturadipiscingelit…</p>
</div>
```

And your style should look as shown in following code snippet:

```css
<style>
@media screen and ( max-width: 800px ) {
        .small-menu {
                display: inline;
        }
        .large-menu {
                display: none;
        }
}
@media screen and ( min-width: 801px ) and ( max-width: 1024px ) {
        .small-menu {
                display: none;
        }
        .large-menu {
                display:inline;
                width: 100%;
        }
        .large-menu ul {
                list-style-type: none;
        }
        .large-menu ul li {
                display: inline;
        }
        .content: {
                width: 100%;
        }
}
@media screen and ( min-width: 1025px ) {
        .small-menu {
                display: none;
        }
        .large-menu {
                display: inline;
```

```
        float: left;
        width: 20%;
    }
    .content{
        float: right;
        width: 80%;
    }
}
</style>
```

The final result is a page with three different versions of the navigation. Your audience will be amazed when given an optimized version of the menu for each particular browser window size. You can see the navigation elements in all their glory in the following screenshot:

How it works...

Each version of the navigation utilizes the media query CSS3 property to maximize the space available for the menu and the content. In the smallest window, below `801px`, the navigation is packed neatly inside a `select` form element. The medium window, ranging from `801px` to `1024px`, the navigation is inline and spans across the top of the page, and is followed by the content. Finally, in the widest browser widths (more than 1025px), the menu floats on the left-hand side and takes only 20 percent of the horizontal screen space, while the content is maximized on the remaining 80 percent (right-hand side) of the wide-browser window. This technique requires more planning and effort, but is well worth it to deliver the best possible viewing to your audience.

Making a responsive padding based on size

To complement a responsive width image element, relative padding can be added. With a static width padding, the image padding may appear too thick in smaller browser windows and overcrowd any other elements nearby, or may push the image off the screen.

Getting ready

A good place to start is with some understanding of the calculation of the box model properties. The total width an object takes is its actual width plus its padding, border, and margin on both sides, or *2 x (margin + border + padding) + content = total width*.

How to do it...

For an image that is 200px wide in its normal non-responsive state, your typical padding may be 8px, therefore using the previous box model, the formula can be framed as follows:

```
2 x ( 0 + 0 + 8px ) + 200px = 216px
```

To find the percentage of padding, divide the padding by the total width, `8 / 216 = 0.037%` rounded to `4%`.

We created this CSS and HTML earlier when we created the responsive percent-width image. Add to the image class a padding of `4%`.

```
<style>
p.text {
      float: left;
      width: 60%;
   }
div.img-wrap{
      float: right;
      margin: 0px;
      width: 38%;
   }
img.responsive {
      max-width: 100%;
      height: auto;
      padding: 4%;
   }
</style>

<p class="text">ipsum dolor sit amet, consecteturadi…</p>
<div class="img-wrap">
```

```
        <img alt="robot image" class="responsive" src="robot.png">
        <p>ipsum dolor sit amet, consecteturadipiscingelit…</p>
    </div>
```

To help you see the actual padding width change as you change the browser window's size, add a background color (`background-color: #cccccc;`) to your image CSS.

How it works...

The image padding set at 100 percent will stick to the edge of its parent element. As the parent element size changes, the image padding adjusts accordingly. If you have done your box model math properly, your layout will successfully respond to your browser window's changing width.

Making a CSS3 button glow for a loading element

Your website, like many others, may cater to impatient people. If your site has a submitable form, your users may find themselves clicking the "submit" button a number of times impatiently if your page does not load the new content quick enough. This can be a problem when it causes multiple form submissions with the same data.

Getting ready

You can stop this behavior by adding some simple visual cues that tell the user something is happening behind the scenes and to be a little patient. If it's a little bit flashy, it might even bring a little sunshine into their otherwise hurried lives. This recipe does not require any images, we are going to create a handsome gradient submit button using CSS only. You may want to pause and go get a cup of coffee, as this is the longest recipe in this chapter.

How to do it...

You can start by creating a form with some text boxes and a submit button. Then, make the form really cool, use the HTML5 placeholder property for the label. Even with the placeholders, the form is pretty boring.

Note that this is not yet supported in Internet Explorer 9.

```
<h1>My Form<h1>
<form>
    <ul>
        <li>
```

```
        <input type="text" placeholder="Enter your first name"/>
      </li>
      <li>
        <input type="text" placeholder="Enter your last name"/>
      </li>
   </ul>
<input type="submit" name="Submit" value="Submit">
</form>
```

By adding CSS properties we can start giving the button some life:

```
input[type="submit"] {
      color: white;
      padding: 5px;
      width: 68px;
      height: 28px;
      border-radius: 5px;
      border: 1px;
      font-weight: bold;
      border: 1px groove #7A7A7A;
}
```

This is illustrated in the following screenshot:

The button can become even more shiny when we add a CSS3 gradient effect. To accomplish this, there must be a different line of CSS for each browser rendering engine: Opera, Internet Explorer, WebKit (Chrome and Safari), and Firefox. You can add as many gradient shifts as you like, simply by adding a `color` phase and the % location from the top, each shift separated by a comma, as shown in the following code snippet:

```
<style>
input[type="submit"] {
      background: -moz-linear-gradient(top, #0F97FF 0%, #97D2FF
   8%,#0076D1 62%, #0076D1 63%, #005494 100%);
```

```
      background: -webkit-gradient(linear, left top, left bottom,
color-stop(0%,#0F97FF), color-stop(8%,#97D2FF)color-stop(50%,#0076D1),
color-stop(51%,#0076D1), color-stop(100%,#005494));
      background: -webkit-linear-gradient(top, #0F97FF 0%,#97D2FF
8%,#0076D1 62%,#0076D1 63%,#005494 100%);
      background: -o-linear-gradient(top, #0F97FF 0%,#97D2FF 8%,#0076D1
62%,#0076D1 63%,#005494 100%);
      background: -ms-linear-gradient(top, #0F97FF 0%,#97D2FF
8%,#0076D1 62%,#0076D1 63%,#005494 100%);
      background: linear-gradient(to bottom, #0F97FF
0%,#97D2FF 8%,#0076D1 62%,#0076D1 63%,#005494 100%);filter:
progid:DXImageTransform.Microsoft.gradient( startColorstr='#0f97ff',
endColorstr='#005494',GradientType=0 );
}
</style>
```

This effect is illustrated in the following screenshot:

Another effect can be added to the button by CSS, the `hover` effect. With this property, when the pointer moves over the button, it looks like it is being pressed in. The following CSS will help you add that dark border to the button:

```
input[type="submit"]:hover {
    border: 2px groove #7A7A7A;
}
```

This is displayed in the following screenshot:

Using CSS3 Box Shadows and jQuery we can make a simple animation of a pulsing halo around the **Submit** button after you pushed it. Create an event listener with jQuery that listens for the button's `click` event, and on that `click` event a series of class changes on the form button element. The `partial-fade` class will be added by the script to the button element.

Don't forget to add a link in your `head` tag to the jQuery source:

```
<scriptsrc="http://code.jquery.com/jquery-latest.js"></script>
```

Then, insert the following script after the form closes:

```
<script >
//Submit Glow
$('input[type="submit"]').click(function() {
$(this).addClass('partial-fade');
    $(this).animate({
        opacity: 0.1
    }, 8).animate({
        opacity: 0.9
    }, 226).animate({
        opacity: .5
    }, 86);
    setTimeout(function () {
        $('input[type="submit"]').removeClass('partial-fade');
    }, 366).animate({
        opacity: 1
    }, 86);
});
```

```
</script>
```

To finish making the button glow when you click it, add the new class `partial-fade`, to your CSS file and give it a CSS3 Box Shadow Property, and change the border properties.

```
<style>
input[type="submit"].partial-fade {
    border-top: 1px solid #CFF !important;
    border-right: 1px solid #CCF !important;
    border-left: 1px solid #CCF !important;
    border-bottom: 1px solid #6CF !important;
    -webkit-box-shadow: 0 08px 0px #0F97FF, inset 0 0 20px rgba(37,
141, 220, 1);
    -moz-box-shadow: 0 0 8px 0px #0F97FF, inset 0 0 20px
rgba(37,141,220,1);
    box-shadow: 0 0 8px 0px #0F97FF, inset 0 0 20px rgba(37, 141,
220, 1);
}
</style>
```

Now, the **Submit** button will give a flash of blue when pressed. The following screenshot shows the final product:

Whew! This button was a lot of work for such a small detail, but the details like this will really help make a great-looking website. This happens to be one of my favorite details to surprise my audience with.

How it works...

The CSS3 background gradient is an easy way to make a great-looking button consistently across browsers. The gradient is complicated and each browser currently requires its own line for CSS. You can control the gradient breakpoints by adding the percentage and colors manually. Adding box shadow, borders, and jQuery make fun effects on the button when the event is fired.

Responsive Typography

In this chapter, you will learn about:

- ▸ Creating fluid, responsive typography
- ▸ Making a text shadow with canvas
- ▸ Making an inner and outer shadow with canvas
- ▸ Rotating your text with canvas
- ▸ Rotating your text with CSS3
- ▸ Making 3D text with CSS3
- ▸ Adding texture to your text with CSS3 text masking
- ▸ Styling alternating rows with the nth positional pseudo class
- ▸ Adding characters before and after pseudo elements
- ▸ Making a button with a relative font size
- ▸ Adding a shadow to your font
- ▸ Curving a corner with border radius

Introduction

This chapter deals mostly with how to make responsive typography. You will learn recipes for optimizing your text for various types of device, as well as methods to embellish your typography. The technologies involved are simply CSS3 and HTML5's canvas element with JavaScript. With responsive typography, you can apply a number of exciting effects to your text.

When finished with this chapter, you should be armed with a number of techniques that will get you started on the road to making amazing responsive websites. These recipes cover the basics, but when combined together with some creativity, they will enable you to do some fantastic production.

Creating fluid, responsive typography

This recipe is a simple example of responsive typography. It will demonstrate the use of the new size unit REM. REM means Root EM. This simply means that the size of the font is relative to the root's font size, not the parent, as with the EM unit.

Getting ready

Without any further discussion, let's jump into this recipe. Go get some filler text from my favorite Ipsum generator (http://ipsum.com). Generate at least one paragraph and copy the text into your clipboard.

How to do it...

Now, paste the filler text into your HTML document and wrap it in a paragraph tag. Give the paragraph element class= "a", then make a copy and assign the new paragraph class="b", as shown in the following code snippet:

```
<p class="a">
    Lorem ipsum dolor sit amet, consectetur adipiscing elit.
<p>

<p class="b">
    ultricies ut viverra massa rutrum. Nunc pharetra, ipsum ut
    ullamcorper placerat,
<p>
```

Next, create a style for the base HTML font-size property, and then one for the static sized paragraph to compare the font size changes—similar to an experiment's control group:

```
html{font-size:12px;}
p.b{font-size:1rem;}
```

Next create two @media queries, one for orientation:portrait, and the second one for orientation:landscape. In the orientation:portrait media query, style the "a" class paragraph element with a font-size value of 3rem. And in the orientation:landscape media query, style the "a" class paragraph with the font-size value of 1rem.

```
@media screen and (orientation:portrait){
p.a{font-size:3rem;}
}
@media screen and (orientation:landscape){
p.a{font-size:1rem;}
}
```

Now when you resize your browser window from landscape to portrait mode, you will see the font size of the first paragraph goes from a ratio of 1:1 to the base size, to 3:1 of the base size. While this seems very simple, this recipe can be varied and built on to create a number of impressive responsive typography tricks.

How it works...

When your browser makes a request, the CSS3 `@media` query returns some conditional styles based on viewport's width. It loads or builds (rebuilds) on the fly for changes to the viewport's size. While not many in your audience are going to spend much time resizing your website in their browser, it is easy to spend too much time worrying about how your website shifts from one size to the next.

See also

▸ The *Making a button with a relative font size* recipe

Making a text shadow with canvas

HTML5 brings a new element to web design, the `<canvas>` element. This is used to create graphics on a web page on the fly using JavaScript.

Getting ready

The `<canvas>` element creates a rectangular area on your page. It dimensions default to 300px by 150px. You can specify different settings inside the JavaScript. The code in this recipe grows quickly, so you can get the whole code online at the Packt Publishing's website.

How to do it...

To begin, create a simple HTML page with a `<canvas>` element:

```
<!DOCTYPE HTML>
<html>
    <head>

    </head>
    <body>
        <canvas id="thecanvas"></canvas>
    </body>
</html>
```

The JavaScript gets the `canvas` element from the DOM.

```
var canvas = document.getElementById('thecanvas');
```

It then calls the `getContext()` method. The `getContext('2d')` method is the built-in HTML5 object. It has a number of methods to draw text, shapes, images, and more.

```
var ctx = canvas.getContext('2d');
```

Next, start drawing the text within the JavaScript. Here, we create a code to draw the horizontal and vertical shadow offsets, the blur, and the color of the shadow.

```
ctx.shadowOffsetX = 2;
ctx.shadowOffsetY = 2;
ctx.shadowBlur = 2;
ctx.shadowColor = "rgba(0, 0, 0, 0.5)";
```

The text and its properties is written in the JavaScript here, but can be passed in as a variable from the DOM:

```
ctx.font = "20px Times New Roman";
ctx.fillStyle = "Black";
ctx.fillText("This is the canvas", 5, 30);
```

Back in the HTML, add the `onload="drawCanvas();"` script command to the `body` element. When the page loads, the JavaScript fires and draws the text and its shadow onto the canvas. This is illustrated in the following screenshot:

How it works...

Without getting too deep into the gears of JavaScript, the `canvas` element provides a place for the designer to script some content directly to the page on page load. The `body` element's `onload="drawCanvas();"` command fires the JavaScript, which draws the content onto the canvas.

See also

▸   The *Rotate your text with canvas* recipe

Making an inner and outer shadow with canvas

This recipe also uses `canvas` and JavaScript to draw the text and the effects in your browser. There is no direct method to make an inner-glow or inset-shadow effect using `canvas`, however, using the stroke method, you can simulate an inner shadow in your text.

Getting ready

This recipe starts with some already-written code. You can download this from Packt's website. It is also the same code you created in the recipe, *Making a text shadow with canvas*. This code should be run on your local computer without any special web server. You can get the whole code online at the course's website.

How to do it...

To begin, create a simple HTML page with a `<canvas>` element.

```html
<html>
  <head>

  </head>
  <body>
    <canvas id="thecanvas"></canvas>
  </body>
</html>
```

The JavaScript gets the `canvas` element from the DOM.

```javascript
var canvas = document.getElementById('thecanvas');
```

It then calls the `getContext()` method. The `getContext('2d')` method is the built-in HTML5 object. It has a number of methods to draw text, shapes, images, and more.

```
var context = canvas.getContext('2d');
```

This script uses multiple effects combined to make an inner and outer shadow. You add a drop shadow and two different outlines. First, add a drop shadow to the top-left part and make it black with a `context.shadowBlur` value of 2. Building on that, after `context.fillText`, add `context.strokeStyle` and `context.strokeText` to the canvas context.

```
context.shadowOffsetX = -1;
context.shadowOffsetY = -1;
context.shadowBlur = 2;
context.shadowColor = "#888888";
context.textAlign = "left";
context.font = "33px Times New Roman";
context.fillStyle = "#666";
context.fillText("This is the Canvas", 0, 50);
context.strokeStyle = "#555";
context.strokeText("This is the canvas", 2, 50);
context.linewidth = 2;
```

Instead of a raised look, the text appears to be beveled in and has an inner glow or shadow effect. The effect is displayed in the following screenshot:

How it works...

As stated in the beginning of this recipe, there is no true direct method to make an inner shadow in canvas, but there are ways to use the `context.fillText` and `context.strokeStyle` methods together that will create something that sufficiently looks like an inner shadow.

Rotating your text with canvas

The HTML5 canvas methods can do more than just coloring the text or adding drop shadows. You can also use it to move or manipulate the objects in the canvas area. In this recipe, we will rotate the objects in the canvas.

Getting ready

This recipe builds on top of the previous recipes. If you skipped them, that's okay, you can go back to the previous recipe to refer to the complete code.

How to do it...

Once you have your previous recipe's canvas set up, the basic steps for rotation are easy. Add a `rotate` method to the beginning of the function:

```
context.rotate(Math.PI/4,0,0);
```

You will probably notice that the text rotated right off of the canvas. What happened? The `rotate` method rotates the entire canvas and is not aware of what is in it.

The canvas has a small default size of 300px by 150px. Changing the element's size attributes will not affect the canvas size, but distorts the objects drawn on it. To change the size of the canvas and the objects drawn, add the `canvas.width` and `canvas.height` properties in the JavaScript:

```
canvas.width=250;
canvas.height=250;
```

In addition, because the canvas rotates entirely itself, and not the text rotating about an origin, the text location will need to be repositioned to desired location. In this case, change the object offset of the fill and the stroke:

```
context.fillText("This is the Canvas", 140, 1);
context.strokeText("This is the Canvas ", 140, 1);
```

This is depicted in the following screenshot:

How it works...

The JavaScript uses the `rotate` method to rotate the whole `canvas` element and everything drawn inside it. It requires a small amount of forethought when using the `rotate` method in the canvas. It is complex, but is the perfect tool to use in large responsive web projects.

See also

- The *Rotate your text with CSS3* recipe

Rotating your text with CSS3

CSS3 provides an easy way to rotate your text. The `transform:rotate` property is easy to implement and provides a simple solution when the project does not require the complexity of the canvas.

Getting ready

Write a line of text in your HTML document. Brace yourself; you are about to rotate it with CSS3.

How to do it...

Wrap the text in a paragraph tag element:

```
<p class="rotate">I think, therefore I am</p>
```

Then, add the CSS `transform` property to rotate the text. Each browser renders this differently, so each will need its own unique `transform` property. However, each will use the `transform` property's subproperty `rotate`, followed by the degrees of rotation, as shown in the following code snippet:

```
<!DOCTYPE HTML>
<html>
    <head>
        <style>
    .rotate {
/* Chrome, Safari 3.1+*/
-webkit-transform: rotate(-90deg);
/* Firefox 3.5-15 */
-moz-transform: rotate(-90deg);
/* IE9 */
-ms-transform: rotate(-90deg);
/* Opera 10.50-12*/
-o-transform: rotate(-90deg);
/* IE */
transform: rotate(-90deg);
}
        </style>
    </head>
    <body >
        <p class="rotate">I think, therefore I am </p>
    </body>
</html>
```

How it works...

The `transform` property applies a 2D or 3D transformation to an element. Other property changes available are `move`, `skew`, and `perspective`.

See also

▸   The *Rotate your text with canvas* recipe

Making 3D text with CSS3

In previous recipes, we created a drop shadow, bevel, and an inner shadow, using the `canvas` element. With CSS3, we can do this to make your text really stand out. Using the CSS3 `text-shadow` property, we can make your text look as if it is jutting out of the screen towards your viewer.

Getting ready

If you would like to skip ahead, you can get the code online at Packt Publishing's website. Otherwise, if you are the learning-by-doing type, let's make our 3D text. We create the 3D effect by using a combination of CSS3 shadow effects.

How to do it...

In your IDE, create a new HTML document with only a header in the body. Add a `style` section to the `head` tag and assign the header the property, `color:#f0f0f0;`, as shown in the following code snippet:

```
<style>
    h1{ color: #f0f0f0; }
</style>
```

Now add to it a series of seven increasing-decreasing X- and Y- positioned `text-shadow` properties, from `0px 0px0px #666`, to `-6px -6px 0px #666;`.

```
text-shadow: 0px 0px0px #666,
-1px -1px 0px #666,
-2px -2px 0px #666,
-3px -3px 0px #666,
-4px -4px 0px #666,
-5px -5px 0px #666,
-6px -6px 0px #000,
```

Your header now leaps off the screen. Well, almost! To make sure it really pops off the screen, let's give it some more effect. When building any 3D objects on a screen, it is important to give consistent lighting and shadows. Since this text rises above, it needs a shadow.

Add another series of six X- and Y- positioned `text-shadow` properties, only this time give them positive values and a lighter color (`color:#ccc;`).

```
1px 1px 5px #ccc,
 2px 2px 5px #ccc,
 3px 3px 5px #ccc,
```

```
    4px  4px  5px  #ccc,
    5px  5px5px  #ccc,
    6px  6px  5px  #ccc;
```

The drop shadow makes sense, but it still looks a bit fake, well let's take it to another level; let's blur and darken the elements on the background. The third number in your `text-shadow` property creates the blur, so add an increasing blur of 0, 0, 1, 1, 2, 3, and 5, as shown in the following code. Also, change the colors to grow darker as you go back: `#888`, `#777`, `#666`, `#555`, `#444`, `#333`, and `#000`.

```
    text-shadow:0px  0px0px  #888,
    -1px  -1px  0px  #777,
    -2px  -2px  1px  #666,
    -3px  -3px  1px  #555,
    -4px  -4px  2px  #444,
    -5px  -5px  3px  #333,
    -6px  -6px  4px  #000,
```

Now your header has a truly realistic 3D effect. The effect illustrated in the following screenshot:

How it works...

Play around and experiment with variations of this recipe for some very exciting typographic effects. CSS3 brings a whole new level of excitement and depth to typographic design that has always been difficult to achieve, and does it well.

The `text-shadow` property can handle numerous shadow properties. Therefore, you can stack them on top of each other in an increasing distance away from your text. This creates the 3D effect on your text.

Adding texture to your text with text masking

CSS3 also gives you the awesome power of adding an image mask texture to your text with an image. This effect was previously only achievable by creating a static image of your text with an image-editing software.

Getting ready

You'll need an image to use as the texture mask. Using an image-editing software, create a new image with an alpha channel. If you do not have an image-editing software that can create a PNG with alpha channels, you can download an open source, free image-editing software GIMP at `http://www.gimp.org`. To create a quick texture effect, use a scatter-type brush to create a textured area near the top of the image.

Save it as a PNG image type, preserving the alpha channel, in the `images` directory of webhost.

How to do it...

Create your HTML with a header element that will contain the text you want to apply your texture mask to. Then, add some text in it:

```
<h1 class="masked">I think, therefore I am</h1>
```

Then, add your CSS markup. This will include a large font size (to show off your mask texture!), a white color font, padding and alignment, and then, of course the image mask property.

 Note that each browser requires its own prefix for the property.

```
h1.masked{
    font: 140px "Arial";
    color: white;
    -webkit-mask-image: url(images/mask2.png);
    -o-mask-image: url(images/mask2.png);
    -moz-mask-image: url(images/mask2.png);
    mask-image: url(images/mask2.png);
    text-shadow: 0px 0px 10px #f0f0f0;
    width: 100%;
    padding: 12% 0 12%;
    margin:0;
    text-align: center;
}
```

The CSS effect is displayed in the following screenshot:

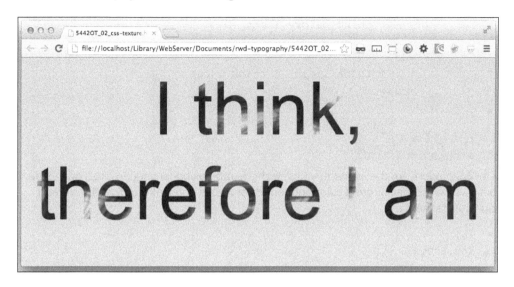

How it works...

The mask image cuts out the visible portion of the element according to the mask image's alpha. When applied over the text in the CSS, it will cut out the masked portions. This works in a very similar way to the image-editing software's alpha channel layer.

Styling alternating rows with the nth positional pseudo class

The positional-pseudo classes in CSS3 offers easy CSS solutions to problems that previously required annoyingly complicated solutions. Until very recently, to style alternating rows of a list or table, if you were fortunate enough to be able to work on a server with some sort of logic, you could at least iterate through a count in a list, or if unlucky, you had to manually numerate your rows.

Getting ready

The CSS3 solution is surprisingly simple. First, create your HTML list of values. This does not necessarily require a name-spaced class, as you might want this to be an universal style throughout your site:

```
<ul>
    <li>
        I think, therefore I am
```

```
        </li>
        <li>
            I think before I act
        </li>
        <li>
            I think I can, I think I can
        </li>
    </ul>
```

How to do it...

Add a CSS property for the list item, `<li>`, with the *n*th positional pseudo-class odd value. Give it a value of a background color and font color that is noticeably different than your default color scheme.

```
    ul{
width:100px;
    }
    li:nth-of-type(odd){
background-color:#333;
color:#f0f0f0;
    }
```

This will auto magically style the odd numbered rows of your list! The following screenshot illustrates this effect:

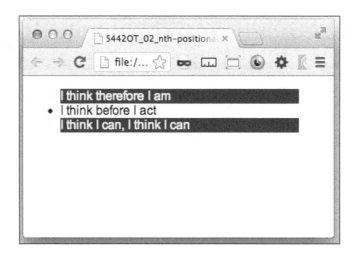

Now take a breath; that was so easy!

How it works...

According to `http://www.w3.org`, the `:nth-of-type(an+b)` pseudo-class notation represents an element that has *an+b-1* siblings with the same expanded element name before it, in the document tree for any zero or positive integer value of *n*, and has a parent element.

What does that mean? It means that as long as it has similar siblings inside the same parent element, you can either enter in a formula like *(-n+2)* for the last two rows of the siblings, or keeping it simple, even or odd, and style those rows via CSS.

Adding characters before and after pseudo elements

In what seems like a lost episode of *The Twilight Zone*, a new property of CSS gives you the ability to add pseudo markup to your content. As strange as it may sound, there are a surprising number of use cases for this sort of styling. You may want to wrap a section of your content in quotes, and not have to deal with the extra coding trouble to put quotes in your content or theme file, which of course is a sensible thing to do. Or perhaps you want to join in with the popularity of Twitter and its hash-tag and the @ markups, you can precede your content with a # or @ symbol, just by using CSS markup, as shown in the following code line:

```
#I think, therefore I am#
```

Getting ready

This requires no server-side logic or fancy footwork of any kind. All you need is to be able to launch the page in your localhost to see it in action.

How to do it...

This is accomplished with CSS only, therefore all you need to create in your HTML is a `class` or `id` property wrapped around the target content:

```
<h2 class="hashtag">I think, therefore I am</h2>
```

The CSS markup is only a bit complicated, in that the inserted symbol adheres to the margin and padding rules of the content. It uses the *n*th `class:before` and `class:after` pseudo classes. So, the CSS for `before` is `.class:before {content:"#";}`. Simply replace # with whatever symbol you want to use. And for `after`, replace `.class:before{}` with `.class:after{}`.

```
.hashtag {
    border:1px solid #ccc;
```

```
        display:block;
        width:200px;
        height:10px;
            }
.hashtag:before{
    content:"#";
            }
.hashtag:after{
    content:"#";
            }
```

How it works...

The `before` and `after` pseudo elements in CSS generates content before or after the element's content. Be careful that they are not real content or elements, and cannot be used for markup or JavaScript event triggers.

Making a button with a relative font size

There are several use cases for having a responsive button font size. A good example of a use case is for mobile versions of your site. When a regular button is viewed on your iPhone, it is tiny and difficult to press. The last thing we want to do is to create a bad experience for mobile device users through our negligence of mobile devices.

Getting ready

The goal of this recipe is to use the new font measure of REM to make a responsive button font size that will grow larger when viewed on your mobile device.

REM is a new unit introduced in CSS3, it stands for Root EM, or relative to the root font size. This is different from EM, which was relative to the parent. One way to use it is to set the size of certain elements to the base size of the body font.

How to do it...

It can be used with the `@media` query to build a responsive button for your desktop and mobile devices. Here's what to do.

First, create a simple HTML page with some filler text (`http://lipsum.com`) and a `input` type of `submit`.

```
<div>
<p>Lorem ipsum dolor sit amet, consectetur adipiscing elit. Vestibulum
vehicula enim at dolor ultricies ut viverra massa rutrum. Nunc
pharetra, ipsum ut ullamcorper placerat,
```

```
    </p>
        <input type="submit">
    </div>
```

Next add CSS for the HTML's base font size at `62.5%`, and a static font size for the paragraph, as an experimental control group:

```
html{font-size:62.5%;}
p{font-size:1.4rem;}
```

The next step is to create your `@media` query for the mobile device, and two different desktop window sizes. I'm adding an additional `@media` query for desktop screens, so if you do not have access to a mobile device you can still see the responsiveness in action.

Set up two `@media` queries for the desktop at `1024px` and `1280px` and two for mobile devices, both with `max-device-width:480px`, one with `orientation:landscape`, and other one with `orientation:portrait`.

```
@media screen and (min-width:1024px){ }
@media screen and (min-width:1280px){ }
@media screen and (max-device-width: 480px) and
(orientation:landscape){ }
@media screen and (max-device-width: 480px) and (orientation:portrait)
{ }
```

In your desktop `@media` queries, add an `input` element to both; and a `font-size:1rem` value to the `min-width:1024px` query, and a `font-size:2rem` value to the `min-width:1280px` query. To both queries add the properties: `width:84px;` and `padding:2%;`.

In the mobile `@media` queries, add the `input` element to both. In the `orientation:landscape` media query, assign the properties: `font-size:2rem;` and `width:25%;`. And in the `orientation:portrait` media query, assign the properties: `font-size:2.4rem;` and `width:30%;`.

```
@media screen and (min-width:1024px){
            input{
                font-size:1rem;
                width:84px;
                padding:2%;}
        }
@media screen and (min-width:1280px){
        input{
            font-size:2rem;
            width:84px;
            padding:2%;
```

```
        }
    }
    @media screen and (max-device-width: 480px) and
    (orientation:landscape){
        input{
            font-size:2rem;
            width:25%;
            padding:2%;
        }
    }
    @media screen and (max-device-width: 480px) and
    (orientation:portrait){
        input{
            font-size:2.4rem;
            width:30%;
            padding:2%;
        }
    }
}
```

Now when you view this page from a mobile device you can see how the REM size unit creates a font, sized relative to the base font. The mobile device may render the font so small it is hardly readable, and the button too small to use without fumbling. Turn the device from portrait orientation to landscape and you will see the button and its font change sizes.

Compare the mobile device button to the desktop versions. You will see the button displays unique properties per device type. And, as you drag the desktop browser window between the 1024px and 1280px sizes the button font changes also.

How it works...

The REM font size unit creates a font size relative to the base font size declared in the HTML or body elements, or if undeclared relative to the built-in base size of the font. The @media query we wrote gives a new relative size for the different devices and orientations.

Adding a shadow to your font

With CSS3 you can easily add a shadow to your text. This effect can be used to either give a special element a highlighted effect, or used throughout your body text to enhance the look of your content. In addition, you can use it to highlight links within your text to help them stand out.

Getting ready

CSS3 makes this easy, so there isn't a big setup. Open your development environment, or a Notepad program and get started. You can also go online to Packt Publishing's web page for this module and get the completed code and take a look inside.

How to do it...

First, create a paragraph element of text; recall that you can get this from our favorite filler text generator, `http://lipsum.com`. And give the text a title header:

```
<h1>I think therefore I am </h1>
<p>Lorem ipsum dolor sit amet...
</p>
```

In your paragraph, insert some links, by wrapping a couple of words in an `href` tag:

```
<h1>I think therefore I am</h1>
<p>Morbi<a href ="#">venenatis</a>Lorem ipsum dolor sit amet...
<a href ="#">scelerisque</a> Lorem ipsum dolor sit amet...</p>
```

First, let's give your paragraph text a drop shadow, this is a simple CSS3 `dropshadow` effect we can use on the text. Add the property `text-shadow` in your CSS. For Internet Explorer, add the `filter` property.

```
text-shadow: 1px 1px 2px #333333;
```

This gives your text a slight shadow that makes it pop off the page. For body text, anything more than a slight shadow will be too much. Foryour links, to make them stand out more, we can add multiple levels of text shadow. Add a shadow similar to the previous example, and then following a comma, add another shadow effect. This example adds a light blue shadow to the link text.

```
text-shadow: 0px 0px 1px blue, 1px 1px 2px #333333;
filter: dropshadow(color=blue, offx=1, offy=1);
```

Let's add an old property to give the page some new shine. Let's make your links flash on the pseudo-action hover (`:hover`):

```
p.shadowa:hover{
text-shadow: 0px 0px 8px #ffff00, 2px 2px 3px #666; filter:
dropshadow(color=#ffff00, offx=1, offy=1);
}
```

This property makes the links in the paragraph flash with a yellow glow, when you hover over them. This effect illustrated in the following screenshot:

How it works...

This recipe is a combination of shadow effects. You can combine multiple shadow effects to create realistic 3D effects for your type. The best way to learn is to experiment until you are extremely satisfied with your 3D effects.

Curving a corner with border radius

Curved corners were at one time the Holy Grail of the web design world. It was always possible, but never simple. A designer had a limited number of bad choices to employ to make an element have a curved corner.

Getting ready

This is now achieved without too much fuss with CSS3. The `border-radius` property is a simple method of creating a rounded corner on an element.

How to do it...

First create your HTML element. This works on any element that can have a border. So let's make a paragraph block of text. You can get filler text at `http://lipsum.com`.

```
<p class="rounded"> Lorem ipsum dolor sit amet…</p>
```

Next add CSS to fill out the paragraph element:

```
.rounded{
        background-color:#ccc;
        width:200px;
        margin:20px;
        padding:20px;
    }
```

Then, to round the corners, add the CSS3 property, `border-radius`. In this example, I used a curve radius of `5px`.

```
border-radius: 5px;
-webkit-background-clip: padding-box;
background-clip: padding-box;
```

This property gives you simple and easy-rounded corners. This is great for a floating element on a page. But what if you wanted to round only the top corners for a menu element? Still easy.

Let's start with a simple inline list:

```
<ul class="inline">
    <li class="rounded-top"><a href="#">menu 1</a></li>
    <li class="rounded-top"><a href="#">menu 2</a></li>
    <li class="rounded-top"><a href="#">menu 3</a></li>
    <li class="rounded-top"><a href="#">menu 4</a></li>
</ul>
```

Next add the CSS to make the list inline, with padding and margins:

```
li.rounded-top{
    display:inline;
    background-color:#ccc;
    margin:3px;
    padding:8px;
}
```

The CSS in the previous example gives you rounded corners for all the corners. To have different rounded corners, specify a radius for each corner.

```
border-radius: 8px 8px 1px 1px;
```

You can achieve the same results by specifying each corner as its own CSS property:

```
border-top-left-radius:8px;
border-top-right-radius:8px;
border-bottom-right-radius:2px;
border-bottom-left-radius:2px;
```

You can take this further by adding another level of curved radius:

```
border-top-left-radius:8px 4px;
border-top-right-radius:8px 4px;
border-bottom-right-radius:2px;
border-bottom-left-radius:2px;
```

The new look is shown in the following screenshot:

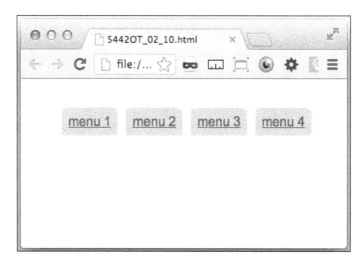

To add another level of responsiveness try replacing the curved radius entries with percentages. Go back to the first example in this recipe and change the CSS to have a percent radius curve:

```
border-radius: 1%;
```

How it works...

The `border-radius` property provides a simple rendering of a curve on an element. This property takes four values, but can be written in the shorthand format with only one curve radius.

3
Responsive Layout

In this chapter, you will learn about:

- ▸ Responsive layout with the min-width and max-width properties
- ▸ Controlling your layout with relative padding
- ▸ Adding a media query to your CSS
- ▸ Creating a responsive width layout with media queries
- ▸ Changing image sizes with media queries
- ▸ Hiding an element with media queries
- ▸ Making a smoothly transitioning responsive layout

Introduction

This chapter has some challenging recipes. Responsive layouts often present some difficult challenges that can push you to create a great solution. With responsive design methods you can do much more, and do it more efficiently. Responsive layouts have introduced a whole new area of challenges to web development and a new dimension of excitement.

Responsive layout with the min-width and max-width properties

Many responsive layout techniques can be quite complex and overwhelming, but in this recipe you will see a fairly simple layout using the `min-width` and `max-width` properties applied to three floating elements. With this very simple responsive layout feature of CSS, you are ready to display your site on mobile devices and desktop screens of various sizes.

Getting ready

Floating elements that collapse from multiple columns into one column on a small viewport is not a new trick. This has been around for years as a standard property of CSS1, however, there was never any reason to consider it useful until the mobile devices became common. So let's combine this old, stale property with some other fresh CSS properties to make a responsive layout.

How to do it...

Create a simple HTML page enclosed in an `article` element, containing a `h1` header and three elements. The first element will contain an image and the second and third will contain filler text. Assign to all of the inner elements a class of `float` and respectively one, `two`, and `three` as their IDs:

```
<article>
    <h1>Responsive Layout with min and max width</h1>

    <div class="one float">
        <img src="images/robot.png">
    </div>

    <div class ="two float">Pellentesqueeleifendfacilisisodio ac
    ullamcorper. Nullamutenimutmassatinciduntluctus...
    </div>

    <div class="three float">Pellentesqueeleifendfacilisisodio ac
    ullamcorper. Nullamutenimutmassatinciduntluctus. Utnullalibero, …
    </div>
</article>
```

Next, create your style for the `.article` element and assign the properties: `width: 100%;`, `max-width: 1280px;`, and auto side margins. Then, center the `h1` title. Assign the `img` element the `width: 100%` and `height: auto;` properties to make it responsive to its parent element. For the floating element containing the `img` element, give it a `min-width` value of `500px`. You could also give each floating element a different background color to make them more discernible, but this is not vital to the layout. To all the floating elements in the `.float` class, add a `max-width: 350px` property, left float, and for clean looks, justify the text.

```
<style>
article{
    width: 100%;
```

```
        max-width: 1280px;
        margin: 0 auto;
}
h1 {text-align:center;}
img {
        width: 100%;
        height: auto;
}
.one {
        background-color: #333;
        min-width: 500px;
}
.two {background-color:#666}
.three {background-color:#ccc}
.float {
        max-width: 350px;
        float: left;
        text-align: justify;
}
    </style>
```

Once everything is put together and you have the HTML document open in your browser, you will see how the layout smoothly goes from a three-column layout to a two-column layout, and then finally to a single-column layout, as shown in the following screenshot:

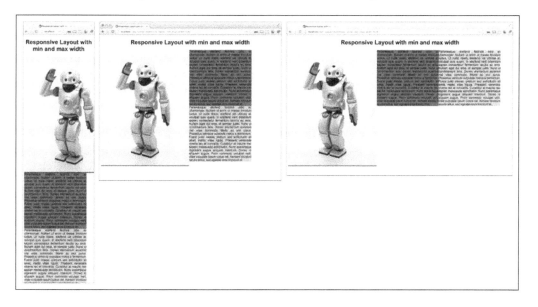

How it works...

The `max-width` property of the columns allows them to have a fluid but a maximum width. This gives you more flexibility in the layout of the columns than you would have with a static width. The image column utilizes the `min-width` property so it can respond to parent element width's changes by growing and shrinking. Finally, the whole layout can smoothly break down from three columns to one column by using the `float` property; once there is not enough room for the elements to float side by side, the last element drops to a new row.

Controlling your layout with relative padding

Let's put together a simple layout for a blog with comments and comment replies. This is possible using only relative padding for the layout. You say, "That's crazy! How can you control a page layout with nothing but padding?" Let's find out.

Getting ready

Of course, a blog is much more dynamic than a static HTML page, so this would be a good part of a comments template section for your favorite blogging software. That being said, this recipe is remarkably easy, and yet effective. So, go get yourself some Ipsum filler text and get ready to troll yourself.

How to do it...

The first step is to create a very simple blog style page with comments embedded in the `div` element. In your HTML body, create the element that will hold everything, the `.content` div. Give it a `h1` title, a paragraph of Ipsum filler text, and follow it with a `.comments` element. Inside the `.comments` element you will build your embedded comments layout.

```
<div class="content">
    <header>Control your layout with relative padding</header>
    <p>
Pellent esque eleifend facilis isodio ac ullam corper. Null amuten
imut massat incident luctus. Utnull alibero, el eifend vel ultrices
at, volut patquis quam...</p>
    <div class="comments">
        <h2>Comments</h2> No 2 x h1
    </div>
</div>
```

Under the `.comments` title, you will add your first comment. And next, inside that comment, immediately after the closing paragraph tag add a comment to that comment:

```
<aside>
    <h1>Comments</h1>
    <div class="comment">
        <p>
Pellent esque eleifend facilis isodio ac ullam corper. Null amuten
imut massat incident luctus. Utnull alibero, et...
        </p>
        <div class="comment">
            <p>
Pellent esque eleifend facilis isodio ac ullam corper. Null amuteni
mut massat incident luctus. Ut null alibero, el eifend vel ultrices
at, volut patquis quam...
            </p>
        </div>
    </div>
</aside>
```

Continuing from there, you can insert more comments the same way to a comment on the parent comment, or add a comment outside of the parent `div` element to make the comment to the parents' parent, all the way up to the original blog post:

```
<aside>
    <h1>Comments</h1>
      <div class="comment">
        <p>
           Pellent esque el eifend facilis isodio ac ullam corper..
        </p>

      <div class="comment">
        <p>
            Null amuten imut massat incident luctus....
        </p>

      <div class="comment">
        <p>
           Ut null alibero, el eifend velul trices at, volut pat quis
quam...
        </p>
      </div>
```

```
        </div>
        </div>
    <div class="comment">
        <p>
            Null ameget dui eros, et semper justo. Nun cut condi mentum
felis...
        </p>
        </div>
        </div>

    </aside>
```

Eventually, you can have many comments and a good looking working layout built simply with only relative padding.

The CSS to make this work is surprisingly easy. Simply add the classes: `.content`, `.comments`, and `.comment`. In the `content` class add some side padding, and in the `comment` add heavier padding to the left.

```
.content {padding:0 5% 0 5%;}
aside {padding:0 10% 0 20%}
.comment {padding:0 0 0 10%}
```

This is illustrated in the following screenshot:

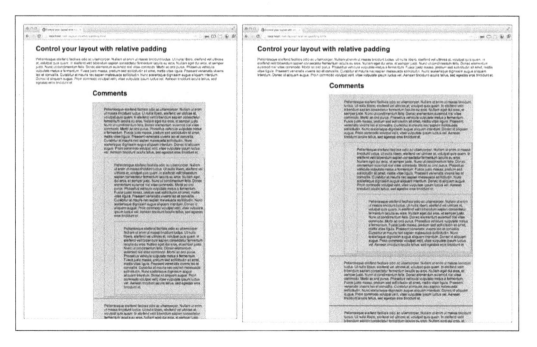

How it works...

The relative padding attribute responds to page width changes by adjusting its own width.

Adding a media query to your CSS

In this recipe, we will explore the awesome power of the media query by rendering a simple web page with every permutation and device available in the universe. Okay, I'm exaggerating a little, I admit. But we will create a simple web page that will respond to several browser window sizes, devices, and other possible presentation methods.

Getting ready

Solely for the purpose of this recipe, go out and purchase one of each of the devices and variations described here. You'll need a new high definition TV, a smart phone, a not-so-smart phone, and at least one printer. No way? Okay, but I'm just trying to help you and the economy. That being said, of course it will be impossible to truly test every media query, but do what you can. There are a surprising number of possibilities. But in most real-life scenarios, you are unlikely to need or care to use most of these. We will at least try to cover the most commonly used media queries.

I will skip over those that I think are unnecessary to you. You can easily access information about these if you find yourself in a project with requirements to create presentations for one of these obscure devices. You never know! The WC3 has all of the detailed information and descriptions of these if you need them at `http://www.w3.org/TR/css3-mediaqueries/`. I will exclude the examples and just for your reference include numerous devices with specific color limitations, including monochrome, print, TV, and handheld. The media queries you will need most likely are `screen` and `print`.

How to do it...

Create a simple HTML page with a `h1` title, and an element wrapping around an image, and a paragraph of text. Get some Ipsum filler text if you don't have any text lying around. It will look just like the following:

```
<body>
    <h1>Add Media Query to your CSS</h1>
        <div class="wrap">
            <img src="images/robot.png"/>
Pellent esque el eifend facilisis odio ac ullam corper. Nullam ut enim
ut massa tincidunt luctus…
        </div>
</body>
```

Next create a series of media queries. In the following list, I will give a brief explanation of what each does:

```
@media print{...}
```

This is applied to the web page when it's printed. You can test this by selecting **File** | **Print** and then view the print preview. This is useful for web pages where users will be printing it as a document to read. You can take advantage of this and change or remove the formatting to make this version as simple as possible.

```
@media (orientation: portrait){...}
```

This is generally applied on any device that shows the document in portrait mode. You can use it for mobile devices to change the look for different orientations. Be cautious because this also will be applied to desktop screens unless you specify it to smaller screens or devices only. The media query orientation's other possible value is landscape.

```
@media (height:500px){...}
```

The `height` and `width` media query allows you to specify style for specific screen dimensions.

```
@media (device-width:500px){...}
```

This media query will apply a style to any page, regardless of browser's window size, that is viewed on a device of the specified dimensions.

```
@media screen and (device-aspect-ratio: 16/9) {...}
```

This media query can be used to define styles for screens (not print) with a view window of the `16/9` ratio.

```
@media tv {...}
```

This aspect ratio would apply only to a device using a television to view.

```
@media screen and (max-width:960px){...}
@media screen and (min-width:961px) and (max-width:1280px){...}
@media screen and (min-width:1281px) and (max-width:1336px){...}
@media screen and (min-width:1336px){...}
```

The `min-width` and `max-width` media queries are the most useful one. Here, you can define a responsive style for any window size including the small-screen mobile devices. I typically start by defining the smallest—or mobiles—viewports breakpoint, and define their styles, and then create breakpoint ranges for the most popular screen sizes, ending with a `min-width` media query to apply to the largest screen sizes.

Once you have created the media queries that you think are useful for your current project, add styles to the media queries with different values:

```
@media tv {
    body {color: blue;}
    h1 {
        font-weight: bold;
        font-size: 140%;
    }
    img {
        float: left;
        width: 20%;
        border: 2px solid #ccc;
        padding: 2%;
        margin: 2%;
    }
    p {
        width: 62%;
        float: right;
        font-size: 110%;
        padding: 2%;
    }
}
@media screen and (max-width: 960px) {
    body {color: #000;}
    h1 {
        font-weight: bold;
        font-size: 120%;
    }
    img {
        float: right;
        width: 20%;
        border: 2px solid #ccc;
        padding: 1%;
        margin: 1%;
    }
    P {
        width: 80%;
        float: left;
        font-size: 60%;
    }
}
```

```
@media screen and (min-width:961px) and (max-width:1280px) {
    body {color: #000000;}
    h1 {
        font-weight: bold;
        font-size: 120%;
    }
    img {
        float: right;
        width: 20%;
        border: 2px solid #ccc;
        padding: 1%;
        margin: 1%;
    }
    P {
        width: 76%;
        float: left;
        font-size: 60%;
    }
}
@media screen and (min-width: 1281px) {
    body {color: #000000;}
    h1 {
        font-weight: bold;
        font-size: 120%;
    }
    img {
        float: right;
        width: 20%;
        border: 2px solid #ccc;
        padding: 1%;
        margin: 1%;
    }
    P {
        width: 70%;
        float: left;
        font-size: 100%;
    }
}
```

The final version of the page is displayed in the following screenshot:

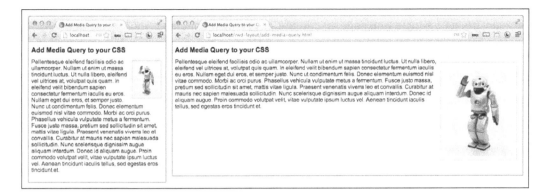

How it works...

Apply these styles and you will find that a different style is applied to different devices. You can combine a number of these in a clever way to create magic responsiveness in your site.

Creating a responsive width layout with media queries

In this recipe we will make a simple responsive width layout that adjusts itself to various screen widths. This layout would be a good starter template for a personal blog or news magazine, where you would want your readers to comment on your content and on each other's comments. It may even be a great theme starter to attract trolls to a flame war. This paragraph just sounds silly, sorry!

Getting ready

This template will work great in a dynamic CMS or blog software, but might not make much sense as a plain HTML page. But most themes work in the same as HTML as far as presentation goes. In most cases, you would simply replace the text and static navigation with template tags. This recipe will need some filler text to demonstrate. If you do not already have some text to work with, go to our old standby Ipsum generator to get some filler text.

How to do it...

To begin, create a simple web page, and in the `style` element create your media queries. You can always link to an external stylesheet, but for the sake of simplicity, this and most of the recipes contain the CSS in the `<style>...</style>` section of your header. Include these standard breakpoints at screen sizes: `960`, `1024`, and `1280`.

```
<style>
@media screen and (max-width: 960px) {…}
@media screen and (min-width: 961px) and (max-width: 1024px) {…}
@media screen and (min-width: 1025px) and (max-width: 1280px) {…}
@media screen and (min-width: 1281px) {…}
</style>
```

The first media query affects all viewports narrower than `960px`. The second from `961px` to `1024px`, the third from `1025px` to `1280px`, and the last affects, all screen sizes larger than `1281px`. Within each media query, you will write a CSS for a different layout. There will be some layout CSS outside of the media query along with your style presentation, but most of them will be defined in the media queries.

The next step is to create your HTML layout. The basic structure starts with these basic `div` elements—`nav`, `content`, and `comments`:

```
<body>
  <nav></nav>
  <div class="content"></div>
  <aside class="comments"></aside>
</body>
```

Next add some filler content to your page. This will aid in the demonstration of the layout.

In the `nav` element, add an unordered list with sample menu links. This will serve as a responsive menu. At the pages' narrowest width, the menu will display vertically. In widths ranging from 961px to 1280px, the menu is displayed inline horizontally on top. For larger widths, we want the menu to return to a vertical display and return to the left-hand side.

In the first two media queries, the `content` and `comments` elements will float left, but with different width ratios. In `960px`, these elements should have a width of `90%`. In the larger widths, set the `content` and `comments` elements at `60%` and `20%`, respectively.

```
@media screen and (max-width: 960px) {
    .content {width: 90%;}
    .comments {width: 90%;}
}
```

```
@media screen and (min-width: 961px) and (max-width: 1280px) {
    .nav ul li {display: inline-block;}
    .content {width: 60%;}
    .comments {width: 20%;}
@media screen and (min-width: 1281px) {
    .content {width: 60%;}
    .comments {width: 20%;}
}
```

To make the menu slide back to the left on the large screens, we will use positioning to create a three column layout. In the `min-width:1281px` media query, add the `.nav` element and styles for absolute positioning and width:

```
.nav{
    position: absolute;
    top: 20px;
    left: 0px;
    width:144px;
}
```

That's almost all the steps necessary to build a responsive layout. To tidy things up, let's add some padding to the layouts. Add the `.nav`, `.content`, and `.comments` elements to the other media queries, and then add padding to those. Refer to the following CSS. The `min-width:1281px` media query will not have a padding for the `.nav` element, and the padding for the `.content` and `.comments` elements are reduced to allow for the vertical menu.

```
@media screen and (max-width: 960px){
    .nav {padding: 1% 5%;}
    .content,.comments {padding: 1% 5%;}
    .content {width: 90%;}
}
@media screen and (min-width: 961px) and (max-width: 1280px){
    .nav {padding: 1% 5%;}
    .nav ul li {display: inline;}
    .content,.comments {padding: 1% 5%;}
    .content {width: 60%;}
}
@media screen and (min-width: 1281px){
    .nav {
        position: absolute;
        top: 20px;
        left: 0px;
        width: 144px;
    }
```

```
.content,.comments {padding: 1% 1% 1% 0;}
.content{
    width: 60%;
    margin-left: 144px;
}
}
```

You can also style the inline menu however you want. For now let's simply add some margins to the `li` elements. Add this element and styles outside of the media queries, `.nav ul li{margin: 2px 10px;}`.

Finally, on to the content and comments, paste your filler text inside the `.content` element. I also added the header and paragraph tags inside. We will do something similar for the comments.

Remember that we want to allow for embedded comments, or people to comment on comments. There will be a possible inherited hierarchy of comments, and we still need this to look good in all browser sizes, so we should add some padding. Adding a static padding to the `.comment` element will not look good in all browser sizes. Instead, add a relative padding to each media query's `.comments` element, so that they take less space as the browser window gets smaller: `90%` for the `max-width:960px` media query and `20%` for all larger sizes. Add outside of the media queries, `padding-left: 8%` to the `.comment` element, and float the `.content` and `.comments` elements to the `left`. You can also `text-align:justify` them to make the text look like a block.

```
@media screen and (max-width: 960px) {
    .nav {padding: 1% 5%;}
    .content,.comments {padding: 1% 5%;}
    .content {width: 90%;}
    .comments {width: 90%;}
}
@media screen and (min-width: 961px) and (max-width: 1280px) {
    .nav {padding: 1% 5%;}
    .nav ul li {display: inline;}
    .content,.comments {padding: 1% 5%;}
    .content {width: 60%;}
    .comments {width: 20%;}
}
@media screen and (min-width: 1281px) {
    .nav {
        position: absolute;
        top: 20px;
        left: 0;
        width: 144px;
    }
```

```
    .content,.comments {padding:1% 1% 1% 0}
    .content {
        width: 60%;
        margin-left: 144px;
    }
    .comments { width: 20%;}
}
.content,.comments {
    float: left;
    text-align: justify;
}
.nav ul li {margin: 2px 10px;}
.comment {padding-left: 8%;}
```

This CSS will make the padding on comments and embedded comments adjust to the changes in the browser window sizes. As a result, the comments section of your page will show the comment parent-and-child hierarchy, as well as a consistent and workable layout for each browser window size. You can see the code in action demonstrated in the following screenshot:

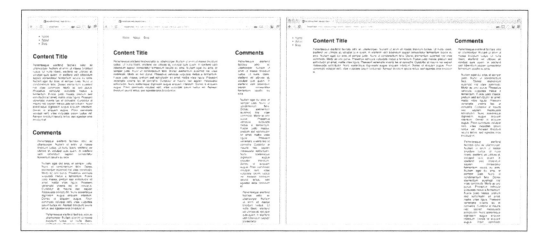

How it works...

In this responsive layout we used a few different techniques. First, the media query offers us limited but useful logic to deploy different layout techniques for different browser window sizes. Second, the fluid and floating elements with size ratios adjust with ease to the new layouts. And last but not least, fluid's percent-based padding gives a consistent ratio of padding to the screen size and layout.

Changing image sizes with media queries

In this recipe, you will learn how to resize an image with a CSS media query. This can be useful in a number of situations, especially those where you want to download only one image and use it in different size versions in your responsive layout.

Getting ready

This is a good method for size variation that can be handled on the client side, but be careful not to abuse this method by causing the client to download a really large image file and do heavy resizing in their browser. There are better ways to do that, which were discussed in *Chapter 1, Responsive Elements and Media*.

How to do it...

I recommend putting together a small HTML page with a h1 title, the wrap element, and inside wrap, an image and a paragraph of text. You really don't need all of this extra stuff to make an image size change in an image query, however, it will help you demonstrate the use of changing an image size in the media query.

Next, create your media queries for the most frequent browser window size breakpoints: 960px, 1024px, 1280px, 1366px, 1440px, and last but not least 1680px. In each of these media queries, add your styles for the elements. In my example, I created media queries at 960px and 1280px:

```
@media screen and (max-width: 960px){
    .wrap {padding:0 5%; width: 90%;}
    .wrap img {
        width: 90%;
        height: auto;
        padding:5%;
    }
    .wrap p {
        width: 90%;
        padding: 5%;
        text-align: justify;
    }
}
@media screen and (min-width: 961px) and (max-width: 1280px) {
    .wrap {
        padding: 0 5%;
        width: 90%;
    }
    .wrap img {
        width: 50%;
```

```
                height: auto;
                max-width: 600px;
                float: right;
                }
        .wrap p {
                width: 50%;
                text-align: justify;
                float: left;
        }
}
@media screen and (min-width:1281px) {
        .wrap {
                padding: 0 5%;
                width: 90%;
        }
        .wrap img {
                width: 40%;
                height: auto;
                max-width: 500px;
                float: left;
        }
        .wrap p {
                width: 60%;
                text-align: justify;
                float: right;
        }
}
```

Now as you resize your page you can see how the image resizes as the browser resizes through the various media queries. This is illustrated in the following screenshot:

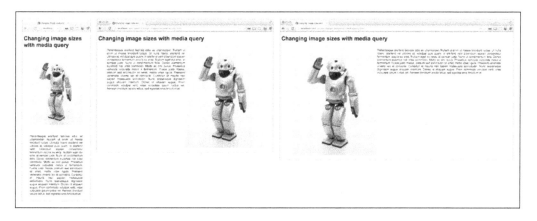

How it works...

The different media queries, when called by the browser, present different sizes for the element's `width` and `height` property. This allows you to optimize your image size for different devices. Use your judgment, and if the original image is too large, look into some server-side resizing as an alternate method.

Hiding an element with media queries

This recipe will show you some very useful tricks with media queries to make elements disappear off the screen, depending on the browser window's size. There are a few different methods of hiding an element on the screen, I will go through three of them in this recipe.

Getting ready

This method can have a number of use cases. One very helpful case is using it to switch out menus on the fly when scaling a page down to a smaller device. You could also use this to change the way your content areas or aside contents are displayed. The possibilities are unlimited when you get creative with the methods.

How to do it...

Set up a simple page for demonstration. In my example, I wrote up a page with a `h1` header, an image, and then two elements with text inside them. Next, add some style to those elements. I added a different background color and width properties to each element, mostly, so that I could keep them apart when they disappeared.

And then add your media queries at a breakpoint. In the example, I'll add a breakpoint at `960px`. And inside the media queries, we're going to take a look at some different methods of getting the element to disappear.

In your first media query, `max-width: 960px`, add the position: absolute and left: 5000px properties for the `img` element; This style will move the element far enough to the left of the screen that it has for all practical purposes, disappeared. Add to that media query a `display: none` style to the `.bar` element. This leaves the element where it is, but renders it invisible. Both of these elements are are effectively gone from the page, leaving only the title and `.foo` elements.

In the second media query, you will try a different way to remove an element from the screen. First, add the `.foo` element to the media query and give it a left margin of `5000px`. That removes it from the screen, however, the next element clears its vertical space and leaves an obvious white space where the element was. Then, float the element to the left and the white space will disappear. This is illustrated in the following code snippet:

```
.foo {
    background-color: #ccc;
    width: 300px;
}
.bar {
    background-color: blue;
    width: 600px;
    color: white;
}
@media screen and (max-width: 960px) {
    img {
        position: absolute;
        left: 5000px;
    }
    .bar {display: none;}
}
@media screen and (min-width: 961px) {
    .foo {
        float: left;
        margin-left: -5000px;
    }
}
```

Congratulations! Open the project in your browser and see if it looks like the following screenshot:

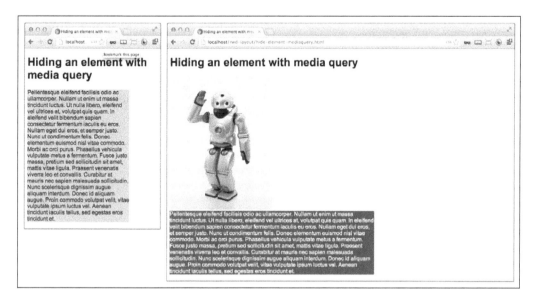

How it works...

Both the absolute position and float do not have a height property, so once applied to an element, they will not occupy any vertical space. This can be an especially useful trick to move elements around on your page. It can also cause some problems when you use floating elements for layout. This behavior can be fixed by inserting a break with a `clear:both` property after the element.

Making a smoothly transitioning responsive layout

In this recipe I will guide you through the creation of a multi-zoned and responsive front page. This one will have a number of elements that are responsive in different ways; giving a rich user experience that delivers an impressive layout. I developed this for a startup I was working on and found that I liked it so much that I continued to develop it further to share with you in this recipe.

Getting ready

This recipe will be a good template for a homepage to a content-heavy site. If you have been building content for a while, this will be perfect for the landing page, and can be modified for a single-item content page easily. If you are just getting started with your site, you can go get some generated text at `http://lipsum.com` like I did for this recipe.

How to do it...

This site breaks down into three HTML elements or a footer, and two elements that sometimes are vertical and sometimes are left and right floats—depending on the screen width. These elements themselves are also divided into smaller elements. So, get started and create a basic page with a top-wrap element, a middle-wrap element, and a footer:

```
<body>
  <header>...</header>
  <div class="content" role="main">...</div>
  <footer>...</footer>
</body>
```

Next, we start the CSS for these items. Add some basic CSS and the following media queries:

```
body{
    margin: 0;
    padding: 0;
}
```

```
footer {width: 100%;}
.clear {clear: both;}
@media screen and (max-width: 1280px) {
    header, .content {width: 100%;}
}
@media screen and (min-width: 1281px) {
    header {
        float: left;
        width: 60%;
    }
    .content {
        float: right;
        width: 40%;
    }
}
```

In this basic layout, the `header` and `.content` rows both occupy `100%` of the page width, while the page is under `1280px`. When the page is larger, they occupy the respective `60%/40%` split and the float `left` and `right`.

Next let's build the menus. This menu will employ a responsive trick of using a media query to hide and show two different menus. Essentially, we will build two different menus, and then use CSS to display the optimized one for each screen. The smallest version will use a multi-select drop-down menu, while the larger menu contains two inline lists. Here's what the HTML looks like inside the top-wrap element:

```
<header>
    <nav>
        <div class="menu small-menu">
            <img src="images/robot-low.png">
            <form>
                <select name="URL" onchange='window.location.
href=this.form.URL.options[this.form.URL.selectedIndex].value'>
                <option value="blog.html">Page 1</option>
                <option value="home.html">Home Page</option>
                <option value="tutorials.html">Tutorials</option>
                </select>
            </form>
        </div>

        <div class="menu large-menu">
            <div class="top-menu">
                <nav>
                  <ul>
```

```
                    <li><a href="login.html">Log In</a></li>
                    <li><a href="account.html">My Account</a></li>
                 </ul>
              </nav>
          </div>
      <div class="bottom-menu"> these should be classes so they can
be reused. Plus the names are too specific.
          <nav>
             <a href="#" class="logo">
                <img src="images/robot-low.png">
             </a>
             <ul>
                <li><a href="blog.html">Page 1</a></li>
                <li><a href="home.html">Home Page</a></li>
                <li><a href="tutorials.html">Tutorials</a></li>
                <li> <a href="news.html">News</a> </li>
             </ul>
          </nav>
        </div>
     </div>
    </nav>
</header>
```

Add the following CSS for the header elements:

```
nav .small-menu img{
     width:9%;
     height:auto;
     float:left;
     padding:0 2%;
}
nav .small-menu select {
     margin: 3%;
     width: 80%;
}
```

This will display two different versions of the menu until we add to our media queries.
Add media queries to switch between displaying the drop-down menu on small browser
windows and the larger inline list menu on larger browser window sizes. Use the display
property to show and hide the menus.

```
@media screen and (max-width: 600px) {
     nav .small-menu {display: inline;}
     nav .large-menu {display: none;}
}
```

```
@media screen and (min-width: 601px) {
    nav .small-menu {display: none;}
    nav .large-menu {display: inline;}
}
```

Under the menus, before the closing `</header>` tag create a space for a large high-quality photo to display on the site. And to prevent it from becoming a wasted space let's put a search box right in the middle of it. We can actually make this search form stick closely to the center of the picture and responsively adjust to screen size changes. This is illustrated in the following simple code:

```
<div class="img-search">classes
    <div class="search">
        <form>
          <input type="text" placeholder="Find a Robot">
          <input value="Search" class="search-input" type="submit">
        </form>
    </div>
    <img class="main-img" src='images/robot-wide.png'>
</div>
```

And of course the magic is in the CSS. Let's use some tricks to make the search form hover in the same spot. First give the outer `div` element a width of `100%`, then the `search` element will get an absolute position and few different properties under different media queries. This combination will keep the search form floating above the middle of the `img` area. Keep in mind that we are adding new CSS to the media queries. The following CSS code reflects only the additions, not what was already there. It gets rather long if I show the entire CSS expanding each time. At the end, I will include the entire CSS as it should be in its final state.

```
.img-search {width: 100%;}
.search {position: absolute; }
.top-menu {
    height: 33px;
    background-color: #ccc;
}
.logo img {height: 87px; float: left;}
.top-menu nav li {display: inline-block;}
.large-menu ul {margin: 0 5px;}
.large-menu li {display: inline;}

@media screen and (max-width: 600px) {
    .search {
        margin-top: 87px;
        left: 22%;}
}
```

```
@media screen and (min-width: 601px) and (max-width: 1280px) {
    .search {
        margin-top: 144px;
        left: 40%;
    }
}
@media screen and (min-width: 1281px) {
    .search {
        margin-top: 144px;
        left: 22%;
    }
}
```

The `.img-search` image element will receive a dynamic width of `100%`, and auto height. And that's it for the large image search field.

Give the next element, `.flip-tab`, a width of `100%`, and any height or other properties you want. You won't have to worry about this again:

```
<div class="flip-tab"><h3>Look Down Here</h3></div>

.flip-tab {width: 100%; height: 54px; text-align: center;}
```

The next element, `.teasers`, will get a `max-width: 1280px` property so it will auto-magically be at `100%` width of its parent element, `top-wrap`, limited to `1280px`. This element is simply a container for the three left-floating `.teaser` elements. These `.teaser` elements will have two different property sets under different media queries for a `600px` breakpoint.

```
<div class="teasers">
    <div class="teaser teaser1">
        <h3>The First Law of Robotics</h3>
            <p>
                Lorem ipsum dolor sit amet,..
            </p>
    </div>
    <div class="teaser teaser2">
        <h3>The First Law of Robotics</h3>
            <p>
                Lorem ipsum dolor sit amet,..
            </p>
    </div>
    <div class="teaser teaser3">
        <h3>The First Law of Robotics</h3>
            <p>
```

```
                    Lorem ipsum dolor sit amet,..
              </p>
       </div>
</div>
.teasers {max-width: 1280px;}
.teaser {float: left;}
@media screen and (max-width: 600px) {
       .teaser {width: 100%;}
}
@media screen and (min-width: 601px) {
       .teaser {
             width: 32%;
             min-width: 144px;
       }
}
```

That concludes everything you will be doing in the header element. Up next is the content element, which wraps the content that will float in the right-hand side columns. What's inside this element is nothing more than a two-column float split at a 60/40 ratio, or if the parent element is narrow, each is 100% wide. The content element will have two different property sets under media queries with a breakpoint at 1280px. These elements have some limited sample content. You can add much more once you deploy the layout:

```
<div class="content" role="main">
       <div class="contact-us">

              <div class="form-wrap">
                    <legend>Find a Robot</legend>

                    <form>
                          <input type="text" placeholder="Robot Search">
                          <input value="Search" class="search-input"
type="submit">
                    </form>
              </div>
                    <h4>Search or Like Us Locally</h4>
              <ul class="local-like">                  <li><a
href="/search/SanFranciso">San Francisco</a><a href="/like/
SanFrancisco">Like</a></li>
                    <li><a href="/search/LosAngeles">Los Angeles</a><a
href="/like/LosAngeles">Like</a></li>
                    <li><a href="/search/Austin">Austin</a><a href="/like/
Austin">Like</a></li>
```

```
                    <li><a href="/search/Houston">Houston</a><a href="/like/
Houston">Like</a></li>          </ul>
      </div>
      <divclass="cities"> really?
            <p>Loremipsumdolor sitamet, consecteturadipiscingelit.
Nunc non felisutmetusvestibulumcondimentumuteueros.Nam id ipsumnibh.
Praesent sit ametvelit...
            </p>
      </div>

   </div>
```

This CSS is more complicated, but remember, you can access this entire work online. As you can see, the elements do zig and zag around a bit, but each breakpoint will have an optimized display.

```
.contact-us {float: left;}
.cities {float: left;}
@media screen and (max-width: 600px) {
      .contact-us {width: 100%;}
      .cities {width: 100%;}
}
@media screen and (min-width: 601px) and (max-width: 1280px) {
      .contact-us {width: 40%;}
      .cities {width: 60%;}
}
@media screen and (min-width: 1281px) and (max-width: 1366px) {
      .contact-us {width: 100%;}
      .cities {width: 100%;}
}
@media screen and (min-width: 1367px) {
      .contact-us {width: 40%;}
      .cities {width: 60%;}
}
```

Finally, the footer! (The end of the page!) The footer breaks down into a `100%` wide outer `<footer>`, and then a `footer-wrap` wrap with a `100%` width, `max-width` of `1280px`, dynamic side margins, and inline-block display. Inside are three elements that always have the property `display:inline-block`. When the display is small, these elements are each `100%` wide, otherwise they are `33%` wide, left-floating, with a minimum width of `144px`:

```
<footer>
      <div class="footer-wrap">
            <div class="footer-1 footer-third">
                  <ul>
```

```
            <li><span class=""><a href="#">FaceBook</a></span></li>
            <li><span class=""><a href="#">Google +</a></span></li>
            <li><span class=""><a href="#">Twitter</a></span></li>
            </ul>
        </div>
        <div class="footer-2 footer-third">
            <ul>
              <li><span class=""><a href="#">Link1</a></span></li>
              <li><span class=""><a href="#">Privacy Policy</a></span></li>
              <li><span class=""><a href="#">Terms of Use</a></span></li>
            </ul>
        </div>
        <div class="footer-3 footer-third">
            <ul>
                <li><span class=""><a href="#">Link1</a></span></li>
                <li><span class=""><a href="#">Link2</a></span></li>
                <li><span class=""><a href="#">Link3</a></span></li>
            </ul>
        </div>
    </div>
</footer>

.footer-wrap{
    width: 100%;
    max-width: 1280px;
    margin :0 10%;
    display: inline-block;
}
.footer-third {display: inline-block;}

@media screen and (max-width: 600px) {
    .footer-third {width :100%;}
}
@media screen and (min-width: 601px{
    .footer-third {
        float: left;
        width: 33%;
            min-width: 144px;
    }
}
```

As I promised previously, here is the full CSS code:

```css
body{margin:0;padding:0;}
.img-search {width: 100%}
.search {position:absolute;}
nav .small-menu img{width:9%;height:auto;float:left;padding:0 2%;}
nav .small-menu select {margin: 3%; width: 80%;}
.main-img {width: 100%; height: auto;}
.top-menu {height: 33px; background-color: #ccc;}
.top-menu nav li {display: inline-block;}
.logo img {height: 87px; float: left;}
.large-menu ul {margin: 0 5px;}
.large-menu li {display: inline;}

.flip-tab {width: 100%; height: 54px; text-align: center;}
.teasers {max-width: 1280px;}
.teaser {float:left;}
.contact-us {float:left;}
.cities {float:left;}

footer {width:100%}
.footer-wrap {width: 100%; max-width: 1280px; margin: 0 10%; display:
inline-block;}
.footer-third {display:inline-block;}


@media screen and (max-width: 600px) {
 nav .small-menu {display: inline}
 nav .large-menu {display: none}
 .search {margin-top: 87px; left: 22%;}
 .teaser {width: 100%}
 .contact-us {width: 100%;}
 .cities {width: 100%}
 .footer-third {width: 100%}
}
@media screen and (min-width: 601px) and (max-width: 1280px){
    .search {margin-top: 144px; left: 40%}
    .contact-us {width: 40%;}
    .cities {width: 60%}
}
```

```
@media screen and (min-width: 601px) {
 nav .small-menu{display: none}
 nav .large-menu{display: inline}
 .teaser {width: 32%; min-width: 144px;}
 .footer-third {float: left; width: 33%; min-width: 144px;}
}
@media screen and (max-width: 1280px) {
 header, .content {width: 100%;}
}
@media screen and (min-width: 1281px) {
 header {float: left; width: 60%;}
 .content {float: right; width: 40%;}
 .search {margin-top: 144px; left:22%;}
}
@media screen and (min-width: 1281px) and (max-width: 1366px){
 .contact-us {width: 100%}
 .cities {width:100%}
 }
@media screen and (min-width: 1367px) {
.contact-us {width: 40%}
.cities {width: 60%}
}
```

This one was long and difficult; thanks for hanging in there! The effect is illustrated in the following screenshot, compare this with your output:

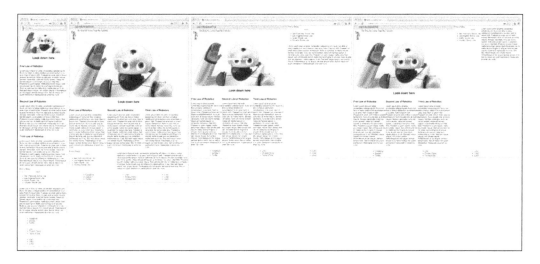

How it works...

These CSS and media queries, when combined together, make a responsive footer that can stay centered through all the screen sizes, and collapse down for small mobile-sized browser windows.

Responsive layout is an exciting new area of web development methodology. The responsive methodology allows the designer and developer to create for multiple devices, especially mobile devices, without the expense of developing native apps. Very soon, if not already, you can expect many companies to want to take a responsive approach to their site redesigns.

There's more...

You created a very simple method of responsive almost completely using CSS. I would challenge you to take this one step further by eliminating the dual menus in the `nav` element. Look in the *Adding JavaScript for mobile browsers only* recipe, in *Chapter 5, Making Mobile-first Web Applications*, to add a jQuery method to replace the large menus with the `<select>` element in mobile browsers. This will prevent any potential search engine penalty from having duplicate content in the menus.

First, cut out the `smallMenu` div element and its children, and paste it somewhere in the header, or top of the body, inside a `<script>` `</script>` element as a variable, `smallMenu`.

```
var smallMenu = '<div class="menu small-menu">...</div>'
```

Next write the script that will be called to remove the `large-menu` div element and append to the `nav` element the `smallMenu` variable.

```
$(document).ready(function() {
    $('.large-menu').remove();
    $('nav').append(smallMenu);
});
```

Now, when the page loads on a mobile device, the script will replace the navigation with a scaled-down mobile version, and you will not lose any sleep over your SEO!

4
Using Responsive Frameworks

In this chapter, you will learn about:

- ▶ Using the Fluid 960 grid layout
- ▶ Using the Blueprint grid layout
- ▶ Fluid layout using the rule of thirds
- ▶ Trying Gumby, a responsive 960 grid
- ▶ The Bootstrap framework makes responsive layouts easy

Introduction

The **layout** frameworks have become increasingly useful and widespread in layout design and development. Many web developers have found that by adapting their designs to a framework, they can speed up their production dramatically.

There are a number of good frameworks out there, which at first glance may seem like too much effort to spin up, otherwise you will have to sacrifice too much of your design to adapt to someone else's methodology. At least, that's what I thought at first. In practice, what I found was that learning and using frameworks allowed me to focus more on the parts of the project I enjoyed, and helped me get the project done faster. In essence, using a framework may cause your final products to look like the framework. Sometimes, this may not be such a terrible notion, that is, having a toolset at your disposal that helps you develop faster and better websites. There are many frameworks available; some are bare-bones, and require that you invest more time in design and development but you have more control over the final product; conversely, some provide more features, but the framework guides your design and it will be difficult to change without a full redesign.

So, which framework is right for you? The answer is of course; it depends on what is best for the project requirements. I suggest trying out the recipes in this chapter and having a number of tools at your disposal and ready to build with.

Using the Fluid 960 grid layout

The **960 Grid System** has been around for a while and has already proven useful in deploying new projects quickly. It is fairly simple to learn, and after a quick learning curve you can jump right into using it.

The only snag in this is that it is not responsive. In fact, it behaves much like a table using column, spanned over fixed-width table headers. It lays out nicely in a 960px-wide window, and that's it, you are stuck with a good view in only one browser window size. So why even discuss the 960 grid at all in a module about responsive design? The answer is that some people liked it so much that they decided to fix the problem.

Getting ready

There are good solutions for this, and hopefully you can find them in this chapter. Bear with me and I'll show you one of the simpler versions of it in this recipe. The simple responsive version of 960 Grid System could actually be more accurately described as a **fluid grid**. It replaces much of the fixed-width grid elements with percentage width, left-floating element. This works pretty well but when the columns get narrow, it can become difficult to read. We can fix this rather easily with some additional CSS.

What we eventually want for our page is to respond to the screen changes by exerting more granular change over how the grid is laid out in different screen sizes.

First, go get the Fluid 960 Grid System at `http://www.designinfluences.com/ fluid960gs/`. Then, download and expand the archived files. Copy the `grid.css` file from the archived `CSS` folder into your project's `CSS` folder. Next, create a new CSS file in your `CSS` directory called `responsive.css`. We'll come back to that later.

How to do it...

Create a new HTML file in your IDE. Add links to the file `grid.css`, and to your new CSS file, `responsive.css`:

```
<link rel="stylesheet" href="css/grid.css" media="screen" />
<link rel="stylesheet" href="css/responsive.css" media="screen" />
```

Next, create some content within your HTML body. Then, to make the Fluid 960 Grid work, you first add a wrapping `div` element with a class to define the number of columns inside it. For this recipe use the class `containter_16`, for a total of 16 usable columns. You also have the option of having 12 columns by assigning to the `div` element the `container_12` class.

Inside the `container_16` element, first create a container for a header. Create a new `div` element with a class `grid_16`. You probably have already guessed that the `grid_16` class takes the whole width of the `container_16` div. That was a pretty good guess; you are 98 percent correct; it actually takes 98 percent of the width, or all 16 columns with 2 percent outer padding. If you had instead used the `grid_11` class it would have taken up 11 columns, or 66.75 percent with 2 percent padding on the outside.

To create a new line, we add the another `div` element, this time with the class `clear`. This works in a similar way to the *Enter* key on your keyboard, or a newline (\n) in some programming languages. This `clear` element is necessary between rows because their position is set by a `left:float` property, which does not have a vertical space.

```
<div class="clear"></div>
```

The same could be accomplished by using an uncomplicated break, as follows:

```
<br class="clear">
```

You will need to add the `clear` div or break between every row.

Now, we will focus onto the content! Following your `clear` element, add six new `div` elements. Give the first element a `grid_3` class, the second element the `grid_5` class, and the rest of the elements the `grid_2` class. The order does not matter, as long as the number following the `grid_*` adds up to 16. Insert a few lines of Ipsum filler text (`http://lipsum.com`) inside the `div` elements. Your code will look something like this:

```
<div class="container_16">
<div class="grid_16">
<h2>Fluid Grid</h2>
</div>
<div class="clear"></div>
<div class="grid_3">Loremipsum dolor sit amet...</div>
<div class="grid_5">Curabitursapien ante, pretium...</div>
<div class="grid_2">tiam quam tortor, necsagittis ...</div>
<div class="grid_2">Donecmollisconsequatarcuvel...</div>
<div class="grid_2">Nullam sit amet magna dui. In dictum...</div>
<div class="grid_2">Etiamsuscipitvariuspharetra...</div>
</div>
```

In the following screenshot, you can see how the fluid grid breaks down on smaller viewports:

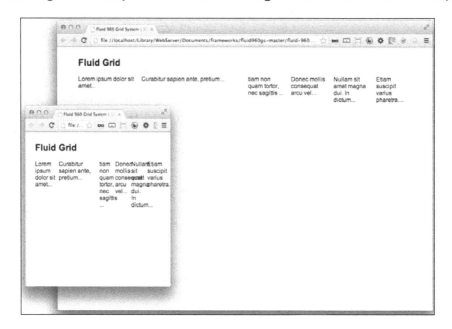

The next step is to update your CSS to add some responsiveness to the fluid layout. Now, open your `responsive.css` file in your IDE to edit it. Add media queries to cover the smaller screen breakpoints: `1024px`, `600px`, and `420px`, as shown in the following code snippet:

```
@media screen and (max-width:420px){...}
@media screen and (max-width:600px) and (min-width:421px){...}
@media screen and (max-width:1024px) and (min-width:601px){...}
```

Our intent is to make some new CSS that will override the fluid grid and make new sticking breakpoints for content elements. At narrower widths we want an element to have a greater percentage width, or a fixed width. To make the override, we will add a new class to the media queries: `.break-column`.

Next add to the `max-width:420px` media query a `min-width` value of `360px` for the `.break-column` element class. Then, add to the new media queries, `max-width:600px` and `min-width:421px`, add the `.grid_2.break-column`, `.grid_3.break-column`, and `.grid_5.break-column` element classes and their `width:48%` property. In the largest of the three media queries, add the class with a property of `width:30%` followed by the `!important` override (be sure it is inserted before the semicolon), as shown in the following code snippet:

```
@media screen and (max-width:420px){
    .break-column{min-width:360px; }
}
```

```
@media screen and (min-width:421px) and (max-width:600px){
    .grid_2.break-column, .grid_3.break-column, .grid_5.break-
column{width:48%;}
}
@media screen and (max-width:1024px) and (min-width:601px){
    .break-column{width:30% !important;}
}
```

One last step to a responsive fluid grid! Open your HTML file again and add to each of the six `div` elements a class of `break-column`. And the recipe is complete. Refresh your browser, or open the HTML to view it. As you scale down your browser window or open the file in a mobile device, you will see the layout responds with a more optimized layout for the smaller views. The fluid grid is illustrated in the following screenshot:

How it works...

When you open the un-updated (fluid and non-responsive) HTML file in your browser, you will see your six columns, and they will fluidly retain their same proportional width as the browser window or the device gets smaller. When viewed in a small window or mobile device, it will display six unreadable narrow columns.

Adding the media queries works by overriding the style properties of the `div` elements. I demonstrated overrides with three different methods: first, the `min-width` method overrides the percent width; next, as the `responsive.css` file follows the `grid.css` file and the CSS is explicitly name-spaced (`.grid_2.break-column`, `.grid_3.break-column`, and `.grid_5.break-column`), it overrides the fluid width declared in the `grid.css` file, and in the last case, the `!important` declaration trumps all in the override cascade.

Using the Blueprint grid layout

The **Blueprint CSS** framework is another popular static CSS grid system. There may be a case where you come across a need to make the static Blueprint CSS grid framework into your very own responsive Blueprint framework. This one is pretty easy to break apart into a responsive layout. There are only a few simple CSS breaks to insert and you have a responsive framework.

Getting ready

First go and get a hold of the Blueprint CSS framework. You can download it at `http://www.blueprintcss.org/`. This framework works similarly to other static CSS grid frameworks.

How to do it....

Once you have downloaded the Blueprint framework, extract the files and copy the `blueprint` folder into your `CSS` directory. Next we'll start building the HTML file to work with the Blueprint CSS framework. Create a new HTML file in your IDE. Inside the body, add a title, and then an `hr` element.

"Huh? A what?", you may ask. It's a horizontal rule—a thematic break. Let me explain.

In previous versions of HTML, `hr` was a horizontal rule. Meaning it acted like a break, but places a horizontal line across the page. It got an upgrade in HTML5, and is now a thematic break. So what's the difference? It still, by itself, does the same thing putting a horizontal line across the page. However, in the past it was used to define the layout, but now it emphasizes a change in theme or content.

However, in Blueprint CSS, the `hr` element is used specifically to capture a row. Okay? Let us get back to our task at hand.

After your `hr` element, you can start a row of content. First create a three-column layout for the first row. Then, insert some Ipsum (`http://Ipsum.com`) text into the three `div` elements. This, like the 960 Grid, works like a table `colspan`, you assign a class to the `div` element corresponding to the number of columns you want the element to span across. The total number of columns is 22. The first three classes will be: `span-7`, `span-8`, and `span-7`. Follow the same steps with another thematic break:

```
<h1>Blueprint CSS Framework Responsive<h2>
<hr>
  <div class="span-7">Loremipsum dolor sit amet,
   consecteturadipiscingelit...</div>
  <div class="span-8">Etiamegettortorlectus, et
   variusnibh...</div>
  <div class="span-7">Duis sit
   ametfelislobortisfeliscommodolacinia...</div>
<hr>
```

In your next row, add two large columns. Add two divs with the classes `span-15` and `span-7` in them. In the left-hand side `div` element, add a paragraph of Ipsum text and an image. In the right-hand side column, add an unordered list of Ipsum text sentences. Then close the row with a horizontal rule:

```
<hr />
<div class="span-15">
    <img src="test.jpg" class="top pull-1 left" alt="test">
    <p>Loremipsum dolor sit amet, consectetueradipiscingelit...</p>
</div>
<div class="span-7">
<ul>
<li>Loremipsum dolor sit amet, consectetueradipiscingelit...</li>
<li>Loremipsum dolor sit amet, consectetueradipiscingelit...</li>
<li>Loremipsum dolor sit amet, consectetueradipiscingelit...</li>
</ul>
</div>
<hr />
```

This is most of the HTML we want to build for this recipe. If you want more, you can see the `sample.html` file in the `tests` folder of the archive you downloaded.

In your HTML header, add links to the Blueprint CSS framework stylesheets in the `css/Blueprint/` directory.

Next, let's add our own stylesheet to make the framework a responsive one. Add a new link to the new stylesheet, `responsive.css`, in your header. If you have not already added the CSS file, then add the new `responsive.css` stylesheet:

```
<link rel="stylesheet" href="css/responsive.css"  >
```

Open the `responsive.css` stylesheet. Create a media query for the smallest breakpoint, and for the next breakpoint. Make the media query breakpoints at `600px` and `1024px`, as follows:

```
@media screen and (max-width:600px) {...}
@media screen and (min-width:601px) and (max-width:1024px) {...}
```

Inside it we're going to use a CSS trick called an **attribute selector**. This is like using a wildcard `*`. To make a property apply to all of the column span classes in the Blueprint CSS grid, such as `span-1`, `span-2`, `span-3`, and more, you write it like this: `div[class*='span'] {...}`. This is a wonderful trick for making responsive overrides in a CSS grid.

At the `600px` media query, add CSS with the attribute selector, and add a width of `90%`. This will make all the spans expand to 100 percent when the browser window is less than `600px` wide. Do the same in the `1024px` media query with a width of `42%`. If you were expecting nice round numbers such as 100 percent and 50 percent, you may be surprised; but keep in mind that Blueprint CSS adds padding already.

```
@media screen and (max-width:600px){
    div[class*='span-']{width:90%;}
}
@media screen and (min-width:601px) and (max-width:1024px){
    div[class*='span-']{width:42%;}
}
```

Open the HTML in your browser or refresh your screen and you'll see that when you change the browser width, the spans adjust automatically to the new width.

You may notice that the second row leaves too much white space when you hit that `1024px` breakpoint. Let's fix that. Copy your attribute selector CSS line in the `1024px` media query and paste it beneath. Append a `.wide` class to the attribute selector. Give it a width of `90%`.

In your HTML file add a `wide` class to the first span after the second thematic break (`hr`), the one with the image inside it.

This works great on the most recent browsers, but not yet in old browsers. We'll need to add just a few lines of CSS to make this work in more browsers. In your `responsive.css` file, add on the first line the class `.container`, and give the attribute a width of `960px`. Then inside each media query add the same class, but change the width to `100%`.

```
.container{width:960px}
@media screen and (max-width:600px){
    div[class*='span-']{width:90%;}
    .container{width:100%}
}
```

```
@media screen and (min-width:601px) and (max-width:1024px){
    div[class*='span-']{width:42%;}
    div[class*='span-'].wide{width:90%;}
    .container{width:100%}
}
```

That will help it from breaking in older browsers that don't support media queries.

For some extra fun, add some CSS3 transition to the spans. This will make a smooth animated transition to the width of the affected spans. Do this outside of any media queries.

```
div[class*='span-']{

-moz-transition: width 0.1s; /* Firefox 4 */
-webkit-transition: width 0.1s; /* Safari and Chrome */
-o-transition: width 0.1s; /* Opera */
transition: width 0.1s;

}
```

With this extra tidbit you can do some fancier responsive design in each media query. The new responsive Blueprint is illustrated in the following screenshot:

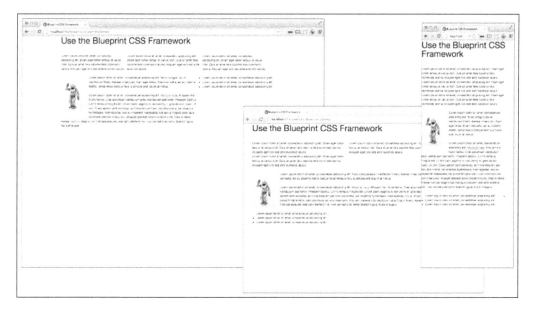

How it works...

To make the Blueprint CSS framework responsive, we first changed its container width from a static width to a fluid maximum width, and added media queries at breakpoints. The key ingredient in this recipe was the attribute selector that allowed us to throw a wildcard at the CSS and avoid having to recode each span's property.

Fluid layout using the rule of thirds

The **rule of thirds** is a design methodology that states that a layout or an image can be made more interesting if it is divided into three parts horizontally or vertically. And like everything else related to the Internet, there is endless discussion and debate on it. For the purpose of this module, all we care about is how to make it useful.

There is no indexed in search results, at least that I've seen, responsive and fluid layout based on the rule of thirds. However, there is a good static framework based on the Rule of Thirds. It's called the **Golden Grid**.

Getting ready

Search for `Golden Grid`, and `http://code.google.com/p/the-golden-grid/` should be the first result. From the top navigation, go to the **Downloads** page and get the latest version.

How to do it...

Look inside the extracted files for a `CSS/golden-base` directory. Inside it, copy the `golden.css` file into your development directory. You will use this CSS file as your base framework for layout.

In a new HTML file add a link to the `golden.css` stylesheet.

```
<link rel="stylesheet" href="CSS/golden.css" media="screen,
projection">
```

Open this CSS file and edit the property of the `.main` class. Change `width:970px` to `max-width:970px`. This will break the static page template and allow the outer wrap to adjust as the browser's window shrinks.

While you have the `golden.css` stylesheet open, take a look at how this works. It's very simple; three vertical lines, and then for each division divide the page layout by half, and then in half again. The class spans start at `70px` width with the `80px` increments until they fill up their `width:950px;` attribute. To assign the `width` property to your element, assign it a class starting with the letter g plus the width and `10px` for a margin. These also have the `float:left;` and `display:inline;` styles. Because they are left-floating inline elements, when they run out of horizontal room, they will take a new line. Since they are left floated, they are aligned left, to move them to the right, you can either put empty elements in front of it, or use the framework's `.margin` class to put a left margin in front of it.

The margins work much like the grid span's widths, they increment by `80px`, the only difference is that they start at `90px` instead of `70px`. The difference is accounted for in the element's `margin-left:10px` property.

The elements line up in rows, and like the other frameworks we have worked with them in this chapter, it uses an element to clear the end of the row, before starting a new one. In this case, the framework uses a div with a `clear:both` property.

Let's now get back to editing the HTML file and create a responsive layout using the Rule of Thirds. We will start by creating a static layout. Create a header (H1) with a style of `width:100%`, and then add three divs to clear new rows.

```
<body>
<div class="g960"><h1>Golden Grid CSS Layout</h1></div>
    <div class="clear"></div>
    <div class="clear"></div>
    <div class="clear"></div>
</body>
```

After the first clearing `div` element, add a `div` element with the class `.g960`, and we will insert a large image in which we will create responsiveness characteristics. You can refer to the *Resizing an image using percent width* recipe in *Chapter 1, Responsive Elements and Media*, for a refresher on to making images responsive:

```
<div class="clear"></div>
<div class="g960">
<img src="robot-large.png" class="resp" alt="robot picture"/>
</div>
<div class="clear"></div>
```

After the next break, insert six `div` elements, each with the class `g160`. Inside each, insert a paragraph of Ipsum text. For a more informative example, replace one of the `.g160` elements with an 80px-wide class. Be sure to also include the class for the margin, `ml80`, as follows:

```
<div class="clear"></div>
<div class="g160"><p>Loremipsum dolor sit amet...</p></div>
<div class="g160"><p>Loremipsum dolor sit amet...</p></div>
<div class="g160"><p>Loremipsum dolor sit amet...</p></div>
<div class="g160"><p>Loremipsum dolor sit amet...</p></div>
<div class="g80 ml80"><p>Loremipsum dolor sit amet...</p></div>
<div class="g160"><p>Loremipsum dolor sit amet...</p></div>
<div class="clear"></div>
```

That's likely enough for the HTML to get a clear demonstration of how to make this work. Let us now move on to adding our CSS to make this a responsive design.

Add a new CSS file to your `CSS` directory, `responsive.css`, and link to it in your HTML head.

```
<link rel="stylesheet" href="CSS/responsive.css" media="screen,
projection">
```

Here, we'll add some CSS properties to make the CSS framework responsive. First, let's take care of that large image. We'd rather not let it stay large when the browser gets smaller.

```
.resp{
    width:100%;
    height:auto;
}
```

Next, add media queries at two breakpoints, `600px` for mobile and `1024px` for tablets. You can add more as you like for larger screens, but for this recipe we're just covering the basics.

```
@media screen and (max-width:600px){...}
@media screen and (min-width:601px) and (max-width:1024px){...}
```

For all screens smaller than `600px`, we want all the `div` elements to default to the full width of the screen. Do not forget that we have classes with left-margin properties; we'll want to shrink those to zero. To keep the new CSS minimal, let's use the CSS attribute selectors to wildcard select all the grid classes. Add `div[class*='g']{...}` and assign a width of 90%, and `div[class*='ml'] {...}` to assign a left margin of 0.

```
@media screen and (max-width:600px){
    div[class*='g']{width:96%;}
    div[class*='ml']{margin-left:0;}
}
```

For screens ranging from 600px to 1024px, add the same but change the grid class' width to `48%`. For this `@media` query, we don't want every element to drop to half of the screen. That would kill all of the joy of this responsive framework. After your attribute selector, add `.wide` to make a distinct CSS property for this distinct class. Then, give it a width of `96%`. In your HTML, add the `wide` class to the title and the image parent `div` elements (they are the elements with the `g960` class).

```
div[class*='g'].wide{width:96%;}
```

The following screenshot illustrates the Golden Grid behavior:

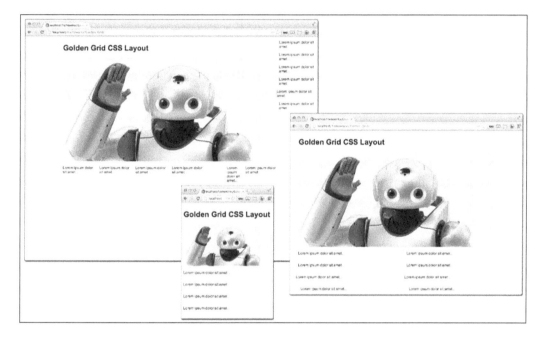

How it works...

The attribute selectors give us a tidy trick to break apart a rigid framework across limited column spans into a full width across the screen. Combine this with your custom media queries to only change the HTML on smaller screens, and you have an easy recipe for a responsive, and potentially visually, compelling layout for all sizes. This same technique can be used for a number of different frameworks.

There's more...

Let's have some fun and take this a little further. We've so far in this chapter dealt mostly with making static frameworks that run on a mobile device. Let's do an experiment together to make the Golden Grid do something cool when displayed on a large screen. Add a new media query for the `1280px` breakpoint.

```
@media screen and (min-width:1280px){...}
```

This extra section of the recipe goes a little deeper into attribute selectors. It may be a bit disturbing at first to see basic logic in your CSS, but bear with me and you'll find some new tools for your toolbox, which you will find very useful. But, first let's add some more content and an HTML structure.

Copy the last row of your HTML and append it to the HTML page right after where you have copied it. Give it a parent `div` element with a class of `g960`. To the preceding `div` element, add the class `last clear`.

```html
<div class="last clear"></div>
<div class="g960">
    <div class="g160"><p>Loremipsum dolor sit amet...</p></div>
    <div class="g160"><p>Loremipsum dolor sit amet...</p></div>
    <div class="g160"><p>Loremipsum dolor sit amet...</p></div>
    <div class="g160"><p>Loremipsum dolor sit amet...</p></div>
    <div class="g80 ml80"><p>Loremipsum dolor sit amet...</p></div>
    <div class="g160"><p>Loremipsum dolor sit amet...</p></div>
</div>
```

Back to your CSS. The attribute selectors now allow more conditions, such as parents, children, and precedence. Let's use this to apply CSS properties to the grid element preceded by the `.last` div. To do this we use a ~ symbol; the syntax is as follows:

```
DIV.preceding~DIV.following
```

We want this element to change into a column on the right-hand side when the screen is bigger than 1280px to maximize our viewing area.

```css
div.last~div[class*='g']{position:absolute;right:0;top:0;width:14%;max-width:226px;}
```

Next, we want all its children to line up nicely and take up the available space, as well as remove any margins from the `ml` classes. This syntax is much like the preceding one, but uses a > symbol; and is written like this `DIV.parent>DIV.child`.

```css
div.last~div[class*='g']>div[class*='g']{display:block;float:none;width:100%;}
div.last~div[class*='g']>div[class*='ml']{margin-left:0;}
```

We also need to prevent the wrapping `g960` grid element from being affected by the wildcard in the `max-width:1024px` media query. Add the same attribute selector to the grid div element preceded by the `.lost` div element and give it a width of `100%`, this is shown in the following code line:

```
div.last~div[class*='g']{width:100%}
```

Now refresh your browser's window and expand it past the `1280px` breakpoint. You'll see that the last row move into a sidebar position. Who says frameworks are too rigid to be responsive?

Now, you already know that media queries are not supported in old browsers, so since we care for all of our audience we want to give some love to the steadfast users of old browsers. Copy the CSS from the `1280px` media query breakpoint, and add it to a pre IE9-only stylesheet. Then make a conditional link to the stylesheet in your header:

```
<!--[if lt IE 9]>
  <link rel="stylesheet" type="text/css" href="IE8.css" />
<![endif]-->
```

This will take care of the old-browser-support issues and your site will still look good in the older browsers.

Trying Gumby, a responsive 960 grid

The Gumby framework is a continued effort on the good old reliable static 960 Grid framework. It was brought to you by the nice folks at Digital Surgeons. The framework itself has been updated, and a good number of bells and whistles have been added. There are, of course more features than we have time to go through in this recipe, so we're going to stick solely to the improved layout structure of the framework.

Getting ready

Let's take a look at the Gumby 960 Responsive framework's website `gumbyframework.com/`. As you go through it, you can see the modernized framework features in action. The layout snaps nicely to a mobile version at 767px, and in addition transforms the menu into a usable mobile navigation. There are several useful UI elements included that you will want to spend some time to getting familiar with.

Click on the highly prominent **Download Gumby 2** button on the navigation to acquire the Gumby's master version archive. Included inside the package are Photoshop files to help you design your layout, the actual framework CSS, JavaScript, image files, and sample HTML files. The `demo.html` file could be a good place to examine the source and make some discoveries about how the framework is used.

But save the poking around for later, let's jump right into building a page.

How to do it...

Start by creating a new page in your HTML editor. This framework has a lean method of importing in your CSS scripts inside a singular link to `css/imports.css`. Inside that file, the different stylesheets are imported. This is a helpful concept in case you need to change or add stylesheets in the future, you can control it in this CSS file.

```
<link rel="stylesheet" href="css/imports.css">
```

This is what the CSS looks like:

```
@import url('gumby.hybrid.css');
@import url('ui.css');
@import url('style.css');
@import url('text.css');
```

Just so you don't forget, add your links to a jQuery library and the included JavaScript files: `gumby.min.js`, `plugins.js`, and `main.js`, at the end of the page directly before the closing `body` tag. You will need these later.

```
<script src="http://ajax.googleapis.com/ajax/libs/jquery/1.7.2/jquery.
min.js"></script>
<script src="js/libs/gumby.min.js"></script>
<script src="js/plugins.js"></script>
<script src="js/main.js"></script>
</body>
```

Now that the basics are taken care of, let's move on to some development. The Gumby Responsive Grid framework can use either 12 or 16 columns. Start with building a 12-column layout and later we will make the page a hybrid one by adding a 16-layer section.

Inside your HTML body, add a `div` element with the class `container`. The default layout inside the `container` class element is 12 columns. Next, inside the `container` class element, add a new `div` element with a `row` class assigned. The `row` class element encapsulates each entire range of the 12 column spans. Inside each row, you have 12 column spans to work with, to build your content divs with.

Insert inside the `row` class element three new div elements with classes, `four columns`, `three columns`, and `five columns`. The column classes can be of whatever number your design requires, as long as they together are equal to 12. The number label of the class determines the number of column spans the element occupies. Inside each of these elements add a paragraph of Ipsum filler text (`http://ipsum.com`), to help give a more illustrative demonstration of the layout.

```
<div class="container">
        <div class="row">
```

```
<div class="four columns"><p>Loremipsum dolor sit amet,
consecteturadipiscingelit. …</p></div>
<div class="three columns"><p>Loremipsum dolor sit amet,
consecteturadipiscingelit. …</p></div>
<div class="five columns"><p>Loremipsum dolor sit amet,
consecteturadipiscingelit. …</p></div>
        </div>
</div>
```

Feel free to launch this page in your browser now and see how it looks. Test its responsiveness to see how it behaves on the smaller screens. The CSS for the class, columns, looks as follows:

```
.column, .columns {
margin-left: 2.127663%;
float: left;
min-height: 1px;
position: relative;
-webkit-box-sizing: border-box;
-moz-box-sizing: border-box;
box-sizing: border-box;
}
```

The CSS for the number classes look as follows:

```
.row .two.columns {
width: 14.893641%;
}
.row .three.columns {
width: 23.404293%;
}
.row .four.columns {
width: 31.914945%;
}
.row .five.columns {
width: 40.425597%;
}
....
And so on.
```

As you can see, the columns class gives a relative position and floats the element to the left, with padding and some other style.

Next add another `div` element with the `row` class. And inside the `row` div, add a row of the six smaller `div` elements. Each of the new `div` elements will have the classes, `two` and `columns`. These together will take up a span of 12 columns. Include a short paragraph of text inside each element.

```
<div class="row">
<div class="two columns"><p>Loremipsum dolor sit amet...</p></div>
<div class="two columns"><p>Cum sociisnatoquepenatibus et...</p></div>
<div class="two columns"><p>eufacilisis sem. Phasellus...</p></div>
<div class="two columns"><p>Loremipsum dolor sit amet...</p></div>
<div class="two columns"><p>Cum sociisnatoquepenatibus et...</p></div>
<div class="two columns"><p>eufacilisis sem. Phasellus...</p></div>
</div>
```

In your browser, you can see that these align nicely into six columns of content. When you go to a small browser window, you will see that they jump to 100 percent width.

So far, the grids work in an orderly fashion if you have designed all your element to float against the left-hand side of the screen. However, that is not always the case; there will always be uses for content to be right, center, or some other arbitrary alignment. Don't worry, the Gumby 960 Responsive framework has thought of that. Let's add some more rows that demonstrate how to do that.

In the first row, we'll make two `div` elements, one on the left-hand side, and one on the right-hand side. Add a new `row` div element, and inside it, add two more `div` elements. Give the first one, which will lie on the left-hand side of the screen, the classes `two` and `columns`. With these two classes, the first `div` element floats left and spans across two columns. We want the next `div` element to only take up six columns, give it the classes, `six` and `columns`. We do not want this next column to float towards the left; instead, it should have some space between the previous `div` element and itself. To make this, there is a series of classes that have only a set percentage left-margin. In this case, we need to push the element four column spans to the right. To do so add the class, `push_four`.

```
<div class="row">
<div class="two columns"><p>Loremipsum dolor sit amet...</p></div>
<div class="six columns push_four"><p>Consecteturadipiscingeli...</p>/
div>
</div>
```

The following is the CSS for the `push_four` class:

```
.row .push_four {
margin-left: 36.170271%;
}
```

To make a column span of content *centered*, there is a special class for that. I put center in quotes, because it's not really centered, it's pseudo-centered. Instead of using a `text-align:center` or `float:center` property, the Gumby Grid uses a smart left-margin system. The CSS for the centered `six column` div element looks as follows:

```
.row .six.centered {
margin-left: 25.531956%;
}
```

It follows the same pattern as the number classes, a centered `five column` row has a greater left margin: `margin-left: 29.787282%`.

Finally, before we end this recipe, let's make use the framework to build a responsive menu. This is worth the little extra time to show at least one of the responsive UI elements included in the framework.

Since the CSS is already built we'll just go through the HTML to build this menu. Back at the top of the `container` div element, add a `row` div element. In the `row` div element add a `nav` element with the `id` value of "prettynav" and the `pretty navbarclearfix` class. Next, inside the `nav` element, add an `a href` tag with a `link` value equal to #, a `toggle` class, and a `data-for` value as #prettynav>ul element tag. Instead of text inside the `a href` element, add the image inside that is included in the `img` directory, `img/icon_nav_toggle.gif`.

```
<div class="row">
<nav class="pretty navbarclearfix" id="prettynav">
<a href="#" class="toggle" data-for="#prettynav&gt; ul"><img src="img/
icon_nav_toggle.gif"></a>
</nav>
</div>
```

The `a href` element works as a button to display the navigation menu, when it is hidden in the mobile version of the menu.

Following the `a href` element, add an unordered list (`ul`) with list items (`li`) that contain the links of your navigation:

```
<ul>
   <li><a href="#">First Item</a></li>
   <li><a href="#">Second Item</a></li>
   <li><a href="#">Third Item</a></li>
   <li><a href="#">Fourth Item</a></li>
</ul>
```

This alone creates a nice responsive menu system and that would be exciting enough, but there's still more. You can add a submenu to each one of those menu list items. To add one submenu, add a `div` element with a class `dropdown`. Inside that `div` element, add a submenu `ul` with list items similar to the parent. They automatically are converted to a hidden submenu!

```
<li>
<a href="#">Second Item</a>
<div class="dropdown">
<ul>
<li><a href="#">Dropdown item</a></li>
<li><a href="#">Dropdown item</a></li>
</ul>
</div>
</li>
```

The following screenshot illustrates the Gumby framework:

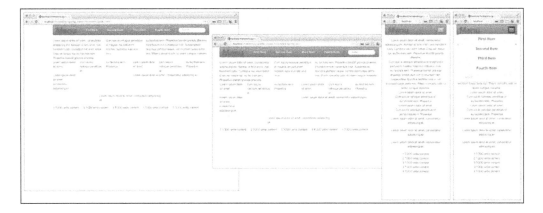

How it works...

The Gumby 960 Grid framework was designed and built to be an elegant and easy layout and element framework. There is not much needed to know how to make it work. First, learn how to class your `div` elements to make them work within the framework. Secondly, build it. Understanding how to use the UI elements included in the framework will require some more involvement, but it will be well worth your time.

The Bootstrap framework makes responsive layouts easy

The Bootstrap framework (formerly known as the **Twitter Bootstrap** framework) stands out from most other frameworks, as it is completely responsive out of the box. You can either use it as a static framework, or use their additional files to quickly deploy a fully responsive site. This is a great tool to use when you need to produce fast and good sites, and you are willing to make minimal design adjustments to an external standard.

Acquiring the framework is as easy as searching for `Bootstrap Framework` and going to the first link, `http://twitter.github.com/bootstrap/`, and clicking on the big **Download Bootstrap** button. The package includes CSS files, images, and JavaScript, but no documentation. There is, however, plenty of good documentation online at their site, and the source of their examples is highly coherent. This recipe will get you started along the path of using the Bootstrap framework.

Getting ready

Building with the Bootstrap framework is remarkably easy; you can get a template spun up in a matter of minutes. That being said, let's push through it. Spin up a new HTML file and get started. First, add a link in your header to the Bootstrap CSS files so we can on occasion see our work in action:

```
<link href="css/bootstrap.css" rel="stylesheet" media="screen">
<link href="css/bootstrap-responsive.css" rel="stylesheet"
media="screen">
```

Let us start with a simple page with a top navigation and content. The navigation will respond to the screen's width and optimize for each display. The navigation `div` element uses several classes to achieve the desired results; they are `navbarnavbar-inverse navbar-fixed-top`. Inside it, add a `div` element with the class `container`. Inside the `container` div element, there is a button graphic that is displayed in the mobile version. When clicked, it displays the mobile version of the menu. The menu is displayed in an optimized manner for both mobile and desktop versions. Pretty cool, eh!

Following is a sample menu to show how it is put together:

```
<div class="navbarnavbar-inverse navbar-fixed-top">
    <div class="navbar-inner">
      <div class="container">
```

```
        <a class="btnbtn-navbar" data-toggle="collapse" data-
target=".nav-collapse">
          <span class="icon-bar"></span>
          <span class="icon-bar"></span>
          <span class="icon-bar"></span>
        </a>
        <a class="brand" href="#">Project name</a>
        <div class="nav-collapse collapse">
          <ul class="nav">
            <li class="active"><a href="#">Home</a></li>
            <li><a href="#about">About</a></li>
            <li><a href="#contact">Contact</a></li>
          </ul>
        </div><!--/.nav-collapse -->
      </div>
    </div>
  </div>
```

Then, insert into your header, a link to the jQuery library.

```
<script src="http://code.jquery.com/jquery-latest.min.js" ></script>
```

Then, at the bottom of your HTML, right before the closing body tag, add a link to the js/bootstrap.js file.

```
<script src="js/bootstrap.js"></script>
```

Finally, if you haven't already copied the JS directly into your webroot, do so.

Now, check your slick responsive navigation.

That was great, wasn't it? Now that we're both excited about the Bootstrap framework, let's get to work on some responsive content layout. Next, let's go through and build what Bootstrap calls a basic marketing site.

First thing to do is add a div element with the container class. If you look back at our menu, you'll find that this class is a clever re-usable layout element used throughout, to control the responsive width of the containing elements. Inside the container element, add a new div element and give it a class, hero-unit. Inside the hero-unit class, add some content that you want to display in a large billboard style on the screen:

```
<div class="container">
<div class="hero-unit">
<h1>Hello World</h1>
<p>Loremipsum dolor sit amet...</p>
</div>
</div>
```

Refresh your browser and try that on for size. Everything looks great without much effort. Beneath that we want to add some columns of the teaser text. This is starting to look like a good landing page. Aren't you glad you are doing this?

The Bootstrap framework uses a `div` element with a `row` class to outline its column spans. So to create a new *row* of content, add a new `div` element with the `row` class. Inside the row you have 12 spans available to work your content into. For this recipe, let's stick with simple, so insert three new `div` elements, each with a `span4` class, inside the `row` div element. Inside each `span4` element, add a secondary header and a paragraph of Ipsum (`http://lipsum.com`) filler text.

```
<div class="row">
<div class="span4">
<h2>Header</h2>
<p>Loremipsum dolor sit amet, consecteturadipiscingelit...</p>
</div>
<div class="span4">
<h2>Header</h2>
<p>Loremipsum dolor sit amet, consecteturadipiscingelit...</p>
</div>
<div class="span4">
<h2>Header</h2>
<p>Loremipsum dolor sit amet, consecteturadipiscingelit......</p>
</div>
```

Open up your browser window or refresh it and see this nice layout in action. The newest row takes up three columns and collapses nicely into a single column, when you go to a mobile browser or windows with a smaller widths.

You could copy the entire `row` class element and inner HTML, and paste it to add a whole new row of content, and it will behave nicely.

Now that we have made a good looking page and it did not take any earth-shattering exertion, let us add another level to the page. This part is an excellent demonstration of the flexibility of the Bootstrap framework. Next, you are going to add a side navigation to the page.

In the second `container` class element, wrap the `hero-unit` and `row` elements in a new `div` element and assign that element a `span9` class. Next, insert before your new element another `div` element with the class `span3`. That should take care of the change in layout of the page; next we are going to rapidly build a menu inside it.

Add a new `div` element inside your `span3` div class, and give it the classes: `well` and `sidebar-nav`. These give the sidebar navigation a good-looking style. Now, onto the menu list, add an unordered list (`ul`) with the classes, `nav` and `nav-list`. You can add list section headers by assigning a class `nav-header` to a list item. Add in each of the list items, a `href` link for the navigation items:

```
<div class="well sidebar-nav">
    <ul class="navnav-list">
        <li class="nav-header">Navigation 1</li>
        <li><a href="#">Nav Link</a></li>
        <li><a href="#">Nav Link</a></li>
        <li><a href="#">Nav Link</a></li>
        <li class="nav-header">Navigation 2</li>
        <li><a href="#">Nav Link</a></li>
        <li><a href="#">Nav Link</a></li>
        <li><a href="#">Nav Link</a></li>
    </ul>
</div>
```

You're almost done; there are only a couple of more steps in this recipe. Wrap your two new `span*` elements in another `div` element with a `row` or `row-fluid` class. Finally, change the `row` div element class name that contains the teaser content's elements to `row-fluid`.

```
<div class="container">
        <div class="row">
          <div class="span3">
          <div class="well sidebar-nav">
            <ul class="navnav-list">
              <li class="nav-header">Navigation 1</li>
              <li><a href="#">Nav Link</a></li>
              <li><a href="#">Nav Link</a></li>
              <li><a href="#">Nav Link</a></li>
              <li class="nav-header">Navigation 2</li>
              <li><a href="#">Nav Link</a></li>
                  <li><a href="#">Nav Link</a></li>
                  <li><a href="#">Nav Link</a></li>
              </ul>
          </div>

        </div>
        <div class="span9">
        <div class="hero-unit">
  <h1>Hello World</h1>
      <p>Loremipsum dolor sit amet, consecteturadipiscingelit...</p>
        </div>
          <div class="row-fluid">
            <div class="span4">
              <h2>Header</h2>
              <p>Loremipsum dolor sit amet, consectetur adipiscing
  elit...</p>
```

```
            </div>
            <div class="span4">
              <h2>Header</h2>
              <p>Loremipsum dolor sit amet,
consecteturadipiscingelit...</p>
            </div>
          </div>
        </div>
      </div>

</div>
```

Congratulations, you are done! You now have a firm base to a professional-looking responsive layout and design. You could only make a few modifications to this and have a finished product. The following screenshot shows the base Bootstrap framework:

How it works...

Like magic! No really, the Bootstrap framework has to be one of the easiest and well thought-out frameworks I've worked with yet. Once you go through the recipe and their documentation to get familiar with the classes and layout, it's very easy to rapidly develop your projects.

There are some specific items I want to discuss. First the responsive menu; the top `div` element inside the `container` class is `button`, which is displayed only in the mobile version, and its purpose is, when clicked, to reveal the hidden menu `div` element, `nav-collapse`, in a mobile style.

This, by itself, gives you a great starter for a usable and very elegant responsive menu. However, you will find that the button does not work by itself, that's because we need to add some JavaScript to make this battle-station fully operational.

The responsive layout does heavy lifting behind the scenes for you also. Each row of the columns you create takes up the specified columns, but collapses nicely into a single column when you go to a mobile browser, or a window with small width.

There's more...

There is so much more you can do with this framework. There are rich elements, menus, UI functions, and animations galore included in the Bootstrap framework. Take some time and get a more in-depth understanding of the framework and you will be happy you did. After learning this I found that I could deploy new work much more quickly and with a much less frustrating process.

5
Making Mobile-first Web Applications

In this chapter, you will learn about:

- ▶ Using the Safari Developer Tools' User Agent switcher
- ▶ Masking your user agent in Chrome with a plugin
- ▶ Using browser resizing plugins
- ▶ Learning the viewport and its options
- ▶ Adding tags for jQuery Mobile
- ▶ Adding a second page in jQuery Mobile
- ▶ Making a list element in jQuery Mobile
- ▶ Adding a mobile native-looking button with jQuery Mobile
- ▶ Adding a mobile stylesheet for mobile browsers only using the media query
- ▶ Adding JavaScript for mobile browsers only

Introduction

In this chapter, we will focus our efforts on mobile-first Responsive Design. By this, we mean first designing your site for the mobile device, and then applying variation or even a wholly different look for the desktop. We'll cover a few recipes on jQuery Mobile, a free and open source library of mobile UI elements and widgets. In addition, we'll build some client-side scripting to handle a unique look only for mobile devices.

Using the Safari Developer Tools' User Agent switcher

For developing mobile-first applications, you will need to deploy them locally and test the various features you have developed. Many of the responsive web recipes we have worked on so far relied on media queries to determine layout based on size to deliver the optimized view of your site. This is not the only way in which apps can deliver mobile layout, there are more. One method is, by sniffing the **user agent**.

You may already know about the user agent, but let's assume you don't. Besides, knowing everything already simply defeats the purpose of buying the this course, now doesn't it? The user agent exists in the request header and identifies the client software making the request. It contains information about your processor, operating system version, browser, rendering engine, IP address, and other identifying information.

According to the needs of the project or the preference of the developer, some websites are designed to display different template files for mobile devices, or based on other details of the user agent data. This method requires a different server or client intelligence to read the user agent and interpret its data to deliver the presentation for that scenario.

So you've created a new web application, and the software displays the mobile template when the user agent details a mobile device. However, you want to be able to test it on the fly and not have to spin up a web server, so the next best thing is to use the user agent masking feature in Safari.

Using the Safari browser user agent switcher is a win-win, because not only does it mimic the user agent of the mobile Safari browser on iOS devices, but it also mimics the user agent of the Android browsers. So you can be at peace because the Android user agent was changed to say that it is also Mobile Safari, just to make your life easier. Wasn't that nice of them?

 It's a good practice to clearly specify in your scope of work which browsers and user agents you will be testing for.

Getting ready

On an Apple computer, it's already installed. You are ahead of the game. So hang on while the Windows people catch up.

It looks unlikely that Apple will continue developing Safari for Windows. In fact, when you search for `Safari Windows`, the first link is not to the Safari homepage, but to an Apple support page with a link to the last Safari for Windows version, Safari 5.1.7 for Windows, not to the latest version (Version 6). But for the point of the recipe, let us continue.

How to do it...

First, open the Safari browser; you will want to go to a website that works as a demonstration for reading the user agent. Go to `http://whatsmyuseragent.com`, and the page will show you details of your user agent.

In Safari, go to **Safari | Preferences**, or press *Command + ,*. In the **Advanced** tab, select the **Show Develop menu in menu bar** checkbox. You can see this illustrated in the following screenshot:

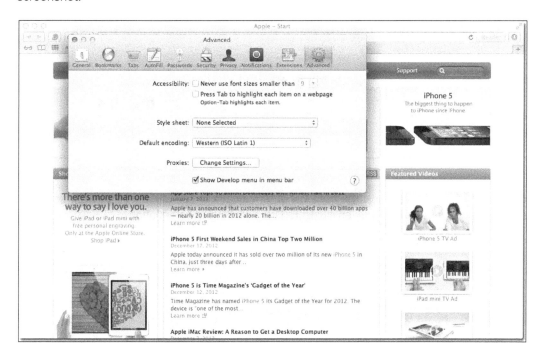

Now the menu bar shows the menu option **Develop**. Click on it and select **user agent**; a sub menu appears with different user agent options. There are a number of useful options here, but for this recipe, the most contextually useful ones are **Safari iOS 5.1 - iPhone** and **Safari iOS 5.1 - iPad** (it is very likely that you may have a version other than Version 5.1). This is demonstrated in the next screenshot:

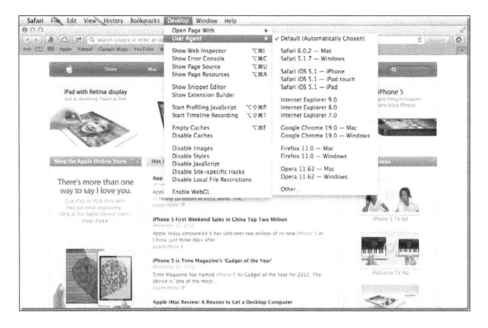

Select one of the iOS versions; the page will automatically be refreshed. You will now see the new user agent information, as illustrated in the following screenshot:

How it works...

I know it doesn't look like much happened, but what did happen was pretty big. The browser gave the server information about your computer and browser, and it served you a different web page as a result. You could build logic that delivers a special stylesheet, template, scripts, or completely different page content for mobile browsers.

Masking your user agent in Chrome with a plugin

The Chrome browser is rich with a multitude of plugins that you can use for just about any purpose under the sun. Let's explore a user-agent masking plugin to mask your user agent.

Why would you want to "mask" your user agent? Isn't that dishonest? Okay I'll admit it, it is. But here is one of the few cases where the ends genuinely justify the means. Besides, there's no harm done; it's not like the server figures out that your browser was lying to it and feels deceived and hurt. Masking your user agent gives you the power to convince the web server that your desktop browser is really a mobile browser. If the server believes you are using a mobile browser and its logic dictates that it should deliver a mobile version, then that's what you will get.

Getting ready

We want to find a way to be able to toggle between different user agents, and we want it to be really simple. In fact, we want it to be a button on the browser that we can press and switch. So where will we get this awesome bit of technological trickery? At the Chrome Web Store!

I've tried a few different Chrome browser plugins and have found one that has become a favorite in my responsive toolkit. The **User-Agent Switcher** for Chrome offers a snappy method to toggle between a comprehensive list of user agents. To get it, take the easier path and do a search for `Google UA Spoofer`.

How to do it...

The first search result should be a link to the User-Agent Switcher in the Chrome Web Store. If it is, go to it and click on the **ADD TO CHROME** button. That's all you need to do to install it. Using it will be easier.

Now look at the topmost section of your browser, to the right of the address bar, and find a new icon in the shape of a tiny mask. When you click on it, a menu of different browsers pops up, with submenus for available versions. We tested it, it is easy. See the following screenshot for proof:

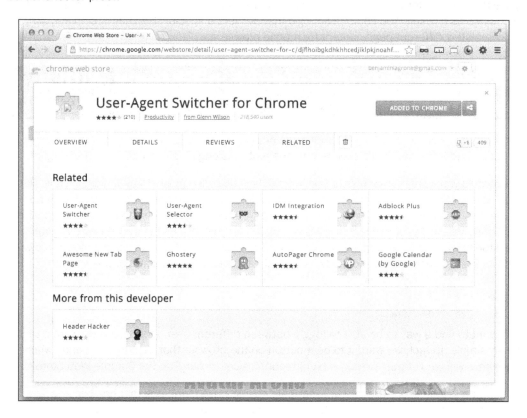

How it works...

The Chrome User Agent Spoofer browser plugin intercepts the normal browser user agent information in the request header and replaces it with the spoofed user agent information. So far, we've merely discussed how to test the user agent spoofer. How you will design your site to handle different user agents is a completely different subject.

To see it in action, go to `http://whatsmyuseragent.com/` and then toggle the browser plugin, from **iOS** to **iPhone**. You will see the user agent information change to **iPhone**. Try some more experiments and see how the masked user agent affects your favorite sites.

There's more...

Take a look at some of the various popular sites around the Web and you'll see how they handle different user agents. Some serve a different theme, while some redirect your browser to a subdomain for their mobile version. For example, `http://facebook.com` redirects to `http://m.facebook.com/?_rdr` for the iOS user agent, and `https://plus.google.com/` redirects to `https://plus.google.com/app/basic/stream` for a mobile version of their site.

The following screenshot shows how the masked user agent displays the page differently:

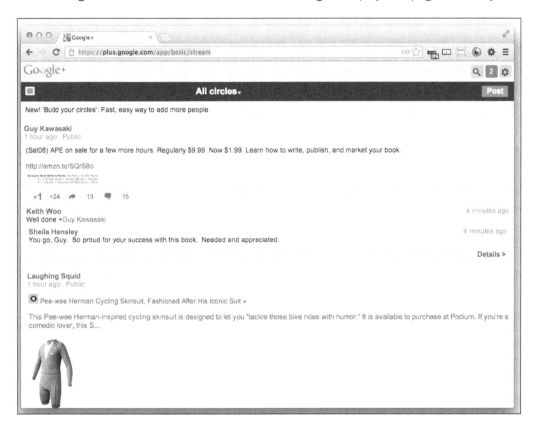

Using browser resizing plugins

I'll be frank with you; this recipe is about installing and using the browser resizing plugin that I use. If you have a better one, tell me about it. The one I have chosen after searching is called "Window Resizer".

Apart from testing on the target device, resizing the window with the plugin is the most accurate method of testing your media query. It is, however, only part of the testing you should put your responsive site through. Be sure to test it with emulators, and of course, actual devices, before deploying it. There's nothing worse than deploying a live site and watching it crash and burn after someone brings it to your attention.

Getting ready

Google is your friend. Search for `Window Resizer`. The first search result should be the Window Resizer plugin in the Chrome Web Store. There it is, like a beacon in the night! It has five stars, it's free; how could you not have clicked on that link already?

How to do it...

You will find yourself at the install page in the Chrome Web Store if you have gone along with me. You will see an attractive, wide, and calming deep blue button that says **+ ADD TO CHROME**. You are drawn to it and feel the need to click on it. You see in the blue, the sky at night that you look up to and wonder how far you will travel one day. You think about all the different sizes your browser could be. You think about the pain you feel while dragging the corners of your window, trying to guess its size. You can't take it anymore. Click on the button!

A flutter of movement across your browser window indicates that changes are being made. In the end, the blue button turns green. You are done here.

In your browser window, a new icon that looks like a tiny browser window has found its home on the right-hand side of your address field. Curiosity dictates that you need to know what this thing can do.

This is a virtually perfect way to test different media queries and responsive versions of your website, second only to testing it directly on the target device.

How it works...

Use the button to test your responsive designs to pixel-perfect precision. When you click on it, it unveils a list of different browser window sizes. Each one is perfectly measured and will bend your browser's size according to your will. The browser plugin does all of the guesswork and precise measuring for you, as it directly affects the browser window size at the click of a button! See the following screenshot:

Learning the viewport and its options

If nothing else, it can be said that the purpose of the viewport is to tame the mobile browser window. The viewport is vital to determining how your mobile browser renders the mobile web page.

Getting ready

If you are using an Apple computer, an iOS simulator can be obtained by downloading Xcode from Apple. It is part of the Xcode package. I usually get to it by using Spotlight. Press *Command* + the Space bar; the Spotlight search field appears in the top-right corner of your screen. Start typing in `iOS Simulator`, and it will appear in the search results. Click on it to spin up the iOS simulator.

How to do it...

Open up one of the responsive projects that you've done from a previous recipe project. I suggest opening up the `resp-width-layout-media-query.html` project from the *Creating a responsive width layout with media query* recipe.

To get an iOS simulator for Windows, you'll need to find one on the Web. After searching, I found a good one at `http://iphone4simulator.com/`, and another at `http://iphonetester.com/`. To use them, you'll need to upload your project files to a web host before this web simulator can view it. The simulator cannot read files from your local hard drive, unless you are running a local web server.

First, for comparison, view the file in your browser. Then in your iPhone simulator, enter the URL of the files, and you'll discover the shock and horror of seeing your site looking just like the desktop version. I experienced the same frustration when my early responsive projects did not work the way I wanted them to. The problem is that the mobile browser does not know what size you want it to be. It is smart but not clever. Like all software, it needs good instructions. So take a deep breath and we will fix it together. The problem is illustrated in the following screenshot:

You can tell the mobile browser what it should do by configuring the viewport. First add the simple viewport `<meta>` tag:

```
<meta name="viewport">
```

Before we go any further, I should tell you about this caveat. If you don't intend to do a design for the mobile device, then leave out the viewport `<meta>` tag. It can cause unintended consequences on your page delivery. In fact, it might just show a sliver of your page and not allow the viewer to pan out our scroll to view the whole page.

Now we will discuss its options. First, the width; I'm a big fan of the K.I.S.S. principle (keep it short and simple). Unless you have a reason for specifying a particular width, enter the device width as the viewport width. This way, it will read the device width and set that as the page width. Setting a specific width, `1000px` for example, will look okay on your iPad, but on your phone devices it will render too wide and nullify the media queries smaller than that width.

```
<meta name="viewport" content="width=device-width">
```

Once you've made the change, open your iOS simulator's browser and view the file. You can see the fixed version in the following screenshot:

Next, let's talk about scaling. Let's assume you have no special request to do anything weird, like starting the scale with any value other than one. Add to the viewport `<meta>` tag, the initial scale value of `1`.

Okay, I know I said don't do anything weird, but just for demonstration, change your initial scale to `2`. Refresh your screen.

Next, change it to `0.4`. Remember this is just for demonstration. Please refresh your screen again. In the portrait view, you can see that the web page uses the small screen media query. Now, change the orientation of the simulator to bring it to landscape mode. You will now see that the larger media query is active. That was an interesting experiment; now change your initial scale back to `1`.

Finally, do you want your viewers to be able to zoom in and out using the multi-touch pinch? Use the meta attribute `maximum-scale` to limit how much zooming you want to allow. Set the maximum scale to `1` if you want to disallow zooming.

```
maximum-scale=1
```

How it works...

The viewport `<meta>` tag was included in the Safari Mobile browser by Apple initially, and was then added to other browsers. It is used to define the width the page should be read in. When the browser sees the viewport `<meta>` tag with the width attribute defined, it loads the page at the scale defined in that width setting, coupled with the initial scale attribute.

Adding tags for jQuery Mobile

This recipe jumps deep into a new area of responsive design, that is, mobile-first. Mobile-first, in a nutshell, means that you would first design for a mobile version of the site and then make modifications for the desktop. Now, this does not mean that you are designing a "mobile only" website, only that designing your layouts and styles for mobile comes first.

Mobile-first may require rethinking your designs, or at least designing from a different perspective. But isn't change good? Can't we all improve our design skills by trying out new approaches? Isn't Darwinism merely the survival of those who are best suited to adapt to change?

So let's go ahead with an open mind and try some mobile-first development.

Getting ready

First, hop on over to the jQuery Mobile site. It is at `http://jquerymobile.com`. Otherwise, you can simply search for `jQuery Mobile` if you are lazy like me. I'll provide the direct link if you don't want to search for it and because you are my special buddy. The direct link to the site is `http://lmgtfy.com/?q=jquery+mobile&l=1`. I'll even shorten that for you; go to `http://bit.ly/TMpuB8`.

Here, you can download the library if you want to host your files locally (and there are some very good reasons to do that); for this recipe, however, we can do it the more expedient way and let someone else host all the necessary files.

The jQuery Mobile site has a veritable cornucopia of docs and samples. It even has download builders, so you can scale down the necessary libraries to just those that are needed to run your mobile web app.

How to do it...

First, create a new HTML document in your IDE. Add the viewport `<meta>` tag to your header:

```
<meta name="viewport" content="width=device-width, initial-scale=1">
```

Next, include links to the jQuery Mobile CSS and JavaScript files.

```
<link rel="stylesheet" href="http://code.jquery.com/mobile/1.2.0/
jquery.mobile-1.2.0.min.css" />
<script src="http://code.jquery.com/jquery-1.8.2.min.js"></script>
<script src="http://code.jquery.com/mobile/1.2.0/jquery.mobile-
1.2.0.min.js"></script>
```

It's worth it to pause for a pedagogical minute and talk about your stylesheets. In the previous piece of code, we are linking to a remote jQuery CSS. I would recommend you (if you are going to host this file locally) to leave it as is and add all of your new CSS for your elements in an entirely different stylesheet. Additionally, if you want to make any changes to jQuery's CSS, add another CSS file and make explicit namespaced overrides, or use the `!important` override. Name this something like `jQuery-mobile-changes.css`. I don't expect that you will need to do this, but just in case you do, this is a good way to handle it. I recommend this because when a new version of jQuery is released, you won't need to break your site when you upgrade.

That covers most of your header. Now let's create some basic content for the page. First, let's wrap the page with a `<div>` element:

```
<body>
    <div>

    </div>
</body>
```

One of the really great features of jQuery Mobile is that it uses tags, which you can put inside the HTML elements that are not used to render your page. The benefit is that you can use the same template for your desktop site just by swapping out the jQuery Mobile scripts and styles for your own. Next, add some tags to your wrapping `<div>` element that tell jQuery Mobile to act on this page. Add `data-role="page"` to the element.

```
<div data-role="page">
```

Let's demonstrate by building a sample text page.

Add a new `h1` header title wrapped in a `<div>` element. To the `<div>` element, add a `data-role="header"` attribute. Then, open the file in a browser to see the jQuery Mobile theme.

```
<div data-role="header">
    <h1>Adding tags for jQuery Mobile</h1>
</div>
```

That's a good start; let's continue by adding some more examples of page structure in jQuery Mobile.

 You can also give these elements IDs and classes for your desktop version.

Next, add a body. Add a paragraph of some filler text and then wrap the paragraph in a `<div>` element. Assign an HTML5 data attribute `data-role:"content"` to the `<div>` element.

```
<div data-role="content">
  <p>
     Lorem ipsum dolor sit amet, consectetuer adipiscing elit. Aenean
commodo ligula eget dolor. Aenean massa....
  </p>
</div>
```

Similarly, add a footer. Wrap a simple text in an `h4` tag, and wrap that in a `<div>` element. Now give that `<div>` element the attribute `data-role="footer"`:

```
<div data-role="footer">
  <h4>The Footer</h4>
</div>
```

That's all there is to it. The jQuery Mobile site has great documentation and examples on how to further build mobile sites using their framework. We will be going through more jQuery Mobile recipes in this chapter. Go check them out. This is how your page will look with jQuery Mobile:

How it works...

jQuery Mobile uses HTML5 data attributes to fire the scripts for markup and widgets. The script will automatically act when you place the data attribute in the element.

Adding a second page in jQuery Mobile

There is a really cool feature in jQuery Mobile that allows you to divide a bigger HTML page into smaller, digestible parts. Imagine you have a page that has a lot of content and you don't want to force your audience to keep scrolling down to read. Consider using jQuery Mobile's multipage template structure. The user experience of a web page on a mobile device is very different from that of the one on a desktop. On the old desktop Web, it was often said, "Content is king"; now that the Web is mobile, there is limited space, and it's easy for all that content to become too much content. You may want to consider limiting some of what is displayed on each page. In this recipe, we will use jQuery Mobile to divide a large page with lots of data into smaller digestible bits.

Getting ready

In the previous recipe, we built a simple page using jQuery Mobile tags. Let's dig up the file from that recipe and save it as a new file to work on. This will serve as a starting point for this recipe.

How to do it...

Add an ID of p1 to the outer, wrapping `<div>` element (with the page `data-role`). This will help jQuery identify and transition between the multipage elements.

```
<div data-role="page" id="p1">
```

You have created what jQuery Mobile will recognize as the first page among the multiple pages. Let's create the next one. Create new opening and closing `<div>` elements right before the closing `<body>` tag. Give this `<div>` element a `data-role="page"` element just like the previous instance, and an ID of p2.

```
<div data-role="page" id="p2">
```

This page will need `data-role="header"`, `data-role="content"`, and `data-role="footer"`, just like the previous `<div>` element `data-role="page"`. You can also simply copy the previous section and paste it into the "p2" `<div>` element.

```
<div data-role="page" id="p2">
  <div data-role="header">
    <h1>The second page</h1>
  </div>
  <div data-role="content">
    <p> Lorem ipsum dolor sit amet...</p>
  </div>
  <div data-role="footer">
    <h4>The Footer</h4>
  </div>
</div>
```

We are almost done; we only need to link the pages together. In the "p1" content, right before the closing `<div>` element, add an `href` anchor tag linking to "#p2":

```
<a href="#p2">Page 2</a>
```

In the "p2" `<div>` element, inside the `data-role="content"` `<div>` element, add another link, linking back to the first page ID:

```
<a href="#p1">Back to Page 1</a>
```

Now save the file and launch it. You'll see it create a nice and native-looking mobile website. Click on the **Page** links and you'll see that there is a smooth fade transition between the multipage pages. You will also notice that the back button works as well. If you think about it, this behavior is very useful for the native app look and feel of our website. See the first page in the next screenshot:

The second page is illustrated in the following screenshot:

How it works...

jQuery Mobile can load multiple pages within a single HTML page and present them as multiple pages or subpages. To link between them, simply add HREF="#page". When that link is clicked, jQuery Mobile will look for an internal page with that ID and smoothly write it to the viewport.

Making a list element in jQuery Mobile

Let me be the first to say this: I love unordered lists. Conversely, I have an equally intense aversion to "programmer art" tables. In fact, I've earned a reputation with the people I work with as a "destroyer of tables". There are very few sets of things in HTML that can't be displayed using a good list, which is why I adore the way in which jQuery Mobile handles lists. jQuery Mobile lists, in my opinion, prove why a list is the superior way to present data, menus, navigation, and so on. Enough of my abnormal obsession with unordered lists, let's go through a recipe about jQuery Mobile lists together.

Getting ready

Think about how many awful tables you have put out on the Internet and what terrible things all of that deadweight code has turned into. That's enough admonishment for the crimes of your past, let's move forward and make some jQuery Mobile lists!

How to do it...

Create a new page with the necessary header information that jQuery Mobile wants. Include the viewport <meta> tag and the links to the jQuery Mobile stylesheet, the jQuery JavaScript, and finally, the jQuery Mobile JavaScript. You can host these locally on your own server or use those hosted at http://code.jquery.com.

```
<meta name="viewport" content="width=device-width, initial-scale=1">
<link rel="stylesheet" href="http://code.jquery.com/mobile/1.3.0-
beta.1/jquery.mobile-1.3.0-beta.1.min.css" />
<script src="http://code.jquery.com/jquery-1.9.min.js"></script>
<script src="http://code.jquery.com/mobile/1.3.0-beta.1/jquery.mobile-
1.3.0-beta.1.min.js"></script>
```

Next create a <div> element with the data-role="page" attribute. This is an HTML5 attribute that jQuery Mobile uses to deploy style, elements, and widgets.

```
<div data-role="page"></div>
```

Inside that `<div>` wrap, create an unordered list of your favorite robots.

```
<ul>
  <li>Hero 1</li>
  <li>Bender</li>
  <li>Optimus Prime</li>
  <li>Soundwave</li>
  <li>Wall-E</li>
  <li>Maximillian</li>
  <li>R2-D2</li>
  <li>GORT</li>
  <li>Cat Quadcopter</li>
  <li>Robocop</li>
  <li>The Maschinenmensch</li>
</ul>
```

Let's not launch this right now. We both already know that this will look like a plain old list. If you were making a separate CSS for a desktop version, you could style this list there.

Add the attribute `data-role="listview"` to your unordered list. Now you can launch this and see that it looks like a styled list of robots.

Let's keep going. Because this is a list, and we love lists, we're going to just keep playing with it and see what jQuery Mobile can do with it. Add another attribute, `data-inset="true"`. Now your list has a cool wrap border around it so each item does not stretch to the edge of the screen.

Sometimes, you may end up with a really long list, like when you make a list of cool robots, because robots are cool, and you don't want to have to keep scrolling and scrolling to select your favorite robot. jQuery Mobile has a built-in solution for this, a filtering element. Invoke it by adding a new attribute, `data-filter="true"`. Refresh your mobile browser; you will see an input at the top to enter a `filtertext` element. The Search widget uses a client-side search/filter to filter out list items. No longer will you have to scroll down to find that awesome robot at the bottom of your list.

Let's take this to the next level. What if we want to be able to filter the robots by some other data that we don't want to display, such as the robot manufacturer? You can add the attribute `data-filtertext=""` to each list item. It would look something like this:

```
<li data-filtertext="Mom's Robots"><a href="#">Bender</a></li>
<li data-filtertext="Hasbro"><a href="#">Optimus Prime</a></li>
```

See the following figure for a demonstration:

This list can even be styled differently by assigning a theme in the data attribute. Try adding `data-theme="a"` to the unordered list. Now try using the letters `b` through `f`. Each one has a different theme that you can apply to the list.

Here is the unordered list with the different attributes we have used so far. The figure after the following piece of code shows the different themes in action.

```
<ul data-role="listview" data-inset="true" data-filter="true" data-theme="g">
```

Next let's see what happens when these list items become links. Add an `href` anchor tag to each item.

```
<li><a href="#">Bender</a></li>
```

When you refresh your screen, you will see how it adds the icon to indicate that it is a clickable link. However, since `href` links to #, it does not load a new page. See the following screenshot for the illustrated example:

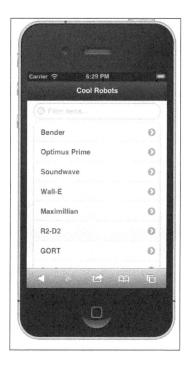

Let's break this list apart, into two groups, the "destroy all humans" group and the "workerbot" group. Add another list item for the first group to the top of the list, with the attribute `data-role="list-divider"`.

```
<li data-role="list-divider">destroy all humans</li>
```

Add another similar list item about halfway down the list.

```
<li data-role="list-divider">workerbot</li>
```

This is shown in the next screenshot:

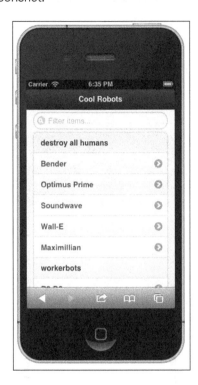

You might feel the need to organize your robots into these groups if it makes you feel good. We can take this impulse further and make the lists nested. Add a `ul` element to the `list-divider` that you just made, and then cut and paste the first half of the robots' `li` code into this `ul` element.

```
<li data-role="list-divider">destroy all humans
  <ul>
    <li><a href="#">Bender</a></li>
    <li><a href="#">Optimus Prime</a></li>
    <li><a href="#">Soundwave</a></li>
    <li><a href="#">Wall-E</a></li>
    <li><a href="#">Maximillian</a></li>
  </ul>
</li>
```

Do the same for the next list section. Then, refresh to see the new results. Check out the following figure:

You can add an `h3` header title wrap to the parent list items, and even a description wrapped in a paragraph element. These lists keep getting fancier and fancier.
See the following screenshot:

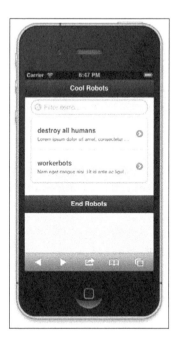

So let's do one final list feature and call it a recipe. This is a gorgeous widget for handling lists. You can make a list of collapsible list elements. We're going to change the ul and li list item attributes. First, make the outer ul list element contain the attributes data-role="collapsible-set", data-theme="b", and data-content-theme="d".

```
<ul data-role="collapsible-set" data-theme="b" data-content-theme="d">
```

Each of the two direct child li elements of that ul element should have the attribute data-role="collapsible".

```
<li data-role="collapsible"><h2>workerbots</h2><p>...<p>
```

Give the attributes data-role="listview" and data-filter="true" to the child ul element of that collapsible li list item.

```
<ul data-role="listview" data-filter="true">
```

The whole unordered list list will look like this:

```
<ul data-role="collapsible-set" data-theme="b" data-content-theme="d">
  <li data-role="collapsible">
    <h2>destroy all humans</h2>
    <p>Lorem ipsum dolor sit amet, consectetur adipiscing elit.
Integer consectetur quam in nulla malesuada congue volutpat mi
molestie. Quisque faucibus, nisi ut malesuada volutpat</p>
    <ul data-role="listview" data-filter="true">
      <li><a href="#">Bender</a></li>
      <li><a href="#">Optimus Prime</a></li>
      <li><a href="#">Soundwave</a></li>
      <li><a href="#">Wall-E</a></li>
      <li><a href="#">Maximillian</a></li>
    </ul>
  </li>
  <li data-role="collapsible" >
    <h3>workerbots</h3>
    <p>Nam eget congue nisi. Ut id ante ac ligula congue auctor a et
lacus. Suspendisse varius sem sed elit tincidunt convallis.</p>
    <ul data-role="listview" data-filter="true">
      <li><a href="#">R2-D2</a></li>
      <li><a href="#">GORT</a></li>
      <li><a href="#">Cat Quadcopter</a></li>
      <li><a href="#">Robocop</a></li>
      <li><a href="#">The Maschinenmensch</a></li>
    </ul>
  </li>
</ul>
```

The finished list has been depicted in the following figure:

How it works...

That was amazing. You did not have to do much apart from making a good list. No table could have pulled that off, ever. As long as you use the HTML5 data attributes in your elements, jQuery Mobile will do the heavy lifting and turn your list into a sleek, native-looking web app. jQuery Mobile takes the data attribute (which doesn't affect the layout or style), and from it, it rewrites the HTML and CSS for the mobile version.

Adding a mobile, native-looking button with jQuery Mobile

Let's make buttons! Making a button may seem like a very trivial part of the design, but contrarily, when you are building a web application, a button can be a very important part of the site's usability.

jQuery Mobile has an impressive array of button invocations, and they are all easy to use. They are usable within many other jQuery Mobile widgets as well. In addition, it is just as easy to make a button from a link as it is to make one from a `form input` element.

Getting ready

In your IDE or text editor, spin up a new HTML document and add the requisite header tags. First add the viewport `<meta>` tag, followed by links to the jQuery Mobile CSS and the JavaScript libraries jQuery and jQuery Mobile.

```
<meta name="viewport" content="width=device-width, initial-scale=1">
<link rel="stylesheet" href="http://code.jquery.com/mobile/1.2.0/
jquery.mobile-1.2.0.min.css" />
<script src="http://code.jquery.com/jquery-1.8.2.min.js"></script>
<script src="http://code.jquery.com/mobile/1.2.0/jquery.mobile-
1.2.0.min.js"></script>
```

In your HTML `<body>` tag, add a `<div>` element with the HTML5 attribute `data-role="page"`. Inside it, add an h1 header and wrap it with a `<div>` element with the `data-role="header"` attribute. Following the header element, add a `<div>` element with the `data-role="content"` attribute. See the following code snippet:

```
<div data-role="page">
  <div data-role="header"><h1>There be buttons</h1></div>
  <div data-role="content">...</div>
</div>
```

How to do it...

Let's compare some different methods to create a basic button. First, there is the HTML5 element `<button>`, various `<input>` form elements `button` and `submit`, and an `href` pseudo button. Put one of each inside your content `<div>` element.

```
<button>HTML5 Button</button>

<input type="button" value="Input Button" />

<input type="submit" value="Submit Button" />

<a href="#" data-role="button">Link button</a>
```

Launch your new page. You will see four new buttons that look identical (with the exception of the text). You can see that each of these methods is delivered the same way. This is impressive, as your non-mobile version of the template file may require you to use a certain type of `submit` element (which is not exactly mobile-first, but no one is perfect). See the following screenshot:

Let's continue with this recipe now by demonstrating how to add icons to the buttons using jQuery Mobile. This is a simple, one-step process; it uses an HTML5 data attribute, the `data-icon` attribute. In your first button, add the `data-icon="delete"` attribute; in the next one, add the `data-icon="check"` attribute; add `data-icon="plus"` to the next one; and finally, add `data-icon="arrow-l"` to the last button in this set of buttons. There is a list of icons that you can put in there; you can find them in the documentation.

```
<button data-icon="delete">HTML5 Button</button>

<input type="button" value="Input Button" data-icon="check" />

<input type="submit" value="Submit Button" data-icon="plus"/>

<a href="#" data-role="button" data-icon="arrow-l">Link button</a>
```

The following screenshot shows the new buttons:

You can also make a button smaller by adding the `data-mini="true"` attribute and position the icon at the right, left, top, or bottom corners of the button using the `data-iconpos` attribute. Otherwise, you can use the `data-iconpos="notext"` attribute to only show the icon. See the following screenshot:

The default behavior for these jQuery Mobile buttons is to stretch across the whole screen. You can change this by adding the attribute `data-inline="true"`.

```
<button data-icon="delete" data-mini="true" data-inline="true">HTML5
Button</button>

<input type="button" value="Input Button" data-icon="check" data-
iconpos="right" data-inline="true"/>

<input type="submit" value="Submit Button" data-icon="plus" data-
iconpos="top" data-inline="true"/>

<a href="#" data-role="button" data-icon="arrow-l" data-
iconpos="notext" data-inline="true">Link button</a>
```

It's messy, but you can see it in action here:

They will become inline elements, similar to the list items that are displayed as inline. We're almost done, but there's still some fun to be had. We can also make button groups easily. Remove the `data-inline="true"` attribute that you added in the previous section. Next, wrap the button elements with a `<div>` element, with the attribute `data-role="controlgroup"`.

```
<div data-role="controlgroup">

    <button data-icon="delete" data-mini="true" >HTML5 Button</button>
```

```
    <input type="button" value="Input Button" data-icon="check" data-
    iconpos="right"/>

    <input type="submit" value="Submit Button" data-icon="plus" data-
    iconpos="top" />

    <a href="#" data-role="button" data-icon="arrow-l" data-
    iconpos="notext" >Link button</a>

</div>
```

Now you can see the potential for creative button groups and keeping them together in a pretty package. Let's add some more effects to the button group. If you add `data-type="horizontal"` to the `"controlgroup"` `<div>` element, you'll make a mess that you'll need to clean up. One way to clean this up would be to change all of the `data-iconpos` attributes to `"notext"`.

Finally, as we have seen in the previous jQuery Mobile recipes, the `data-theme` attribute can make your buttons colorful. To quickly show this effect, add a different `data-theme` attribute (a, b, c, e) to each of the buttons (I skipped d, it looked too much like c). These are illustrated in the next screenshot:

How it works...

All you really need to know about how this works is which data tags to use to make jQuery Mobile pick up the HTML elements and turn them into mobile-native buttons. It happens auto-magically actually, when you have the correct attributes, and it works no matter what method of the `submit` button it is applied to. jQuery Mobile fires an event on the HTML5 attributes and adds the HTML and styles to the rendered page.

Adding a mobile stylesheet for mobile browsers only using the media query

In this recipe, we want to be able to use a stylesheet in the template only for use by mobile browsers. JavaScript aside, there is no way in client-side rendering to listen for the user agent and deliver some logic or special template for mobile browsers. Let's take the K.I.S.S. approach and get as close as we can with a media query.

Of course, there are numerous ways to write JavaScript to detect a user agent, and we will cover that in a later recipe, but for now let's write a killer media query to lock down the mobile browser for a specific CSS. In the previous recipes, our media queries were performed inside a stylesheet. This one will be different as we will put it inside the HTML header link. Change is good, do not worry. The reason we are putting the media query within the HTML link to the CSS file is that we want to call that CSS file only under special circumstances. This recipe is especially useful when you are using mobile-first design and technologies like jQuery Mobile.

Getting ready

Fire up your handy IDE and start a new HTML page. Be sure to add your viewport `<meta>` tag. If you like, you can add a paragraph of text in the HTML body.

How to do it...

In the `<body>` tag of your new HTML file, add two paragraphs of text. Each with a different class (`class="a"` and `class="b"`). This will be enough HTML to demonstrate the media query at work.

```
<p class="a">Lorem ipsum dolor sit amet, consectetur adipiscing
elit.</p>
<p class="b">Nulla ante tortor, rutrum eu sollicitudin eget, vehicula
quis sem. Nullam cursus placerat luctus.</p>
```

Now back to the `<head>` tag. First, let's add the viewport `<meta>` tag. Include the content attribute `"width=device-width"`. Next, add some simple style for the font (`font-size: 100%`).

```
<style>
  html{font-size:100%}
</style>
```

Next we're going to add the link to the mobile CSS stylesheet with a media query. The basic stylesheet link contains `rel="stylesheet"` and the path. Add to it the conditions it needs to satisfy to use that stylesheet. Add a media query for `screen` and `max-device-width=320px`. Your CSS link should look like this:

```
<link rel="stylesheet" media="screen and (max-device-width:320px)"
href="mobile.css" />
```

There's nothing more for us to do in the HTML file, so create a CSS file in the same directory and name it `mobile.css`. Open it to edit it. We don't need to do much here, only one line is sufficient. Add a line for the `b` class paragraph and give it an attribute of `2rem` for the font size. REM means Relative EM, or relative to the root font size (in case you skipped the responsive typography recipes).

```
p.b{font-size:2rem}
```

Now let's try it out. Open your HTML file in a browser, and then open it in your mobile device simulator. Here, you can see the mobile device has a unique presentation with a different font size for the `b` class paragraph. See this recipe illustrated in the following screenshot:

How it works...

The media query is designed to become active only on devices that have a screen resolution of 320px or lesser. Anything greater than that ignores (it still does get downloaded) the CSS file linked. You could additionally write media queries for other specific devices as well.

Adding JavaScript for mobile browsers only

In the previous recipe, we wrote a media query inside a stylesheet link. This was useful for our own mobile-first responsive web development. However, when using JavaScript code specifically for mobile platforms, such as jQuery Mobile, you might not want to have them initiated on desktop computers. Let's build a tiny JavaScript code that detects the mobile device screen size and then deploys jQuery Mobile for it but not for the desktop.

Getting ready

Mobile-first technologies like jQuery Mobile are amazing tools when you have a server-side technology. They do need server-side logic to work the best. If you are not fortunate enough to have access to server-side logic, you can employ some client-side tricks to work your magic.

How to do it...

If you have not looked through the jQuery Mobile recipes, take a look now; we're going to reuse one of the recipes that we have used already.

Open up one of the files that you created in the previous recipe using jQuery Mobile. You can use the *Adding a mobile, native-looking button with jQuery Mobile* recipe. If you worked through this recipe on making a mobile, native-looking button, use it to follow along.

When we last saw this file, the jQuery Mobile script took your plain old boring HTML buttons and turned them into cool jQuery Mobile buttons. All you needed was to include the HTML5 data attributes in your elements, and jQuery Mobile did the rest auto-magically. So what if you only want this to happen on a mobile device?

Well, you would be in trouble if it weren't for the magic of client-side scripting. We first want the script to be aware that it is dealing with a mobile device. One way is by querying the user agent of the DOM element. I've seen a few people do that, but it's complicated enough to be bug-prone. So instead, let's detect the size of the device screen. Most mobile viewports are at most 600 pixels wide or smaller; so for now, you are safe if you are developing applications assuming that that is the correct maximum size.

So let's make the script get the screen width from the DOM; if it's smaller than 600px, go get jQuery Mobile script. First, using jQuery, fire a function when the document loads.

```
$(document).ready(function(){
  //
});
```

Inside the function, write a conditional statement; if the screen is smaller than 600, then do something.

```
$(document).ready(function(){
  if (window.screen.width < 600){
    //Do something!
  };
});
```

That's a good start, but let's be more specific about "doing something". What we want the script to do is fetch and run the jQuery Mobile script. A good method for that is jQuery's `$.getScript()` function. So put that in the `if` condition, including the jQuery Mobile source URL.

```
$(document).ready(function(){
  if (window.screen.width < 600){
    $.getScript("http://code.jquery.com/mobile/1.2.0/jquery.mobile-1.2.0.min.js");
  };
});
```

Now load the page in your mobile device emulator.

How it works...

If the emulator successfully spoofs the device width in the request, you will see the jQuery Mobile version of the HTML page. In your desktop browser, no matter what size your browser window is, you will not be able to load the jQuery Mobile script.

jQuery's `$.getScript()` is a function that loads an external script into the header. You can use it like we did in the recipe, to conditionally load an external JavaScript and additionally execute functions on its successful loading.

6
Optimizing Responsive Content

In this chapter, you will learn about:

- ▸ Responsive testing using IE's Developer Tools
- ▸ Browser testing – using plugins
- ▸ Development environments – getting a free IDE
- ▸ Virtualization – downloading VirtualBox
- ▸ Getting a browser resizer for Chrome

Introduction

The recipes in this chapter cover a broad range of topics. There is no code covered in this chapter, but the recipes fall under a more functional umbrella. This chapter talks more about the tools you will use to develop and test code. Here we will make sure that our code works the way we want it to. While this topic may seem uninteresting, it is as important as honing your skills in design and development. No amount of confident boasting makes a frontend developer immune to errors, and there are simply too many things that can go wrong as a project grows. Please go through these recipes and try out the tools, they will make your work easier and less prone to errors down the line.

Responsive testing using IE's Developer Tools

Having a responsive design also includes having an optimized design for all of the prolific browsers, which is without equivocation, the least exciting aspect of Responsive Design. There is no way to sugarcoat this, many features of HTML5 and CSS3 are not supported even in the future versions of Internet Explorer, and those that are supported can sometimes be rendered incorrectly. To add more madness, Versions 7, 8, and 9 all behave differently, and there are countless users who just cannot or will not update their browsers. There's also the problem of a number of companies having invested in web software that only runs on older versions of Internet Explorer. This lack of updating has been solved by other browsers such as Chrome and Firefox; the Internet Explorer team really needs to catch up. However, because you want your work to always look good no matter what browser it's in, the responsibility is yours to make it work for every browser.

Getting ready

Talk to your clients and fellow designers on the project about what levels of support you want to provide for Internet Explorer users. There are a few strategies possible for supporting the older versions of Internet Explorer. Talk about how much additional work each will require to support older versions of Internet Explorer, how much it should cost, and who should pay for it. The last thing you want is to launch your clients' brand new web project and them starting to complain that it looks broken in their favorite, degraded old browser.

The first question to ask is: what can you do with Internet Explorer F12 Developer Tools? The answer is, you can use it to debug the rather wonkish way in which Internet Explorer is displaying your code, and to toggle between the different versions of Internet Explorer to see how your site looks in each.

How to do it...

If you don't use a Windows computer, you won't be able to natively get a hold of Internet Explorer F12 Developer Tools. That doesn't mean that you simply forget about testing for IE and hope what you do works. There are legions of web pages and plugins that promise to accurately emulate the quirks of IE's multitude of versions. I have tried many and found that there was not one that actually stood up to testing against the original IE Developer Tools. So after much trial and failure, I found that the only dependable way to test for IE, without having to go and buy several computers just for testing, was to use virtualization. I have a few instances of Windows on virtual machines, with different versions of Internet Explorer installed. I have found that it's the only way to be sure. If you want to learn how to get started with virtualization, see the *Virtualization – Downloading VirtualBox* recipe in this chapter.

So once we have started up our Windows machine and updated to the latest version of Internet Explorer, let us see what the F12 Developer Tools can do for us. Either press *F12* on your keyboard or click on the gear icon on the toolbar at the top-right corner of the screen to display the F12 Developer Tools. This is demonstrated in the following screenshot:

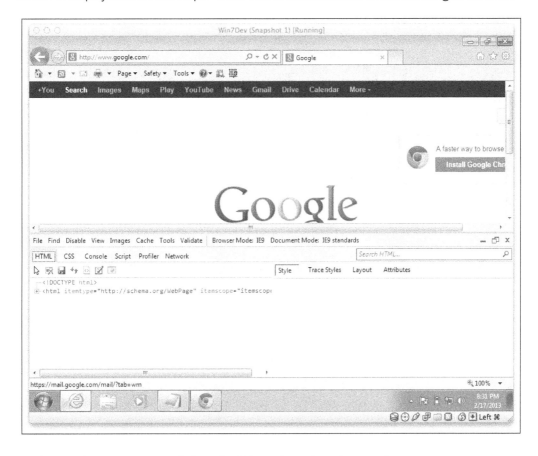

The first useful thing you can do here is click on the pointer icon and move your mouse over the browser window to the element that is misbehaving. While the mouse is traveling, you will see that the element your mouse is moving over gets a white border around it. Once you see the white border around the element you want to inspect, click on it; the HTML pane will then bring that line of HTML code into focus in the left-hand side window, and its CSS on the right. In the CSS pane, you can edit the tree of CSS attributes for each element.

If you want to add a CSS attribute, click on the **Attributes** button. By scrolling down to the bottom of the page, you can add a new name and value pair for the attributes. You can use these two tools to test out different CSS attribute variations or debug some strange IE behavior.

The other useful tool is the **Browser Mode** select menu. You can use this tool to toggle between the different browser versions. This is a good tool to do on-the-fly checking of your work. Here, you can also test out your IE-specific stylesheets. You can see this in following screenshot:

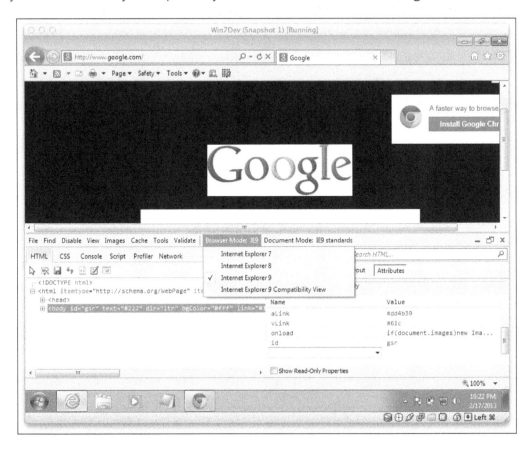

How it works...

According to MSDN, the F12 Developer Tools represents the actual way in which the Document Object Model (DOM) interprets the page, and not the code you actually wrote.

There's more...

An additional pitfall you may fall into occurs when you are designing a site that may be accessed as internal software or on the same domain as the intranet. Internet Explorer will use Internet Explorer 7 Compatibility View as the default rendering view.

Compatibility mode was a feature added in IE 8 so that websites that were developed for the older standards could still work in the new browsers. Often, people's browsers are set to render intranet sites in compatibility mode. To make a site that is built for IE 7 work in the most recent Internet Explorer, you would have to set this `<meta>` tag to render it at the desired rendering version. To force the browser to always render this using the most recent rendering engine, you'll need to specify the following `<meta>` tag to prevent this.

```
<meta http-equiv="X-UA-Compatible" content="IE=edge,chrome=1">
```

Browser testing – using plugins

Testing is a big deal in any and all development processes. For some, the idea of testing is incorrectly perceived as a sign of poor workmanship or criticality of their work. This idea could not be more wrong. On the contrary, rigorous and thorough testing is the only way to ensure that your software approaches a state of perfection. I consider myself very fortunate to work with QA testers whose role is to test the work of the development team. Having had to do all of my own testing (in a previous life), I can say that this is a luxury.

In this recipe, we will discuss a specific area of testing, cross-browser testing. Not too long ago, this was less complicated, and more challenging at the same time. The idea of testing a web project for mobile devices was not very common; it was simply not expected to look remotely similar, or even display the same content. Therefore the number of devices you needed to test for were usually limited to what you could spin up in a virtual environment, and they were all desktop devices. The tools were also limited, and were often only virtual desktops with older browser versions. Remember those stubborn people who refused to move beyond IE6?

One approach to browser testing is to simply get your credit card out and buy every device you think it would be plausible for your software to be viewed on. I have never actually met anyone who has done this, but I think one or two of the fairy tales I read to my children spoke of this sort of phenomenon happening. This is not a practical solution for people who work for money. This has resulted in a market of paid and free cross-browser testing tools popping up on the Internet.

Getting ready

If you were starting to think that this is going to be an expensive recipe, calm down. There will be no need to go out and buy every new mobile device on the market. There are plenty of emulators that will cover most of your bases.

How to do it...

I have scoured the Internet and built a list of free tools for you to use for testing. Go through the list with me and check them out. Open one of your previous responsive web design (RWD) recipe project files in a browser tab to continue. For each of the simulators, you will have to open the file by entering it into the simulated browser's address bar. If you have not done any of these or simply do not have the files handy, go to the Packt website and download them. On to the simulators.

First let's look at online browser simulators. Go to `http://theleggett.com/tools/webapptester`. Here you can test you RWD site on a web simulation of iOS devices. It can read your localhost files. You can toggle between the portrait and landscape modes and choose iPhone versus iPad. It's simple enough and you don't need to install any complicated applications or plugins. This is good if you need something in a pinch, want to test fast, and don't want to install anything. You can see the simulator in action in the following screenshot:

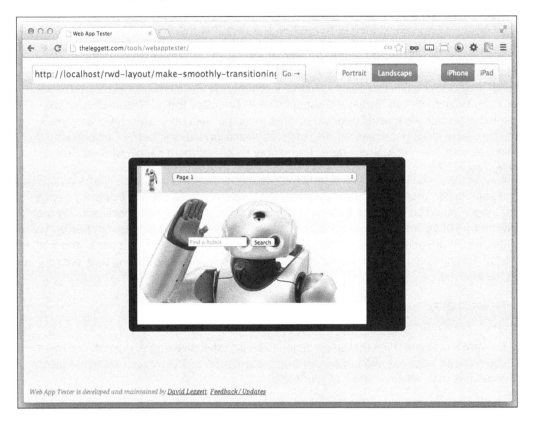

There is another handy web-based iOS simulator at `http://ipadpeek.com`. You can get the portrait versus landscape and iPad versus iPhone (including iPhone 5) options here as well. This one too can view your localhost server. I keep mentioning this because there are too many web-based emulators that did not make it to this list for that reason, including some commercial emulators. The next screenshot displays this web-based emulator:

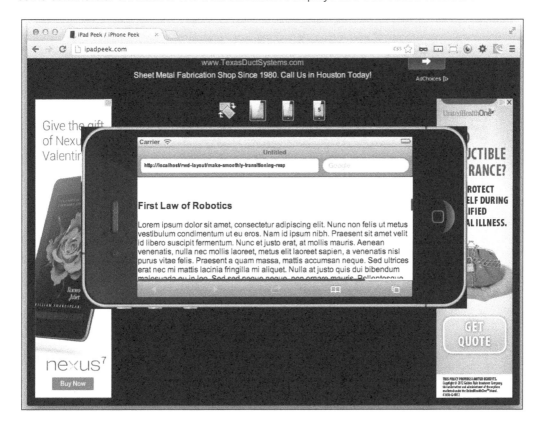

Next let's look at some application-based browser testing tools.

The Ripple browser plugin is an excellent testing tool. It can be downloaded at `https://chrome.google.com/webstore/detail/ripple-emulator-beta`. This emulator blows the others out of the water. First, it does the same job as the others (that is, emulating the iOS devices), but it does it well. This one does so much more than what you need, but it will do everything you need for testing for the future mobile integration of your web apps. Let us get started by finding and installing the Ripple browser plugin. That's an easy task. Just go search for it. Remember when things used to be hard?

Once you get to the Google Chrome Web Store, click on the big blue button and install the browser plugin. See the following screenshot:

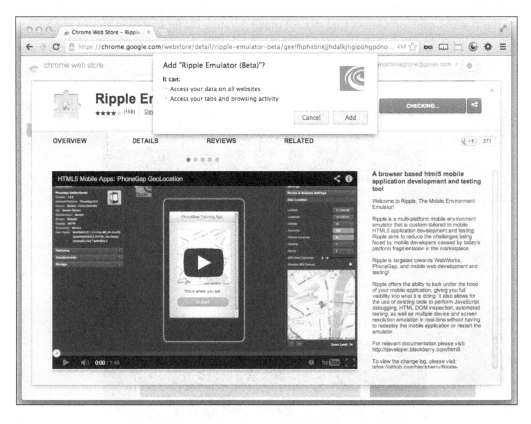

Once it is installed, you will see a new browser button with blue ripples appearing next to the address bar of your Chrome browser. In your browser, go to your responsive web app. Next, click on the **Ripple plugin** button, and then click on **Enable** when a menu pops up asking whether you want to enable the Ripple plugin. The contents of the browser window transform to display an emulation of the device, which displays the mobile version of your page. In addition, you will notice a number of toolbars full of amazing settings and tools. Let's explore some of these. Most of them are beyond the scope of what we are doing, but you should still take note of these. These come in handy as you develop more advanced mobile web apps. You can see the numerous settings for Ripple in the next screenshot:

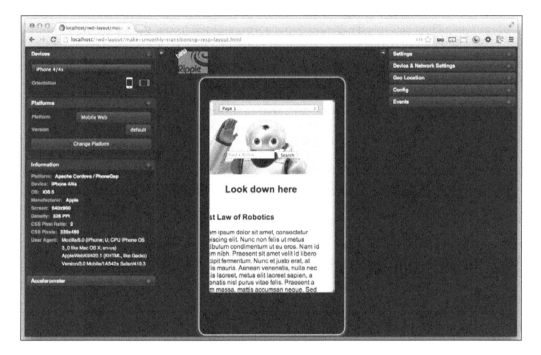

First, click on the menu at the top-left corner of the screen to reveal a number of different mobile devices. Under that, you can select either the landscape or portrait orientation. As you go through the different simulated devices, you will see that there is an information panel that gets updated with the technical specs of the current simulated device. When you are done testing, simply click on the Ripple button again and select the **Disable** option.

There are a number of other awesome tools in this simulator that are outside the scope of this module. Spend some more time on your own to discover useful tools to use for future mobile web app projects. Now let's move on to the next browser testing tool.

The Opera Mobile Emulator is located at `http://www.opera.com/developer/tools/mobile`. When I first saw this, I nearly skipped it, because it's Opera. Even though it's a serious browser project, I had gotten used to ignoring it for testing. It really is a respectable browser for mobile devices. I'm happy that I tried it out anyway. I was surprised to find that it has a number of options, and you really could use it to simulate a number of devices. It turns out to be a good mobile device browser testing tool to test a project on multiple Android devices. That's an important statement; note that I said Android devices, it means that it only tests those devices. It does, however, allow you to create and save custom screen sizes and settings. Let's jump straight to installing it and setting some custom screen sizes.

To find it, use your favorite search engine and type in `Opera Mobile Emulator`. This should lead you to a page to download the Opera Mobile Emulator specific to your operating system (`http://www.opera.com/developer/tools/mobile/`). Once you have downloaded and installed it, launch the application.

When the application loads, you can see that there are a number of defined devices you can choose from on the left-hand side of the screen. Select any one of those devices and then click on the **Launch** button. See the following screenshot for demonstration:

We can also create custom device profiles and save them. Since there are no iPhone device settings, we will setup a custom screen for the iPhone. Select **Custom** from the **Profile** list. Next, in the **Resolution** drop-down menu, select a resolution of 320 x 480. Then under the **Pixel Density** drop-down menu, click on **Add**, and add 326. Now click on **Launch**. You can also click on the **Save** or **Save As...** buttons to save your profile. The dimensions for iPhone 4 are 640 x 960, and 640 x 1136 for iPhone 5. This is displayed in the following screenshot:

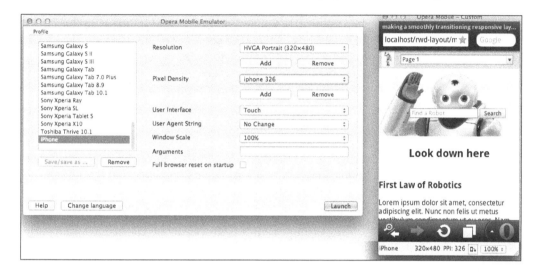

One important feature of the Opera Mobile browser for your desktop is that you can use it to debug your code! To use this tool, download and install Opera for desktop devices; go to www. opera.com. Next, open it and then under **Menu**, go to **Tools | Advanced | Opera Dragonfly**. In Opera Dragonfly, in the right-hand side window, find and click on the **Remote debug configuration** button, and then click on **Apply**. Then in your mobile browser emulator, in the address bar, enter opera:debug and click on **Connect**. Now you can debug your mobile code.

Development environments – getting a free IDE

Throughout this module, I've often referred to developing code in an IDE, or integrated development environment. The IDE is the toolset of the developer to create and manage code. There are many out there, free and paid, which you can use to help produce good code. Which IDE should you choose? That depends on a number of factors. Cost would be an important factor; Visual Studio can cost hundreds of dollars, and even more for additional auto-suggest plugins. The expensive IDEs are great as long as someone else is paying for them!

Getting ready

For this recipe, let us take the easier, cheaper route and install a good, free IDE. I spent some years working as a scientist, and because nine out of ten scientists prefer NetBeans, you might hypothesize that I use NetBeans. I can tell you that your hypothesis is empirically correct with a 90 percent probability.

You might think that an enhanced notepad is a sufficient tool to build your applications. This may be the truth; your notepad is sufficient to write some code. But using a development environment brings much more than just a big program to write your code in. There are features such as enhanced project organization, autosuggest, and community-developed plugins for nearly every type of project or special function imaginable.

How to do it...

To get NetBeans, you can go straight to the NetBeans site at `www.netbeans.org` and click on the big orange **Download** button. The next page has a grid of options for the NetBeans download; you can either select the PHP option, or the "All" option to get the IDE package you need for frontend development. But before you download anything, there is another piece to the puzzle. NetBeans runs on Java, and both OSX and Windows do not come with Java preloaded. See the following screenshot:

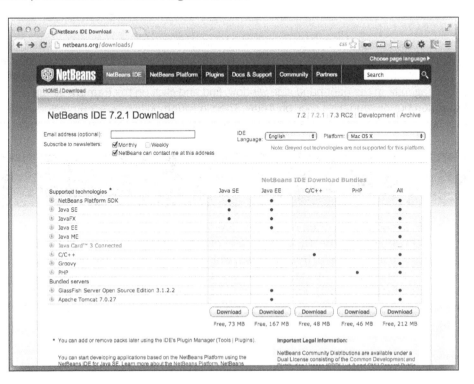

If you already have Java Development Kit installed, continue with the download and install process. If not, go to the Java JDK site instead at `http://www.oracle.com/technetwork/java/javase/downloads/index.html` (if that URL does not work, just search for Java JDK, and then click on the **Downloads** link). Here you can download a package of the latest stable NetBeans release with JDK. It's a large file, so start the download and go get some coffee.

Expand the downloaded package; the install process will take care of the installation of the IDE and JDK.

Next, open NetBeans. You should see the file and project browser on the left-hand side pane of the IDE. If not, and you are unable to open any of your projects, then it does not have the Web Development plugins activated. Open the **Tools** menu and select **Plugins**. In **Available Plugins**, find the PHP plugin and activate it. Your IDE will ask to restart. After restarting, you will see the **Projects** and **File** panes on the left-hand side in the IDE. This is displayed in the following screenshot:

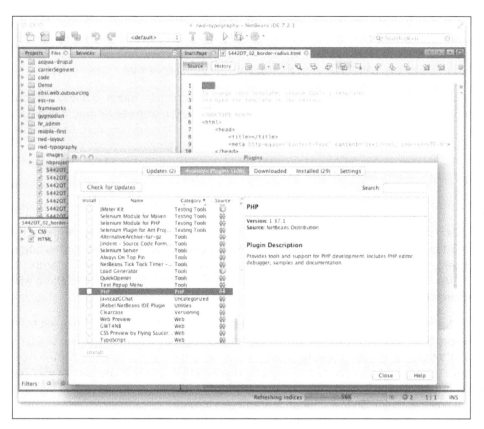

How it works...

The NetBeans Integrated Development Environment is built in Java and therefore needs JDK to run. It comes as a base IDE; you download and install the plugins you need for your specific project. Additionally, because it is open source, people can develop more cool and useful plugins. There are testing, autosuggest, language, and other plugins continuously being developed. So try to be brave and experiment with some to see whether they enhance your development work.

Virtualization – downloading VirtualBox

Virtualization is one of the keystone tools in the developer's toolbox. It is used in a number of different phases of the development process. Our focus for this recipe will be on testing. But first, I want to mention how it can be used further upstream in the process. Setting up virtual machines allows you to use your preferred operating system and toolset in a shop that only provides and supports different ones. For example, if you need to be able to use Visual Studio but don't want to use Windows, you can spin up a virtual machine and develop applications on it. You can also use a LAMP stack on a virtual machine and spin it up.

Virtualization is a resource-intensive computing task. It won't take much to bog down your system when you are running a virtual machine with an IDE, a web server, and a remote desktop viewer, and it might just drag your system down to a screeching halt. So my advice is to load up on memory before you try to load up multiple VMs.

Getting ready

Before we go on to the simple task of spinning up a new VM, let us explore some of the rationale behind what we are about to embark on. The first reason is, Internet Explorer. Do I need to say anything else? I will anyway, for the uninitiated. There is an earth-shattering collective groan whenever a designer has to make his beautiful modern website terrible for it to work in any version of Internet Explorer. It isn't enough that it looks good in IE9; we will also be required to make it look presentable in IE8.

Why is this the reality of web development? Because people are slow when it comes to upgrading; businesses are even worse in this matter. To get a picture of the ratio of your site's visitors that are using deprecated browsers, install Google Analytics and monitor the types of browsers used to visit your page. You might be horrified to find that 20 percent of your traffic is using Internet Explorer 7, and you need to market to them. You cannot run IE7 along with IE9 on the same computer. So the solution is starting to visualize its problem.

To be able to test your site to make sure it's optimized, or at least, degrades well for every old version of Internet Explorer, or is responsive for mobile devices, you can employ virtualization. Spin up a new virtual machine for each different browser version that you need to test for. For the rest of this recipe, we will go through the process of creating new virtual machines.

How to do it...

VirtualBox is a free software made available by Oracle. There are other virtualization software out there, such as VMware, which are not free. To download VirtualBox, go to www.VirtualBox.org and download it from the **Downloads** page.

Once downloaded, the install process is as straightforward as anything else. In OS X, unpack it and drag it into the Applications folder. In Windows, it gives different options. I would not try anything tricky at this point; it will work great with the default options. Both versions will set up directories for the virtual machines in your profile's home directory.

Next, you will need the operating system install disk or disk image (ISO) for the guest operating system you want installed on the virtual machine. When you are ready and have your OS installation software ready at hand, click on the **New** button at the top-left corner of **Oracle VM VirtualBox Manager**. This will start up a wizard called **New Virtual Machine Wizard**. See the following screenshot:

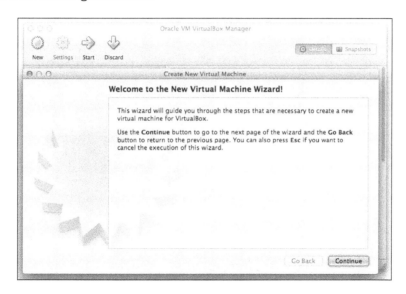

You will be asked to enter a name and OS type on the next screen. Next, select the memory to allocate for the VM. The recommended base memory size is 192 MB. The next screen asks you to either create a new disk or use an existing disk. When installing a new OS from a disk or image, you will want to select **Create new hard disk**. On the next screen, use the already selected default, **VDI** (VirtualBox Disk Image), and then select **Dynamically Allocated**.

You will then be asked to name the folder that holds the virtual image, and also the size of the virtual disk; the default is 10 GB. The summary pages follow, where you can review your choices before you proceed. Thus far, we have only created the virtual machine, the equivalent of turning on a new computer with no operating system.

To finish what we have started, we need to start up your new virtual machine and install Windows on it. Select your new virtual machine and start it to initiate the **First Run Wizard**. It will prompt you for the installation media; here you select your disk or image ISO. Select your installation media, continue to the **Summary** page, and then on to the OS installation process. This goes pretty fast since it is a virtual drive. I'll skip the ins and outs of installing your Windows Desktop Operating System software; there are no secret best practices here, just click through the defaults and keep going.

While I was writing that paragraph, my VM finished installing the OS. I told you it was fast. Once it starts up, you can use the default browser version or get an updated version. This depends on the needs of your project. I recommend having a separate VM for IE9, IE8, and even IE7. Once you get it running, you should have a good, clean, working version of Windows XP. See the following screenshot:

Now that the virtual machine has its OS installed, fire up the browser and point it to the IP address of your host computer. If you have your local web server running, and have not monkeyed around with your VirtualBox network settings, you should see the files on your local web server.

You can use this to test your web design to make sure the desktop version works well for all of your desktop audience, even those using IE7.

You don't need to host multiple versions of Chrome or Firefox anymore, they have all started auto-updating. The old Firefox version is a thing of the past.

That covers testing for desktop. Before we move on to the next chapter, let us take a look at how we can use VirtualBox to test for mobile devices as well.

There exist out there on the Internet, downloadable virtual machines that already have Android installed. I found a few downloadable resources at `http://www.android-x86.org/download`. By doing a search for `Android-v4.7z`, I found a good download link here: `http://www.vmlite.com/index.php?option=com_kunena&func=view&catid=9&id=8838`. It offers you a link to download it from `http://www.vmlite.com/vmlite/VMLite-Android-v4.0.4.7z`. Download and extract the virtual image to your hard drive.

Let us see what happens when we open up one of these Android images with VirtualBox. After you have downloaded an Android image, spin up a new virtual image. When asked to select the OS type, choose **Linux** from the list of operating systems in the drop-down list and choose **Other Linux** for **Version**. See the following screenshot for demonstration:

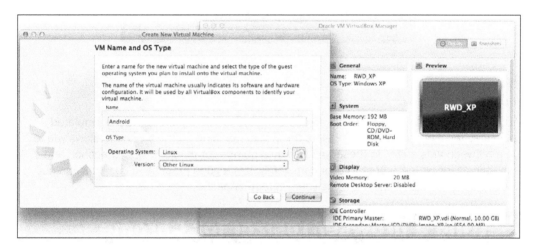

On the **Virtual Hard Disk** screen, select **Use existing hard disk**, and then in the select dialog box, browse to the folder you extracted to your drive. Inside it is a `*.vmdk` file. Select it to load it into your new virtual machine, and click on **Continue**.

Continue beyond the **Summary** page, and your Android emulator will spin up and be fully operational. Now you can test your apps on a true Android emulation as shown in the next screenshot:

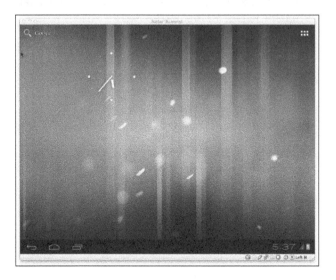

How it works...

Virtual machines allow you to install an operating system on a generic type of emulated computer. You can copy, edit, and delete the virtual machine on the fly, and it allows you to jump between VMs easily. In these, you can do a number of things; take a snapshot, and if something goes wrong, just start over completely. It is a good practice to use VMs and not need to worry too much about getting your OS to run Apache.

Getting a browser resizer for Chrome

Imagine yourself dragging your browser window's bottom corner left and right to resize it over and over again, watching for the points where your best visual estimation tells you it should be hitting the breakpoint of your media query and eloquently respond by showing a new optimized display of your website. The far from small problem that you have is you have no idea where your breakpoints will hit because you have no real clue of your current browser size, and no reliable way to set it to its desired size. Looks silly doesn't it? The co-worker sitting behind you thinks so too.

There has to be a better way. There is! Now you can stop your co-worker from laughing at your browser window antics.

Getting ready

There are some websites out there in Internet-land that can resize your browsers to the most popular breakpoints. However, these are difficult to find and are not reliable. I have found that the best option is to install a good browser resizer plugin.

How to do it...

The best solution I have found is the Chrome Window Resizer plugin. To get it for Chrome, search for `Window Resizer` in your favorite search engine and click on the link to go to the plugin's page at the Chrome Web Store. Click on the big blue button that says **Add to Chrome**.

It's a fairly brief and easy installation. Go through the process and say yes every time you are prompted. See the resizer in action in the following screenshot:

Once you are done, you will see the world's tiniest browser perched next to the address bar of the Chrome browser; no, just kidding, it's an icon. When you click on it, you will see a drop-down menu of different window sizes. These sizes were chosen as they are the most common size screens found in the wild of Internet-land.

If you have an analytics tool such as Google Analytics installed in your web project, you can get a good picture of what your viewers are like. With respect to this recipe, you would want to look at the browser screen sizes. Navigate to the **Audience** tab and expand the **Technology** toggle element to expose the **Browser & OS** link. You will see the breakdown of your audience's browsers. On that page, change the **Primary Dimension:** to **Screen Resolution**. Now you will be able to see the most common screen sizes of your site's visitors. This tool should give you an insight into areas to concentrate on in your design. See the following screenshot:

 Analytics will provide some good intelligence about your user's screens, but remember that people often use only part of their screen for the browser window.

Back to the browser resizer plugin; try out some of the built-in sizes on your project and see how it responds. This tool will be a great testing tool in your Responsive Design toolbox.

In addition to the set sizes, you will see that the drop-down menu also has an **Edit resolutions** menu item. Here you can add any screen sizes that you discover on your analytics screen. Based on my analytics report, I might want to start by adding `1920 x 1080`, `960 x 1080`, `1772 x 1038`, and `886 x 1038`. I have demonstrated this option in the next screenshot:

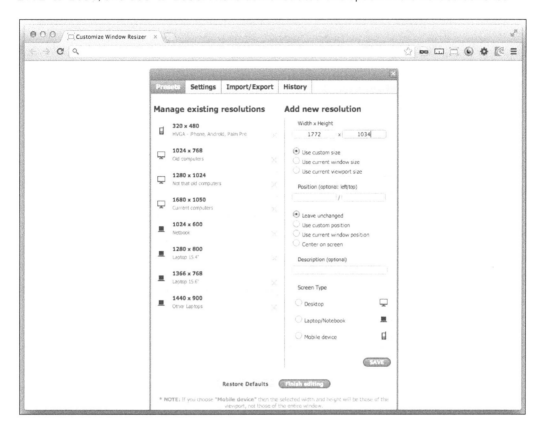

How it works...

This highly useful tool plugs right into your browser to work its magic by emulating different screen resolutions. It's not really magic, even though good software can appear to be magical sometimes. With Analytics tools, you can design specific optimizations for your website viewer's screens.

7

Unobtrusive JavaScript

In this chapter you will learn:

- ▶ Writing "Hello World" unobtrusively
- ▶ Creating a glowing "submit" button with the event listener
- ▶ Making a button stand out when you hover over it
- ▶ Resizing an element with unobtrusive jQuery
- ▶ Masking a password with unobtrusive JavaScript
- ▶ Using an event listener to animate an image shadow

Introduction

The concept of unobtrusive JavaScript fits right into responsive design. By keeping your interaction layer at an arm's length from your presentation layer, you can build a great degree of flexibility into your web app. Because mobile devices have very different input methods, you may need to call a function through a different event. You may want to create a desktop version of a page with JavaScript and use jQuery Mobile instead for your mobile version; with the same template files, by using unobtrusive JavaScript, this is not a difficult task.

Writing "Hello World" unobtrusively

An important facet of responsive design is interaction. As we know that mobile devices and desktops have very different user interfaces, we cannot expect that our JavaScript interaction scripts will work across all devices. An illustrative example is the `.mouseover()` or mouse hover event listener. The mouse is not attached to a touch screen device, so any misdirected attempt at the `.mouseover()` event would likely function as a `.click()` event. The solution to this is to fully remove your interaction script from your templates.

Getting ready

This method is referred to as "Unobtrusive JavaScript". Here, instead of embedding scriptlets like `onclick()` in your HTML template, you can create an external JavaScript that runs through a series of event listeners to set up your interaction.

How to do it...

Let's start with a simple example; we will create only a button and an alert. Many JavaScripts start as a test; in essence, I will create an event listener and then debug it with an alert. We start by creating an HTML page with a simple `submit` button.

```
<body>
<input type="submit">
</body>
```

There you go, that was a simple task, but not very exciting. That's just a basic `submit` button, even though it did not submit anything. So let's make this more interesting, one step at a time. Start by adding some custom text to the button, so that we at least have some expectation of what might happen when this page is ready. We add `value="Say Hello"`. That's enough for the `body` tags, next we add a `script` tag to the header:

```
<script></script>
```

Inside the script tags, you will need to add an event to start the JavaScript. The script would otherwise not run without the `$(document).ready(function(){...});` function:

```
$(document).ready(function(){
//do something here
};
```

Inside this function, replace `//do something` with a listener for the `:submit` button click event that fires a function to somehow put Hello World on the screen:

```
$(":submit").click(function() {
//write "Hello World"
});
```

So far, we have created a JavaScript that loads as the page loads and listens for when the user clicks on the button. When the `click` event occurs, a function executes, but right now that function is empty. Our next task is to create the method of adding the "Hello World" text to the page.

Inside the function, we want to append the "Hello World" text to the parent element of the `:submit` button. Since the `:submit` button is the object from which the method is firing, we can reference it by using `$(this)` in jQuery. To attach the "Hello World" text, use the jQuery `.append()` method:

```
$(this).parent().append("Hello World");
```

The jQuery will append the "Hello World" text to the end of HTML's `body` tag. To have more control over where the text is appended, wrap the button in a parent `div` element.

Open the HTML file in the browser and test the button's functions. If pressing the button does not make the text **Hello World** appear under the button, then something has gone wrong. Go back through the tutorial and see where you went astray.

Before continuing, we can't just let the text be plain text. We want to be able to do more with this later. Mark it up with a paragraph tag that includes an `ID` attribute, `helloWorld`.

At this point, we have accomplished our basic intention, to clicks a button, and write Hello World. That is good, but not good enough; because we always over-deliver, don't we?

Outside the `.click()` event function, add a variable `foo` for the string `Hello World`. Next, replace the `.append(...)` function's internal Hello World text with the `foo` variable. Removing the text from the method and replacing it with a variable makes things easier to work with, and is only a small step towards improving this function. Refresh and test your page to make sure everything still works.

Inside the `body` tags, we are now going to personalize this page by sending the text to the script through a form `input` element. Inside your HTML body tags, enter a text `input` element with `id="bar"` and `placeholder="Enter your name"`.

To receive the text from our input box, we need to add a new variable bar inside your function. Set it equal to the value of the input:

```
var bar = $('input').val();
```

Next, update your `.append()` method by changing it to include `foo`, `bar`, and some new text, all wrapped in a styleable element:

```
$(this).parent().append("<div class='newText'>" + bar + " says " + foo
+ "!</div>");
```

Now, when you refresh this page, you see that the text box has been added. Try it out by entering your name in the input box and watch the results.

This is great, but not complete. Now it's time for some cleanup. Let's go through some scenarios that we want to avoid. We do not want to be able to submit an empty input or keep adding more lines of **Hello World**.

First, take care of the blank input box. Let us add an `if` condition to check that the input text is not blank before we append it to the HTML. After the line that gets the input value, add a new line with the conditional statement checking that the variable is not a blank string. This condition wraps the `append` statement. Also add an `else` statement for when the input is a blank string. Inside it, copy the `.append()` method with text reminding the user to enter a value in the text input.

```
var bar = $('input').val();
if (bar != "") {
$(this).parent().append("<div class='newText'>" + bar + " says " + foo
+ "!</div>");
} else {
$(this).parent().append("Please enter a your name!")
};
```

This adds some validation to your form that will nag your user to enter your name if the **submit** button is clicked with a blank text box. There are two more clean-up items left, so hang on for a few more minutes.

First, we want the appended HTML to reset each time. So add a line right after your `if` conditional statement and before the `else` statement, removing the `.newText` element added earlier.

```
$(".newText").remove();
```

Finally, right before the end of the `if` conditional, reset the input form to have a blank value by using the `.val()` method. Also add an `ID` attribute to the text input to connect the value to the input.

```
$('input#fooBar').val("");
```

That's it! We have kind of over killed it, but we have a pretty good Hello World web app.

How it works...

Unobtrusive JavaScript works by loading up the script on page load and operates by using listeners to wait for specific events to occur on the page. This may be an adjustment in how you write, but then there is an advantage in being able to separate the interaction from the presentation.

Creating a glowing "submit" button with the event listener

Working with forms is often an overlooked aspect of most web design topics, even more so, responsive web design. Often non-transactional pages do not use forms beyond the simple **Contact Us** page, therefore the form design is often an afterthought. However, in the realm of transactional e-commerce and Software as a Service industries, forms are the most important elements the user interacts with. In this world, responsive design is more than just responsive layouts and images, it includes thoughtful interaction. In this recipe we can imagine a scenario where a user is at the end of a form process and is ready to submit the form.

It's not an uncommon occurrence to see a person rather comically click the **submit** button and watch the page just sit there, seemingly doing nothing (but it is actually performing the `post` action of the form) and react by clicking the same button again and again and again. In the simple **Contact Us** scenario, this could generate some additional form submission e-mails, but in the transactional situation, this could activate a long string of business logic and become disruptive to other processes.

On the user side, there can be the idea that if nothing happens immediately after clicking the **submit** button, something has gone wrong and the site has failed; and the end result is the abandoned transaction and the damaged trust of your site. There are a number of things you can and should do about this. One of them is adding visual cues to let the user know that they have successfully clicked the button, and something is going to happen. Consider the transaction being performed behind the scenes and the time it will take. If you anticipate a long wait, be aware that your user might not know this. People usually expect that in the Internet world of instant gratification everything is instant, and anything that isn't instant is broken.

Getting ready

In the *Writing "Hello World" unobtrusively* recipe, we wrote a simple submit button function. We can use this as the basic building block for this recipe. If you do not have that code handy, you can get the finished version of it online at Packt Publishing's website (`http://www.packtpub.com/`).

How to do it...

First we need to break out the meat of the submit function into a separate function that is called by the `.click()` event function. Cut out everything from inside the function and paste it outside the `$(document).ready(function() {...});` function. Replace everything that you have cut out with a function call to the new function. In the function call, include the declared variable `foo` with the ID value of `$(this)` by the `.attr()` method. Then, wrap the code you pasted in a new function of the same name, and assign it to receive the two variables. Finally add an ID attribute to your submit input. Your code should look similar to the following:

```
$(document).ready(function(){
```

```
        var foo = "hello world ";
        $(":submit").click(function(){
            formAction(foo,$(this).attr("id"));
        });
    });

    function formAction(foo,id){
        var bar = $('input').val();
        if (bar != ""){
            $(".newText").remove();
            $("#" + id).parent().append("<div class='newText'>" +
            bar + " says " + foo + "!</div>");
            $('input#fooBar').val("");
        } else {
            $(".newText").remove();
            $("#" + id).parent().append("<div class='newText'>
            Please enter a your name!</div>");
        };
    };
```

First things first, remove the `bar` variable from the `formAction()` function and paste it inside the `.click()` event listener function. This builds the variable on every click event. Now onto building new functions; add a new function to the JavaScript called `buttonAnimate()` and call it after the `formAction()` call in the `.click()` event listener. In the `buttonAnimate()` function call, send the `bar` variable. Finally, add the `bar` variable to the `formAction()` function call and the function declaration variables. The key development is that we have added the input value as a variable in the `.click()` event listener function and sent it to the two function calls.

With that out of the way, we can now start writing in our new function of animating effects on the button. Take a small break and get some coffee. We are going to temporarily shift gears and write some CSS.

Add a stylesheet to your project; inside the stylesheet, add two classes, `.valid` and `.invalid`, which will act on the button for its two different response states, `valid` and `invalid`. The `pass` scenario occurs when the text is entered into the form when submitted and the `fail` scenario occurs when the **submit** button is pressed without the text being entered in the `form` element.

```
.valid{...}
.invalid{...}
```

In the `valid` state, we have submitted the form with text in the input box. We want to add CSS to the button that represents a positive state; the button has been activated, indicating that something correct has happened. I have added a border, shadow, text-shadow, background color, text color, and border-radius. This will be a sufficient indicator that something expected has happened.

```
.valid{
    border:2px solid #000;
    -webkit-box-shadow: 1px 1px 5px 3px #0000ff;
    box-shadow: 1px 1px 5px 3px #0000ff;
    text-shadow: 1px 1px 1px #666666;
    filter: dropshadow(color=#666666, offx=1, offy=1);
    background-color:rgb(150, 150, 255);
    color:#ffffff;
    -webkit-border-radius: 5px;
    border-radius: 5px;
}
```

We add the same CSS style types to the `invalid` state, where the user has submitted the form with no text in the input box. In this instance, we want to give visual clues that something has gone wrong, and prompt the user for their attention to try again. In this scenario, orange and red are good colors to signal that an error has been made. In addition, we also add a CSS blur effect with a transition.

```
.invalid{
    border:2px solid #ffff00;
    -webkit-box-shadow: 1px 1px 5px 3px rgb(255, 0, 0);
    box-shadow: 1px 1px 5px 3px rgb(255, 0, 0);
    background-color:rgb(255, 133, 0);
    color:#ffffff; -webkit-border-radius:
    5px; border-radius: 5px;
    -webkit-filter: grayscale(0.1) blur(1px);
    -webkit-transition: border 0.2s ease;
    -moz-transition: border 0.2s ease;
    -ms-transition: border 0.2s ease;
    -o-transition: border 0.2s ease;
    transition: border 0.2s ease;
    text-shadow: 1px 1px 1px #666666;
    filter: dropshadow(color=#666666, offx=1, offy=1);
}
```

That is all the CSS we are going to write for this recipe. Next, we are going to write the JavaScript to connect the two different styles to the actual states. Way back earlier in this recipe, we created an empty function called `buttonAnimate()` that received the variable `bar`, now it's time to build that out. Inside it, add the same `if` conditional statement to check if `bar` is an empty string. If it is, add the `valid` class to the `submit` button, and if it is not, add the class `invalid`. This added `invalid` class alerts the user that something has gone awry, and an action needs to be taken.

```
if (bar!= "") {
        $(":submit").addClass("valid");
} else {
        $(":submit").addClass("invalid");
};
```

When the appropriate action is taken, that is, when the user clicks on the form element to enter text, the button should be reset to its original state; technically, the new added class should be removed. That code is as follows:

```
$('input#fooBar').focus(function() {
        $(":submit").removeClass('invalid')
});
```

The final bit of cleanup left is to remove either or both classes from the beginning of the `if` and `else` conditions. Use the `.removeClass()` method on the `submit` element twice to remove the class opposite to the class to be added.

```
function buttonAnimate(bar) {
        if (bar!= "") {
                $(":submit").removeClass("invalid");
                $(":submit").addClass("valid");
        } else {
                $(":submit").removeClass("valid");
                $(":submit").addClass("invalid");
                $('input#fooBar').focus(function() {
                        $(":submit").removeClass('invalid')
                });
        };
};
```

Now reload and test out the page and see the magic you created. It will look like the following screenshot:

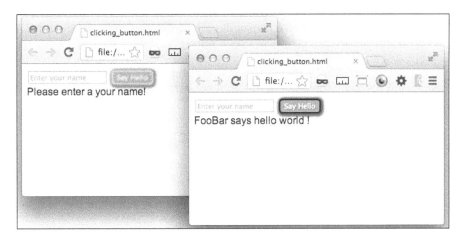

How it works...

jQuery is a great library that does the heavy lifting for you to create great web apps quickly and with very little code. In the old world of plain old JavaScript, this functionality would have cost you much more code and time. It has the library functions to read the form's values, append HTML easily, and toggle the CSS classes on and off. All you need is to implement some jQuery methods and CSS, and the rest is done for you.

Making a button stand out when you hover over it

Sometimes the big challenge in responsive design is being able to really over deliver a project when the requirements are only to build something that is just good enough. A button is an opportunity where you can deliver that extra level of polish for a product that astonishes the users. If we were not over delivering, we could just throw a :hover selector at this and be done. However, in this recipe, we're going to make a button that shines like a boss when you hover over it.

Getting ready

Know the pitfalls of over delivering. Giving more than asked is something we should all strive for, but beware of setting unreasonable expectations that you cannot meet, and drive an otherwise successful project into failure.

In a previous recipe, we created a form with a button that animated when you clicked on it. For this recipe, you can continue working with that code. You can also go and download the code for that recipe, or this recipe for that matter.

Or you could just make a form and button element. It's not that hard.

How to do it...

We are essentially starting with a page with two form elements; an input box and a submit button. As I mentioned earlier, these were built in a previous recipe; you could also just build them here. The JavaScript we built in the recipe will work with the new interaction, but is not required. The `input` element has the `id` attribute `fooBar`, and the button has the `id` attribute `submit`.

```
<input id="fooBar" type="text" placeholder="Enter your name">
<input id="submit" type="submit" value="Say Hello">
```

Let's start by making the default look of the button more interesting. Add to your CSS a style for the `input#submit` element. Inside the style, add a blue background color, a white font color, an 8-point border radius, a 14-pixel font size, and padding of 5 pixels and 8 pixels. This can be done using the following code:

```
input#submit{
    background-color:blue;
    color:white;
    border-radius:8px;
    font-size:14px;
    padding:5px 8px;
}
```

Now that the button's default look is defined, let's talk about the interactive design. Here, we get into the actual advantage of using JavaScript for a `.mouseover()` event instead of a CSS `:hover` selector. I would like to interact with the `form` element and query if text has been entered in it or not. If text is entered, we want a special visual cue indicating that the form is ready to be submitted; if no text is submitted, a strong visual cue should tell the user to stop and go back to check their form again.

First, if the form is ready to be submitted, the button will appear to extend out towards the mouse pointer and turn green. The CSS will include a green background color with the `!important` override, a box shadow, and a text-shadow. See the following code snippet for the exact CSS syntax:

```
.buttonLight{
    background-color:green !important;
    -webkit-box-shadow: 1px 1px 2px 1px green;
    box-shadow: 1px 1px 2px 1px green;
    text-shadow: 1px 1px 2px #666666;
    filter: dropshadow(color=#666666, offx=1, offy=1);
        }
```

Alternately, if the form input is empty, the button will turn red and retract away from the mouse pointer. This CSS will have a red background color with the `!important` override, and inset shadow, and a text shadow that makes the text blurred.

```
.redButtonLight{
    background-color:red !important;
    -webkit-box-shadow:inset 1px 1px 3px 2px #663535;
    box-shadow:inset 1px 1px 3px 2px #663535;
    text-shadow: 0px 0px 2px #fff;
    filter: dropshadow(color=#fff, offx=0, offy=0);
}
```

That's the extent of the CSS we are creating. It's time to build the interactivity. In your header, if you have not already done so, create the opening and closing `<script>` tags. First, we create the `(document).ready` listener:

```
$(document).ready(function(){
    //do some things here
});
```

That does not do much, but it is a start. So let us move forward to building the interactivity. Inside the `(document).ready` listener function, add an event listener for the `.mouseover()` event and one for the `.mouseout()` event. The `.mouseover()` listener replaces the hover in function, and will both animate the button and add one of the CSS classes we built earlier, while the `.mouseout()` listener completes the hover out function, and will ultimately remove the `class` attribute of the `.mouseover()` function that was added.

```
$(document).ready(function(){
    $("#submit").mouseover(function(){
        //do something
    });
```

```
$("#submit").mouseout(function(){
    //do something else
});
});
```

Moving forward, let us build the `.mouseover()` event listener function first. At its core, it performs two functions; first, it queries the value of the form `input` element, and then changes the `submit` button based on the value of the form `input` element. The first part, querying the value of the input, will look like the following:

```
if($('input').val()!="")
    //do something
} else {
    //do something else
}
```

The first condition, when the value of the form is not an empty string, should create new variables, `classtoAdd = "buttonLight"` and `paddingAdd = "5px 8px 5px 9px"`. The other condition, when the value of the form is an empty string, creates the same variables, `classtoAdd = "redButtonLight"` and `paddingAdd = "5px 9px 5px 7px"`. These will be applied to the `submit` button in the next part of this function.

The next part of the function starts by animating the opacity and padding of the button with the `.animate()` method, and adding the class determined by the `classtoAdd` variable. The animation should be somewhat quick, say 100 milliseconds.

```
$("#submit").animate({opacity: 0.7, padding: paddingAdd},
100, function(){
    $("#submit").addClass(classtoAdd);
});
```

That is all that is required for the `.mouseover()` event. What is needed next is the `.mouseout()` function's inner workings. Again, animate the `submit` button's `position` and `padding` attributes, but for a longer time, and then remove the `class` attributes.

```
$("#submit").mouseout(function(){
    $("#submit").animate({opacity: 1, padding :"5px 8px"},
    300, function(){
        $("#submit").removeClass(classtoAdd);
    });
});
```

And that is it. Launch the page and watch the interaction of the button. The following screenshot is illustrating the same:

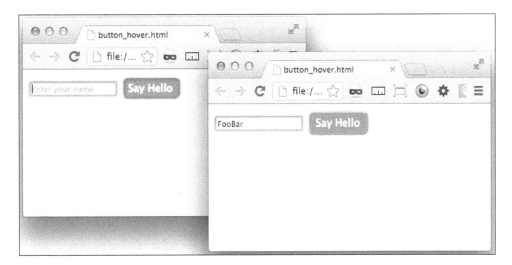

How it works...

This recipe uses event listeners to replace the simple CSS `:hover` selector that can only deploy with limited logic with a `.mouseover()` event listener that can make a query against the form `input` element to see if the form data is not empty. Based on the page's form state, the script can assign a different CSS class to the button. This adds another level of logic to the client side of the application and a richer interactivity to your application.

Resizing an element with unobtrusive jQuery

The purpose of this recipe is to build a smart image element handler in your project. This will be a simple element that can respond to your screen size. We can do all this with an unobtrusive jQuery script.

In a previous recipe, we resized an image with server-side scripting using PHP. This recipe is going to achieve a similar result, but it will be client side instead of server side, and it will be for a mobile-first responsive design.

This recipe is a good tool for mobile-first responsive design. For instance, if you want a scaled down image to display the loading of the document first, and if the screen is large, the script will replace the image with a larger version of the image. The unobtrusive aspect of this means that the script can easily be called by adding a `class` attribute to the image.

Getting ready

This recipe starts from scratch, so you won't be required to go download anything to get started. You do, however, need to plug in to the jQuery libraries to make this work. In your header, include the path to the jQuery libraries online:

```
<script src="">
```

How to do it...

Once you have your header set up with the path to the jQuery libraries, add a script element to the HTML header. Inside the `<script>` tags, we will shortly add some event listeners and a function that will resize an element.

In your HTML body, add a div element to wrap the child elements in the page. Give that the class `wrap`. Inside the `.wrap` div element, add two child div elements.

Inside one of those div elements, we will insert an image. We want to have two versions ready and available for the page to display, so open your image editing software (if you do not have one, go to `www.gimp.com` and download it) and create two versions, a large one and a small one, of the image you want displayed.

Name the two images `imagename-small` and `imagename-large`. The images I created for the recipe are `robot-small.png` and `robot-large.png`. Add the small image with an image element, and add to the image element the class, `scalable`.

```
<img src="robot-small.png" class="scalable" />
```

Now that we have the basic HTML, let us do some slight CSS layout and styling. Add the `<style>` tag to your header. Inside, add a style for the `div.wrap` element to be `75%` wide. Float its first child element to the left and assign `50%` width. Do the opposite for the second child element. You can add different colored backgrounds to each just to see the division between the two elements. Finally, for `img`, add a responsive `100%` width and `auto` height. The CSS is displayed as follows:

```
div.wrap{width:75%;}
div.wrap div:first-child{float:left;width:50%;background-color:#ccc;}
div.wrap div:nth-child(2){float:right;width:50%;background-
color:#666;}
div.wrap div img{width:100%;height:auto;}
```

Now that the page layout is ready, it is time to build the JavaScript. The most important function, the utility function, to replace the image should be created next. It will be called from within a separate function with parameters of whether to replace it with the large or small version.

```
function replaceImage(size){...}
```

Inside the function, first we need to see if the parameter sent is large or small. Create a simple `if` conditional statement with an `else` condition to check this.

```
if (size == 'small') {…} else {…};
```

If the parameter is `small`, then the function works to replace the image in HTML with the small version. First, for the sake of preventing the function from replacing the small version with the small version unnecessarily, add another `if` condition to check if the `img` element with the class `scalable` has the string `large` in the `src` attribute using the `.indexOf()` method. If the `.indexOf()` method finds the string present, it will return the index number of where it is found in the `img.scalable` object. The specific `if` condition will ask if the index is greater than 1; if it is greater than **1**, the `if` condition would be true.

```
if($("img.scalable").attr("src").indexOf('large')>1){…}
```

Inside the conditional statement, create a new variable, `newImageReplace`, this will create a string to set the `src` attribute to in the next line. Set the variable's value to get the `img.scalable` object's `src` attribute and replace the string section `-large.` with `-small.` (I included the trailing period just in case your original image name included `-large.`).

```
var newImageReplace = $("img.scalable").attr("src").replace("-large.",
"-small.");
```

The next line uses the `.attr()` method to update the value of the `img.scalable` object's `src` attribute to the value of the variable created earlier, `"robot-small.png"`.

```
$("img.scalable").attr({src:newImageReplace});
```

That is it for the `if` conditional, and there is no method to act on as there is no `else` condition. Next, for the parent element's `else` condition, if the `size` parameter is not `small`, the function will do exactly the opposite as before. Use the `.indexOf()` method to check if the `small` image is present, and if so, change the `src` attribute to point to the `large` image.

```
} else {
    if($("img.scalable").attr("src").indexOf('small')>1){
        var newImageReplace =    $("img.scalable").attr("src").
        replace("-small.", "-large.");
        $("img.scalable").attr({src:newImageReplace});
    };
};
```

This completes the most important action function. Now let us backtrack to create the function that calls it with the parameter. This function will have to get some intelligence about the screen width, therefore, call it `measureWindow()`. Inside, first gather the intelligence by measuring the window width into a variable called `getWindowWidth`. If the window width is small, say smaller than 600 px, and you want it to call up the small image, it should thus call the `replaceImage()` function with a parameter, `small`. If larger than 600 px, call the function with the parameter `large`.

```
function measureWindow() {
    var getWindowWidth = $(window).width();
    if (getWindowWidth < 600) {
        replaceImage("small");
    } else {
        replaceImage("large");
    };
};
```

That function which measures the screen width, and then calls the resize function, itself needs to be called. It does not just fire itself. And we would not want it to be constantly measuring the screen width. We only want it to occur in two scenarios. First, on page load, when we want to check if the screen is large, and quickly replace the low-resolution image with a higher one. For this instance, the call is as follows:

```
$(document).ready(function() {
    measureWindow();
});
```

The second scenario is when the screen width is changed by the user. We will use the `.resize()` listener to fire a function when the window is resized.

```
$(window).resize(function() {
    measureWindow();
});
```

Now we are really finished, and that was short enough. Launch the file and open your inspector or debugger to watch the image `src` change when you resize your screen below 600 px. You could build on this to deliver a few different sizes if you wanted.

How it works...

This recipe gives a usable example of client-side responsive image delivery using unobtrusive JavaScript. It measures the screen width whenever there is some change, and updates the image source appropriately.

Masking a password with unobtrusive JavaScript

The most common way to handle masking a password is to use the password type when creating an input element. This is the best practice when used on a desktop. When entering a password on a mobile device however, there is a high potential for input error on the device's touch input. These input errors are often not caught because you cannot see the encrypted text. This is a problem that the designers of iOS really got right. They created an input where the input text is visible for a short time before turning into a *, or changes upon entry of the next character.

In this recipe, we will create a password input that mimics this solution for your password input.

You can use this form element to mask other form entries as well. But be sure you understand that the underlying hidden form contains the entry to be transmitted. It is not encrypted unless you specify so. This only prevents the password from being seen visually.

Getting ready

You don't need to get any files locally to get started. Only, in your header, include the link to the jQuery libraries. This will allow you to plug in to the jQuery libraries and use them to extend the functionality of your code.

```
<script src="http://code.jquery.com/jquery-1.8.2.min.js"></script>
```

How to do it...

The first task is to create in your HTML body, two `input` elements. The first has the attributes of `type` and `ID` of the password. This will be the encrypted version submitted in the form, but will ultimately be hidden from view. The second will have the ID `altDisplay` and be disabled, so the user cannot click inside it. This one will be displayed on top of the other one and it will appear to be the one the user is typing into. At the end, we will add a style to hide the password field.

That is all that is needed for the HTML body of the recipe, of course you can add other form elements as needed.

In the header, add a JavaScript `<script>` element, and inside add the jQuery `$(document).ready` function. Inside it, add a listener to the `#password` input for the `.keyup()` event. This occurs after the key is pressed down, and when the key is let up, the event fires.

But there is a small bump in the road to manage before we get into the meat of this recipe. First, not all keys pressed enter a letter; there are *Shift*, *Tab*, and function keys, and then there is the *Delete* key. Each key has a numerical identifier, and you can find it by logging in the console e.which. You will need the numerical key identifiers to write a condition to filter out non-character keyup events.

First we should make a series of if conditions to make sure that we are not getting a keystroke that is not an actual character. Inside that, create an additional if statement to check that the *Delete* (8) key was not entered. If not, we can proceed with the function to handle a regular character keyup event, otherwise we will need to add functionality to handle the delete keyup event (that will come later).

```
$(document).ready(function(){
    $("#password").keyup(function(e){
        if (e.which!=16 && e.which!=27 && e.which!=91 &&
        e.which!=18 && e.which!=17 && e.which!=20 ){
            if (e.which!=8){
                //do something for the character key
            }else{
                //Do something for the delete key
            }};
        });
    });
```

In the condition of a character keyup, we will get the current values of both input fields into variables altDisplayVal and passwordVal. The value present in the #altDisplay input is taken and it's values are all changed to * in a regular expression and stored in the regAltDisplayVal variable. The value in the #password is taken and the last letter is taken out and put into a new variable with the .charAt() method. These two new variables are added together to become the new value of the #altDisplay input.

```
var altDisplayVal = $("#altDisplay").val();
var passwordVal = $("#password").val();
var regAltDisplayVal = altDisplayVal.replace(/./g,"*");
var passwordValLastLetter = passwordVal.charAt( passwordVal.length-1
);
$("#altDisplay").val(regAltDisplayVal + passwordValLastLetter);
```

That handled keyup on a character key, next let's write functionality for the delete key. The delete key is different in that it removes the last character in the character string. To handle the delete keyup event, get the last character in the #password input with the .charAt() method and hold it in the delLast variable.

Then use the `.slice()` method to first get through the next-to-last characters for the `delTxt` variable. Use a regular expression to change the characters into * and store them in the `regDelTxt` variable. Finally, add the `regDelTxt` and `delLast` variables to make the new value of the `#altDisplay` input element.

```
var delLast = this.value.charAt(this.value.length-1);
var delTxt = this.value.slice(0,this.value.length-1);
var regDelTxt = delTxt.replace(/./g,"*");
$("#altDisplay").val(regDelTxt + delLast);
```

And that takes care of the JavaScript. You can now launch the page and see both the input elements on the page. Enter the text in the first input element, and then it will enter into the second as *. Now the only problem is that having two side-by-side form elements in the page does not make this an iOS style password element. To make it really work, we need to overlay the `#password` input over `#altDisplay` and make it invisible. You can do this with some CSS, as follows:

```
div input:first-child{
    position: relative;
    left: 131px;
    background: transparent;
    color: transparent;
}
```

There, try that. On refreshing your screen, you will see only one input element. When you enter text into it, it transforms into stars.

How it works...

This does not actually change the input submitted; it only hides it, and translates the values in the hidden field into star characters. It should be a good mimic of the iOS password entry.

Using an event listener to animate an image shadow

Since this is the last recipe, it should be a fun recipe. This one takes a responsive image, like the one we built back in *Chapter 1*, *Responsive Elements and Media*, and uses jQuery event listeners and CSS3 to animate a shadow to follow your cursor.

This is a simple recipe, but it still works in a responsive way. The image will respond to the page width, while the jQuery is written such that it still measures the image position and mouse position on every mouse movement.

Getting ready

This recipe needs you to work with jQuery. So in the header of your new file, add a link to the jQuery libraries. Other than that, you are ready to go.

```
<script src="http://code.jquery.com/jquery-1.8.2.min.js"></script>
```

How to do it...

First, create the body of your HTML file using a div element with the class `wrap`. Inside it, add an image with the class `topRight`. Next up; the CSS.

```
<div class="wrap">
    <img class="topRight" src="robot-small.png"/>
</div>
```

Add a section for the CSS. First, add a `text-align: center` style to the body. Next, give the `.wrap` div element a width of `30%`, and an automatic horizontal width. This is shown in the following code snippet:

```
body{text-align:center;}
.wrap{
    width:30%;
    margin:0 auto;
}
.wrap img{
    width:100%;
    height:auto;
    margin:80px 1%;
    border-radius:50%;
    -webkit-border-radius:50%;
    border:1px dotted #666;
}
```

The next set of CSS is varying the image class variations that will be assigned by the jQuery script depending on the mouse position. Each contains a differently angled `box-shadow`. Name the different classes `topLeft`, `topRight`, `bottomLeft`, and `bottomRight`. Each will have a shadow offset of 5 pixels, a spread of 2 pixels, and blur radius of 2 pixels.

```
img.topLeft{
    border-top: 5px solid #666;
    border-right:5px solid #999;
    border-bottom: 5px solid #999;
    border-left:5px solid #666;
    -webkit-box-shadow: -5px -5px 2px 2px #666;
```

```
        box-shadow: -5px -5px 2px 2px #666;
    }
    img.topRight{
        border-top: 5px solid #666;
        border-right:5px solid #666;
        border-bottom: 5px solid #999;
        border-left:5px solid #999;
        -webkit-box-shadow: 5px -5px 2px 2px #666;
        box-shadow: 5px -5px 2px 2px #666;
    }
    img.bottomLeft{
        border-top: 5px solid #999;
        border-right:5px solid #999;
        border-bottom: 5px solid #666;
        border-left:5px solid #666;
        -webkit-box-shadow: -5px 5px 2px 2px #666;
        box-shadow: -5px 5px 2px 2px #666;
    }
    img.bottomRight{
        border-top: 5px solid #999;
        border-right:5px solid #666;
        border-bottom: 5px solid #666;
        border-left:5px solid #999;|
        -webkit-box-shadow: 5px 5px 2px 2px #666;
        box-shadow: 5px 5px 2px 2px #666;
    }
```

Excellent work so far. Now it is time to build the JavaScript. Inside your `script` tag, create the standard `$(document).ready` event function. Then, to start add a `.mousemove()` event listener function to the body. Inside it, create two new variables `imgHorz` and `imgVert` for the horizontal and vertical positions of the `.wrap img` div element.

```
$("body").mousemove(function(e){
    var imgHorz = ($(".wrap img").offset().left);
    var imgVert = ($(".wrap img").offset().top);
});
```

Next, after the variables have been created, we create some conditions based on the variable values compared to the position of the mouse at the time of the event. If the results are true, then remove all CSS classes before adding one of the image classes.

```
if(e.pageX < imgHorz && e.pageY < imgVert){
    $(".wrap img").removeClass();
    $(".wrap img").addClass("bottomRight");
};
```

Then you will want to add three additional `else`/`if` conditions to add the other classes. The following code snippet shows the four conditions displayed:

```
if(e.pageX < imgHorz && e.pageY < imgVert){
    $(".wrap img").removeClass();
    $(".wrap img").addClass("bottomRight");
} else if (e.pageX > imgHorz && e.pageY < imgVert) {
    $(".wrap img").removeClass();
    $(".wrap img").addClass("bottomLeft");
} else if(e.pageX > imgHorz && e.pageY > imgVert) {
    $(".wrap img").removeClass();
    $(".wrap img").addClass("topLeft");
} else if(e.pageX < imgHorz && e.pageY > imgVert) {
    $(".wrap img").removeClass();
    $(".wrap img").addClass("topRight");
};
```

And that wraps up the JavaScript.

One last thing, we also need to animate the transition between CSS styles. So, instead of adding more JavaScript, add a CSS transition to the `.wrap img` element (each browser needs its own transition command).

```
-webkit-transition: all .5s linear;
-o-transition: all .5s linear;
-moz-transition: all .5s linear;
-ms-transition: all .5s linear;
-kthtml-transition: all .5s linear;
transition: all .5s linear;
```

That was a fairly simple recipe, and the end result is a fun image element where the shadow follows the mouse around. The following screenshot is an illustration of this recipe:

How it works...

This recipe measures the location of the image and the mouse on every `.mousemove()` event. The result of each is that a new shadow is applied to the object. Now it is important to think about what events are appropriate for mobile devices versus desktops. A `.mousemove()` event won't work as there is no mouse attached to a mobile device. From here, I would refer to *Chapter 5, Making Mobile-first Web Applications*, for a refresher on how to load JavaScripts such as jQuery Mobile for mobile devices.

We built simple UI interactions using unobtrusive JavaScript. I hope that these simple scripts are not only useful examples that you could actually use in a project, but they also demonstrate effectively how to write JavaScript that could live outside of your template files. This fits into your responsive design when you pair it with mobile versions of the script that can be called to the mobile devices. Going forward, this will help you create more responsive and fluidly transitioning web projects.

Live long and prosper, my friends.

Bibliography

This Learning Path is a blend of content, all packaged up keeping your journey in mind. It includes content from the following Packt products:

- *Responsive Web Design by Example Beginner's Guide - Second Edition, Thoriq Firdaus*
- *Responsive Web Design with HTML5 and CSS3 - Second Edition, Ben Frain*
- *HTML5 and CSS3 Responsive Web Design Cookbook, Benjamin LaGrone*

Index

title tag 402
tooling editors 233
top bar 171, 172
transforms
  matrix 439
  rotate 439
  scale 439
  skew 439
  translate 439
transitions and animations
  reference 446
translate
  used, to center absolutely positioned
    elements 440-442
translate3d
  reference 450
tweening 417
Typekit
  reference 362

U

Ubuntu
  Node.js, installing in 33
  XAMPP, installing in 25, 26
Ultimate CSS Gradient Editor
  reference 379
Uniform Resource Identifier (URI) 408
unobtrusive JavaScript
  about 663, 664
  used, for creating password 679-681
unobtrusive jQuery
  element, resizing with 675-678
Unsplash
  reference 49
user agent
  about 608
  masking, in Chrome 611-613
User Agent switcher
  using 608-611
user experience
  delivering 492
  tiering 492

V

validators
  about 500, 501

reference 500
value
  generating, with mathematical
    operations 135
values, box-sizing property
  border-box 11
  content-box 11
  padding-box 11
Varela Round
  references 74, 147
variables
  about 128, 129
  interpolation 192, 193
  used, for storing value 191, 192
  used, in import statement 137
Velocity.js
  reference 421
vendor prefix, CSS3
  -moz 64
  -ms- 64
  -webkit- 64
video
  adding, in HTML5 325, 326
  responding, to screen width 513, 514
video-hosting sites 513
video tag 513
video-wrap element 514
viewport
  about 7, 236, 615
  content, displaying 499
  content, hiding 499
  content, loading 499
  heavy lifting, with CSS 500
  options 616, 618
  references 8
viewport meta tag
  about 5, 6, 261, 262
  reference link 262
  screen size 7
  viewport 7
VirtualBox
  about 655
  downloading 655-658
  download link 655
virtualization 654
Visual Studio 651
VMware 655

W

W3C
  reference 119
W3C validator
  reference 310
Web Accessibility Initiative-Accessible Rich
  Internet Applications (WAI-ARIA)
  about 306, 322, 323
  ARIA 324
  correct elements, using 324
  reference 324
  roles, avoiding for semantic elements 323
Web Content Accessibility
  Guidelines (WCAG)
  about 306, 322, 323
  references 322, 323
WebDesignServed
  reference 17
Webicons
  reference 174
WebP
  about 303
  reference 303
web pages
  SVG, inserting 405
WebPagetest
  reference 502
Webshims lib
  references 478, 479
website
  customizing 207
  fine-tuning 220
  styling 207-218
  styling, with media queries 220-224
website layout
  examining 164-167
website styles
  composing, with LESS syntax 147-158

web typography
  @font-face 362-364
  @font-face CSS rule 361
  about 361
  custom @font-face typography 364
Wells
  reference 124
whitespace 273
Windows
  Node.js, installing in 31, 32
  XAMPP, installing in 22, 23
WinLESS
  reference 28
word wrapping
  about 336, 337
  horizontal scrolling panels,
    creating 338-340
  text ellipsis 337, 338
Working Draft (WD) 248

X

XAMPP, local server
  installing, in OS X 24, 25
  installing, in Ubuntu 25, 26
  installing, in Windows 22, 23
  reference 22

Y

YSlow! performance rules
  reference 67

Z

Zurb Responsive
  reference 17

Thank you for buying

HTML5 and CSS3: Building Responsive Websites

About Packt Publishing

Packt, pronounced 'packed', published its first book, *Mastering phpMyAdmin for Effective MySQL Management*, in April 2004, and subsequently continued to specialize in publishing highly focused books on specific technologies and solutions.

Our books and publications share the experiences of your fellow IT professionals in adapting and customizing today's systems, applications, and frameworks. Our solution-based books give you the knowledge and power to customize the software and technologies you're using to get the job done. Packt books are more specific and less general than the IT books you have seen in the past. Our unique business model allows us to bring you more focused information, giving you more of what you need to know, and less of what you don't.

Packt is a modern yet unique publishing company that focuses on producing quality, cutting-edge books for communities of developers, administrators, and newbies alike. For more information, please visit our website at www.packtpub.com.

Writing for Packt

We welcome all inquiries from people who are interested in authoring. Book proposals should be sent to author@packtpub.com. If your book idea is still at an early stage and you would like to discuss it first before writing a formal book proposal, then please contact us; one of our commissioning editors will get in touch with you.

We're not just looking for published authors; if you have strong technical skills but no writing experience, our experienced editors can help you develop a writing career, or simply get some additional reward for your expertise.

CPSIA information can be obtained
at www.ICGtesting.com
Printed in the USA
LVHW100144091118
596520LV00003B/35/P

9 781787 124813